Natural Resources

Neither Curse nor Destiny

Natural Resources

Neither Curse nor Destiny

Edited by

Daniel Lederman
William F. Maloney

A COPUBLICATION OF STANFORD ECONOMICS AND FINANCE,
AN IMPRINT OF STANFORD UNIVERSITY PRESS, AND THE WORLD BANK

A copublication of Stanford Economics and Finance, an imprint of Stanford University
Press, and the World Bank.

Stanford University Press	The World Bank
1450 Page Mill Road	1818 H Street NW
Palo Alto CA 94304	Washington DC 20433

World Rights except North America	*North America*
ISBN-10: 0-8213-6545-2	ISBN-10: 0-8047-5709-7 (soft cover)
ISBN-13: 978-0-8213-6545-8	ISBN-10: 0-8047-5708-9 (hard cover)
eISBN-10: 0-8213-6546-0	ISBN-13: 978-0-8047-5709-6 (soft cover)
eISBN-13: 978-0-8213-6546-5	ISBN-13: 978-0-8047-5708-9 (hard cover)
DOI: 10.1596/978-0-8213-6545-8	

Library of Congress Cataloging-in-Publication Data
Natural resources, neither curse nor destiny / edited by Daniel Lederman,
William F. Maloney.
    p. cm. -- (Latin American development forum)
  Includes bibliographical references and index.
  ISBN-13: 978-0-8213-6545-8
  ISBN-10: 0-8213-6545-2
  1. Economic development. 2. Natural resources. I. Lederman, Daniel, 1968–
  II. Maloney, William F. (William Francis), 1959–
  HD82.N36 2006
  333.7--dc22
                                                            2006048227

Latin American Development Forum Series

This series was created in 2003 to promote, debate, and disseminate information and analysis and convey the excitement and complexity of the most topical issues in economic and social development in Latin America and the Caribbean. It is sponsored by the Inter-American Development Bank, the United Nations Economic Commission for Latin America and the Caribbean, and the World Bank. The manuscripts chosen for publication represent the highest quality in each institution's research and activity output and have been selected for their relevance to the academic community, policy makers, researchers, and interested readers.

Advisory Committee Members

Contents

TABLES

Foreword

This book addresses two key questions for policy makers in natural resource–rich regions such as Latin America: First, is natural resource wealth an asset or a liability for development and, if potentially the former, how can its contribution be enhanced? And second, can countries rich in natural resources efficiently diversify toward manufacturing or service-sector exports?

The first question may seem surprising to many: why would anybody doubt that wealth (of a particular form) is bad? The reality is that specialization in natural resource–based activities has suffered from a kind of "yellow press" among economists for a long time, beginning with Adam Smith.[1] In particular, the work of Prebisch convinced generations of Latin Americans that natural resource–based activities were somewhat inferior to manufacturing, both because of their assumed lack of "technological intensity" and because of the low elasticity of world demand, which would lead to a long-run trend of deteriorating relative prices. Prebisch's articles were a key intellectual driving force behind the decades of Latin American "import substitution" policies that taxed natural resource–based activities and protected manufacturing. Even today, based on the work of several contemporary authors who have argued that resource-rich developing countries have grown more slowly than other developing countries since around 1960,[2] many in Latin America and Africa feel that these countries should do whatever is needed to shift toward manufactured-led exports. Given the persistence of these views in our region, some years ago the Chief Economist Office of the World Bank began a research program on these issues; the first results were published in the report "From Natural Resources to the Knowledge Economy."[3] The current book collects updated versions of some of the background papers originally committed for that report and other recent contributions on the subject.

It is true that wealth can be wasted and can lead to destructive behaviors. There are many examples in the developing world of natural resource–rich societies that have become immersed in "rent-seeking" activities and even in civil strife. But is this the general rule? Isn't it true that many of the present-day richest countries (such as the United States, Canada, Australia, and the Scandinavian countries) became rich and technologically developed precisely through a judicious use of their natural resource wealth? In the first two parts of this book, the editors and authors examine this question in a rigorous way both from a historical perspective and with the help of cross-country econometrics. The conclusion seems quite robust: overall, natural resource wealth is good for development. However, more important, these studies show that natural resource wealth becomes a real development asset when coupled with investments in skills and technological capacities and with good macroeconomic institutions and management.

The chapters in this book help to dispel many myths about natural resources. In particular, they show that activities based on natural resources need not be technologically backward. For example, total factor productivity (TFP) growth has been consistently higher in agriculture than in manufacturing in the last decades (although, of course, this would not be true when agriculture was compared to the higher technological end of manufacturing). Indeed, it is perplexing that modern agriculture, forestry, and fisheries based on transgenetics and biotechnology, as well as modern oil and mineral exploration and production based on major scientific and technological advances in geology and other earth sciences are still routinely classified as "low-technology" activities by most of our fellow economists. It is each country's choice either to exploit their natural resources with outdated technologies or enclave production systems, or to invest in related skills in transfer, adaptation, and creation of more productive technologies and in the setting of adequate institutions for the efficient and sustainable use of natural resources and of the public revenues associated with oil and mineral activities. When natural resource–rich societies take appropriate complementary policies, they indeed become very rich and grow fast; when they don't, they can certainly waste the great development opportunities that nature holds out for them.

Similarly, one of the papers in part II shows that commodity prices seem to have had a downward structural break around 1921, with *no* trend, positive or negative, before or since, in real terms. A major question arises: is the current commodity prices boom an accident in a random-walk process, or is it an upward structural break linked to the growing weight of East Asia (a region with high income elasticity of consumption of commodities but poor in natural resource endowments) in the world economy and trade?

With regard to the question of whether countries rich in natural resources can efficiently diversify toward manufacturing or service-sector exports, the papers in part III show that natural resource–rich societies diversify their economies toward other activities as they increase their physical and human capital stocks, liberalize their trade, reduce their transport and transaction costs, and accelerate transfer and adaptation of technologies. Indeed, they give empirical support to the predictions of the "new trade theory," which argues that comparative advantages can be created

through the process of capital and skill accumulation, innovation, and reduction of transaction costs.

In summary, as the editors conclude: "natural resources are assets for
development that require intelligent public policies that complement natural riches with human ingenuity."

Guillermo Perry
Chief Economist for Latin American and the Caribbean
The World Bank
October 2006

Notes   ·

1. Adam Smith said "Projects of mining, instead of replacing capital employed
in them, together with ordinary profits of stock, commonly absorb both capital and
stock. They are the projects, therefore, to which of all others a prudent law-giver,
who desired to increase the capital of his nation, would least choose to give any extraordinary encouragement . . ." (quoted in chapter 1).
2. See quotations in chapter 1.
3. de Ferranti, David, Guillermo Perry, Daniel Lederman, and William Maloney. 2001. *From Natural Resources to the Knowledge Economy.* Washington,
DC: World Bank.

About the Contributors

Magnus Blomström is a professor in the Stockholm School of Economics, Sweden; president of the European Institute of Japanese Studies, Stockholm School of Economics; a research associate with the National Bureau of Economic Research, Cambridge, Massachusetts; and a research fellow with the Centre of Economic Policy Research, United Kingdom.

Claudio Bravo-Ortega is an assistant professor in the Department of Economics at the University of Chile, Santiago.

John T. Cuddington is the William J. Coulter Professor of Mineral Economics and professor of economics and business at the Colorado School of Mines in Golden, Colorado.

Jesse Czelusta is a doctoral candidate in economic history at Stanford University, California.

José de Gregorio is vice-governor of the Central Bank of Chile, Santiago.

Shamila A. Jayasuriya is an assistant professor in the Department of Economics at Ohio University, Ohio.

Ari Kokko is a professor in and director of research of the European Institute of Japanese Studies at the Stockholm School of Economics, Sweden, and an associate professor in Åbo Akademi University, Finland.

Daniel Lederman is senior economist in the Office of the Chief Economist for Latin America and the Caribbean and the Development Economics Research Group, World Bank, Washington, DC.

Rodney Ludema is an associate professor in the Department of Economics and Edmund A. Walsh School of Foreign Service at Georgetown University, Washington, DC.

William F. Maloney is lead economist in the Office of the Chief Economist for Latin America and the Caribbean, World Bank, Washington, DC.

Ozmel Manzano is principal economist at the Andean Development Corporation (CAF), Coordinator of the Research Program, and an associate professor at Universidad Católica Andres Bello in República Bolivariana de Venezuela.

Will Martin is lead economist in the Development Economics Research Group, World Bank, Washington, DC.

Roberto Rigobón is an associate professor (with tenure) in the Sloan School of Management at the Massachusetts Institute of Technology and a faculty research fellow at the National Bureau of Economic Research in Cambridge, Massachusetts.

Anthony Venables is chief economist in the Department for International Development (DFID), London, and Yu Kuo-Hwa Professor of International Economics at the London School of Economics and Political Science at the University of London, United Kingdom.

Gavin Wright is the William Robertson Coe Professor at Stanford University; a senior fellow in the Stanford Institute for Economic Policy Research at Stanford University, California; and on the board of directors of the National Bureau of Economic Research, Cambridge, Massachusetts.

L. Colin Xu is a senior economist in the Development Economics Research Group, World Bank, Washington, DC.

Abbreviations

ANOVA	analyses of variance
ARMA	autoregressive moving average
BACE	Bayesian averaging of classical estimates
CGE	computable general equilibrium
CIF	cost, insurance, and freight
COMTRADE	UN Commodity Trade Statistics database
CORFO	Corporación de Fomento de la Produción (Chile)
DS	difference stationary (model)
FDI	foreign direct investment
FE	fixed effects
FGLS	feasible generalized least squares
GATS	General Agreement on Trade in Services
GDP	gross domestic product
GLS	generalized least squares
GMM	generalized method of moments
GNP	gross national product
GSP	Groupe Speciale Mobile
HOV	Heckscher-Ohlin-Vanek (model)
ICRG	International Country Risk Guide (database)
ICT	information and communications technologies
IIT	intra-industry trade
IMF	International Monetary Fund
INIA	National Institute of Agricultural Research (Chile)
ISI	import substitution industrialization
LDC	least developed country
LMC	low- and middle-income countries
MAS	Minerals Availability System
MUV	manufacturing unit value
NMT	Nordisk MobilTelefoni
NR	natural resources
NRX	natural resource exports

OECD	Organisation for Economic Co-operation and Development
OLS	ordinary least squares
OPEC	Organization of Petroleum Exporting Countries
R&D	research and development
RD	relative demand
RE	random effects
REER	real effective exchange rate
RS	relative supply
SEK	Swedish Krona
SITC	Standard International Trade Classification
SSA	Sub-Saharan Africa
SUAS	Swedish University of Agricultural Sciences
SX-EW	solvent extraction-electrowinnowing (process)
TFP	total factor productivity
TRIMs	trade-related investment measures
TS	trend stationary (model)
UNCTAD	United Nations Conference on Trade and Development
UNSW	University of New South Wales
USGS	United States Geological Survey

1

Neither Curse nor Destiny: Introduction to Natural Resources and Development

*Daniel Lederman and William F. Maloney**

FOR ALMOST AS LONG AS ECONOMICS has been a profession, the role of natural resources in the promotion of economic growth has been among the core issues of development theory and practice. Adam Smith argued, "Projects of mining, instead of replacing the capital employed in them, together with the ordinary profits of stock, commonly absorb both capital and stock. They are the projects, therefore, to which of all others a prudent law-giver, who desired to increase the capital of his nation, would least choose to give any extraordinary encouragement. . . ." In the 1950s, analysts expressed similar concerns in strikingly parallel forms. Prebisch (1959), observing slowing Latin American growth, argued that natural resource industries had fewer possibilities for technological progress and, further, were condemned to decreasing relative prices on their exports. Moreover, these qualities imply that real exchange-rate appreciations driven by natural resource booms—the so-called "Dutch Disease"—in developing countries could have negative effects on long-term development by reducing the relative size of manufacturing exports and production (See Gylfason, Herbertsson, and Zoega 1999; Sachs and Warner 2001). The potential for productivity growth of resource-intensive industries remains a central axis of the debate about their impact on development and a principal focus of this book.

In a different vein, another important body of literature suggests that natural riches produce institutional weaknesses (see, among others, Auty 2001; Ross 1999; Gelb 1988). Tornell and Lane (1999) described the phenomenon where various social groups attempt to capture the economic rents derived from the exploitation of natural resources as the "voracity

1

effect." Subsequent refinements have focused on how "point-source" natural resources—those extracted from a narrow geographic or economic base, such as oil or minerals—and plantation crops have more detrimental effects than resources—such as livestock or agricultural produce from small family farms—that are more diffuse (Murshed 2004; Isham et al. 2005). Mehlum, Moene, and Torvik (2006) have argued that, even if the direct evidence for institutional degradation is weak, poor institutions cannot prevent rent-seeking activity that, as Torvik (2002) argues, can offset the gains from natural resource abundance.

Motivated by these critiques, Gylfason, Herbertsson, and Zoega (1999), Neumayer (2004), Mehlum, Moene, and Torvik (2006), and arguably most influentially, with several authors drawing on their data and approach, Sachs and Warner (1995, 2001) have argued empirically that since the 1960s the resource-rich developing countries have grown more slowly than other developing countries. Consequently, we find ourselves in a time when the conventional wisdom again postulates that natural resources are a curse for development, contradicting the common-sense view that natural riches are riches, nonetheless.

On the policy front, belief in the alleged curse of natural resources was one of the underlying intellectual justifications for the imposition of various barriers to international trade and foreign-exchange restrictions. Subsequently, disenchanted with the inefficiencies of protectionism and the consequences of populist macroeconomic policies many developing countries changed policies during the past quarter century. During this time, the example of East Asia's rapid export-led growth also inspired openings to international trade. However, the liberalizing economies, with some notable exceptions, did not become manufacturing dynamos, or major participants in what is loosely called the "knowledge economy." Further, growth results were not impressive and, in the case of Africa, dramatic falls in commodity prices contributed to negative growth rates. Both led to the reemergence of the fears that natural resource–abundant countries were doubly cursed. First, resource-based industries were poor platforms for growth, and second, it appeared difficult for resource exporters to change their export structure. Continued specialization in natural resources seemed to doom numerous developing economies to be left behind in the boom-and-bust "old" economy. Hence, the two fundamental concerns about the role of natural resources in development seem to have survived with as much relevance today as in Adam Smith's time: are natural resources a curse, and are they destiny?

This book revisits these questions, focusing primarily on the first set of issues and, in particular, on the interaction between natural resources, technology, and insertion in the global economy. It brings together a variety of analytical perspectives, ranging from econometric analyses of economic growth to historical case studies of successful development experiences in countries with abundant natural resources. Our reading of the evidence is that natural resources are neither curse nor destiny. In other words, we find empirical and historical evidence showing that natural resources do spur economic development when combined with the accumulation of knowledge for economic innovation. Even if we fail to convince our readers that natural resources are a blessing, however, this book also presents evidence suggesting that natural resource abundance need not be the only determinant of the structure of production and diversification in developing countries. In fact, the accumulation of knowledge, the level of infrastructure, and the quality of governance all seem to determine not only what countries produce and export, but also how firms and workers produce any particular type of good.

The book is divided into three parts. In Part I, chapters 2–4, the authors assess the relationship between natural resource abundance and economic growth or the growth rate of gross domestic product (GDP) per person. These chapters are tied together by their empirical methodology, which relies on cross-country growth regressions. Part II encompasses chapters 5–8; while all of these chapters take a long historical viewpoint, only one relies exclusively on econometric analysis. Part III includes chapters 9–11, which employ a variety of analytical tools to help us understand the determinants of the patterns of trade and production in developing countries. The rest of this introduction reviews the main findings of the book.

Are Natural Resources a Curse? Econometric Evidence

Is there actually empirical evidence for a resource curse? Consensus about what the available statistical analysis tells us has been complicated by, among other issues, conceptual disagreements over the correct measure of resource abundance, as well appropriate statistical technique for measuring its impact. Further, where a negative impact of natural resources has been identified, the postulated channels through which it may work vary widely, and hence, the implications for policy remain unclear. The three papers in this section revisit both sets of issues.

In chapter 2, Lederman and Maloney examine the empirical relationship between various structural aspects of international trade, ranging from natural resource abundance to export diversification and subsequent economic growth. The central finding is that, regardless of econometric technique and particularly in a panel context allowing better control for unobserved fixed effects, dynamics, and endogeneity, several plausible indicators of the incidence of natural resource exports seem to have a *positive* rather than a negative effect on subsequent economic growth. Put bluntly, *there is no resource curse*. The critical difference with many previous works arises from the fact that, in constructing their cross-country database, Sachs and Warner selectively replace their principal measure of resource abundance—natural resource exports as a share of GDP—with *net* resource exports as a share of GDP for two countries, Singapore and Trinidad and Tobago. This is perhaps understandable as Singapore's privileged position as an entrepot implies re-exports of natural resource–intensive commodities, which leads to its counterintuitive classification as a resource-abundant country. However, a more consistent treatment of data is desirable, and as an alternative proxy with strong theoretical grounding that ameliorates the Singapore anomaly, Lederman and Maloney argue in favor of Leamer's measure of resource abundance—net exports of natural resource–intensive commodities per worker—derived from the standard neoclassical model of international trade. Yet, when they replicate the Sachs-Warner cross-section regressions with this measure (or the Sachs-Warner proxy without the two substitutions), they find that the negative impact of natural resource abundance on growth disappears.

Perhaps as important, chapter 2 also finds that the main structural feature of international trade that is associated with increases in the pace of development is export diversification. This finding is important for an emerging literature that links productive diversification to the process of development.[1] Further, this finding also seems to lie behind Sachs and Vial's (2001) finding that an alternate measure of resource abundance—share of natural resource exports in total exports—affects growth negatively. Once the Hirfindahl index of general export concentration is included in the regression, natural resources no longer have a significant negative effect. This finding is consistent with Auty's (2000) concern about a resource drag on growth arising from the limited possibilities of diversification within commodities. However, as we argue in this volume, diversification into nonresource sectors from a strong resource base is both feasible and historically common. In sum, three measures of natural resources prove to have either a positive effect or no effect on growth. Though several postulated channels of negative impact—depressing effects on capital accumulation, terms of trade, and macroeconomic volatility—often do appear important, overall, natural resources are good for growth.

The next two chapters can be seen as broadly supporting these findings, but also asking what lies behind the negative findings for the cross-country sample used by Sachs and others. Manzano and Rigobón, the authors of chapter 3, work with resource exports as a share of GDP and conclude that natural resources per se are not responsible for the fact that resource-rich developing countries have experienced lackluster growth since the 1970s; this leads them to focus instead on the role of international debt and imperfect credit markets. They first find, consistent with Lederman and Maloney, that when we move from Sachs and Warner's cross-sectional regression to a panel context and use standard fixed-effects corrections for unobserved country characteristics that may be confused with natural resource endowments, the resource curse again disappears. Seeking to explain Sachs and

Warner's cross-sectional evidence for a curse, however, they find that resource-rich economies accumulated foreign debt during periods when commodity prices were high, especially during the 1970s. Manzano and Rigobón present econometric evidence showing that, as commodity prices declined in subsequent years, these economies suffered from a debt "overhang" that stifled growth beyond the slowdown expected due to declining prices, an overhang that is analogous to those arising from bubbles in the real estate or stock markets. These results are important, not only because they dispel the alleged curse of natural resources, but especially because the policy implication is that the right levers to dealing with the lackluster performance of resource-rich developing countries in recent decades lies in the realm of macroeconomic policy rather than in trade or industrial policies.

Bravo-Ortega and de Gregorio provide yet another theoretical and empirical assessment of the alleged resource curse in chapter 4. This article makes two important points. First, as perhaps the only article in the volume that accepts at face value and models Adam Smith's concerns noted earlier, the authors find that, while it is theoretically plausible that natural resources could reduce the rate of economic growth by a "Dutch disease" effect working through the absorption of human capital in the resource sector, this partly results from the fact that natural riches make countries richer. That is, resources produce a higher level of development in the long run (or in the steady state of an economy), even if they reduce the rate of change of income per person in the short run.

Second, again using Sachs and Warner's resources over GDP proxy in their truncated sample, as well as resource exports over total exports, they confirm empirically that the effect of natural resources on the pace of growth crucially depends on the availability of human capital. As the stock of human capital rises, the marginal effect of the stock of natural resources on income growth rises and becomes positive. This is broadly consistent with Gylfason (2001), and Gylfason, Herbertsson, and Zoega's (1999) argument that a national effort in education is especially necessary in resource-rich countries, although without their hypothesis that resource-rich sectors intrinsically require, and hence induce, less education. More generally, Bravo-Ortega and de Gregorio's findings can be seen as suggestive empirical support for the emphasis many of the subsequent papers place on the role of human capital broadly construed as getting the most out of natural resources. In addition, however, they find that the point at which resources begin to contribute positively to growth occurs at around three years of education, a level achieved by all but the poorest countries. Consequently, it is misleading to speak of an inevitable resource curse, for human capital and natural resources seem to be complements. Further, the solution to slow growth in resource-rich economies is to combine human capital and knowledge with natural resources.

Though the political-economy channel is not dealt with specifically in any of these articles and, as stressed earlier, is not the focus of the volume, it is a potentially important channel through which the resource curse might operate. Unfortunately, the dearth of time series of institutional indicators of significant span makes this empirical agenda especially challenging. Most works, including Easterly and Levine (2003), which finds a measure of crops and minerals positively affecting the level of development through the institutional channel, or Isham et al. (2005), which finds that point-sourced resources have a negative impact on institutions and hence depress growth, have worked with a single cross-section of countries. Murshed (2004) broadly concurs with Isham et al., working in a panel context that reduces the concerns of bias due to unobserved country characteristics, although at the price of a much-reduced set of institutional variables. That said, the evidence of an overall positive impact of resources on growth suggests that the institutional channel is not strong enough to breathe new life into the curse and seems more consistent with the Easterly and Levine finding. Earlier, we argued that the combined impacts of natural resource endowments on growth were negligible or positive; Sala-i-Martin, Doppelhofer, and Miller (2004), as a result of running millions of regressions, classify natural resources as among the most robust estimates in empirical studies on economic growth, but explicitly note that the fraction of GDP in mining, the quintessential point-sourced resource, enters *strongly and robustly positively*. This is broadly consistent with Davis (1995) and, more recently, Stijns (2005), who finds that fuel and mineral reserves have not been a deterrent to growth (although, arguably, land—not generally considered a point-source resource—has been).[2]

Are Natural Resources a Curse? Lessons from History

The articles in this section take a historical view of the experience of resource-led development and why it has worked in some countries and not in others. In general, they place heavy emphasis on the role of knowledge and of openness to the international product and knowledge market as keys to success.

First, however, chapter 5 addresses the evolution of prices of natural resource commodities relative to the prices of manufactures. More specifically, Cuddington, Ludema, and Jayasuriya address a key concern about commodity specialization in developing countries by revisiting the argument of Prebisch (1950) that, over the long term, declining terms of trade would frustrate development efforts in economies with abundant natural resources. Thus, the chapter has two main objectives. The first is to clarify the issues raised by Prebisch and Singer (1950) as they relate to the commodity specialization of developing countries (and Latin America in particular). The second is to reconsider empirically the issue of trends in commodity prices, using long-run historical data and modern econometric techniques. The authors show that, rather than a downward trend, real primary prices over the last century have experienced one or more abrupt shifts—or "structural breaks"—downwards, while the data-generation process seems to follow a random walk. The preponderance of evidence therefore points to a single break in 1921, with *no* trend, positive or negative, before or since. This evidence is of practical interest, because it tells us that the best predictor of future relative prices of commodities is today's prices, although random breaks that push prices down or up could occur, as has happened since 2001; these breaks, however, tend to be unpredictably random and thus are irrelevant for policy formulation.

The next three chapters can be seen as historical documentation of the centrality of technological progress to successful natural resource–based growth. Chapter 6, written by Maloney, argues that Latin America missed opportunities for rapid resource-based growth that similarly endowed countries and regions, such as Australia, Canada, and Scandinavia, were able to exploit. Fundamental to this poor performance was deficient technological adoption driven by two factors. First, deficient national "learning" or "innovative" capacity, arising from low investment in human capital and scientific infrastructure, led to weak capacity to innovate or even take advantage of technological advances abroad. Second, the period of inward-looking industrialization discouraged innovation and created a sector whose growth depended on artificial monopoly rents rather than on the quasi-rents arising from technological adoption, and, at the same time, it undermined natural resource–intensive sectors that had the potential for dynamic growth. Indeed, Latin America's missed opportunities could have been tremendous during the heyday of protectionism in the 1950s and 1960s, even when some countries, such as Brazil and Mexico, grew rapidly, because the reconstruction of Europe and Japan implied an unprecedented (and still unreplicated) expansion of world demand.[3] Consequently, Latin America's resource-based and export-led growth during that time could have been even better than it was if it had allowed exports, including commodities, to rise in accordance with growing world demand.

Wright and Czelusta examine experiences of resource-led growth from a historical perspective, with a focus on mineral-rich countries, in chapter 7. The chapter highlights several cases of successful resource-based development. The first is the historical experience of the United States from the mid-19th to the mid-20th centuries. Not only was the United States the world's leading mineral economy in the period during which the country became the world leader in manufacturing (roughly from 1890 to 1910), but linkages and complementarities to the resource sector were vital in the broader story of American economic success as well. Demurring from Bravo-Ortega and de Gregorio's pessimism about the replicability of such experiences, the authors describe successful modern development of the minerals sector in South American and African countries, leading up to a more detailed look at the remarkable rejuvenation of minerals in Australia—a country that had earlier consigned the resource-based phase of its development to history. Consistent with the previous paper is their emphasis on the essential complementarity of innovation in the dynamism of extractive industries, citing for instance the "glass earth" project, a complex of six new technologies that allows analysts to peer into the top kilometer of the earth's crust to locate new mineral deposits. The broad lesson is, again, that what matters for resource-based development is not the inherent character of resources, but the nature of the learning process through which their economic potential is achieved.

Blomström and Kokko concur with this argument in chapter 8, stressing the central role of the expansion of industries based on domestic raw materials such as timber and iron ore in the Scandinavian development experience. From a position as suppliers of intermediate products to more advanced economies in Western Europe, Sweden and Finland were able to upgrade the technological level of their raw-materials industries and establish a foundation for a more diversified economy, eventually successfully entering related activities such as machinery, engineering products, transport equipment, and various types of services. Nevertheless, industries that depend on raw materials still account for a significant share of manufacturing activity and experience high rates of productivity growth. Focusing particularly on forestry products, they argue that there is every expectation that natural resource sectors will continue to play an important role in the future, despite the increased competition from lower-wage producers in Chile, Brazil, or Eastern Europe.

The key to the success of these resource-based sectors has been the incessant process of technological upgrading in the context of knowledge clusters of universities, private think tanks, and within-firm research units. The authors use the cases of sawn wood products vs. pulp and paper to illustrate how important these clusters are to the long-run performance of the sector. The export, production, and employment shares of knowledge-intensive manufacturing and service sectors have grown rapidly in recent decades, and the chapter elaborates on the emergence of Nokia, a global telephony giant that traces its corporate lineage back to one of Finland's first pulp mills in a village of that name. While documenting Nokia's evolution from resource-based to electronics-based firm, the authors show that the strategies for technological upgrading in the Swedish forestry and Finnish electronic industry are similar: high levels of human capital, internationalization of both markets and sources of technological progress, and flexibility in adjusting to shifts in demand or technology.

All three chapters in this section stress the high degree of complementarity between natural resources and knowledge, broadly consistent with the empirical findings of Bravo-Ortega and de Gregorio. Further, all provide case studies that support the plausibility of the findings from the Lederman and Maloney piece that, in fact, natural resource abundance is good for growth. Finally, both the discussion of the role of mining in economic development and the role of forestry in Scandinavia suggest the possibilities for economic diversification from a solid natural resource–based platform, which is the main topic addressed by the chapters in the last part of the book.

Are Natural Resources Destiny?

Chapter 9, written by Venables, provides a review of the theoretical literature concerning the determinants of the patterns of trade, the location of economic activity, and development. With a lucid exposition, the author takes us from traditional endowment-based trade theory to the role played by geography and market size as equally if not more important factors determining comparative advantage (or the pattern of international trade). Moreover, recent theoretical advances have highlighted that comparative advantage is endogenous, which means that it can be created by capital accumulation and skills acquisition. The main driving forces in many of these models are spillovers or linkages across firms that produce increasing returns to scale. An important contribution of this literature has thus been to connect the concepts of development economics (and its traditional emphasis on backward and forward linkages) with the ideas of business economists that emphasize the formation of industrial clusters. In any case, this emergent literature has produced testable hypotheses that predict that natural endowments might not be the most important determinants of the patterns of trade.

Lederman and Xu provide an empirical counterpart in chapter 10 to some of the ideas put forth by new theories of trade and development. After a careful assessment of various econometric techniques, the authors provide a rich set of results concerning the empirical determinants of trade structure and trade intensity across countries and over time. The results suggest that the traditional concepts of factor endowments, such as land and capital per worker, do help explain observed patterns of trade, but that their role is not as important as previously thought. For some industries, the patterns of trade (that is, which countries are net exporters) are also affected by domestic infrastructure, the quality of public institutions and governance, investments in knowledge accumulation such as research and development, and macroeconomic volatility. The authors also provide evidence showing that complex interactions between the scale effects, volatility, and institutions and the trade intensity, which is the incidence of international trade in the national economy. Hence, nontraditional factors help explain not only what countries buy and sell from each other, but also how much they trade. Thus, some of the new theories that predict that the patterns of trade are endogenous not only to trade policies and factor endowments but also are affected by transport and transaction costs seem supported by econometric evidence. All of this clearly points to the role of public policy in shaping the productive structure of open economies in the era of globalization.

The book's final chapter, written by Martin, addresses a related question: how do countries reduce their dependence on natural resources during the process of development? This question is relevant even if we do not believe in the alleged curse of natural resources, because policymakers may still want to help the process of productive diversification. This is so either because policymakers might be believers in the curse or because dependence on certain types of commodities, such as oil or minerals, can also be associated with capital-intensive development with unwanted social side effects such as rising inequality when the rents of natural resources are not redistributed. In any case, the chapter by Martin examines four changes that reduce dependence on natural resources by reducing their share in national output. These are (i) accumulation of capital and skills, (ii) trade liberalization that reduces the indirect taxation of exporters, (iii) differential rates of technical change, and (iv) declines in transport costs. In practice, developing countries as a group have made enormous progress in diversifying their exports away from natural resources in recent decades. These trends seem to have been propelled by the accumulation of capital and skills in some countries and by trade liberalization, both of which more than compensated for biased technical change that favored agriculture. Thus, it is a bit ironic that trade reforms have supported diversification away from natural resources while technical progress has been fastest in agriculture, which depends on a key natural resource, namely, land. This last observation is also directly in contradiction with some version of the resource-curse hypothesis, which implies that technological progress is fastest in manufacturing activities.

In sum, this book provides ample statistical, historical, and theoretical evidence to suggest that natural resources are neither curse nor destiny for developing countries. Nor are they a short-cut to equitable and sustainable long-term development. Natural resources are assets for development that require intelligent public policies that complement natural riches with human ingenuity. It is only through these complex interactions that resource-led growth can take off.

Notes

* This volume was supported by the Regional Studies Program of the Office of the Chief Economist for Latin America and the Caribbean of the World Bank. We are grateful for incisive feedback on the overall project from Guillermo Perry and two anonymous referees.

1. The seminal contribution seems to be Imbs and Wacziarg (2003), who show that employment and production concentration across industries tends to decline with the level of GDP per capita up to a point over $10,000, after which specialization tends to rise and diversification falls. Moreover, it is related to an influential theory proposed by Hausmann and Rodrik (2003), which argues that economic development is brought about by a messy process of economic "self discovery" that, as with other elements of innovation, is plagued by appropriability market failures. The robust empirical finding that export diversification is associated with improvements in the pace of economic growth lends support to these types of growth models, since the process of export diversification in developing countries seems tightly linked to the introduction of new exports (Klinger and Lederman 2006). Furthermore, these results are consistent with the work by Kahn (2004), who shows that the introduction of new products is associated with capital accumulation, which then accelerates GDP growth.

2. Natural resources over exports enters less robustly but negatively as they assert, although, as we suggest, this effect appears to largely reflect export concentration per se. Since our understanding that none of the regressions includes fixed effects, we remain circumspect on both points.

3. The average rate of growth of GDP per capita (at constant national prices) in Latin America during the decade of the 1960s was around 2.4 percent per year. Mexico grew at an average annual rate of around 3.5 percent, while Brazil achieved a rate of 2.9 percent. In contrast, the world's GDP per capita grew by 3.5 percent per year during the same decade. World growth declined to 2.1 percent in the 1970s, to 1.3 percent in the 1980s, and to around 1 percent during 1990–2002. These trends are not altered if we use PPP-adjusted or constant-dollars data.

References

Auty, Richard M. 2000. "How Natural Resources Affect Economic Development." *Development Policy Review* 18: 347–64.

———. 2001a. "The Political Economy of Resource-Driven Growth." *European Economic Review* 45: 839–46.

———. ed. 2001b. *Resource Abundance and Economic Development.* New York: Oxford University Press.

Davis, Graham A. 1995. "Learning to Love the Dutch Disease: Evidence from the Mineral Economies." *World Development* 23 (10): 1765–79.

Easterly, William, and Ross Levine. 2003. "Tropics, Germs, and Crops: How Endowments Influence Economic Development." *Journal of Monetary Economics* 50 (1): 3–47.

Gelb, Alan. 1988. *Oil Windfalls: Blessing or Curse?* New York: Oxford University Press.

Gylfason, Thorvaldur. 2001. "Natural Resources, Education, and Economic Development." *European Economic Review* 45: 847–59.

Gylfason, Thorvaldur, Tryggvi Thor Herbertsson, and Gylfi Zoega. 1999. "A Mixed Blessing, Natural Resources, and Economic Growth." *Macroeconomic Dynamics* 3: 204–25.

Hausmann, Ricardo, and Dani Rodrik. 2003 "Economic Development as Self-Discovery." *Journal of Development Economics* 72 (2): 603–33.

Imbs, J., and R. Wacziarg. 2003. "Stages of Diversification." *American Economic Review* 93 (1): 63–86.

Isham, Jonathan, Michael Woolcock, Lant Pritchett, and Gwen Busby. 2005. "The Varieties of Resource Experience: Natural Resource Export Structures and the Political Economy of Economic Growth." *World Bank Economic Review* 19 (2): 141–74.

Kahn, Faruk A. 2004. "New Product Technology and Factor Accumulation." Williams College, Massachusetts. http://www.williams.edu/Economics/khan/.

Klinger, Bailey, and Daniel Lederman. 2006. "Diversification, Innovation, and Imitation inside the Global Technological Frontier." Policy Research Working Paper 3872, World Bank, Washington, DC.

Mehlum, Halvor, Karl Moene, and Ragnar Torvik. 2006. "Institutions and the Resource Curse." *The Economic Journal* 116: 1–20.

Murshed, S. Mansoob. 2004. "When Does Natural Resource Abundance Lead to a Resource Curse?" Environmental Economics Programme Discussion Paper 04-11, International Institute for Environment and Development, The Hague.

Neumayer, Eric. 2004. "Does the 'Resource Curse' Hold for Growth in Genuine Income as Well?" *World Development* 32 (10): 1627–40.

Prebisch, Raúl. 1959. "The Economic Development of Latin America and its Principal Problems." Reprinted in *Economic Bulletin for Latin America* 7 (1): 1–22, 1962.

Ross, M. L. 1999. "The Political Economy of the Resource Curse." *World Politics* (51): 297–322.

Sachs, Jeffrey D., and Andrew Warner. 1995 (revised in 1997). "Natural Resource Abundance and Economic Growth." National Bureau of Economic Research Working Paper 5398, Cambridge, MA.

———. 2001. "The Curse of Natural Resources." *European Economic Review* 45: 827–38.

Sala-i-Martin, Xavier, Gernot Doppelhofer, and Ronald I. Miller. 2004. "Determinants of Long-Term Growth: A Bayesian Averaging of Classical Estimates (BACE) Approach." *American Economic Review* 94 (4): 813–35.

Singer, Hans W. 1950. "U.S. Foreign Investment in Underdeveloped Areas: The Distribution of Gains between Investing and Borrowing Countries." *American Economic Review, Papers and Proceedings* 40: 473–85.

Stijns, Jean-Phillipe C. 2005. "Natural Resources and Economic Growth Revisited." *Resources Policy* 30: 107–30.

Tornell, Aaron, and Philip Lane. 1999. "The Voracity Effect." *American Economic Review* 88 (5): 22–46.

Torvik, Ragnar. 2002. "Natural Resources, Rent Seeking, and Welfare." *Journal of Development Economics* 67 (2): 455–70.

Part I

Are Natural Resources a Curse? Econometric Evidence

2

Trade Structure and Growth

Daniel Lederman and William F. Maloney*

Introduction

IN RECENT YEARS, A VAST BODY of literature has studied the impact of trade openness or magnitude of trade flows on income levels (see, for example, Frankel and Romer 1999; Ferreira and Trejos 2002; Wacziarg and Welch 2003) and on the rate of economic growth (see Rodrik and Rodriguez 2000; Jones 2000; Wacziarg 2001; Wacziarg and Welch 2003). This paper investigates a far less studied issue, namely the impact of trade *structure*—particularly natural resource specialization, export concentration, and intra-industry trade—on growth. Though these variables clearly do not exhaust the possible dimensions of trade structure, they have received extensive attention in the recent literature.

In spirit and approach, this chapter can be seen as the trade analogue to recent empirical work that, for instance, looks at the impact of a set of financial development proxies on growth (Levine, Loayza, and Beck 2000). We follow what has become the standard practice of assessing the robustness of econometric results by examining how they change as the set of control variables (Levine and Renelt 1992; Sala-i-Martin 1997, among many others) and the estimation techniques (Caselli, Esquivel, and Lefort 1996; Levine, Loayza, and Beck 2000) are modified.

We find that, regardless of the estimation technique, trade structure variables are important determinants of growth rates and probably should be in the conditioning set of growth regressions. However, we also find that many of the stylized facts, particularly those surrounding natural resource specialization, are not robust to estimation technique or conditioning variables. In particular, both our preferred measure of natural resource abundance and even Sachs and Warner's proxy natural-resource exports over GDP appear to be *positively* correlated with economic growth, and this effect plausibly arises from a greater potential for productivity growth. We also find that concentration of export revenues reduces growth by hampering productivity and that this, rather than natural resources per se, drives Sachs and Vial's (2001) finding of a negative impact of natural resource exports over total exports, a proxy that we, in the end, see as measuring concentration. In sum, we find no evidence of a resource curse using any of these three measures of resource abundance.

The incidence of intra-industry trade is generally associated with good growth performance, but the channel may be largely through its correlation with export concentration.

Trade Variables and Growth

Natural Resource Abundance

We begin with those variables relating to natural resource abundance and specialization that, from Adam Smith to, more recently, Auty (1998) and Sachs and Warner (1997b, 2001), have been viewed as having detrimental impacts on growth. Numerous channels through which this might occur have been suggested, and here we offer an incomplete list.

First, beginning with Smith,[1] observers have argued that natural resources are associated with lower accumulation of human and physical capital, lower productivity growth, and lower spillovers, although the case is far from proven. Martin and Mitra (2001) find total-factor-productivity growth to be higher in agriculture than in manufactures in a large sample of advanced and developing countries. Wright and Czelusta (in chapter 7) and Irwin (2000) argue that, contrary to Smith's prejudice, mining is a dynamic and knowledge-intensive industry critical to U.S. development. In chapter 8, Blomström and Kokko argue the same for forestry in Scandinavia. And, as Torvik (2002) argues, these findings are important as, in the presence of a sufficiently dynamic resource sector, the behavior of an economy experiencing a resource boom differs radically from the standard Dutch disease model.

Second, Prebisch (1959), among others, popularized the idea that the terms of trade of natural resource exporters would experience a secular decline over time relative to those of exporters of manufactures. However, Cuddington, Ludema, and Jayasuriya (chapter 5) find that they cannot be rejected that relative commodity prices follow a random walk across the 20th century, with a single break in 1929.

Third, either reasons of history or Dutch disease may result in high levels of export concentration, which may lead to higher export price volatility and hence greater macro volatility.[2] Fourth, an extensive literature (see, for example Easterly and Levine 2002) examines how the rents arising from resource extraction may lead to institutional failures. Finally, Manzano and Rigobón (2001) argue that imperfect international capital markets allow countries experiencing commodity price booms to overborrow, eventually requiring policies that restrict growth when credit dries up during the inevitable downturns.

There is as yet limited consensus on the appropriate empirical proxy for measuring resource abundance. Leamer (1984) argues that standard Heckscher-Ohlin trade theory dictates that the appropriate measure is net exports of resources per worker. Though this measure has been the basis for extensive research on the determinants of trade patterns (for example, Trefler 1995; Antweiler and Trefler 2002; Estevadeordal and Taylor 2002),[3] to date there has been essentially no empirical work testing its impact on growth.[4] A look at the unconditional correlation in figure 2.1a suggests that the most resource-abundant country is Norway, followed by New Zealand, Trinidad and Tobago, Canada, Finland, and Australia. Though these countries are mostly well off, there is overall no obvious relationship between the Leamer measure and growth.

In fact, the best known formal empirical tests for the resource curse are found in the work of Sachs and Warner (1995a, 1995b, 1997a, 1997b, 1999, 2001), who employ natural resource exports as a share of GDP as their proxy. Using cross-sectional data employed previously by Barro (1991); Mankiw, Romer, and Weil (1992); and DeLong and Summers (1991) across the period 1970–1990, they persistently find a negative correlation with growth, much to the alarm of many resource-abundant developing countries.[5] Figure 2.1b suggests that, with this proxy, the most natural resource "abundant" countries by far are the Republic of Congo and Papua New Guinea, with Finland, Norway, and Canada nowhere to be found.

This variable is of intrinsic interest although, as Sachs and Warner suggest, it leads to counterintuitive results as a measure of resource abundance. Figure 2.1b shows that Singapore, due to its substantial re-exports of raw materials, appears very resource abundant and, given its high growth rates, even seems to impart a positive relationship between resource abundance and growth. Because this gross measure is clearly not capturing the country's true factor endowments, Sachs and Warner replaced the values of Singapore and Trinidad and Tobago with net resource exports as a share of GDP (see data appendix in Sachs and Warner 1997a). This measure, in fact, approximates Leamer's, and it is not clear why net values should only be used for these two cases. Numerous countries in Asia and Latin America have a large presence of export processing zones that would, using the gross measure, overstate their true abundance in manufacturing-related factors. The variable also shows substantial volatility over time, reflecting terms of trade movements, and hence the average for the period is probably a better

Figure 2.1a Growth vs. NR Net Exports/Labor Force, 1980–99

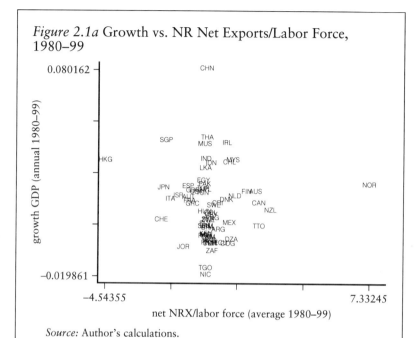

Source: Author's calculations.

Figure 2.1b Growth vs. NR Exports/GDP, 1980–99

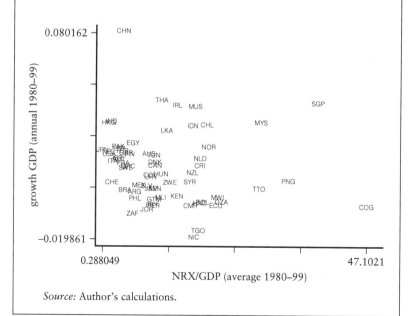

Source: Author's calculations.

measure than the initial period value that was used by Sachs and Warner in several of their papers.

Finally, in an effort using more disaggregated data, Stijns (2005) finds no correlation of fuel and mineral reserves on growth between 1970 and 1989. This confirms earlier work by Davis (1995), which found that mineral-dependent economies, defined by high share of minerals in exports and GDP, did well relative to other countries across the 1970s and 1980s.

Export Concentration

The next set of variables focuses on export concentration. Clearly, dependence on a single export, whether it's copper in Chile or potentially microchips in Costa Rica, can leave a country vulnerable to sharp declines in terms of trade. The presence of a single, very visible, export may also give rise to a variety of political economy effects that are deleterious to growth. On the other hand, specialization is often associated with scale economies and, hence, higher productivity.

We employ two measures to capture different dimensions of concentration. First, we construct a Herfindahl index using export data disaggregated at 4-digit SITC. The index ranges from zero and one and increases with concentration.[6] This index is widely used in studies that focus on general indicators of economic concentration (for example, Antweiler and Trefler 2002). Figure 2.1c suggests a downward sloping relationship with growth.

Second, we employ the share of natural resource exports in total exports. This was employed by Sachs and Vial (2001), again, as a measure of resource abundance and was found to have a very robustly negative relationship to growth in a panel specification in differences. Again, we would argue that this measure has intrinsic interest, but as a specific measure of concentration of exports in one particular industry. Figure 2.1d also suggests a negative relationship with respect to economic growth. However, it also shows a significant re-ranking of countries compared to the previous resource measures. Papua New Guinea, Malawi, Nicaragua, and Togo, among others, now appear as high-value cases, while Finland and Singapore have fallen among the lower-value cases.

Intra-Industry Trade

The final trade measure we employ is the Grubel-Lloyd (1975) index of intra-industry trade (IIT).[7] The scale economies arising from IIT are thought to lead to more rapid productivity gains and, hence, faster growth (see, for example, Krugman 1979). Because the incidence of IIT is high among manufactures, there is a sense in which this measure is a broad

Figure 2.1c Growth vs. Export Herfindahl, 1980–99

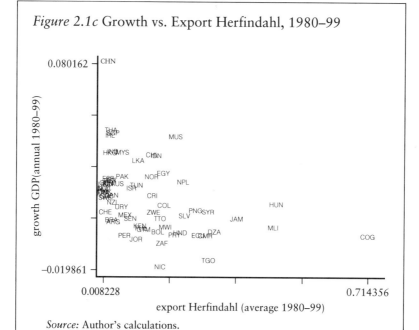

export Herfindahl (average 1980–99)

Source: Author's calculations.

Figure 2.1d Growth vs. NR Exports/Total Merchandise Exports, 1980–99

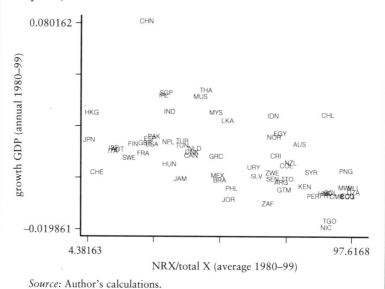

NRX/total X (average 1980–99)

Source: Author's calculations.

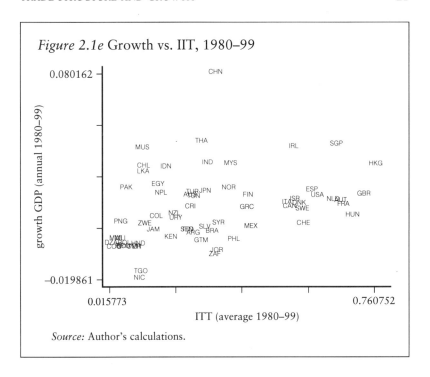

Figure 2.1e Growth vs. IIT, 1980–99

Source: Author's calculations.

complement to those above. No obvious unconditional relationship appears in figure 2.1e.

Each of these variables is of interest in itself. However, each also may represent a channel through which the other variables of interest affect growth. For instance, resource abundance may also imply a high level of export concentration or a low level of intra-industry trade. We attempt to disentangle these effects as well.

Estimation Techniques

We begin with a basic specification that can nest much of the existing work on the empirics of economic growth:

$$\dot{y}_{i,t} = \gamma y_{i,t-1} + \beta' X_{i,t} + \alpha \tau_{i,t} + \mu_t + \eta_i + \varepsilon_{i,t} \qquad (2.1)$$

Where $\dot{y}_{it}$ is the log difference of per capita GDP of country i in period t, $y_{i,t-1}$ log income per capita at the beginning of the period, X_{it} the matrix of conditioning variables, and τ the particular trade variable of interest. μ_i

is a country fixed effect, μ_t is a sample-wide time effect, and ε_{it} is a classical error.

Most of the previous work discussed above—and in fact much of the growth literature until recently—has been based on estimations of an equation similar to (2.1) using cross-sectional regressions data that lack any time dimension, although the drawbacks are well known.[8] As Levine and Renelt (1992) first pointed out in the growth context, cross-country growth regressions are sensitive to the variables included in the specification. Further, substantial bias may be induced by the correlation of unobserved country-specific factors and the variables of interest; $E(\mu_i, \tau_{it})$, may be large. Caselli, Esquivel, and Lefort (1996), for instance, pointed out that the difference with respect to the highest level of income in the sample of countries (that is, the level to which the other countries are converging) acts as a proxy for country-specific effects in cross-sectional regressions, and thus the resulting estimates are inconsistent. Closer to the present paper, Manzano and Rigobón (2001) found in a 1980–90 cross-section that Sachs-Warner's negative correlation of natural resources with growth disappears when they control for the initial ratio of foreign debt to GDP.

Cross-sectional regressions clearly suffer from endogeneity problems as well. In the growth context, Knight, Loayza, and Villanueva (1993) point out that, by construction, the initial level of income is correlated with the growth variable. However, the problem is much larger, as Caselli, Esquivel, and Lefort (1996) note, extending (as is often the case in macroeconomic studies) to the interdependence of virtually all of the relevant growth-related variables. Other papers on economic growth attempting to deal with both unobserved country-specific effects and endogenous explanatory variables include Easterly, Loayza, and Montiel (1997); Levine, Loayza, and Beck (2000); and Bond, Hoeffler, and Temple (2001).

Panel data offer a potential solution to the endogeneity problem through the use of lagged values as instruments for endogenous variables. The issue of unobserved country-specific effects can also be addressed, although the standard fixed or variable effects estimators are not consistent in the present context, where we implicitly include a lagged dependent variable—the initial level of GDP per capita. The assumption of a lack of correlation between μ_i and the explanatory variables required for variable effects estimators is not defensible in this context, since both $\dot{y}_{it}$ and y_{t-1} are a function of μ_i. However, ordinary least squares (OLS) is clearly inconsistent and feasible generalized least squares (FGLS) is also, should the errors show either heteroskedasticity or serial correlation (Sevestre and Trognon 1996). Further, the usual elimination of μ_i by subtracting off the time mean induces a negative correlation between the transformed error and the lagged dependent variables of order $1/T$, which, in short panels such as those used here, remains substantial.

Following Anderson and Hsiao (1982), Arellano and Bond (1991), and Caselli, Esquivel, and Lefort (1996) in the growth literature, we therefore difference the data to eliminate μ_i, yielding:

$$\Delta \dot{y}_{i,t} = \gamma \dot{y}_{i,t-1} + \beta' \Delta X_{i,t} + \alpha \Delta \tau_{i,t} + \Delta \mu_t + \Delta \varepsilon_{i,t} \qquad (2.2)$$

Any unobserved country fixed effects disappear in the differenced errors. However, unless the idiosyncratic error followed a random walk, this differencing necessarily gives the transformed error a moving-average, MA(n), structure that is correlated with the differenced lagged dependent variable. Under the assumption that ε is not serially correlated and that the explanatory variables X are weakly exogenous,[9] following Arellano and Bond (1991), we can employ lagged levels dated $t - n$ and earlier as instruments in a generalized method of moments (GMM) context using the following moment conditions:

$$E(y_{it-s}, \Delta \varepsilon_{it}) = 0 \text{ for } s \geq 2, \ t = 1,...T.$$
$$E(x_{it-s}, \Delta \varepsilon_{it}) = 0 \text{ for } s \geq 2, \ t = 0,...T.$$

However, in growth regressions where the explanatory variables (for example, schooling, natural resource endowments) show little variation across time, levels are often poor instruments. Bond, Hoeffler, and Temple (2001) show that the "weak instruments" problem can be severe in cross-country growth regressions with panel data. For this reason, Levine, Loayza, and Beck (2000), in their examination of the impact of financial variables on growth, follow Blundell and Bond (1998) and Arellano and Bover (1995) in employing a system estimator that rescues some of the cross-sectional variance that is lost in the differences GMM estimator by estimating a system of equations that also includes equation (2.1) in levels, but with the lagged differences of the endogenous variables as instruments. These, again, are not correlated with the unobserved country effect, so that we can use the following moment conditions as the second part of the system:

$$E(\Delta y_{it-s}, \eta_i) = 0 \text{ for } s \geq 1, t = 0, ...T.$$
$$E(\Delta x_{it-s}, \eta_i) = 0 \ \text{ for } s \geq 1, t = 0, ...T.$$

The assumption that there is no correlation between the differences of the variables and the country-specific effect is valid as long as the correlation between the fixed effect and the levels of the variables is constant over time, as explained by Levine, Loayza, and Beck (2000) and others.

The moment conditions effectively give us T–1 equations in first-differences followed by T equations in levels. The solutions to these equations are then weighted by the inverse of a consistent estimate of the moment condition covariance matrix in a two-step method broadly analogous to generalized least squares (GLS).

Working in the differenced panel context raises other concerns. Griliches and Hausman (1986) pointed out that differencing decreases the signal-to-noise ratio in the data, increasing the de facto measurement error and potentially biasing coefficients toward zero. More recently, Prichett (2000) argued that moving to higher-frequency growth data, as we move for example from 20-year averages with cross-sectional data to five-year averages in the panel data set, highlights the short-run relationships (that is, cyclical elements) among variables relative to the long run (growth). The GMM systems estimator, in theory, addresses these problems. However, to err on the side of caution and to be comparable with previous work, we present the OLS cross-sectional results along with the system estimates.

Estimation and Results

The empirical strategy is to introduce the trade variable of interest first to a set of core conditioning variables, and then to progressively add new variables, many now standard in the literature, to examine both robustness and suggestive channels of influence of the trade variable of interest. The basic conditioning set includes initial income of the period to capture standard convergence effects. Because the paper focuses on trade structure and not openness, we include a policy-based index of openness provided by Sachs and Warner (1995a). Although the literature has been highly critical of virtually all such measures of openness (see, for example, Pritchett 1996; Rodrik and Rodriguez 2000), to ensure consistency with the natural resource literature of Sachs and Warner, we use their measure. Nevertheless, it is worth pointing out that Wacziarg (2001) shows that the estimated effects of the trade-to-GDP ratio are virtually identical when the ratio is instrumented by the Sach-Warner index as when it is instrumented by other policy indicators such as average tariffs and the non-tariff barrier-coverage ratio.

The second conditioning set adds variables related to the accumulation of physical and human capital: the average ratio of investment/GDP and log of years of schooling of the adult population, which is the preferred measure of the stock of human capital (for example, Barro 2001). The third set adds growth in the terms of trade as a possible channel through which natural resource variables may affect growth. Finally, as a measure of macrostability of particular importance to the trade sector, we then include the standard deviation of the real effective exchange rate (REER) over the period, calculated from monthly data. As numerous authors (see, for example, Servén 1998) suggest, macroeconomic volatility reduces investment and thus growth. However, other studies show that macroeconomic factors that are likely to be associated with REER volatility, such as episodes of high inflation, are related to both the level of investment and the rate of productivity growth (for example, Fischer 1993; Bruno and Easterly 1998). This may also prove a channel through which our trade variables work. Time dummies are included in all of the regressions that rely on panel data.

Data

The core data set is that of Heston and Summers (1991) updated to 2000, and the trade variables were constructed as in table 2.1. We construct panels of five-year periods extending from 1975 to 1999. We lose one observation to instruments, leaving a 20-year span to estimate from 1980 to 1999. Because we are interested in seeing how sensitive the results are to estimating technique, we use the same sample for both the cross-section and panel exercises. Table 2.2 presents the summary statistics of both the cross-section and panel data sets. The list of countries in the sample is found in the annex.

Tables 2.3a and 2.3b present the cross-sectional and panel results, respectively. The tables report the coefficient and significance level on the particular trade variable in a regression containing the control variables listed in the first column. Hence, the next column reports the coefficient on the Leamer measure first for the basic conditioning variables, then with human capital and investment, then with terms of trade, and so on. This is done for each variable as we move across the top of the table. Below the double line (under the section labeled "Additional controls"), we combine the variables of interest along with the full conditioning set as tests of possible channels through which the principal variable of interest works. For instance, we add the export Herfindahl to the Leamer regression as a test of whether whatever effect resource abundance has on growth may work through export concentration.

As tests of the validity of the instruments, and hence the consistency of the GMM estimator, we report the two specification tests suggested by Arellano and Bond (1991) and Blundell and Bond (1998): the Sargan test for overidentifying restrictions and tests for first- and second-order serial correlation.[10] Finally, we employ Windmeijer's (2005) correction of the standard errors for small sample size.

In both the OLS and panel exercises, the key conditioning variables entered either with the expected sign or statistically insignificantly (results available on request). For instance, in most specifications, initial GDP per capita enters negatively and significantly; the stock of human capital enters positively and significantly; and the Sachs-Warner measure of openness enters positively and significantly.

Table 2.1 Definitions and Sources of Variables

Variable	Definition	Source
Real per capita GDP and growth rates (1985 US$ PPP)	Ratio of total GDP to total population. GDP is in 1985 PPP-adjusted US$. Post-1990 GDP per capita growth rates are obtained from constant 1995 US$ per capita GDP series. Post-1990 GDP per capita levels were calculated applying growth rates to 1985 PPP-adjusted series.	Data provided by Loayza, Fajnzylber, and Calderon (2004). Based on Heston and Summers (1991)
NRX/total exports	Primary exports[a] divided by total merchandise exports	WDI and UN COMTRADE
NRX/GDP	Primary exports[a] divided by GDP	WDI and UN COMTRADE
Net NRX/labor force	Net primary exports[b] divided by the labor force	WDI and UN COMTRADE
Openness (S&W)	Percentage of years with open economic regime	Sachs and Warner (1995a)
Investment	Natural log of the ratio of gross domestic investment (in 1995 US$) to GDP (in 1995 US$)	From Loayza, Fajnzylber, and Calderon (2002)
Growth of terms of trade	Growth of the external terms of trade, defined as the ratio of an export price index to an import price index	WDI
Log years of schooling	Natural log of years of schooling	Barro and Lee (2000)
Real exchange rate volatility	Standard deviation of monthly interannual changes in real effective exchange rates	Authors' construction using IMF and JP Morgan databases
Export Herfindahl	Herfindahl index of export value.	WDI and UN COMTRADE
Grubel-Lloyd IIT index	Grubel and Lloyd intra-industry trade index	WDI and UN COMTRADE

a. Primary exports comprise the commodities in SITC sections 0, 1, 2 (excluding 22), 3, 4, and 68.
b. Net primary exports also include sections 63, 64, and 94.

Table 2.2 Descriptive Statistics

Panel data variable	Countries	Obs	Mean	Std Dev	Minimum	Maximum
Growth of real GDP per capita	65	143	1.81	2.43	–4.69	10.19
Log of real GDP per capita	65	143	8.39	0.99	6.19	9.83
NRX/total exports	65	143	0.49	0.29	0.04	0.99
NRX/GDP	65	143	0.11	0.10	0.00	0.62
Net NRX/labor force	65	143	0.23	1.18	–7.30	11.11
Openness (S&W)	65	143	0.81	0.38	0.00	1.00
Investment	65	143	3.10	0.23	2.62	3.71
Growth of terms of trade	65	143	0.00	0.03	–0.13	0.06
Log years of schooling	65	143	1.68	0.58	–0.63	2.48
Real exchange rate volatility	65	143	0.08	0.08	0.01	0.66
Export Herfindahl	65	143	0.11	0.13	0.01	0.74
Grubel-Lloyd IIT index	65	143	0.30	0.21	0.01	0.83

Cross-section variable	Countries	Mean	Std Dev	Minimum	Maximum
Growth of real GDP per capita	65	1.38	1.74	–1.99	8.02
Log of real GDP per capita	65	8.17	0.95	6.30	9.61
NRX/total exports	65	0.55	0.28	0.04	0.98
NRX/GDP	65	0.12	0.09	0.00	0.47
Net NRX/labor force	65	0.22	1.42	–4.54	7.33
Openness (S&W)	65	0.62	0.37	0.00	1.00
Investment	65	3.09	0.21	2.64	3.65
Growth of terms of trade	65	0.00	0.02	–0.07	0.02
Log years of schooling	65	1.47	0.67	–0.73	2.47
Real exchange rate volatility	65	0.12	0.23	0.02	1.91
Export Herfindahl	65	0.13	0.13	0.01	0.71
Grubel-Lloyd IIT index	65	0.30	0.21	0.02	0.76

Source: Authors' calculations.

Table 2.3a Estimated Effect of Trade Structure on Growth (Cross-Section, 1980–99)

	Natural resource dependence		Export concentration		Intra-industry trade
	Net exports/labor force	NRX/GDP	Export Herfindahl	NRX/total exports	Grubel-Lloyd index
Basic conditioning	-0.38	-0.89	-4.98**	-3.66***	3.26*
	(-0.20)	(-0.31)	(-2.02)	(-3.12)	(1.79)
+ Capital accumulation	-0.12	-3.66	-5.80***	-3.10***	3.09**
	(-0.47)	(-1.44)	(-3.72)	(-3.65)	(2.12)
+ Growth in terms of trade	-0.35	-3.01	-5.62***	-3.09***	2.85*
	(-0.15)	(-1.29)	(-3.28)	(-3.51)	(1.99)
+ Macro stability	-0.09	-3.40	-6.50***	-2.99***	2.67*
	(-0.878)	(-1.37)	(-3.92)	(-4.37)	(1.90)
Additional controls					
NRX/GDP			-6.52***		2.23*
			(-3.93)		(1.67)
Leamer index			-6.56***		3.76*
			(-3.85)		(1.88)
Export Herfindahl	0.45	0.05		-2.10***	1.86
	(0.81)	(0.03)		(-2.69)	(1.63)
NRX/total exports			-4.93***		-0.20
			(-3.91)		(-0.14)
Intra-industry trade	1.40	-2.23	-6.03***	-3.07***	
	(1.43)	(-1.02)	(-4.68)	(-3.11)	
IIT+export Herfindahl	1.56*	0.92		-2.07**	
	(1.79)	(0.60)		(-2.32)	

Source: Authors' calculations.

Note: The dependent variable is the GDP per capita growth rate. Basic conditioning set includes the log of initial income of the period and a measure of openness. Capital accumulation includes average ratio of investment/GDP and log of years of schooling. Growth of terms of trade refers to the growth of the ratio of price index to import price index over the period. Macrostability includes the standard deviation of the real exchange rate over the period. t-statistics shown in parentheses. * significant at 10 percent, ** significant at 5 percent, *** significant at 1 percent.

Natural Resource Abundance

In cross-section, the Leamer measure is never significant until the introduction of the IIT and Herfindahl in the final exercise, and then it is positive at the 10 percent level. The panel results are dramatically different, suggesting the presence of the omitted variables and simultaneity biases discussed earlier. Net natural resource exports appear positively although not quite significantly at the 10 percent level with the core conditioning variables. However, including the capital accumulation variable increases the significance and magnitude somewhat, suggesting that there may be some depressing effect on human and physical capital accumulation. The terms of trade variable similarly suggests a depressing effect of volatility and makes natural resource abundance significant at the 5 percent level. Macrostability seems to have a slight effect in the opposite direction. Taken together, these appear to be channels through which resources may negatively affect growth. Consistent with the cross-sectional results, a large increase appears when the export Herfindahl or the IIT variable or both are added, suggesting that resource-abundant countries may have more concentrated export structures, or have a lower incidence of IIT. Teasing out the implications of this must wait until these variables are examined on their own later. However, the mystery now is no longer what the channels are through which resources reduce growth, but rather why, once we have controlled for these channels, resource abundance continues to have such a positive impact on growth. One possibility is through higher rates of productivity growth, which would be consistent with Martin and Mitra (2001).

The results are broadly similar to the Sachs and Warner proxy, resource exports over GDP. Resources never appear significantly with any conditioning set in cross-section. This is not due to the shifting of the sample period forward 10 years. When we replace Singapore's value with *net* exports, as they do, we again find Sachs and Warner's negative and significant impact of resources. Simply put, whatever the conceptual appeal of this measure, used in its unadjusted form in cross-section, it shows no impact.[11]

This conclusion changes in the panel context. Natural resource exports enter positively and significantly at the 1 percent level with the basic conditioning set. Adding the capital accumulation variable makes their impact less *positive* and significant at the 10 percent level. This may suggest some stimulative impact of resource exports on physical and human capital accumulation. Further controlling for terms of trade variations and macrostability, export Herfindahl, and intra-industry trade variables lead to no further changes, suggesting that these are not especially important channels.

Table 2.3b Estimated Effect of Trade Structure on Growth (Panel Data [System Estimator], 1980–99)

	Natural resource dependence						Export concentration						Intra-industry trade		
	Net exports/labor force			NRX/GDP			Export Herfindahl			NRX/total exports			Grubel-Lloyd index		
		Sargan	Serial correlation		Sargan	Serial correlation		Sargan	Serial correlation		Sargan	Serial correlation		Sargan	Serial correlation
Basic conditioning	1.33 (1.52)	0.20	0.27	0.94*** (3.57)	0.48	0.49	−3.42 (−1.18)	0.38	0.35	−0.12 (−0.82)	0.17	0.34	2.37 (0.71)	0.47	0.42
+ Capital accumulation	2.87* (1.93)	0.39	0.53	0.68** (2.49)	0.29	0.83	−11.40*** (−3.04)	0.31	0.75	−0.57*** (−2.67)	0.32	0.36	8.64** (2.28)	0.35	0.80
+ Growth of terms of trade	3.50** (2.10)	0.45	0.48	0.65** (2.36)	0.40	0.71	−9.43** (−2.48)	0.51	0.76	−0.36** (−2.51)	0.37	0.60	8.29** (2.63)	0.50	0.92
+ Macrostability	2.66* (1.83)	0.50	0.56	0.69** (2.62)	0.56	0.71	−8.79** (−2.30)	0.52	0.72	−0.34** (−2.08)	0.31	0.57	8.21** (2.63)	0.54	0.85
Additional controls															
NRX/GDP							−10.32*** (−2.79)	0.58	0.70				7.80** (2.50)	0.49	0.81
Leamer index							−9.70*** (−2.78)	0.53	0.63				8.28** (2.61)	0.62	0.94
Export Herfindahl	3.05** (2.09)	0.42	0.61	0.65** (2.11)	0.35	0.62				−0.24 (−1.53)	0.21	0.55	6.12* (1.75)	0.42	0.81
NRX/total exports							−8.92** (−2.12)	0.53	0.79				6.05** (2.19)	0.41	0.74
Intra-industry trade	4.46** (2.40)	0.33	0.71	0.64** (2.36)	0.52	0.79	−8.93** (−2.02)	0.49	0.73	−0.21 (−0.88)	0.29	0.77			
IIT+export Herfindahl	4.41** (2.31)	0.32	0.66	0.62** (2.02)	0.36	0.68				−0.18 (−0.85)	0.28	0.80			

Source: Authors' calculations.

Note: The dependent variable is the GDP per capita growth rate. Basic conditioning set includes log of initial income of the period and a measure of openness. Capital accumulation includes average ratio of investment/GDP and log of years of schooling. Growth of terms of trade refers to the growth of the ratio of exports price index to import price index over the period. Macrostability includes the standard deviation of the real exchange rate over the period. t-statistics shown in parentheses. *significant at 10 percent, **significant at 5 percent, ***significant at 1 percent.

Export Concentration

For both measures of concentration, the cross-section and panel results are somewhat more consistent. With the basic conditioning set, the export Herfindahl is of the same order of magnitude and negative in both regressions at the 10 percent level. Adding the capital accumulation variables increases the magnitude (in absolute value) dramatically and makes concentration significant at the 1 percent level in both cases. In cross-section, the addition of new conditioning variables has limited effect on the coefficient value or significance. There is a marginally significant change in value of the OLS estimate with the introduction of the resource exports/exports variable.

The panel findings, however, suggest a significant positive impact of concentration on capital accumulation. There is some negative impact of terms of trade and macrostability of lower magnitude, suggesting an important channel through volatility as well. Among the additional controls, the introduction of NRX/GDP drives the Herfindahl coefficient even more negative, suggesting that, in fact, natural resource abundance partly *offsets* the negative impact of concentration.

The natural resources exports over total exports variable shows less similarity between the two estimation techniques. In cross-section, it is uniformly negative and appears insensitive to the addition of any of the controls or concentration measures or IIT measures. This would seem to suggest some intrinsic effect of a high natural resource concentration in exports that is not accounted for by any of the usual channels. However, again, the panel results cast some doubt on this conclusion. The variable enters negatively and insignificantly with the basic conditioning variables. The introduction of capital accumulation, however, makes the coefficient strongly significant and negative, suggesting that, again, concentration has a positive effect on capital accumulation. The introduction of terms of trade volatility, again, has a modest effect of reducing, again, the size of the coefficient, suggesting a deleterious effect on growth. The influence of natural resource exports over exports weakens with the introduction of the additional controls. Introduction of the export Herfindahl makes the coefficient insignificant, suggesting that it is concentration, and not resources itself, that drives the result.

In sum, to the degree that there is any evidence of a negative impact of natural resources, it is not happening through productivity growth as Sachs and Warner (1995b, 1999), among others, argue. Further, the only natural resource–related variable that enters with a significant and negative sign, natural resources as a fraction of exports, appears due to its proxying for export concentration and not natural resources per se.

Intra-Industry trade

Both regression techniques suggest a positive impact of IIT as the literature suggests, although beyond this, they suggest somewhat different stories. In cross-section, IIT has a positive and generally marginally significant impact that is relatively insensitive to the inclusion of additional control variables. The introduction of the export Herfindahl does push it across the 10 percent line into insignificance, but it is the resource exports/exports variable that renders it completely insignificant.

The panel results, however, find IIT significant with the basic conditioning variables, and it becomes more so with the introduction of the capital accumulation variable. This suggests that IIT has a depressing effect on capital accumulation. The estimates remain reasonably insensitive to the inclusion of the other explanatory variables.

Conclusions

This paper suggests that trade variables related to natural resource abundance, export concentration, and intra-industry trade affect growth. Further, many of its findings are sharply at odds with some of the conventional wisdom.

In the case of natural resources, Sachs and Warner's assertion that resource abundance adversely affects growth is found not to be robust to a variety of measures of resource abundance or estimation technique. The measure with the strongest theoretical foundation, Leamer's net natural resource exports per worker, is slightly significant in one specification in cross-section, and strongly significant in the systems panel estimator, but always *positive*. This remains the case after controlling for several channels through which natural resources have been postulated to affect growth. Strikingly, broadly similar findings emerge using Sachs and Warner's measure of resource exports over GDP once enforcing a consistent processing of the data: there is no evidence in cross-section of a negative impact of this variable on growth, and in the panel systems estimator, again, it enters positively always, if not always significantly. At very least we should abandon the stylized fact that natural resource abundance is somehow bad for growth and even perhaps consider a research agenda on the channels through which it may have a positive effect, possibly through inducing higher productivity growth.

Export concentration, both measured as a Herfindahl index and as natural resource exports as a share of exports, has a predicted negative effect that is extremely robust in cross-section but less so in the panel. The Herfindahl remains significant and negative with most control sets. However, the only specifications for which the resource export measure remains significant are poorly specified, and the result disappears when the Herfindahl measure of overall concentration is included Arguably, it is concentration per se, and not natural resources in particular, that is negatively correlated with growth.

To summarize the last two paragraphs, we can find no evidence of a negative impact of natural resource abundance on growth. *There is no resource curse.*

Intra-industry trade shows positive impacts on growth as predicted by theory, although the preferred specifications leave some doubt about whether the effect is really through the increased productivity effects postulated in the literature or is simply due to that fact that countries with more IIT also tend to be more diversified.

Annex

Table 2A.1 List of Countries in Heston and Summers Sample

	Country	Code		Country	Code
1	Argentina	ARG	34	Japan	JPN
2	Australia	AUS	35	Kenya	KEN
3	Austria	AUT	36	Sri Lanka	LKA
4	Bolivia	BOL	37	Mexico	MEX
5	Brazil	BRA	38	Mali	MLI
6	Canada	CAN	39	Mauritius	MUS
7	Switzerland	CHE	40	Malawi	MWI
8	Chile	CHL	41	Malaysia	MYS
9	China	CHN	42	Nicaragua	NIC
10	Cameroon	CMR	43	Netherlands	NLD
11	Congo, Rep. of	COG	44	Norway	NOR
12	Colombia	COL	45	Nepal	NPL
13	Costa Rica	CRI	46	New Zealand	NZL
14	Denmark	DNK	47	Pakistan	PAK
15	Algeria	DZA	48	Peru	PER
16	Ecuador	ECU	49	Philippines	PHL
17	Egypt, Arab Rep.	EGY	50	Papua New Guinea	PNG
18	Spain	ESP	51	Paraguay	PRY
19	Finland	FIN	52	Senegal	SEN
20	France	FRA	53	Singapore	SGP
21	United Kingdom	GBR	54	El Salvador	SLV
22	Greece	GRC	55	Sweden	SWE
23	Guatemala	GTM	56	Syrian Arab Rep.	SYR
24	Hong Kong, China	HKG	57	Togo	TGO
25	Honduras	HND	58	Thailand	THA
26	Hungary	HUN	59	Trinidad and Tobago	TTO
27	Indonesia	IDN	60	Tunisia	TUN
28	India	IND	61	Turkey	TUR
29	Ireland	IRL	62	Uruguay	URY
30	Israel	ISR	63	United States	USA
31	Italy	ITA	64	South Africa	ZAF
32	Jamaica	JAM	65	Zimbabwe	ZWE
33	Jordan	JOR			

Notes

*The authors thank Pablo Fajnzylber, Norman Loayza, Osmel Manzano, Guillermo Perry, Luis Servén, and L. Colin Xu for helpful discussions. Gabriel Montes and Mariano Bosch provided impeccable research assistance. Fajnzylber, Loayza, and César Calderón graciously shared their data. Two anonymous referees also provided useful comments.

1. More than 200 years ago, Adam Smith wrote: "Projects of mining, instead of replacing the capital employed in them, together with the ordinary profits of stock, commonly absorb both capital and stock. They are the projects, therefore, to which of all others a prudent law-giver, who desired to increase the capital of his nation, would least choose to give any extraordinary encouragement. . . ." More recently, Auty (1998, viii) wrote that "since the 1960s the resource-rich developing countries have under-performed compared with the resource-deficient economies."

2. Sachs and Warner (1995b) argue that Dutch disease leads to concentration in resource exports, which they assume to have fewer possibilities for productivity growth.

3. Assuming identical preferences, a country will show positive net exports of resource-intensive goods if its share of productivity-adjusted world endowments exceeds its share of world consumption. Usually, the net exports are then measured with respect to the quantity of other factors of production, such as the labor force.

4. It is worth mentioning that the cited references show that the HO model of factor endowments performs relatively well for natural resources net exports, but it performs less well for manufactures. The current debate in the trade literature revolves around the question of how the HO model might be amended (by considering, for example, technological differences across countries or economies of scale) to help predict better the observed patterns of net exports across countries. There is, however, no debate about the use of net exports as a proxy for revealed comparative advantage in this literature.

5. The other papers by Sachs and Warner (1995b, 1997b, 1999, 2001a) contain the basic results of 1997a, at times using a slightly longer time span (1965–1990 instead of 1970–1989) and often including additional time-invariant explanatory variables such as dummies identifying tropical and landlocked countries, plus some additional social variables.

6. The index is defined as:

$$H = \sum_i^n \left(\frac{x_i}{\sum_i^n x_i} \right)^2 ,$$

where subscript i stands for a particular product and n is the total number of products. When a single export product produces all the revenues, $H = 1$; when export revenues are evenly distributed over a large number of products, H approaches 0.

7. The index is defined as:

$$IIT = 1 - \frac{\sum_i^n |X_i - M_i|}{\sum_i^n (X_i + M_i)} ,$$

where i indicates a product category and n is the total number of products. This index varies between 0 and 1, and it shows the share of total trade that is conducted among identical products (that is, imports and exports of the same product category).

8. More recently, distinguished economists have raised serious concerns about the general practice of testing a plethora of hypotheses about economic growth by relying exclusively on cross-country growth regressions. See, for example, Solow (2001).

9. The explanatory variables are assumed to be uncorrelated with future realizations of the error term.

10. With regressions in differences, however, first-order serial correlation is to be found by construction, so the relevant specification test is that of second-order serial correlation, which does support the reported results.

11. With the Sachs and Warner 1997b data, our sample of countries yields their results. Hence, the difference in findings is not due to the sample of countries.

References

Anderson, T. W., and Cheng Hsiao. 1982. "Formulation and Estimation of Dynamic Models Using Panel Data." *Journal of Econometrics* 18: 47–82.

Antweiler, Werner, and Daniel Trefler. 2002. "Increasing Returns and All That: A View from Trade." *American Economic Review* 92 (1): 93–119.

Arellano, Manuel, and Stephen Bond. 1991. "Some Tests of Specification for Panel Data: Montecarlo Evidence and an Application to Employment Equations." *Review of Economic Studies* 58 (2): 277–97.

———. 1998. "Dynamic Panel Data Estimation Using DPD98 for Gauss a Guide for Users." Institute for Fiscal Studies, London.

Arellano, Manuel, and Olympia Bover. 1995. "Another Look at the Instrumental-Variable Estimation of Error Component Models." *Journal of Econometrics* 68 (1): 29–52.

Auty, Richard M. 1998. *Resource Abundance and Economic Development.* Helsinki: UNU World Institute for Development Economics Research.

Barro, Robert J. 1991. "Economic Growth in a Cross Section of Countries." *Quarterly Journal of Economics* 106: 407–44.

———. 2001. "Human Capital: Growth." *The American Economic Review: Papers and Proceedings.* May: 12–17.

Barro, Robert J., and Jong-Wha Lee. 2000. "International Data on Educational Attainment: Updates and Implications." NBER Working Paper 7911. National Bureau of Economic Research, Cambridge, MA.

Blundell, Richard, and Stephen Bond. 1998. "Initial Conditions and Moment Restrictions in Dynamic Panel Data Model." *Journal of Econometrics* 87: 115–43.

Bond, Stephen R., Anke Hoeffler, and Jonathan Temple. 2001. "GMM Estimation of Empirical Growth Models." CEPR Discussion Paper 3048, London.

Bruno, Michael, and William Easterly. 1998. "Inflation Crises and Long-Run Growth." *Journal of Monetary Economics* 41 (1): 3–26.

Caselli, Franceso, Gerardo Esquivel, and Fernando Lefort. 1996. "Reopening the Convergence Debate: A New Look at the Cross-County Growth Empirics." *Journal of Economic Growth* 1 (3): 363–89.

Davis, Graham. 1995. "Learning to Love the Dutch Disease: Evidence from Mineral Economies." *World Development* 23 (10): 1765–79.

De Ferranti, David, Guillermo Perry, Daniel Lederman, and William Maloney. 2002. *From Natural Resources to the Knowledge Economy: Trade and Job Quality.* World Bank: Washington, DC.

De Long, Bradford, and Lawrence Summers. 1991. "Equipment Investment and Economic Growth." *Quarterly Journal of Economics* 106(2): 445–502.

Easterly, William, and Ross Levine. 2002. "Tropics, Germs, and Crops: How Endowments Influence Economic Development." NBER Working Paper, Cambridge MA.

Easterly, William, Norman Loayza, and Peter Montiel. 1997. "Has Latin America's Post-Reform Growth Been Disappointing?" *Journal of International Economics* 43: 287–311.

Estevadeordal, Antoni, and Alan M. Taylor. 2002. "A Century of Missing Trade?" *American Economic Review* 92 (1): 383–93.

Ferreira P. C., and A. Trejos. 2002. "On the Growth Effects of Barriers to Trade." Working Paper, Department of Economics, Northwestern University.

Fischer, Stanley. 1993. "The Role of Macroeconomic Factors in Growth." *Journal of Monetary Economics* 32: 485–512.

Frankel, Jeffrey A., and David Romer. 1999. "Does Trade Cause Growth?" *American Economic Review* 89 (3): 379–99.

Griliches, Zvi, and Jerry A. Hausman. 1986. "Errors in Variables in Panel Data." *Journal of Econometrics* 3: 93–118.

Grubel, Herbert G., and P. J. Lloyd. 1975. *Intra-Industry Trade: The Theory and Measurement of International Trade in Differentiated Products.* New York: John Wiley & Sons.

Heston, Alan, and Robert Summers. 1991 "The Penn World Table (Mark 5): An Expanded Set of International Comparisons, 1950–1988" *Quarterly Journal of Economics* 106 (2): 327–68.

Irwin, Douglas. 2000. "How Did the United States Become a Net Exporter of Manufactured Goods?" NBER Working Paper, Cambridge, MA.

Jones, Charles. 2000. "Comment on Rodriguez-Rodrik, 'Trade Policy and Economic Growth: A Skeptic's Guide to the Cross-National Evidence.'" In *NBER Macroeconomics Annual 2000,* ed. Ben Bernanke and Kenneth Rogoff. Cambridge, MA: MIT Press.

Knight, Malcolm, Norman Loayza, and Delano Villanueva. 1993. "Testing the Neoclassical Theory of Economic Growth: A Panel Data Approach." *IMF Staff Papers* 40: 512–41.

Krugman, Paul. 1979. "Increasing Returns, Monopolistic Competition, and International Trade." *Journal of International Economics* 9: 469–79.

Lane, Philip, and Aaron Tornell. 1999. "The Voracity Effect." *American Economic Review* 89: 22–46.

Leamer, Edward. 1984. *Sources of International Comparative Advantage: Theory and Evidence.* Cambridge, MA: MIT Press.

Levine, Ross, and David Renelt. 1992. "A Sensitivity Analysis of Cross-Country Growth Regressions." *American Economic Review* 82 (4): 942–63.

Levine, Ross, Norman Loayza, and Thorsten Beck. 2000. "Financial Intermediation and Growth: Causality and Causes." *Journal of Monetary Economics* 46: 31–77.

Loayza, Norman, Pablo Fajnzylber, and Cesar Calderon. 2004. "Economic Growth in Latin America and the Caribbean: Stylized Facts, Explanations, and Forecasts." Working Paper 265, Central Bank of Chile, Santiago.

Maloney, William. 2002. "Missed Opportunities: Innovation, Natural Resources and Growth in Latin America." *Economia* 3 (1): 111–69.

Mankiw, Gregory, David Romer, and David Weil. 1992. "A Contribution to the Empirics of Economic Growth." *Quarterly Journal of Economics* 106 (2): 407–37.

Manzano, Osmel, and Roberto Rigobón. 2001. "Resource Curse or Debt Overhang." NBER Working Paper 8390, Cambridge, MA.

Martin, William, and Devashish Mitra. 2001. "Productivity Growth and Convergence in Agriculture and Manufacturing." *Economic Development and Cultural Change* 49 (2): 403–22.

Prebisch, Raúl. 1959. "Commercial Policy in the Underdeveloped Countries." *American Economic Review, Papers and Proceedings* 49 (2): 251–73.

Pritchett, Lant. 1996. "Measuring Outward Orientations in LDCs: Can It Be Done?" *Journal of Development Economics* 49 (2):307–35.

———. 2000. "Understanding Patterns of Economic Growth: Searching for Hills among Plateaus, Mountains, and Plains." *World Bank Economic Review* 14 (2): 221–50.

Rodrik, Dani, and Francisco Rodriguez. 2000. "Trade Policy and Economic Growth: A Skeptic's Guide to the Cross-National Evidence." In *NBER Macroeconomics Annual 2000,* ed. Ben Bernanke and Kenneth Rogoff, Cambridge, MA: MIT Press.

Sachs, Jeffrey, and Joaquín Vial. 2001. "Can Latin America Compete?" In *The Latin American Competitiveness Report, 2001–2002,* ed. J. Vial and P. Cornelius, 10–29. Cambridge, MA: Center for International Development and World Economic Forum.

Sachs, Jeffrey, and Andrew Warner. 1995a. "Economic Reform and the Process of Global Integration." *Brookings Papers on Economic Activity,* 25th Anniversary Issue, Washington, DC: Brookings Institution, 1–118.

———. 1995b. "Natural Resource Abundance and Economic Growth." NBER Working Paper 5398, Cambridge, MA.

———. 1997a. "Natural Resource Abundance and Economic Growth—Revised." Working Paper, Center for International Development, Harvard University, Cambridge, MA.

———. 1997b. "Fundamental Sources of Long-Run Growth." *American Economic Review, Papers and Proceedings* 87 (2): 184–88.

———. 1999. "The Big Push, Natural Resource Booms and Growth." *Journal of Development Economics* 59: 43–76.

———. 2001. "Natural Resources and Economic Development: The Curse of Natural Resources." *European Economic Review* 45: 827–38.

Sala-i-Martin, Xavier. 1997. "I Just Ran Two Million Regressions." *American Economic Review, Papers and Proceedings* 87: 178–83.

Sevestre, Patrick, and Alain Trognon. 1996. "Dynamic Linear Models." In *The Econometrics of Panel Data: Handbook of Theory and Applications,* 2nd revised edition, ed. L. Matyas and P. Sevestre, 120–44. Dordrecht, Netherlands: Kluwer.

Servén, Luis. 1998. "Macroeconomic Uncertainty and Private Investment in Developing Countries: An Empirical Investigation." Policy Research Working Paper 2035, World Bank, Washington, DC.

Smith, Adam. [1776] 1976. *An Inquiry into the Nature and Causes of the Wealth of Nations*. Oxford, U.K.: Clarendon Press.

Solow, Robert. 2001. "Applying Growth Theory across Countries." *World Bank Economic Review* 15 (2): 283–89.

Stijns, Jean-Philippe. 2005. "Natural Resource Abundance and Economic Growth Revisited." *Resources Policy* 30 (2): 107–30.

———. 2006. "Natural Resource Abundance and Human Capital Accumulation." *World Development*. 34 (6): 1060–83.

Torvik, Ragnar. 2002. "Natural Resources, Rent Seeking, and Welfare." *Journal of Development Economics* 67 (2): 455–70.

Trefler, Daniel. 1995. "The Case of the Missing Trade and Other Mysteries." *American Economic Review* 85 (5): 1029–46

Wacziarg, Romain. 2001. "Measuring the Dynamic Gains from Trade." *World Bank Economic Review* 15: 393–430.

Wacziarg, Romain, and Karen Horn Welch. 2003. "Trade Liberalization and Growth: New Evidence." NBER Working Paper 10152, Cambridge, MA.

Windmeijer, F. 2005. "A Finite Sample Correction for the Variance of Linear Efficient Two-step GMM Estimators." *Journal of Econometrics* 126 (1): 25–51.

3

Resource Curse or Debt Overhang?

Ozmel Manzano and Roberto Rigobón*

Introduction

As SEVERAL CHAPTERS IN THIS VOLUME note, the concern that resource-abundant economies grow more slowly than other economies has a long history. However, Sachs and Warner's attempt (in 1995b, later updated in 1997 and 2001) to empirically formalize the relationship between natural resource abundance and growth has reenergized the debate. Figure 3.1 plots primary exports as a share of gross domestic product (GDP)—their measure of resource abundance—on the x-axis, against the growth rate in per capita GDP on the y-axis, and table 3.1 confirms their finding of a negative relationship between the two. The results suggest that an increase in a country's primary exports equivalent to 1 percent of the gross national product (GNP) reduces its growth rate between 0.07 percent and 0.10 percent.

Table 3.2 provides some examples to illustrate this relationship. For example, according to the table, Tunisia will grow between 0.72 percent and 1.03 percent less than a country that has similar income, investment rates, external sector rules, and rule of law, but has no primary exports. This number can be as high as 3.8 percent to 5.4 percent for countries such as Zambia. Sachs and Warner argue that the deleterious effects are due to the concentration in resource exports, which they assume provide fewer possibilities for productivity growth than, for instance, the manufacturing sectors.

However, another body of literature, some of which is found in this volume, has questioned the validity of this finding on several grounds. As Maloney observes in chapter 6 and Wright and Czelusta note in chapter 7, there is a long history of literature that questions the detrimental impacts of natural resources, and these authors, along with Blomström

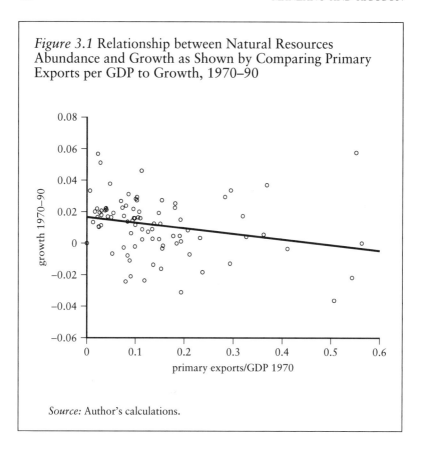

Figure 3.1 Relationship between Natural Resources Abundance and Growth as Shown by Comparing Primary Exports per GDP to Growth, 1970–90

Source: Author's calculations.

and Kokko in chapter 8, stress the numerous success stories among advanced and emerging resource-abundant countries. This has given rise to a line of research investigating the drivers of differential performance, including institutions, poor policy, or endogenous technological progress.

Even the conclusion that, on average, resource-abundant countries grow more slowly has come under assault. For instance, Doppelhofer, Miller, and Sala-i-Martin (2000), using a Bayesian approach to their study, found that mining production as a share of GDP was among the four extremely robust variables positively affecting growth, a finding broadly confirmed by Davis (1995). In chapter 2, Lederman and Maloney learn that Sachs and Warner's finding is not robust to measures of resource abundance, small changes in sample, or estimating technique.

This chapter simply asks the question, "taking Sachs and Warner's data set and estimating approach as given, is there any other explanation for their

Table 3.1 Results from Sachs and Warner Illustrating the Negative Relationship between Resource Abundance and Growth

Dependent variable: Average annual GDP growth rate (1970–89)[a]				
Log. GDP 1970[b]	–0.0011	–0.0096	–0.0134	–0.0179
	(0.55)	(–5.16)	(–7.77)	(–8.82)
Primary exports/	–0.0943	–0.0696	–0.0729	–0.1026
GNP 1970[c]	(–4.75)	(–4.55)	(–0.242)	(–6.89)
Years open		0.0306	0.0242	0.0134
1970–89[d]		(8.05)	(7.06)	(3.44)
Log. investment/			0.0125	0.0081
GDP 1970–89[e]			(5.63)	(2.63)
Rule of law[f]				0.004
				(3.94)
Growth in terms				0.0009
of trade[g]				(1.85)

Source: Sachs and Warner 1997.
Note:
a. Average growth rate for the GDP per economically active population.
b. Logarithm of the GDP per economically active population in 1970.
c. Share of primary exports to GNP in 1970.
d. Percentage of years open in the period of 1970–89.
e. Average of the period of the logarithm of the investment-to-output ratio.
f. Index that measures the rule of law.
g. Average growth rate for the terms of trade.

Table 3.2 Sample Effects of Sachs and Warner's Findings in Selected Countries

Sample position	*Country*	*Effect*
1%	India	–0.11 to –0.16
	United States	–0.09 to –0.13
50%	Tunisia	–0.72 to –1.03
	Ecuador	–0.48 to –0.81
99%	Malaysia	–2.5 to –3.6
	Guyana	–3.5 to –5.0
	Zambia	–3.8 to –5.4

Source: Authors' calculations based on table 3.1.

observed relationship besides the low-productivity-growth story?" We confirm Lederman and Maloney's finding that Sachs and Warner's results are not robust when unobserved heterogeneity is controlled for in a panel data context. However, while acknowledging Lederman and Maloney's concerns about the adjustments Sachs and Warner made to the data (see chapter 2), we confirm that *when using Sachs and Warner's data,* even after dealing with some potential statistical pitfalls, the resource curse continues to exist in the cross-section. In this chapter we seek to explain this relationship, examining several common hypotheses in the growth literature and, in the end, arguing that the resource curse is, in fact, not about resources per se, but about imperfect credit markets. To summarize our argument briefly: in the 1970s commodity prices were high, which led developing countries to use them as collateral for debt.[1] The 1980s saw a significant fall in those prices, leaving developing countries with a considerable amount of debt and a low flow of foreign resources to pay them. Thus, in the sample, the low-growth curse appears to be a debt-overhang problem.

The rest of the chapter is organized as follows. We begin by explaining the problems associated with growth regressions, then move on to reestimating the findings in the literature, using alternative approaches. Next, we review alternative explanations for the findings and, last, present our conclusions.

The Problems of Estimating the "Resource Curse"

We begin by examining a few statistical issues that may be artificially generating the resource curse. The empirical literature on growth starts with the following estimation:

$$\ln y_{i,t} - \ln y_{i,t-\tau} = \alpha \ln y_{i,t-\tau} + \beta X_{i,j} + \eta_i + \varepsilon_{i,t} \qquad (3.1)$$

where $y_{i,t}$ represents output for country i at period t, X represents a series of variables that explain growth, η_i is a country-specific effect, and $\varepsilon_{i,t}$ represents the error term. In Sachs and Warner, this estimation is made using total GDP growth as an independent variable for a cross-section of countries. This gives rise to two issues—the possibility of unobserved variables correlated with research and development and the possible misspecification induced by using total GDP—that may bias our coefficients.

The first issue arises because cross-sectional estimators assume that individual effects are not correlated with other right-hand-side variables.[2] If there were some unobservable characteristics that were correlated with the right-hand-side variables, the coefficients would be biased. As explained in Caselli, Esquivel, and Lefort (1996), this problem is likely to be particularly acute within the dynamic framework of a growth regression, but it can be solved by using panel data that allows the elimination of individual effects.

The second issue arises from the fact that total GDP includes the resource sector of the economy. Thus, there are compositional effects that may yield an artificial relationship between resource endowments and growth. Table 3.3 shows the change of per capita production of seven commodities over time. We use per capita production because this is what the left-hand side of equation (3.1) tries to capture. The table indicates that, in general, the production of natural resources per capita has fallen: only one commodity (gold) has a growth rate greater than the average growth rate of the total GDP (1.1 percent) in our sample of countries. The table also illustrates another point: If we divide the countries into two groups—the five or six countries where the ratio of commodity production to GDP is the highest, and the rest of the world—it is clear that, with the exception of lead and silver, the growth rate in production of the countries with the highest dependency is lower than that in the rest of the world. These results lead one to

Table 3.3 Commodity Production per Capita

Average annual growth rate (1978–96)

| | | Group | |
| | | *Countries with the* | |
Commodity	World	*highest dependency*[a]	Other countries
Oil	−1.5	−3.4[b]	−0.6
Tin	−1.4	−5.9[c]	4.9
Zinc	−1.0	−1.2[d]	−0.9
Lead	−3.1	−3.0[e]	−3.2
Silver	−0.1	1.3[f]	−0.9
Copper	0.1	−2.3[g]	1.8
Gold	1.3	−3.8[h]	4.9

Sources: Financial Times (various years), OPEC (various years), and Summers and Heston 1995.

Note:

a. Countries that had the highest production-to-GDP ratio in 1978.

b. Actual OPEC members: Algeria, Indonesia, Islamic Rep. of Iran, Iraq, Kuwait, Libya, Nigeria, Qatar, Saudi Arabia, United Arab Emirates, República Bolivariana de Venezuela.

c. In order of dependency: Bolivia, Malaysia, Republic of Congo, Rwanda, Thailand, Indonesia.

d. In order of dependency: Republic of Congo, Zambia, Peru, Namibia, Ireland, Canada.

e. In order of dependency: Namibia, Peru, Morocco, Zambia, Canada.

f. In order of dependency: Peru, Republic of Congo, Namibia, Chile, Mexico, Dominican Republic.

g. In order of dependency: Papua New Guinea, Zambia, Republic of Congo, Chile, Peru, Philippines.

h. In order of dependency: South Africa, Papua New Guinea, Zimbabwe, Ghana, Dominican Republic, Philippines wonder whether previous estimations of the effect of natural resources are simply capturing the fall in per capita production of the resource sector.

A Reestimation

For the reasons outlined earlier, in this section we reestimate Sachs and Warner (1995b). First we use panel estimation in this task, then we apply different measures of the nonresource side of the economy.[3]

A Panel Estimation

We estimate a panel using alternative data sets, one with at least two time elements and another with four time elements. The results are shown in table 3.4.[4] The first set of regressions, from (1.1) to (1.3), indicates that the negative impact of natural resources is statistically significant in the cross-section of this subsample but that the effect disappears in the two-element panel controlling for fixed effects. In columns (2.1) to (2.3) we use the sample with four time elements. This allows for the presence of more observations to use in calculating the fixed effect, but there are fewer countries with information available for doing this regression. Again, the effect is statistically significant in the cross-section—although only at the 2.5 percent level—and then insignificant in a panel with fixed effects, while the remaining variables continue to be significant with the expected signs and even with the expected relative size.[5] The fact that the impact of resource abundance disappears once fixed effects are introduced implies that this variable is correlated with unobservable characteristics.

A natural concern is whether we are merely estimating the fixed effects of a country's resource richness, a fact that is time-invariant. Figure 3.2 shows the shocks to the share of primary products in exports (measured as the standard deviation) compared to the share in 1970, and it indicates that the biggest shocks are not concentrated on the biggest producers. However, the cross-section measures the ranking of the countries from low exporters to high exporters, and in this sample it changes substantially from period to period.[6]

To summarize, in the panel we see that there are no effects from primary exports changing through time; this casts some doubts on the validity of the conclusions derived from the cross-sectional regressions.

Growth in the Nonresource Sector

In this section we deal with the other issue related to estimating the effect of resource abundance, namely, the inclusion of the resource sector in total GDP, by using alternative measures of the nonresource side of the econ-

Table 3.4 Effect of Natural Resources: Cross-Section vs. Panel

Dependent variable: Average annual GDP growth rate

	Using sample where a panel with t = 2 can be estimated Panel			Using sample where a panel with t = 4 can be estimated Panel		
	Cross-section (1.1)	Pooled (1.2)	Fixed effect (1.3)	Cross-section (2.1)	Pooled (2.2)	Fixed effect (2.3)
Primary exports/GNP	-0.0636*** (-4.578)	-0.0565*** (-3.796)	-0.0015 (-0.051)	-0.0454** (-2.346)	-0.01963 (-1.037)	0.0669* (1.786)
Log. GDP 1970	-0.0136*** (-6.687)	-0.0153*** (-5.679)	-0.0720*** (-7.995)	-0.0154*** (-6.726)	-0.0208*** (-6.776)	-0.0811*** (-7.672)
% years open 1970–90	0.0247*** (6.223)	0.0197*** (3.954)	-0.0124 (-1.043)	0.0252*** (6.420)	0.0255*** (5.597)	0.0246** (2.576)
Log. invest./GDP 1970–89	0.0140*** (5.514)	0.0190*** (5.783)	0.0199** (2.003)	0.0126*** (3.715)	0.0220*** (5.335)	0.0477*** (4.698)
Hausman test			63,52			50,78
F test all $u_i = 0$			2,11			1,98
Observations	74	148	148	54	216	216
N	74	74	74	54	54	54
T	1	2	2	1	4	4

Source: Author's calculations.

Note: t-statistics shown in parentheses.

*significant at 10 percent, **significant at 5 percent, ***significant at 1 percent.

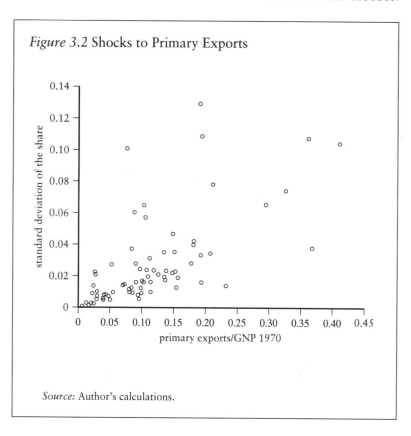

Figure 3.2 Shocks to Primary Exports

Source: Author's calculations.

omy. We present only the results for the panels of 10-year periods because when a panel of five-year periods is used, the negative effect of natural resources is lost even in the cross-sections.

First we construct GDP net of resource exports as a measure of the non-resource sector of the economy. Arguably, this tends to eliminate the resource sector in those countries where the sector is large relative to the rest of the economy.[7] Table 3.5 shows that in cross-section the previous results for total GDP still hold in this reduced sample, and the coefficients in column (1) are actually not significantly different from those in column (3) of table 3.1. We then repeat the estimation with the nonresource side of the economy. The results in column (2) seem to suggest that there is still a negative effect on growth in the nonresource side of the economy. Table 3.6 shows that, again, in the panel context, the resource curse disappears.

In the previous estimations we constructed the "nonresource GDP" with the nominal share of primary exports to GNP. This might be problematic if relative prices changed considerably, and ideally we would correct for this

Table 3.5 Nonresource Growth: Cross-Section

Dependent variable: Average annual GDP growth rate

	Using total GDP	Using nonresource GDP
Primary exports/GNP	–0.0763***	–0.0643***
	(–5.677)	(–4.409)
Log. GDP 1970	–0.0123***	–0.0130***
	(–6.186)	(–6.002)
% years open 1970–90	0.0233***	0.0275***
	–5.667	(6.157)
Log. invest./GDP 1970–89	0.0114***	0.0090***
	(4.583)	(3.349)
N	66	66
R^2	0.61	0.56

Source: Author's calculations.
Note: t-statistics shown in parentheses.
*significant at 10 percent, **significant at 5 percent, ***significant at 1 percent.

Table 3.6 Nonresource GDP: Cross-Section vs. Panel

Dependent variable: Average annual GDP growth rate

		Panel	
	Cross-Section	Pooled	Fixed effect
Primary exports/GNP	–0.0401**	–0.0351**	0.0061
	(–2.44)	(–2.061)	(0.175)
Log. GDP 1970	–0.0126***	–0.0139***	–0.0785***
	(–5.796)	(–4.879)	(–6.468)
% years open 1970–90	0.0261***	0.0256***	0.0008
	(5.840)	(4.607)	(0.055)
Log. invest./GDP 1970–89	0.0100***	0.0117***	0.0007
	(3.815)	(3.384)	(0.046)
Hausman test			34.58
F test all $u_i=0$			1.27
Observations	58	116	116
N		58	58
T	2	2	

Source: Author's calculations.
Note: t-statistics shown in parentheses.
*significant at 10 percent, **significant at 5 percent, ***significant at 1 percent.

using the respective deflators. Regrettably, these do not exist for primary exports. For that reason, we repeated the construction of nonresource GDP, taking into account changes in relative prices using the deflator for total exports compared to the GDP deflator. Our assumption was that the deflator for total exports would capture the change in prices for primary exports in countries where primary products are the main export. For purposes of abbreviation, we called this variable the "real" nonresource growth.[8]

The cross-section estimations are shown in table 3.7. Column (1) shows that the effect is still present in this subsample, and column (2) indicates that the negative effect persists on the "real" nonresource side of the economy, even with a bigger impact than in any other estimation.

In moving to the panel estimations we have two choices: one is to continue using the nominal share of primary exports to GDP as an explanatory variable, and the other is to use the real share. The two measures have different interpretations: the former measures the "windfall" effect, while the latter measures the presence and activity of a resource sector. In other words, a shock in the first one will measure a price windfall, while a shock in the second one will measure the discovery of new reserves. Table 3.8 presents the results using both shares.

As in previous regressions, we started with the cross-sections to check whether the effect was present in the sample.[9] Table 3.8 shows that the effect is present—although weak—in the respective cross-sections.[10] However,

Table 3.7 "Real" Nonresource Growth: Cross-Section

Dependent variable: Average annual GDP growth rate

	Using total GDP (1)	Using nonresource GDP (2)
Primary exports/GNP	−0.0535***	−0.1117***
	(−3.585)	(−2.959)
Log. GDP 1970	−0.0114***	−0.0259***
	(−5.617)	(−5.036)
% years open 1970–90	0.0226***	0.0569***
	(−5.396)	(5.377)
Log. invest./GDP 1970–89	0.0116***	0.0164***
	(4.794)	(2.683)
N	61	61
R^2	0.61	0.51

Source: Author's calculations.
Note: t-statistics shown in parentheses.
*significant at 10 percent, **significant at 5 percent, ***significant at 1 percent.

Table 3.8 "Real" Nonresource GDP: Cross-Section vs. Panel

Dependent variable: Average annual GDP growth rate

		Panel			
		Using nominal shares		Using "real" shares	
	Cross-section (1)	Pooled (2.1)	Fixed effect (2.2)	Pooled (3.1)	Fixed effect (3.2)
Constant	(-4.578)	(-3.796)	(-0.051)	(-2.346)	(-1.037)
Primary exports/GNP	-0.0894**	-0.0210	0.0456	-0.0378*	0.0678*
	(-2.326)	(-1.042)	(1.396)	(-1.705)	(1.810)
Log. GDP 1970	-0.0249***	-0.0134***	-0.0884***	-0.0141***	-0.08271***
	(-4.748)	(-3.956)	(-8.763)	(-4.190)	(-8.105)
% years open 1970–90	0.0529***	0.0259***	-0.0032	0.0260***	-0.0043
	(4.899)	(3.809)	(-0.220)	(3.981)	(0.295)
Log. invest./GDP 1970–89	0.0172***	0.0100***	0.0101	0.0107***	0.0061
	(2.870)	(2.454)	(0.694)	(2.687)	(0.4428)
Hausman test			69.29		85.09
F test all $u_i = 0$			2.26		2.29
Observations	56	112	112	112	112
N		56	56	56	56
T		4	4	4	4

Source: Author's calculations.

Note: t-statistics shown in parentheses.

*significant at 10 percent, **significant at 5 percent, ***significant at 1 percent.

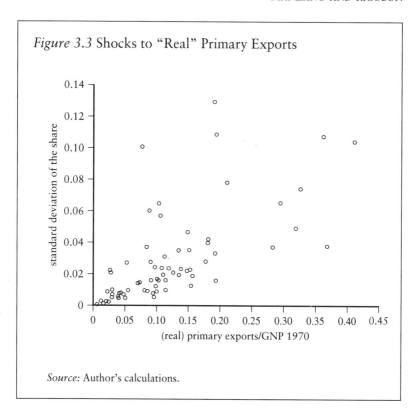

Figure 3.3 Shocks to "Real" Primary Exports

Source: Author's calculations.

again it disappears in the panel context. Moreover, the result from column (3.2) suggests a positive sign.[11]

As in the previous section, there is the concern that once we control for changes in relative prices, the only fixed effect will be whether a country is resource rich, and that variable does not change over time. For that reason, in figure 3.3 we show the shocks to "real" primary exports. We see that this pattern is similar to that found in figure 3.2, in that the biggest shocks are not concentrated on the biggest producers. However, there is a shift in the ranking of the countries.[12] This reflects the findings presented in the introduction to this section, where we showed that the production of commodities is shifting among countries.

In this subsection we reestimated the resource curse, using different approaches to measuring the nonresource side of the economy. We found that there is a negative effect present in the cross-section but not in the panels. As in the previous subsection, the fact that the effect of resource abundance disappears once fixed effects are introduced implies that this variable is correlated with unobservable characteristics.

Dividing Resources by Origin

A final important question is whether the effect is the same for all kinds of exports subsumed under the term "primary exports," which includes agricultural, food, mineral, and fuel exports. Clearly, these are very different products with different profitabilities, different behaviors over time, and so forth. For the purposes of our investigation, we divide exports into categories by type in table 3.9 and rerun the regressions.

In column (2) we divide primary exports between agricultural[13] and nonagricultural exports, and in column (3) we further divide the nonagricultural exports into minerals and fuels. The table shows that, once exports are divided into categories, the resource curse effect is entirely through nonagricultural exports and, in particular, through minerals. This

Table 3.9 Dividing Exports by Origin

Dependent variable: Average annual GDP growth rate			
	(1)	*(2)*	*(3)*
Primary exports/GNP	−0.0643***		
	(−4.409)		
Agricultural exports/GNP		−0.0287	−0.0271
		(−1.583)	(−1.500)
Nonagricultural exports/GNP		−0.1081***	
		(−5.407)	
Fuel exports/GNP			−0.0669*
			(−1.825)
Mineral exports/GNP			−0.1227***
			(−5.414)
Log. GDP 1970	−0.0130***	−0.0121***	−0.0127***
	(−6.002)	(−5.851)	(−6.004)
% years open 1970–90	0.0275***	0.0247***	0.0265***
	(6.157)	(5.717)	(5.891)
Log. invest./GDP 1970–89	0.0090***	0.0113***	0.0110***
	(3.349)	(4.273)	(4.178)
Hausman test		23.22	7.88
N	66	66	66
p-value		0.000	0.096
Adj. R²	0.56	0.61	0.61

Source: Author's calculations.
Note: t-statistics shown in parentheses.
*significant at 10 percent, **significant at 5 percent, ***significant at 1 percent.

Table 3.10 Effects of Different Resource Exports:
Cross-Section vs. Panel

Dependent variable: Average annual GDP growth rate
for nonresource GDP

		Panel	
	Cross-section (1)	*Pooled* (2)	*Fixed effect* (3)
Nonagricultural	–0.0899***	–0.0499***	0.0079
exports/GNP	(–4.319)	(0.722)	(1.151)
Agricultural	0.0026	0.0211	0.1011
exports/GNP	(–2.448)	(–2.794)	(0.227)
Log. GDP	–0.0117***	–0.0128***	–0.0747***
	(–5.814)	(–4.502)	(–5.965)
% years open	0.0222***	0.0225***	0.0054
	(5.231)	(4.004)	(0.339)
Log. investment/GDP	0.0127***	0.0134***	0.0010
	(5.062)	(3.874)	(0.063)
Hausman test			10.23
F test all u_i = 0			1.20
Observations	58	116	116
N		58	58
T		2	2

Source: Author's calculations.
Note: t-statistics shown in parentheses.
*significant at 10 percent, **significant at 5 percent, ***significant at 1 percent.

also reinforces the importance of using nonresource GDP in the regressions. However, again, all results disappear in a panel context (table 3.10).

New Dimensions of the "Curse"

Two striking facts can be derived from the previous exercises: first, in all specifications when fixed effects are included, invariably the natural resource curse disappears. Second, however, in almost all of the specifications the curse persists in the cross-section. In this section, we seek to explain the cross-sectional effect. One explanation could be that most of the source of variation is found in the cross-section and not in the time series variation. A second one, already mentioned above, is that the coefficient in the cross-section may reflect the fact that there is a correlation between omitted variables and resource abundance. In this section we will attempt to find those omitted variables.

The first step is to see which countries are driving the results. We use the specification in column (3) of table 3.9, since the result is clearly driven by nonagricultural exports. Thus, in figure 3.4, we plot the residuals of that regression with all variables except the nonagricultural exports against those nonagricultural exports. We clearly see two groups of countries: one that almost draws a "cone" on the upper-left-hand side of the graph and another on the lower-right-hand side, which seems to be the group of countries driving the results.

First Candidates

Although a first, intuitive explanation is to argue that the cross-section is estimating a difference between developed economies and nondeveloped economies, we find that the results are not driven by the degree of development nor by the quality of the institutions. In table 3.11 we repeat the regression done in column (3) of table 3.9, and then we divide the sample

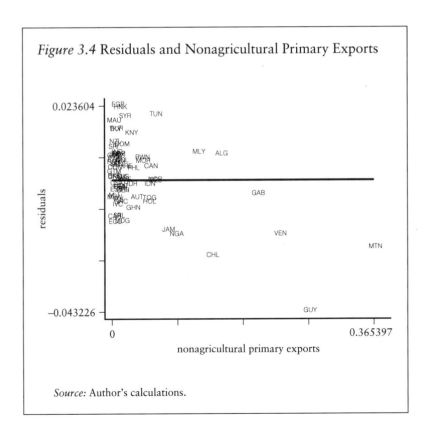

Figure 3.4 Residuals and Nonagricultural Primary Exports

Source: Author's calculations.

between Organization for Economic Co-operation and Development (OECD) countries and non-OECD countries. At the bottom of the table are some summary statistics for the share of primary exports in each subsample.

Non-OECD countries have a higher share of primary exports. While this variable does not seem to have an effect on growth in OECD countries, there is less variance in the share of primary exports in OECD economies. However, since the variable remains significant in the non-OECD sample, the curse cannot simply be capturing some systematic OECD/non-OECD unobserved effect.

Table 3.12 suggests that the impact is not through the quality of institutions and, more specifically, not through bureaucratic quality.[14,15] This variable is measured between 0 and 6, where a high value means low quality of bureaucracy. Since it is usually measured at a point in time, this variable can be used in panels only before the introduction of fixed effects. We

Table 3.11 OECD vs. Non-OECD Countries

Dependent variable: Average annual GDP growth rate

	Sample		
	Total	*OECD*	*Non-OECD*
	(1)	*(2)*	*(3)*
Nonagricultural	−0.1081***	−0.0211	−0.1089***
exports/GNP	(−5.407)	(−0.390)	(−4.116)
Agricultural	−0.0287	−0.0234	−0.0334
exports/GNP	(−1.583)	(−1.212)	(−1.352)
Log. GDP 1970	−0.0121***	−0.0148***	−0.0114***
	(−5.851)	(−4.203)	(−4.898)
% years open	0.0247***	0.0161***	0.0284
	(5.717)	(3.672)	(4.501)
Log. investment/GDP	0.0113***	0.0132*	0.0107***
(average 79–90)	(4.273)	(2.0271)	(3.922)
N	66	21	45
Adj. R^2	0.61	0.73	0.62

Note: *t*-statistics shown in parentheses.
*significant at 10 percent, **significant at 5 percent, ***significant at 1 percent.

Nonagricultural exports/GNP distribution in subsample			
Sample mean	0.0377	0.0180	0.0470
Standard Deviation	0.0688	0.0195	0.0810
Minimum	0.0000	0.0015	0.0000
Maximum	0.3654	0.0590	0.3654

Source: Author's calculations.

Table 3.12 Resource Abundance and Institutions

Dependent variable: Average annual GDP growth rate for nonresource growth

	Cross-section			Panel (pooled)		
	(1.1)	(1.2)	(1.3)	(2.1)	(2.2)	(2.3)
Nonagricultural/ GNP	-0.1222*** (-4.862)	-0.1070*** (-4.090)	-0.1040*** (-3.876)	-0.0381** (-1.899)	-0.0329* (-1.644)	-0.0220 (-1.074)
Agricultural/GNP	-0.0470* (-1.903)	-0.0519** (-2.132)	-0.0531** (-2.157)	-0.0461 (-1.351)	-0.0537 (-1.580)	-0.0509 (-1.523)
Bureaucracy		-0.0023* (-1.730)	-0.0025* (-1.789)		-0.0032* (-1.782)	-0.0035** (-1.981)
Fractionalization			-0.0037 (-0.576)			-0.0173** (-1.994)
Log. GDP	-0.0106*** (-4.449)	-0.0130*** (-4.795)	-0.0139*** (-4.363)	-0.0141*** (-4.519)	-0.0177*** (-4.809)	-0.0219*** (-5.235)
% years	0.0213*** (4.531)	0.0172*** (3.337)	0.0175*** (3.351)	0.0247*** (4.471)	0.0197*** (3.207)	0.0210*** (3.459)
Log inv./GDP	0.0085* (1.952)	0.0066 (1.500)	0.0064 (1.430)	0.0092* (1.776)	0.0070 (1.334)	0.0069 (1.326)
Observations	53	53	53	94	94	94
N				47	47	47
T				2	2	2

Source: Author's calculations.

Note: t-statistics shown in parentheses.

*significant at 10 percent, **significant at 5 percent, ***significant at 1 percent.

also include a variable that measures ethnolinguistic fractionalization, suggested by La Porta et al. (1998),[16] whose idea was to introduce a variable that represents an "exogenous" institutional setting, since it is argued that rents coming from the resource sector might have an impact on the institutional setting.

Introducing the complete set of institutional variables in the panel context largely eliminates the resource curse but it does remain significant in the cross-section. The difference arises because in the panel context, we allow for the fluctuations of the primary exports variable over time, while in the cross-section, the variable serves only to divide the sample into resource-rich and resource-poor countries. Therefore, the cross-section results suggest that there is a difference between countries that is associated with their resource abundance.

Credit Constraints and Debt Overhang

The previous panel exercises suggest that Sachs and Warner's negative correlation of natural resources with growth is probably largely due to some unobserved variable. However, the robustness of the result in cross-section, after controlling for developed or developing countries and institutional quality, suggest that some other dynamic is at play. In this subsection, we present evidence that the results of the "curse" are primarily due to considerations of credit constraints.

Figure 3.5 suggests that many of the countries with strongly negative growth and high resource abundance—Chile, Gabon, Guyana, Jamaica, Mauritania, Nigeria, and República Bolivariana de Venezuela—are also those that showed large increases in their debt-to-GDP ratio from 1975–85. In fact, many of these countries went though either an International Monetary Fund or a World Bank program (including debt relief) as a result. This suggests that the correlation of resource endowments with high and unmanageable indebtedness is an important part of the story.

Figure 3.6 suggests that over the course of our sample period, 1970–90, there were very large swings in nominal commodity prices of coal, copper, iron, and oil (normalized to equal 100 in 1970 for comparative purposes). As can be seen, during the mid-1970s the increases in commodity prices were quite dramatic. Table 3.13 shows that between 1970 and 1975, the prices of coal, natural gas, and iron doubled. Moreover, between 1975 and 1980, oil and natural gas experienced their own "boom." Coal is perhaps the most stable price in this sample, but it still increased by 60 percent in the last five years of the 1970s. These rises induced many resource-abundant countries to use their resources as collateral for investment projects predicated on continuing high prices. However, all commodity prices experienced drops as large as 30 percent during the 1980s: coal, natural gas, iron, and oil experienced an important slowdown in their price increases,

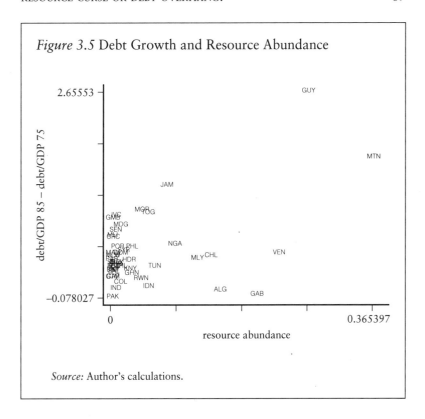

Figure 3.5 Debt Growth and Resource Abundance

Source: Author's calculations.

finishing the decade with declines. Copper is the only exception—it suffered a fall in prices at the beginning of the five-year period and then experienced a recovery. Overall, however, these price falls left many high-borrowing commodity-rich countries with unsustainable balance-of-payments and debt crises.

This story is consistent with the regressions presented in table 3.14. We divide the sample into two periods, 1970–80 and 1980–90. It is clear that the share of nonagricultural exports did not have an effect on growth from 1970 to 1980, but it gained a strong negative coefficient from 1980 to 1990. In column (3) we substitute in the share of nonagricultural exports in 1970 and find that the negative effect increases, as does its statistical significance.[17]

Column (4) includes a variable to capture credit constraints, constructed as the debt/GNP ratio in 1981 for less developed countries and zero (0) for developed countries. This variable emerges as strongly significant, and the nonagricultural exports variable becomes completely insignificant. The results suggest that the unobserved variable correlated

Figure 3.6 Commodity Prices

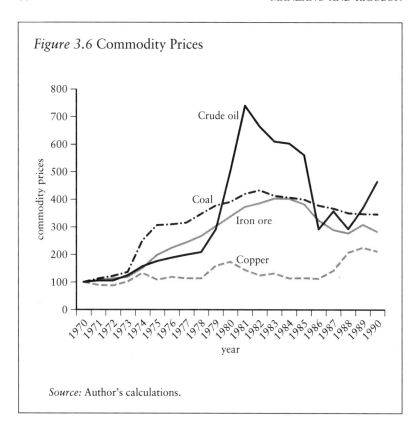

Source: Author's calculations.

Table 3.13 Price Growth Rates Every Five Years

	Coal	Nat. gas	Copper	Iron ore	Crude oil
1970–74	207.6%	163.2%	10.3%	98.2%	76.2%
1975–79	27.3%	253.3%	57.8%	70.8%	185.6%
1980–84	2.4%	57.9%	−33.9%	13.2%	11.6%
1985–90	−13.5%	−31.9%	83.6%	−26.2%	−16.9%

Source: Author's calculations.

with resource abundance was in fact the high indebtedness of these countries at the beginning of the decade.[18] This is also consistent with Maloney's finding that resources were positively associated with growth until the postwar period when Latin America, the region hardest hit by the debt crisis, drove a reversal of sign.

Table 3.14 Natural Resources and Credit Constraints

Dependent variable: Average annual GDP growth rate

	Period: 1970–80	Period: 1980–90		
	(1)	(2)	(3)	(4)
Nonagricultural exports/GNP 1970	-0.0525 (-1.256)		-0.1385*** (-3.385)	-0.0314 (-1.452)
Nonagricultural exports/GNP 1980		-0.0571*** (-2.683)		
Credit constraints (1981)				-0.0524*** (-2.954)
Log. GDP (beginning of period)	-0.0091** (-2.199)	-0.0159*** (-3.988)	-0.0171*** (-4.396)	-0.0206*** (-5.087)
% years open	0.0233*** (3.166)	0.0230** (2.500)	0.0258*** (2.988)	0.0205** (2.376)
Log. investment/GDP (average of the period)	0.0077 (1.540)	0.0189*** (3.700)	0.0199*** (4.015)	0.0205*** (4.279)
Agricultural exports/GNP	0.0674* (1.746)	-0.0366 (-0.790)	-0.0421 (-0.943)	-0.0303 (-0.701)
N	58	58	58	58
Adj. R²	0.23	0.37	0.42	0.45

Source: Author's calculations.
Note: t-statistics shown in parentheses.
*significant at 10 percent, **significant at 5 percent, ***significant at 1 percent.

Conclusions

This chapter considered several explanations for the perceived poor per-formance of resource-intensive economies. It reestimated the effect of nat-ural resource abundance on growth using panel data and improved meas-ures of the nonresource side of the economy. We found that the effect is always present in the cross-section data and is not found in the panel data. We argue that the empirical finding in the cross-section is due to omitted variable biases.

We thoroughly examined the possible candidates to explain the cross-sectional results. And, while we found that the degree of development and the quality of institutions were important determinants of the growth, they were not the cause of the "curse." Rather, we show that the "curse" is due to the fact that these countries decided to take advantage of high com-modity prices in the 1970s to use them as implicit collateral and found themselves on a debt overhang when commodity prices fell in the 1980s.

Therefore, these results seem to point to credit market imperfec-tions—rather than problems associated with the presence of natural resources—as reasons for bad performance. If we think of the commod-ity production of a country as part of its collateral, then an increase in prices relaxes the degree of credit constraint, allowing those govern-ments to increase their foreign debts. During the subsequent slowdown and resulting fall in prices, the countries were unable to continue bor-rowing and had to repay part of their debts. In the end, devaluations and other contractionary measures had to be taken to balance the current accounts, taking their usual toll on growth. Hence, it is the interaction between credit markets and a collateralizable good that is experiencing a bubble that causes the problems in the end. In this respect, a boom-bust cycle in commodity prices is no different from a bubble in stock markets, as was the case of Japan, or a bubble in real estate prices, as was the case in Thailand. Future research should continue to explore the interaction between credit market imperfections and the determinants of growth.

Annex A: Robustness Check

In this annex we test together our reading of the resource "curse" and alternative explanations to it. In table 3A.1, we present the result of repeating the regressions found in table 3.14, but adding institutional per-formance. The degree of financial development should be correlated with the rule of law and the quality of the bureaucracy. In this regression, we test for the robustness in our results regarding the credit constraint results.

Table 3A.1 Credit Constraints and Institutions

Dependent variable: Average annual GDP growth rate

	Period: 1970–80		Period: 1980–90	
	(1)	(2)	(3)	(4)
Nonagricultural exports/GNP 1970	-0.1032** (-1.827)		-0.0848* (-1.842)	-0.0537 (-1.144)
Nonagricultural exports/GNP 1980		-0.0430** (-2.090)		
Credit constraints (1981)				-0.0405** (-2.027)
Bureaucracy	0.0024 (0.893)	0.0029 (1.272)	0.0032 (1.403)	0.0024 (1.097)
Log. GDP (beginning of period)	-0.0095* (-1.733)	-0.0243*** (-5.434)	-0.0233*** (-5.151)	-0.0269*** (-5.717)
% years open	0.0204** (2.198)	0.0197** (2.358)	0.0202** (2.398)	0.0190** (2.338)
Log. investment/GDP (average of the period)	0.0022 (0.262)	0.0144 (2.134)	0.0127* (1.916)	0.0149** (2.298)
Agricultural exports/GNP	0.0368 (0.721)	-0.1161*** (-2.777)	-0.1062** (-2.554)	-0.0958** (-2.373)
N	47	47	47	47
Adj. R^2	0.25	0.44	0.43	0.47

Source: Author's calculations.
Note: t-statistics shown in parentheses.
*significant at 10 percent, **significant at 5 percent, ***significant at 1 percent.

As can be seen, the resource curse survives the inclusion of bureaucracy. The same conclusion as before is found: the effect of primary exports disappears when credit constraint variables are included in the regression.

A second robustness check is to find how sensitive the results are to other variables that explain growth. In particular, resource abundance could be negatively correlated with many different variables that are used to explain growth.[19] In table 3A.2, we test for one of them, education, which, indeed, it is negatively correlated with resource abundance. As seen in the table, the results from table 3.14 do not change with the introduction of education as a variable.

In table 3A.3, we test for another variable used to explain growth— financial development, measured as M2 to GDP Ratio. It is also negatively correlated with resource abundance. As seen in the table, financial development is indeed significant and has a positive effect on growth. However, the results from table 3.14 still do not change with the introduction of financial development. This exercise can be repeated with several other variables that are standard in growth regressions and the results will hold.

In table 3A.4, we test for a variable recently used to explain the curse— a measure of export concentration. Ledeman and Maloney found that this variable explains low growth. Their result shows that, once you control for export concentration, Sachs and Warner's result disappears, and when using Leamer's measure of resource abundance,[20] the latter becomes positive and weakly significant. Ledeman and Maloney do their regressions for the period 1980–2000, and for that reason, we do not present the results for the 1970s. As seen in the table, when we use their measure of export concentration,[21] we do get the result that the negative effect of resource exports disappears. Nevertheless, when we introduce our variable of "credit constraints," the effect of exports concentration disappears and the credit constraint still has a negative effect on growth. Therefore, this might imply that not only resource-abundant countries, but also any country that has export concentration, faces imperfect credit markets that lend to it based on the implicit collateral.

This exercise can be repeated with several other variables that are standard in growth regressions—and the results will hold.

Table 3A.2 Credit Constraints and Education

Dependent variable: Average annual GDP growth rate

	Period: 1970–80		Period: 1980–90	
	(1)	(2)	(3)	(4)
Nonagricultural exports/GNP 1970	−0.0300		−0.1411***	−0.0720
	(−0.697)		(−3.145)	(−1.420)
Nonagricultural exports/GNP 1980		−0.0786***		
		(−3.048)		
Credit constraints (1981)				−0.0518**
				(−2.512)
Secondary enrollment (beginning of period)	0.0040	0.0057	−0.0015	0.00357
	(0.861)	(1.076)	(−0.287)	(0.673)
Log. GDP (beginning of period)	−0.0120**	−0.0195***	−0.0158***	−0.0226***
	(−2.049)	(−3.773)	(−3.137)	(−4.115)
% years open	0.0255***	0.0243***	0.0269***	0.0224**
	(3.356)	(2.671)	(3.013)	(2.594)
Log. investment/GDP (average of the period)	0.0059	0.0147**	0.0184***	0.0171***
	(1.540)	(2.474)	(3.005)	(2.924)
Agricultural exports/GNP	0.0645	−0.0554	−0.0365	−0.0360
	(1.653)	(−1.151)	(−0.789)	(−0.820)
N	55	55	55	55
Adj. R^2	0.35	0.36	0.36	0.43

Source: Author's calculations.
Note: t-statistics shown in parentheses.
*significant at 10 percent, **significant at 5 percent, ***significant at 1 percent.

Table 3A.3 Credit Constraints and Financial Depth Development

Dependent variable: Average annual GDP growth rate

	Period: 1970–80		Period: 1980–90	
	(1)	(2)	(3)	(4)
Nonagricultural exports/GNP 1970	-0.0301 (-0.678)		-0.1221*** (-2.715)	-0.0694 (-1.432)
Nonagricultural exports/GNP 1980		-0.0472** (-2.046)		
Credit constraints (1981)				-0.0453** (-2.285)
M2/GDP	0.0202 (0.965)	0.0425** (2.154)	0.0414** (2.182)	0.0400** (2.218)
Log. GDP (beginning of period)	-0.0121** (-2.490)	-0.0189*** (-4.011)	-0.0194*** (-4.267)	-0.0227*** (-4.984)
% years open	0.0232** (2.474)	0.0133 (1.201)	0.0141 (1.330)	0.0115 (1.139)
Log. investment/GDP (average of the period)	0.0067 (1.278)	0.0191*** (3.446)	0.0204*** (3.781)	0.0216*** (4.206)
Agricultural exports/GNP	0.0867** (2.071)	0.0129 (0.229)	0.0062 (0.116)	0.0129 (0.252)
N	45	45	45	45
Adj. R^2	0.26	0.38	0.43	0.48

Source: Author's calculations.
Note: t-statistics shown in parentheses.
*significant at 10 percent, **significant at 5 percent, ***significant at 1 percent.

Table 3A.4 Credit Constraints and Export Concentration

	Dependent variable: Average annual GDP growth rate		
	Period: 1980–90		
	(1)	*(2)*	*(3)*
Nonagricultural exports/	−0.0842***	−0.0428	−0.0285
GNP 1980	(−3.68)	(−1.35)	(−0.94)
Credit constraints (1981)			−0.0333**
			(−2.48)
Export concentration[a]		−0.0529***	−0.0361
		(−1.81)	(−1.29)
Log. GDP	−0.0218***	−0.0222***	−0.0255***
(beginning of period)	(−5.18)	(−5.42)	(−6.32)
% years open	0.0273***	0.0247***	0.0222***
	(3.12)	(2.87)	(2.76)
Log. investment/GDP	0.0173**	0.0129*	0.0107
(average of the period)	(1.70)	(1.80)	(1.60)
Agricultural exports/GNP	−0.0273	−0.0200	−0.0285
	(−0.64)	(−0.48)	(−0.94)
N	40	40	40
Adj. R^2	0.48	0.51	0.58

Source: Author's calculations.
Note: t-statistics shown in parentheses.
a. See chapter 2, by Lederman and Maloney, for a complete description of this variable.
*significant at 10 percent, **significant at 5 percent, ***significant at 1 percent.

Annex B: Description of the Data

(i)   Total GDP: Growth rates and logarithms of past values are per economically active population. Total GDP is calculated using the GDP per capita constructed by the methodology developed in Summers and Heston (1991) and updated in Summers and Heston (1995). This number is divided by the share of the economically active population in the total population given in World Bank (1999).

(ii)   Primary exports/GNP, agricultural exports/GNP, and nonagricultural exports/GNP: Calculated by using the primary exports and GNP figures given in World Bank (1999).

(iii)   Years open: Percentage of years open in the period of reference. The number of years open is based on the criteria used in Sachs and

Warner (1995a) to determine whether or not a country is open in a certain year.

(iv)   Investment/GDP: Calculated using the values provided by Summers and Heston (1995).

(v)   Manufacturing and services GDP: Calculated using the figures of GDP described in (i) and the shares of the sectors given in World Bank (1999).

(vi)   Nonresource sector: Calculated using the data described in (i) and (ii).

(vii)   "Real" nonresource sector and "real" primary exports share: Calculated using the data described in (i) and (ii) and the ratio of the deflators for merchandise exports and GDP given in World Bank (1999).

(viii) Bureaucracy: Calculated using the 1995 index of bureaucracy quality from Philip Keefer and Stephen Knac (cited by Sachs and Warner, 1995b). The variable in this paper is equal to 6 (maximum possible value) minus the actual value of the index. A lower value means a higher quality of bureaucracy.

(ix)   Fractionalization: Ethnolinguistic fractionalization. Taken from La Porta et al. (1998).

(x)   Credit Rationing: Total external debt divided by the GNP for the countries for which this ratio is available in World Bank (1999). These countries are all less developed countries. For OECD's countries this variable was set to zero.

(xi)   Secondary Enrollment: Percentage of the age group attending secondary school. Taken from World Bank (1999).

Notes

*The authors wish to thank James Poterba, William Easterly, Gaston Gelos, and participants at the Semiannual Meeting of the Center for Energy and Environmental Policy Research (MIT) and at the Latin American and Caribbean Economics Association Session at the American Economics Association Annual Meeting for their comments and suggestions. All remaining errors are ours. The views expressed here are those of the authors and not necessarily those of Corporación Andina de Fomento. This chapter draws extensively from Manzano and Rigobón (2001).

1. We are not saying that there was an explicit use of them as collateral, but most creditors gave loans under the assumption that these countries would have funds to pay back based on their resource wealth.

2. In a cross-section regression, there is only one t. Therefore, it is needed for η_i to be uncorrelated with X_i. Then, the total error term, $\xi_i = \eta_i + e_i$, would be uncorrelated with X_i.

3. There are some problems with the sample used by Sachs and Warner. They modified some countries, such as Singapore, for example, because it has high "gross" resource exports (they changed it to "net" resource exports). This problem is what concerns Maloney (2002). In Manzano and Rigobón (2001), we discuss in detail how we managed to use "unmodified" countries and still got Sachs and Warner's result in the cross-section.

4. In annex B we describe the data used for this chapter.

5. For example, the coefficient of the lagged GDP is expected to be greater the shorter the period of time where growth is measured. For an explanation, see Barro and Sala-i-Martin (1995).

6. We show this in Manzano and Rigobón (2001).

7. In Manzano and Rigobón (2001) we tested for alternative measures of "nonresource" GDP. The results are qualitatively the same.

8. This does not mean that the previous measure of "net-of-exports" GDP was nominal. It was also based on the real GDP, but without taking into account the change of relative prices inside a country.

9. In order to compute the real shares, a base year had to be chosen: we chose 1970.

10. The actual p-value is 2.4 percent.

11. In Manzano and Rigobón (2001), we found that these results also appear with alternative measures of the nonresource GPD.

12. See Manzano and Rigobón (2001).

13. Agricultural exports include raw materials and food.

14. See annex B for a complete description of this variable.

15. In Manzano and Rigobón (2001) we repeat the regressions from this section with alternative institutional variables. These variables are intended to describe corruption, rule of law, risk of expropriation, and risk of government repudiation. There is a problem with these variables, however: the methodology used to construct them is a survey, and the same for all. For that reason, we do not introduce all of them in the same regression since it generates multicollinearity.

These other variables usually have the expected sign, but their significance level is lower. For that reason, we only present here the results for the quality of bureaucracy.

16. See annex B.

17. The p-value for a t-test that they are different is 0.083.

18. In annex A, we also test jointly this explanation with alternative explanations to the "curse." The results confirm the results found here.

19. We thank Bill Easterly for pointing out to us this fact.

20. As we mentioned in the introduction, there is a debate as to whether or not the share of resource exports to GDP is the best measure of resource abundance. In that regard, the alternative proposed by Leamer (1984) seems to be theoretically correct. See Maloney (2002) for more details.

21. We thank Daniel Lederman and William Maloney for sharing their data with us.

References

Barro, Robert, and Xavier Sala-i-Martin. 1995. *Economic Growth*. New York: McGraw-Hill.

Caselli, Franceso, Gerardo Esquivel, and Fernando Lefort. 1996. "Reopening the Convergence Debate: A New Look at the Cross-County Growth Empirics." *Journal of Economic Growth* 1 (3): 363–89.

Davis, Graham. 1995. "Learning to Love the Dutch Disease: Evidence from Mineral Economies." *World Development* 23: 1765–79.

Doppelhofer, Gernot, Ronald I. Miller, and Xavier Sala-i-Martin. 2000. "Determinants of Long-Term Growth: A Bayesian Averaging of Classical Estimates (BACE) Approach." NBER Working Paper 7750, Cambridge, MA.

Financial Times. 1983, 1988, 1993, 1997. *Financial Times International Yearbooks: Mining*. Longmann, Essex, United Kingdom.

La Porta, Rafael, Florencio Lopez-de-Silanes, Andrei Shleifer, and Robert Vishny. 1999. "The Quality of Government." *Journal of Law, Economics, and Organization* 15 (1): 222–79.

Leamer, Edward. 1984. *Sources of International Comparative Advantage: Theory and Evidence.* Cambridge, MA: MIT Press.

Maloney William. 2002. "Missed Opportunities: Innovation, Natural Resources and Growth in Latin America." *Economia* 3 (1): 111–69.

Manzano, O., and R. Rigobón. 2001. "Resource Curse or Debt Overhang?" NBER Working Paper 8390, Cambridge, MA.

Organization of Petroleum Exporting Countries (OPEC). 1983, 1988, 1993, 1997. *Annual Statistical Bulletin,* The Secretariat, OPEC, Vienna.

Sachs, Jeffrey, and Andrew Warner. 1995a. "Economic Reform and the Process of Global Integration." *Brookings Papers on Economic Activity,* 25th Anniversary Issue, The Brookings Institution, Washington, DC, 1–118.

———. 1995b. "Natural Resource Abundance and Economic Growth." NBER Working Paper 5398, Cambridge, MA.

———. 1997. "Natural Resource Abundance and Economic Growth." Working Paper, Center for International Development, Harvard University.

———. 2001. "Natural Resources and Economic Development. The Curse of Natural Resources." *European Economic Review* 45 (2001): 827–38.

Summers, Robert, and Alan Heston. 1991. "The Penn World Table (Mark 5): An Expanded Set of International Comparisons." *Quarterly Journal of Economics* 106: 327–68.

———. 1995. "The Penn World Table (Mark 5.6)." Data set available at http://pwt.econ.upenn.edu/.

World Bank. 1999. "World Development Indicators." (CD-ROM Data) Washington, DC.

4

The Relative Richness of the Poor? Natural Resources, Human Capital, and Economic Growth

Claudio Bravo-Ortega and José de Gregorio *

Introduction

OVER THE PAST DECADE, MANY ECONOMISTS have returned to the familiar question of whether there is any relationship between a country's endowment of natural resources and its rate of economic growth. Few, however, have asked whether—and under what circumstances—natural resources could serve as an engine of growth. In this chapter we examine both questions. Our evidence suggests that natural resources may lead to a *decline* in the rate of growth in countries with very *low levels of human capital,* but in countries with *human capital over a low threshold,* natural resources *propel* economic growth. Furthermore, natural resources also lead to an increase in income, which raises welfare.

The economic history of the past two centuries shows mixed evidence regarding this issue. During the 19th century and the first half of the 20th, several countries with abundant natural resources grew remarkably fast. The most notable cases include Australia, Scandinavia, and the United States (see Wright 1990, Blomström and Meller 1990, among others). However, in the second half of the 20th century many countries with abundant natural resources experienced slow growth.

The literature on economic growth has tended to focus separately on technical change and on the accumulation of physical and human capital, largely disregarding the interaction between these two factors within different economic structures. The main exception has been the research by Edwards (1997) on the effects of openness on economic growth.

71

During the 1970s many economists studied the macroeconomic effects and changes in the productive structure resulting from a shock to the natural resources sector—the so-called Dutch disease. Originally, this conceptual framework explained only the real appreciation of the currency and the process of factor reallocation that accompanies it, without deriving long-run implications for economic growth. More recently, it has been argued that through real appreciation the Dutch disease might be detrimental to export-led growth and development.

To understand the effects of Dutch disease on economic growth, it is necessary to identify the long-run mechanisms that link shocks to the natural resources sector with the country's productive structure and long-run performance. Matsuyama (1992), Sachs and Warner (1995), and more recently Asea and Lahiri (1999), among others, have attempted such an analysis. Yet the gap in our theoretical understanding remains wide.

In this chapter, we try to narrow that gap by developing a stylized model of two productive sectors in order to consider both the dynamic effects of endogenous growth theory and the reallocative effects derived from the Dutch disease literature. We emphasize the interaction between natural resources and human capital and their effects on levels of income and rates of economic growth. Further, we show that under certain assumptions, a high level of human capital may offset any negative effects of natural resources on economic growth.

There are two main reasons why the presence of natural resources might exert negative effects on growth and development. The first is that weak institutions generate conditions that give rise to "voracity effects," through which interest groups devote their energies to trying to capture the economic rents from natural resources (Lane and Tornell 1996). The allocation of talent in such an economy is distorted, and resources are diverted to unproductive activities.

The second reason, which focuses on the productive structure of the economy, is related to the allocation of resources among different activities with different spillover effects on aggregate growth. For example, if a given stock of capital could be allocated either to the exploitation of natural resources or to the production of goods subject to endogenous growth, the presence of abundant natural resources might cause capital to be diverted to their extraction, which would thus diminish the resources available for growth-enhancing activities. In our analysis we pursue this second idea, but because we live in a world with capital mobility, where the constraint on a country's physical capital stock may be relaxed, we focus on the less-mobile human capital (Barro, Mankiw, and Sala-i-Martin 1995).[1]

Our model relies on the following stylized facts:

• The share of natural resources production in total output and the fraction of the labor force working in the natural resources sector both decline over the course of a country's development (Chenery and Syrquin 1975).

• An increase in a country's endowment of natural resources induces a shift in the fraction of human capital working in the industrial sector toward the natural resources sector, as has been traditionally understood in the study of Dutch disease.

One of the foundations of our model is that the rate of growth of an economy is a weighted average of the rate of growth of the natural resources sector and that of the industrial sector. We assume that the natural resources sector uses a constant amount of human capital and does not grow, while the industrial sector can add human capital indefinitely and grow at a positive rate. Thus, a larger endowment of natural resources increases income per capita but reduces the rate of growth of the economy by expanding the natural resources sector. A greater abundance of human capital generates faster growth for a given endowment of natural resources. Hence, natural resources can limit growth only when the level of human capital is very low.

We could also assume decreasing returns in the industrial sector by including physical capital, but that would make the model less tractable and would deviate from our primary focus, the role of human capital. In addition, we could presume that natural resources are also able to generate endogenous growth (for example, by inducing spillovers to other activities through research and development), but, again, we want to focus on the concept of a natural resources sector with a declining share in national gross domestic product (GDP) during the process of development.

After we present the model, we analyze its implications, studying the effects of natural resources on GDP per capita and on its rate of growth. Our finding is that, when interactions with human capital are ignored, an increased abundance of natural resources reduces the rate of growth but increases income. When we add to the regression analysis an interaction between human capital and natural resources, we find that for levels of human capital over a very low threshold, the rate of growth also increases with the abundance of natural resources.

Scandinavia is probably the most striking case of development based on natural resources. In contrast, Latin America's natural resources seem to have failed to spur economic growth. For this reason, in the next section we motivate our theoretical model using the experiences of Scandinavia and Latin America.

Human Capital and Natural Resources: Scandinavia vs. Latin America

A closer look at the history of Scandinavia and Latin America shows that, during the late 19th and early 20th centuries, both groups of countries enjoyed similar levels of GDP per capita and, more important to our analysis, both were primarily exporters of natural resources. In 1870, Finland, Norway, and Sweden had incomes per capita of $1,107, $1,303, and $1,664, respectively, whereas Argentina and Chile had respective incomes per capita of $1,311 and $1,153. However, the long-term economic pattern of the two groups of countries was quite different: the Scandinavian countries developed, but the Latin American countries did not. By 1990, the divergence in income levels was striking. Whereas Finland, Norway, and Sweden by that year had incomes per capita of $16,604, $16,897, and $17,695, respectively, Argentina and Chile had fallen far behind, with respective incomes per capita of $6,581 and $6,380 (table 4.1).[2]

While a variety of factors could explain these differences in growth outcomes, it is beyond the scope of this paper to analyze all of them, and we limit ourselves to the most common factors identified in the literature. We also stress the difference in the countries' initial endowment of human capital, which has not been sufficiently appreciated despite the large differences between the two regions (table 4.2).[3]

Many have argued that the reason for the success of the Scandinavian transformation lies in the openness of these economies. O'Rourke and Williamson (1995) contend that most of Sweden's catch-up was due to mass migration, international capital flows, and trade, and that this experience seems to apply to the rest of Scandinavia as well. This explanation assigns only modest importance to the relatively high level of educational attainment in the Scandinavian countries.

Nevertheless, what has not been widely recognized in the literature is that the Scandinavian countries were not the only resource-rich countries to experience high rates of economic growth—the so-called Scandinavian catch-up—during the late 19th century. Some Latin American countries did so as well. Argentina and Chile experienced rapid growth that, by the late 1920s, had raised their incomes per capita to levels above those in Finland, Italy, Norway, Portugal, and Spain. In these two Latin American countries, as in Scandinavia, international trade played a fundamental role. The openness of their economies and their comparative advantages— in beef and wheat for Argentina and in nitrates for Chile—contributed to that growth. Nevertheless, it is difficult to explain the faster growth of Scandinavia compared with Latin America without highlighting the *educational gap that emerged between the two groups of countries over the period 1870–1910, and which remained large throughout the 20th century* (refer to table 4.2).

This comparison of regional experiences confirms the importance of education in the 19th century. As Blomström and Kokko argue in chapter 8 of this volume, education was central to the development of new industrial activities in Scandinavia and in the economic and political accommodation of external shocks. A well-educated labor force facilitated the movement of workers across economic activities and assisted in sectoral restructuring as new industries developed in the process of natural resource exploitation. Examples include Denmark's shift from the export

Table 4.1 Comparative Evolution of Income and Exports per Capita
(1990 Geary Khamis dollars)

	GDP per capita			Growth GDP 1870–1913	Exports per capita			Exports growth 1870–1913
	1870	1913	1990	1870–1913	1870	1913	1990	1870–1913
Denmark	1,927	3,764	17,953	1.6	166	501	7,642	3.3
Finland	1,107	2,050	16,604	1.4	177	528	5,222	3.9
Netherlands	2,640	3,950	16,569	0.9	478	702	9,346	2.3
Norway	1,303	2,275	16,897	1.3	129	349	9,145	3.2
Sweden	1,664	3,096	17,695	1.5	171	475	6,543	3.1
United Kingdom	3,263	5,032	16,302	1.0	417	923	3,363	2.8
Australia	3,801	5,505	16,417	0.9	281	704	2,732	4.8
Canada	1,620	4,213	19,599	2.2	194	515	4,934	4.1
New Zealand	3,115	5,178	13,994	1.2	344	729	—	—
United States	2,457	5,307	21,866	1.8	62	197	1,765	2.2
Argentina	1,311	3,797	6,581	2.5	124	257	372	5.2
Brazil	740	839	4,812	0.3	87	80	235	1.9
Chile	1,153	2,653	6,380	2.0	85	201	802	3.4
Colombia	—	1,236	4,917	—	48	51	242	2.0
Mexico	710	1,467	4,917	1.7	26	158	341	5.4
Peru	676	1,037	3,000	1.0	78	94	156	5.3

Sources: Maddison 1995 and authors' calculations.
Note: — = not available.

Table 4.2 Social Infrastructure Indicators 1870–1910

	Railroad (km)		Primary enrollment (%)		Literacy rate (%)
	1870	*1910*	*1870*	*1910*	*1870–90*
Denmark	770	3,445	58.3	65.8	99.0
Finland	483	3,356	—	26.4	89.0
Netherlands	1,419	3,190	59.1	70.3	97.0
Norway	359	2,976	60.8	68.6	98.0
Sweden	1,727	13,829	56.9	66.9	98.0
United Kingdom	21,558	32,184	48.7	78.5	96.0
Australia	—	—	69.6	89.2	97.0
Canada	4,211	39,799	75.0	88.2	90.0
New Zealand	—	—	50.0	90.9	—
United States	85,170	386,714	72.0	97.0	88.0
Argentina	732	27,713	20.9	37.0	46.0
Brazil	745	21,326	5.8	10.8	14.8
Chile	732	5,944	18.7	38.8	30.3
Colombia	0	988	5.9	20.8	—
Mexico	349	19,748	16.0	24.8	22.2
Peru	669	2,995	—	15.3	—

Sources: Railroad data from Mitchell 1998a and 1998b. Enrollment rates from Benavot and Riddle 1988. Literacy data from O'Rourke and Williamson 1995, except Brazil, Chile, and Mexico, whose rates were taken from Engerman, Mariscal, and Sokoloff 1999. The figures for Brazil and Chile correspond to 1890, and those for Mexico to 1900.

Note: — = not available.

of grains to the export of livestock in the 1870s, the shift in Sweden and Norway from lumbering to pulp production, and Sweden's adoption and improvement of British metallurgical techniques, which allowed the Swedes to develop their iron and steel industries.[4] While a similar change in Latin America would have provoked a serious social crisis—as happened when the collapse of Chilean nitrates production led to a mass migration to the cities—in Scandinavia such an adjustment would merely be an episode of Schumpeterian creative destruction.

An alternative interpretation, based on an analysis of inequality and growth, is that access to primary education was simply a good proxy for reduced income inequality in Scandinavia. Increased equality would have contributed to a growing domestic market and would have fostered the development of new sectors. It may also have been a proxy, as Maloney argues in chapter 6, for differences in a broader notion of "national learning capacity" or the overall capacity of a country to create and use innovations that would raise the productivity of the natural resource sectors.

Of course, there are many possible reasons why two regions that, more than a century ago, were similar in terms of income per capita and abundance of natural resources subsequently diverged, with very different patterns of development and economic growth. Clearly a salient difference, however, as the empirical analysis of this paper will show, was the level of human capital.

The Model

The model that we present follows from previous work on growth and natural resources, starting with Solow (1974). Unlike Solow, however, we do not consider natural resources to be an essential input for the production of industrial goods.[5]

In our model, we assume a small, open economy with two productive sectors: a natural resources sector and an industrial sector. Both use human capital along with the fixed endowments of the factors specific to each sector. We assume that the natural resources sector exhibits decreasing returns to human capital, whereas the industrial sector exhibits constant returns to scale. All production is sold in the international market, and the proceeds are used to buy a third consumption good. The prices of the three goods are determined in the world market and therefore exogenous in the model. We use the price of the industrial good as a numeraire, and p_1 to denote the price of the natural resources good and p_2 the price of the consumption good.

Thus the production functions for the natural resources and industrial sectors can be expressed as follows:

$$Y_{NR} = R \cdot H_R^{\delta} \; and \; Y_I = a \cdot H_I \qquad (4.1)$$

respectively.

We denote the capital specific to the natural resources sector by R. It represents a measure of the endowment of natural resources and their impact on output. Thus, R considers such factors as the climate and the quality of the soil and mineral deposits.[6] It can be also considered as a fixed technology parameter. This assumption, although questionable, has been standard in the literature, and it will be discussed in light of the results.

The capital specific to the industrial sector is denoted by a and can be interpreted as technological (or social) infrastructure. As usual, the subscripts on R (or I) indicate the productive sector to which the human capital (or labor) is allocated.

Hence, the economy faces the following constraint for the endowment of human capital in each period:

$$H_I + H_R = H \qquad (4.2)$$

To avoid scale effects, we work with just one representative firm for each sector, owned by a representative agent. We assume that the representative agent owns both firms. Total labor in the economy is constant and equal to L, which we normalize to 1, and hence all variables are expressed in per capita terms. The proportion of labor and human capital allocated to the natural resources sector is equal to $L_R = H_I/H$, and that is allocated to the industrial sector is $L_I = 1 - L_R = H_R/H$.

Thus, the representative agent must designate the allocation of human labor across sectors and how much should be invested in human capital. The agent solves the following problem:

$$Max \int_0^\infty \frac{c_t^{(1-\sigma)} - 1}{(1-\sigma)} \cdot e^{-\beta t} dt$$

$$st \quad L \cdot \dot{H}_t = \dot{H}_t = Y - p_2 \cdot c_t \qquad (4.3)$$

$$Y = a \cdot (H_I) + p_1 \cdot R \cdot H_R^\delta$$

$$H_I + H_R = H = L \cdot H$$

From this setup we derive the following five propositions, which are the basis of the empirical analysis presented in the next section. The first four propositions assume conditions for the existence of two productive sectors (assumption 1).[7]

Assumption 1: *The parameters of the model are such that, in equilibrium, both sectors have production greater than zero. This is equivalent to imposing, in period 0,* $H_R = H \cdot L_R = \left(\frac{a}{p_1 \cdot R \cdot \delta}\right)^{\frac{1}{\delta-1}} < H_0$ *and that* $a > \beta$, *where* H_0 *represents the endowment of human capital in the economy at period 0.*

Proposition 1: *In the steady state, the growth rate of income per capita, consumption per capita, and human capital are equal to* $\gamma_{ss} = \frac{1}{\sigma}(a - \beta)$

Note that, in the steady state, the rate of growth of the economy is constant and depends only on the technology used in the industrial sector and not on the endowment of natural resources. This is a direct consequence of the following proposition.

Proposition 2: *In the steady state, the fraction of the labor force allocated to the natural resources sector converges asymptotically to zero. Output and human capital in the natural resources sector are constant.*

Note that L_R, the fraction of the labor force working in the natural resources sector, can be expressed as

$$L_R = \frac{1}{H}\left(\frac{p_1 \cdot R \cdot \delta}{a}\right)^{\frac{1}{1-\delta}} \qquad (4.4)$$

The fraction of the labor force working in the natural resources sector is inversely proportional to the level of human capital per capita, H, and positively related to the amount of the specific factor in the natural resources sector. Hence, as long as human capital increases, the labor force in the natural resources sector decreases proportionately, and the level of human capital remains constant.

Now we turn to the effect of R on the level of income.

Proposition 3: *An increase in the specific factor in the natural resources sector results in an increase in income per capita.*

Proposition 4 considers the growth effect of natural resources and the interplay with human capital. The proof redefines the variables in our system in order to arrive at a system of two nonlinear differential equations, which are then linearized around the steady state of the auxiliary dynamic system.

Proposition 4: *The effect of an increase in the specific factor of the natural resources sector will be a lower growth rate of income per capita in the transition to the steady state. However, for economies with abundant human capital, the growth-reducing effects of an increase in the endowment of natural resources are diminished.*

This result shows, first, that for low levels of human capital the growth effect of natural resources is negative, although the economy has higher income. A larger endowment in natural resources implies a larger share of total output in the natural resources sector, but the greater the level of human capital yields a smaller crowding-out effect on the industrial sector. The impact on growth can be understood by noting that the rate of growth is an average of the rates of growth in both sectors. Given that the natural resources sector has zero growth, only by assumption, the average declines whenever the natural resources share of total input increases. However, when human capital is large, this composition effect is small.[8]

Figure 4.1 illustrates these effects. The economy converges with an increasing growth rate to the steady-state rate of growth.[9] During this process the natural resources sector diminishes in relative importance. For two economies with the same level of human capital, the one with natural resources will have a higher income but will grow more slowly. However, the economy with a higher level of human capital will be closer to the high steady-state rate of growth. For simplicity, and to illustrate these points more clearly, we have abstracted from the convergence effect; however, the model can be interpreted as converging to a Solow-type growth based on the exogenous growth of productivity in the industrial sector, but with a dynamic similar to that described here.

Assumption 2: *The following inequalities hold:*

$$H_R = H \cdot L_R = \left(\frac{a}{p_1 \cdot R \cdot \delta}\right)^{\frac{1}{\delta - 1}} > H_0$$

$$\beta > a$$

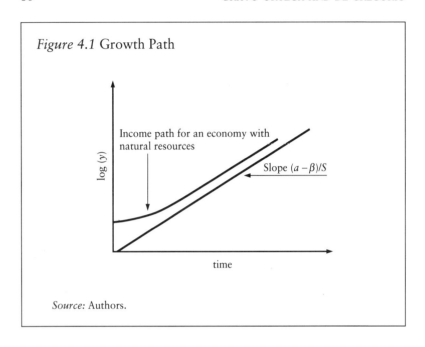

Figure 4.1 Growth Path

Source: Authors.

Note that the first condition simply implies relative abundance of natural resources with respect to the specific factor in the industrial sector, whereas the second implies that the economy will exhaust the returns to human capital in the natural resources sector.

Proposition 5: *Under the conditions of assumption 2, the economy will specialize in the production of the natural resources good, with zero growth of income per capita and zero rate of accumulation of human capital in the steady state.*

So far we have proven that, under the proper assumptions, an increase in the specific factor in the natural resources sector will increase the level of income per capita, but will diminish the rate of growth in the economy. However, as shown in proposition 4, it is possible to reduce this negative effect by increasing the level of human capital per capita. Moreover, as the latter proposition shows, the economy may become stagnant in a no-growth equilibrium when it has a low level of human capital and low industrial productivity.

Finally, an extension of the model would allow us to incorporate the impact of political economy factors on the dynamics of the economy. Suppose that initially the economy produces in both sectors, and consider the existence of interest groups that receive the rents from at least one of the specific factors. Now suppose that these groups are able to tax the return on human capital. The impact of this tax will have three main consequences: first, it will reduce the return and the incentives for human capital accumulation, thereby reducing the growth rate of the economy over the transition and in the steady state. Second, the lower return to human capital will induce, all other things being equal, a larger fraction of the labor force and a larger share of GDP to be allocated to the natural resources sector. Third, under some circumstances, the tax would inhibit the development of the industrial sector, driving the economy into the "poverty trap" described by proposition 5. The same mechanisms operate when the owners of the natural resources sector are able to tax the return to the specific factor in the industrial sector. The tax charged to the specific factor will decrease its return and the productivity of human capital, which will ultimately imply a lower growth rate.

Empirical Evidence

Existing Literature

A series of papers beginning with Sachs and Warner in 1995 has produced the most persuasive evidence to date connecting economic growth and relative abundance of natural resources. Subsequent work includes Lane and Tornell (1996), Feenstra et al. (1997), Gylfason, Herbertsson, and Zoega (1999), Rodriguez and Sachs (1999), Sachs and Warner (1999, 2001), Asea and Lahiri (1999), and Gylfason (2001), among others. Using cross-sectional regressions, Sachs and Warner (1995) find a well-known negative relationship between economic growth and natural resources. They corroborate this relationship with different measures of resource abundance, such as the share of mining production in GDP, land per capita, and the share of natural resources exports in GDP.[10] Finally, Sachs and Warner find that a one-standard-deviation increase in natural resources exports as a fraction of the GDP would imply a slower rate of growth on the order of one percentage point per year. As is done throughout this volume, we test the robustness of this result following the main predictions of our model.

Gylfason, Herbertsson, and Zoega (1999) postulate that the natural resources sector creates and needs less human capital than do other productive sectors. A larger primary sector induces appreciation of the currency, which makes difficult the development of a skills-intensive sector. Thus the model they develop predicts an inverse relationship between real exchange-rate volatility and human-capital accumulation and, hence, growth. Similarly, they predict a positive relationship between external debt and profitability in the secondary (industrial) sector and growth. However, the evidence they provide regarding these two explanatory variables is at best mixed: exchange-rate volatility is not statistically significant, while external debt is statistically significant but has the wrong sign.

According to Gylfason, Herbertsson, and Zoega the share of the labor force in the primary sector can be used as an explanatory variable. However, they find it to be statistically significant only when human capital is excluded from the regressions. This result may be due to multicollinearity, which our model can explain, since the fraction of the labor force (or human capital) employed in the primary sector depends on the level of human capital. Thus Gylfason, Herbertsson, and Zoega (1999) find that "an increase in either the share of the primary sector in the labor force or in the share of the primary exports on total exports from 5 percent to 30 percent from one country or period to another reduces per capita growth by about 0.5 percent per year, other things being equal." In short, the model we have presented is consistent with the results found by Gylfason, Herbertsson, and Zoega relative to the size of the labor force in the primary sector.

In a multisectoral study, Feenstra et al. (1997) test the hypothesis of semiendogenous growth using data on bilateral trade between the United States and South Korea and between the United States and Taiwan. Their study focuses on 16 industrial sectors, for which they test whether changes in the relative varieties of inputs affect the growth rate of relative total-factor productivity between South Korea and Taiwan. They classify seven of these sectors as primary and nine as secondary, defining firms that use raw materials and natural resources as inputs as belonging to the primary sector. Their results show that the variety of inputs affects the growth rate of total factor productivity in seven secondary sectors but in only one primary sector. It is noteworthy to mention that paper and printing (which includes pulp) and chemicals and plastics are classified as secondary sectors, and they show a positive effect. The mining sector displays a positive relationship in several estimations, although two other primary sectors show positive effects, depending on the estimation technique. The remaining sectors in the primary sector present mixed evidence, with a negative or insignificant effect from a variety of inputs on the growth rate of total-factor productivity.

However, not all of the existing evidence supports the hypothesis of a negative impact of natural resources on economic development. Davis (1995) compares the long-run economic-development indicators of minerals-based economies and nonminerals-based developing economies.[11] He finds that the minerals-based economies as a group significantly outperform the nonminerals-based economies. Manzano and Rigobón's contribution to this volume (in chapter 3) finds that Sachs and Warner's results are not robust to small changes in econometric procedure when panel data are used. They specifically analyze the impact on growth of natural resources exports as a share of GDP. They find that when the model is estimated on panel data using fixed effects, the negative impact of natural resources on growth vanishes, but that it remains in the cross-sectional estimations. Manzano and Rigobón argue that the high prices of commodities during the 1970s led developing countries to use them as collateral for debt. During the 1980s, commodity prices fell sharply, leaving developing countries with massive debts and a reduced flow of foreign resources with which to pay them back. Finally, Lederman and Maloney, in chapter 2 of this volume, find that all measures of natural resource abundance appear to be positively correlated with economic growth once all countries' data are handled consistently, and that export concentration reduces growth.

Empirical Methodology and Results

We estimate the main empirical implications of our model using panel data for the period 1970–90. The data used in the regressions are from the Penn World Tables, the Barro and Lee (1994) educational data set, and the World Tables from the World Bank (1993–96). We describe the data and their sources in more detail in the annex.

We regress the growth rate of GDP per capita on various explanatory variables, using random and fixed effects to test the robustness of our measures of natural resources.[12] We also use instrumental variables in order to overcome the possible bias introduced by measurement error in our proxy for human capital.[13] Therefore, in all specifications, we use as instruments the lagged value of government expenditure in education, the lagged value of the average years of secondary and tertiary education in the total population, and the lagged value of number of schooling years on the population over 25 years of age.[14]

Given that we are interested in determining the possible effects of natural resource abundance on economic growth, we extend traditional growth regressions by incorporating the share of natural resources exports in GDP and in total exports as proxies of resource abundance (*Natural*).[15] We must remember from our model that both variables capture the relative sizes between manufactures and natural resources. However, in light of the results, we will discuss which variable seems to be more appropriate. As control variables we use human capital, measured by average years of schooling among the over-25 population (*H*); government expenditure as a fraction of GDP (*G*); openness, measured as exports plus imports divided by GDP (*OPEN*);[16] terms-of-trade shocks (*TT*);[17] investment as a fraction of GDP (*I*); and initial income (*y*). All of the variables are measured at the beginning of each period of the panel. However, as a robustness test, we also estimated regressions using average values of some variables for each period. All of the estimations use period dummies and regional dummies for Africa and Latin America or fixed effects, depending on the estimation technique (*DREG*).[18]

Our benchmark regression for the rate of growth, γ_y, is the traditional growth equation extended by the inclusion of natural resources, as estimated

by several authors and as implied by our model.[19] This regression can be
written as

$$\gamma_{y_{i,t}} = \alpha_{0t} + \alpha_1 \cdot y_{i,t} + \alpha_2 \cdot I_{i,t} + \alpha_3 \cdot H_{i,t} + \alpha_4 \cdot Natural_{i,t} + \qquad (4.5)$$

$$+ \alpha_5 \cdot G_{i,t} + \alpha_6 \cdot OPEN_{i,t} + \alpha_7 \cdot TT_{i,t} + \alpha_8 \cdot DREG_i + \varepsilon_{i,t}$$

Where i is a country index and t indicates the number of the cross-sectional
regression of the panel.

In a second stage, we include an interaction effect between human capital and natural resources. Therefore, we estimate the following regression:

$$\gamma_{y_{i,t}} = \alpha_{0t} + \alpha_1 \cdot y_{i,t} + \alpha_2 \cdot I_{i,t} + \alpha_3 \cdot H_{i,t} + \alpha_4 \cdot Natural_{i,t} +$$

$$+ \alpha_5 \cdot G_{i,t} + \alpha_6 \cdot OPEN_{i,t} + \alpha_7 \cdot TT_{i,t} + \qquad (4.6)$$

$$+ \alpha_8 \cdot H_{i,t} \cdot Natural_{i,t} + \alpha_9 \cdot DREG_i + \varepsilon_{i,t}$$

Equation (4.6) incorporates the interaction term between natural
resources and human capital. This term allows us to test whether the negative effect of natural resources on the rate of growth decreases as human
capital increases, as implied by our model. Hence, we must interpret natural resources exports as a fraction of GDP and total exports as proxies
for the specific factor in our model, R.

Before proceeding with the regression analysis we show in figures 4.2
and 4.3, respectively, scatterplots of growth and income against natural
resources exports in our sample of countries.[20] Figure 4.2 shows a negative relationship. In the case of income, there seems to be no bivariate relationship, although, as shown, this relationship is positive when we control
for other variables.

Table 4.3 presents the results of regressions testing as to whether there
is a negative relationship between natural resources and economic growth
as modeled by equation (4.5); in these regressions we use instrumental
variables in order to overcome the measurement error in our human capital variables, which Krueger and Lindahl (2001) have documented.

In table 4.3 we use both natural resources export share in GDP and in
total exports. We include this first measure for the sake of completeness
and because in our model we do not have a clear prediction of which
measure we should use. As other chapters in this volume have demonstrated, the natural resources export share of GDP is not robust, and thus
our preferred variable is the natural resources export share in total
exports.

Regression 3.1 shows the traditional result of Sachs and Warner for
panel-data estimation. However, regression 3.2 corroborates the results
presented by Manzano and Rigobón in chapter 3; they find that the significance of the share of natural resources exports in total GDP is not
robust to the inclusion of fixed effects. Regression 3.3 instead uses the

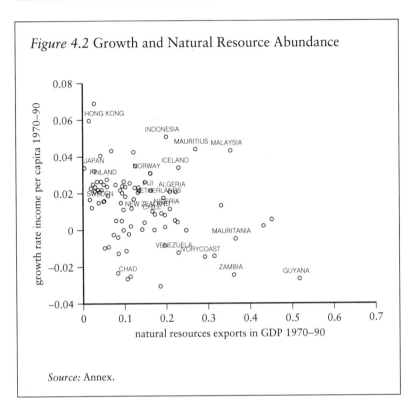

Figure 4.2 Growth and Natural Resource Abundance

Source: Annex.

share of natural resources exports in total exports as a proxy for resource abundance. This variable turns out to be statistically and economically significant and robust to the inclusion of fixed effects, as shown in regression 3.4. This finding is consistent with Sachs and Vial (2001), and with Lederman and Maloney's findings in chapter 2. The fact that the natural resources exports share in GDP is not significant might imply that some of the assumptions of the model do not hold. Perhaps the most sensitive assumption of the model is that the natural resources sector does not present productivity growth. Indeed, Martin and Mitra (2001) and Bernard and Jones (1996) found that total factor productivity (TFP) in the agricultural sector grows faster than it does in manufactures.

Another variable that is not robust to the inclusion of fixed effects is government expenditure as a fraction of GDP. Regression 3.5 excludes this variable without altering the size and significance of the other explanatory variables, as well as without reducing the R^2. Human capital is significant at the 1 percent level in the random-effects estimations, but

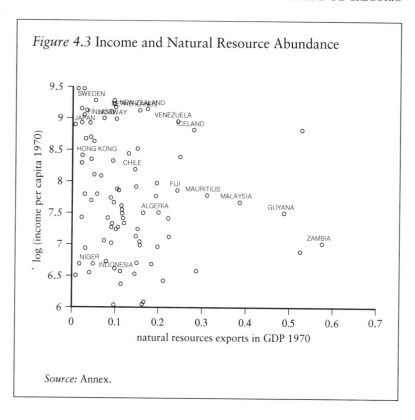

Figure 4.3 Income and Natural Resource Abundance

Source: Annex.

only at the 10 percent level in the fixed-effects estimations. Openness, investment, and the terms of trade are significant, regardless of the esti- mation method. We also performed the Hausman test to determine whether the random effects or the fixed effects specification is more appro- priate for each measure of natural resources. In both cases we reject the null hypothesis that there are no systematic differences in the coefficients estimated by the two methods, and thus we find that the fixed-effects results are more reliable.

The results in table 4.3 show an elasticity of the growth rate with respect to the relative abundance of natural resources (measured as a share of total exports) of around –0.03. The estimations largely support the hypothesis that natural resources affect growth through their impact on the productive structure, even when the estimates control for investment, trade policy, fiscal policy, and shocks to the terms of trade.

Table 4.4 reports the results of regressions using the level of income per capita instead of the growth rate as the dependent variable, controlling for

Table 4.3 Determinants of Economic Growth, Instrumental Variables Estimations

	3.1 Growth Random effects	3.2 Growth Fixed effects	3.3 Growth Random effects	3.4 Growth Fixed effects	3.5 Growth Fixed effects
Log (income)	-0.023 (0.004)***	-0.092 (0.013)***	-0.027 (0.004)***	-0.090 (0.012)***	-0.090 (0.012)***
Openness	0.019 (0.006)***	0.043 (0.017)***	0.008 (0.005)	0.043 (0.015)***	0.043 (0.015)***
Investment	0.063 (0.027)**	0.105 (0.044)**	0.064 (0.027)**	0.088 (0.043)**	0.088 (0.043)**
Government exports	-0.100 (0.025)***	-0.024 (0.048)	-0.106 (0.025)***	-0.012 (0.047)	
Human	0.004 (0.001)***	0.023 (0.012)*	0.005 (0.001)***	0.021 (0.012)*	0.021 (0.012)*
Natural resources ($\frac{X_{NR}}{Y}$)	-0.057 (0.016)***	0.026 (0.035)			
Natural resources II ($\frac{X_{NR}}{TX}$)			-0.029 (0.007)***	-0.031 (0.014)**	-0.032 (0.014)**
Terms of trade	0.195 (0.049)***	0.299 (0.063)***	0.206 (0.048)***	0.285 (0.060)***	0.287 (0.059)***
R^2 within	0.29	0.34	0.33	0.37	0.37
Countries	92	92	92	92	92
Observations	326	326	326	326	326

Source: Authors' calculations.
Note: Standard errors in parentheses. * significant at 10 percent, ** significant at 5 percent, *** significant at 1 percent. All of the random effects regressions are estimated with regional dummies for African and Latin American countries.

the same set of variables as before, with the obvious exception that the lagged value of income replaces that of the growth rate. Regressions 4.1 and 4.2 show that the share of natural resources exports in GDP is positively correlated with income. Whereas in the random-effects estimation this variable is significant at the 1 percent level, in the fixed-effects estimation it is significant only at the 10 percent level. Regressions 4.3 and 4.4 substitute the share of natural resources exports in total exports for the share in GDP as a regressor. In the random-effects and fixed-effects estimations this variable is insignificant at the 5 percent level, although it is still correlated positively with income in the fixed effects estimation.

Thus, the empirical evidence in tables 4.3 and 4.4 confirms two of the predictions of the model: a positive effect of natural resource abundance on income per capita and a much less robust negative effect on the rate of growth. We note that it is the share of natural resources in GDP that is positively correlated with income, but it is the share of natural resources in total exports that might be negatively correlated with the growth rate in our sample. These results may indicate that countries well endowed with natural resources enjoy greater welfare, as indicated by Davis (1995) and suggested by our model. The significance of natural resources exports in explaining the growth rate may fit the predictions of our model. However, it may also indicate that export concentration is damaging for growth, as suggested by Lederman and Maloney in chapter 2.

We also estimated, but do not report, specifications in which we did not control for investment. The natural resources coefficient and its significance remained largely unchanged, which we interpret as indicating that the negative effect of natural resources on growth does not operate through the investment channel but rather through the relative productivity among sectors and, consequently, through their relative sizes.[21]

Table 4.5 shows the effect of the interaction between natural resources and human capital using instrumental variables and fixed effects.[22] In regression 5.1, neither the interaction term nor the human capital variable is statistically significant beyond the 10 percent level, but the null hypothesis that both coefficients are zero is rejected. In regression 5.2, only one interaction term is statistically significant but, again, the null hypothesis that both coefficients equal zero is rejected. In regressions 5.1 and 5.2, the coefficient on the interaction term reaches a higher statistical significance than that on human capital alone. For this reason, and given the specification of our model, we estimate a set of equations (regressions 5.3 to 5.4) that includes human capital only through the interaction effect with natural resources. In these new specifications both the coefficient on natural resources and that on its interaction term are statistically significant at the 5 percent level or higher.

Given the economic significance of the coefficient on the interaction term, we investigate whether it is possible not only to decrease but also to change the sign of the effect of natural resources on growth. Therefore,

Table 4.4 Determinants of Level of Income, Instrumental Variables Estimations

	4.1 Income Random effects	4.2 Income Fixed effects	4.3 Income Random effects	4.4 Income Fixed effects
Openness	0.313 (0.083)***	0.394 (0.094)***	0.396 (0.075)***	0.465 (0.086)***
Investment	1.105 (0.254)***	0.969 (0.256)***	1.075 (0.258)***	0.934 (0.256)***
Government exports	−0.506 (0.271)*	−0.198 (0.283)	−0.496 (0.275)*	−0.203 (0.283)
Human	0.202 (0.022)***	0.180 (0.070)***	0.198 (0.022)***	0.166 (0.070)**
Natural resources ($\frac{X_{NR}}{Y}$)	0.471 (0.192)**	0.398 (0.209)*		
Natural resources II ($\frac{X_{NR}}{TX}$)			−0.027 (0.083)	0.007 (0.087)
Terms of trade	0.833 (0.326)**	0.707 (0.333)**	0.707 (0.326)**	0.572 (0.324)*
R^2 within	0.39	0.39	0.39	0.40
Countries	93	93	93	93
Observations	336	336	336	336

Source: Authors' calculations.
Note: Standard errors in parentheses. * significant at 10 percent, ** significant at 5 percent, *** significant at 1 percent. All of the random effects regressions are estimated with regional dummies for African and Latin American countries

Table 4.5 Determinants of Economic Growth, Interaction Effect between Natural Resources and Human Capital, Instrumental Variables Estimations

	5.1 Growth Fixed effects	5.2 Growth Fixed effects	5.3 Growth Fixed effects	5.4 Growth Fixed effects
Log (income)	−0.096	−0.087	−0.079	−0.082
	(0.015)***	(0.014)***	(0.013)***	(0.013)***
Openness	0.056	0.078	0.044	0.077
	(0.019)***	(0.022)***	(0.013)***	(0.022)***
Investment	0.047	0.120	0.137	0.122
	(0.054)	(0.050)**	(0.049)***	(0.049)**
Natural resources ($\frac{X_{NR}}{Y}$)	−0.138		−0.287	
	(0.134)**		(0.136)**	
(Natural resources)* Human	0.044		0.089	
	(0.033)		(0.038)**	
Human	−0.010	0.016		
	(0.182)	(0.014)		
Natural resources II ($\frac{X_{NR}}{TX}$)		−0.063		−0.064
		(0.020)***		(0.020)***
(Natural resources II)* Human		0.022		0.024
		(0.009)**		(0.009)***
Terms of trade	0.301	0.400	0.360	0.384
	(0.108)***	(0.081)***	(0.075)***	(0.078)***
R^2 within	0.23	0.22	0.24	0.26
Countries	92	92	92	92
Observations	326	326	326	326

Source: Authors' calculations.

Note: Standard errors in parentheses. * significant at 10 percent, ** significant at 5 percent, *** significant at 1 percent. All of the random effects regressions are estimated with regional dummies for African and Latin American countries. Regression 5.1 includes the lagged value of the natural resources variable as instrument.

based on the coefficient of the interaction term, we solve for the number of years of schooling at which it is possible to recover a net positive effect of natural resources on growth. This is equivalent to recovering from our estimations a threshold value for *Human* such that

$$\frac{d\gamma_y}{dNatural} = \alpha_4 - \alpha_8 \cdot Human \geq 0 \qquad (4.7)$$

In table 4.5, we find that human capital always offsets the negative effects of natural resources on economic growth, and this offsetting effect is increasing in the level of human capital. Moreover, it is possible that this negative effect turns positive for economies with enough human capital. The point estimates of the number of years of schooling that fully offset the negative impact of natural resources range from 2.7 years (in specification 5.4) to 3.2 years (in specification 5.3). We prefer to focus our discussion on specification 5.4, given that the share of natural resources exports on total exports is the variable that has shown to be robust across specifications and estimation techniques. On the one hand, this could imply that natural resources hamper economic growth in economies with very *low levels* of human capital. On the other hand, for the case of economies with more human capital, we conclude that the effect of natural resources on growth is positive, given the low level of human capital needed to outweigh the negative impact of natural resources. Indeed, for the last period of our panel there are 60 countries that have a positive impact of natural resources on economic growth according to our preferred specification.[23] Thus, it would be a mistake to consider without any caveat that natural resources are detrimental for growth, given that for *more than two-thirds* of the sample the *impact is positive*.

It is a well-known fact that some countries known to be richly endowed with natural resources, like Australia, Canada, Denmark, Finland, New Zealand, Norway, Sweden, and the United States, are at the top of the list of years of education of the labor force. These countries have had permanent economic growth during the last centuries. In the next paragraphs we discuss the case evidence on the complementarity between human capital and natural resources.

Part of the development success of the United States, it has been argued, is due to its abundance of natural resources. Wright (1990) argues that, over the period 1880–1920, the distinctive characteristic of U.S. exports was their intensity in nonrenewable natural resources. Nevertheless, for the period 1879–99, he finds that net manufacturing exports depended negatively on natural resources, whereas for the period 1909–40, this relationship was reversed. In chapter 7, Wright and Czelusta convincingly argue that the rise and success of the American minerals economy were due to an accommodating legal environment, investment in infrastructure, and education in mining, minerals, and metallurgy. This last point should be emphasized: much of the success of American mining was due not just to mineral discoveries, but also to technical progress, fed by well-qualified human capital.

Wright and Czelusta also discuss Australian mining and economic success. The mining sector is on the technological edge, thanks to the constant innovations fueled by its highly qualified human capital. Indeed, these authors state that in the past 10 years, the income from Australian intellectual property rights in mining has reached $1.9 billion a year, with the research and development expenditure in mining accounting for almost 20 percent of the expenditure for all industries. Furthermore, the mining sector also shows higher spending on employee training than do other industries.

In chapter 8, Blomström and Kokko review the Swedish and Finish development experiences. They present a list of some of the determinants of these countries' successful economic growth; among them, the authors note that "the acquisition of relevant skill and knowledge has been an essential success factor." Human capital has been key not only to the recent development of the telecommunications industry, but has also played a historical role in the development of the agriculture, mining, and forestry sectors at different stages of development. Again, human capital has not only led to technical progress, but it has also created good institutional arrangements for the development of these sectors.

In short, the evidence seems to indicate that natural resources are a hindrance to economic growth in countries with *very low levels of human capital*. Our model predicts that this effect comes about because the natural resources sector draws resources away from other economic sectors that could generate further economic growth. However, as the country's development continues, the accumulation of human capital eliminates this effect. Hence, the negative impact of natural resources can be more than offset through the accumulation of human capital. Thus, our empirical analysis shows that human capital increases the returns to the natural resource sector. Alternatively, this result can also be interpreted as the returns to human capital increasing with the participation of natural resources exports in total exports. This evidence goes against the natural resource "curse" hypothesis. Indeed, natural resources could in this manner be transformed into an engine of growth.

Conclusion

We have found that the relationship between a country's rate of economic growth and the relative abundance of its natural resources depends on each country's level of human capital and on a positive relationship between level of income and natural resources. These findings agree with the main predictions of our model. Moreover, in contrast to other empirical work, we find statistical evidence of a positive relationship between human capital and economic growth after controlling for natural resource abundance.[24] Based on the model's predictions, we have also extended the usual specifications of economic growth regressions by incorporating an interaction term between human capital and natural resources. This allows us to conclude that those countries whose level of human capital is over a given (and low) level will show a positive effect of natural resources on economic growth. This is the case for most of the countries in our sample.

The results indicate that natural resources reduce economic growth in countries with very low levels of human capital, although there is a positive income effect. The negative effects on growth arise as the natural resources sector draws economic resources away from other sectors that would otherwise be capable of generating further economic growth. Our model and the evidence we have presented show that the main resource that is siphoned off from these growth-enhancing activities is human capital. If human capital is relatively abundant, however, this effect is more than outweighed.

Our evidence strongly suggests that abundant human capital not only partially compensates for the negative effects of abundant natural resources on economic growth, as implied by our model, but may actually more than offset it. Further work is needed to fully account for this evidence, however. In particular, further research should account for the existence of economically dynamic natural resources sectors. In a multisector model with close interlinkages between natural resources and industrial activities, it may be possible to formalize the idea of the joint development of an industrial or high-technology sector simultaneously with natural resources, if the economy has enough human capital. This is what may have happened in Scandinavia, where the development of natural resources was accompanied by the growth of an industrial base linked to the natural resources sector—in this case, in forestry (wood and pulp processing) and mining. For such a synergy to occur, however, the country must be well endowed with human capital.

The aggregate data, as well as our review of the Scandinavian experience since the late 19th century, provide supporting evidence for our model. In addition, we have shown that the abundance of natural resources leads to higher income, so that one cannot infer from the growth effects alone what the welfare implications of being rich in natural resources might ultimately be. Indeed, from the perspective of our model, increased natural resources imply higher current and future income, so that welfare increases when natural resources become more abundant. A country would not benefit from giving away its natural resource endowment, as one might mistakenly conclude from models that emphasize only a dubious negative growth effect.

As this chapter has shown, although extremely low levels of human capital may cause an economy to stagnate, a country that is rich in natural resources can start with a high level of income, accumulate human capital, and see its growth accelerate. In this sense, natural resources need not be a curse.

Annex: Data

Penn World Tables, version 5.6: Real GDP per capita in constant dollars, base 1985 (*RGDPCH*), real investment share of GDP (*I*), real government share of GDP (*G*), openness (Exports + Imports)/GDP (*OPEN*).

Barro and Lee Database, 1994: Average years of schooling in the total population over age 25 (*HUMAN*), average years of schooling in the male population over age 25 (*HUMAN (MALE)*), average years of secondary schooling in the total population over age 25 (*SYR*).

World Tables CD Rom, 1993–1996. The following are the variables:

Exports of Fuel: Comprise commodities in SITC Revision 1, Section 3 (mineral fuels and lubricants and related materials) (TX VAL FUEL CD).

Exports of Nonfuel Primary Products: Commodities in SITC Revision 1, Sections 0, 1, 2, 4, and Division 68 (food and live animals, beverages and tobacco, inedible crude materials, oils, fats, waxes, and nonferrous metals) (TX VAL NFPP CD).

Exports of Metals and Minerals: Exports of metals and minerals comprise commodities in SITC Revision 1, Sections 27 (crude fertilizer, minerals), 28 (metalliferous ores, scrap) and 68 (nonferrous metals) (TX VAL MET M CD).

GDP at Market Prices: Measures the total output of goods and services for final use occurring within the domestic territory of a given country, regardless of the allocation to domestic and foreign claims. GDP at purchaser values (market prices) is the sum of GDP at factor cost and indirect taxes less subsidies. Data are expressed in current U.S. dollars.

The figures for GDP are dollar values converted from domestic currencies using single-year official exchange rates. For a few countries where the official exchange rate does not reflect the rate effectively applied to actual foreign transactions, an alternative conversion factor is used.

Merchandise Exports: Merchandise exports refer to all movable goods (excluding nonmonetary gold) involved in a change of ownership from residents to nonresidents. Merchandise exports are valued free on board (f.o.b) at the customs frontier and include the value of the goods, the value of outside packaging, and related distributive services used up to, and including, loading the goods onto the carrier at the customs frontier of the exporting country (TX VAL MRCH CD).

The primary source is the UNCTAD database, supplemented with data from the UN COMTRADE database, IMF's International Financial Statistics, and national and other sources. Because of the source change, the data for some countries may differ significantly from those presented last year. Also, export and import component values may not sum to the total shown.

Merchandise Imports: Merchandise imports refer to all movable goods (excluding nonmonetary gold) involved in a change of ownership from nonresidents to residents. Merchandise imports are valued at their c.i.f. (cost, insurance, and freight) price. In principle, this price is equal to the f.o.b. transaction price plus the costs of freight and merchandise insurance involved in shipping goods beyond the f.o.b. point. Data are in current U.S. dollars.

The primary source is the UNCTAD database, supplemented with data from the UN COMTRADE database, IMF's International Financial Statistics, and national and other sources. Because of the source change, the data for some countries may differ significantly from those presented last year. Also, export and import component values may not sum to the total shown (TM VAL MRCH CD).

All of the previous variables are expressed in current U.S. dollars.

Merchandise Export Price Index: This item is a price index measuring changes in the aggregate price level of a country's merchandise exports f.o.b. over time (TX PRI MRCH XD).

Merchandise Import Price Index: This item is a price index measuring changes in the aggregate price level of a country's merchandise imports c.i.f. over time (TM PRI MRCH XD).

Notes

*The authors would like to thank Daniel Lederman, Bill Maloney, Botond Koszegi, and Maurice Obstfeld for their comments that helped greatly to improve our work. We also would like to thank Pranab Bardhan, Julian di Giovanni, Miguel Fuentes, Patricio Meller, Ted Miguel, David Romer, and participants in numerous seminars and conferences for their helpful comments. Claudio Bravo-Ortega would also like to thank CIEPLAN and Chile's Ministry of the Economy for their support and hospitality during early stages of this research.

1. Even in periods of low capital mobility, foreign direct investment has traditionally been available for exploiting natural resources.

2. All figures come from Maddison (1995).

3. More recently, Maloney (chapter 6) has studied in more detail this and other issues related to the capacity of resource-rich economies to absorb and to develop technology.

4. Heckscher (1968) notes that Sweden built the world's first industrial pulp processing plant and covers the details of Swedish development of metallurgical techniques.

5. More recently, Gylfason and Zoega (2002) also follow Solow's assumption about the essential role of natural resources in production.

6. This assumption is similar to those used by Matsuyama (1992). Allowing for an optimal path of extraction for nonrenewable natural resources would imply, in our setup, a decreasing R over time and, hence, decreasing output in the natural resources sector. This result would reinforce some of the conclusions of our model, for example, proposition 2.

7. The solution to the model and the proofs of the propositions can be obtained from the authors upon request or can be found in Policy Research Working Paper 3484, available through the World Bank's website: www.worldbank.org

8. Interestingly, Vincent (1997) notes that Malaysia's growth has behaved consistently with the assumptions and results of our model. Malaysia has three main regions: the peninsular mainland, Sabah, and Sarawak. Today, peninsular Malaysia's economy is mostly based on manufactures, whereas the other two regions remain natural resources–based economies. Whereas in 1970 the primary sector accounted for 40 to 50 percent of output in all three regions, by 1990 it accounted just for 20 percent in the peninsular region and 60 percent in Sabah and Sarawak. Perhaps most interesting, whereas peninsular Malaysia's economy grew at an average annual rate of 3.8 percent during that period, those of Sabah and Sarawak grew at 2.9 and 3.4 percent, respectively.

9. This feature of our model seems similar to the "convergence from above" of Rodriguez and Sachs (1999). However, in Rodriguez and Sachs' model the main variables exhibit overshooting with respect to the steady-state levels, whereas our model does not exhibit that property. Indeed, our model implies a smooth convergence to the steady state of the economy.

10. It is worth mentioning that the inclusion of natural resources exports (as a fraction of GDP) as an explanatory variable can be derived directly from the model we have developed. For more details, see the annex.

11. These indicators include life expectancy at birth, infant mortality, and share of the population with access to safe water and sanitation.

12. Data limitations prevent estimation by some other procedures recommended in the literature, such as the Generalized Method of Moments, as proposed by Caselli, Esquivel, and Lefort (1996). Hence our results could be biased, because the fixed-effects estimator yields a downward bias in the coefficient of the initial level of GDP per capita.

13. For a revision of this point see, for example, Krueger and Lindahl (2001).

14. For the sake of brevity, we do not report the first stage regressions; however, these can be obtained from the authors upon request.

15. As in most of the recent literature, we use the World Tables CD-ROM as a data source and define natural resources exports as the sum of exports of fuels and nonfuel primary products.

16. We use this variable due to its widespread use, therefore turning out our results comparable with the previous evidence. However, we are aware that it has been criticized on the grounds of being an outcome variable rather than a policy one.

17. We replicate the measure of terms-of-trade shock developed by Easterly et al. (1993). See the annex.

18. For a detailed discussion of the control variables, see Sachs and Warner (1995) and Temple (1999). In our empirical specification we do not rule out the conditional convergence hypothesis; hence, we include the lagged value of income per capita. Given the theoretical framework, it may be possible to recover conditional convergence to a given growth rate after including a decreasing marginal return to capital.

19. Because in our model the economy exports all of its output, we can use either the share of natural resources exports in GDP or the share of natural resources exports in total exports as the proxy for resource abundance, although in reality they are not equivalent since all countries have nontradable sectors.

20. The complete sample list for each regression can be obtained from the authors upon request. Our final sample could be different from the ones used in other chapters in this volume. For example, our sample does not include Singapore, a country with a very high rate of growth and a significant level of gross natural resources exports over GDP. As shown by Lederman and Maloney in this volume, this observation might result in being crucial.

21. Gylfason, Herbertsson, and Zoega (1999) consistently find that the share of the labor force employed in the primary sector (farming, forestry, hunting, and fishing) adversely affects the rate of growth. Indeed, they found this variable to be more robust than the measures of human capital they utilized.

22. We performed the Hausman test to determine whether the random or the fixed effects specification is more appropriate for each measure of natural resources. In both cases we reject the null hypothesis that there is no systematic difference in the coefficients estimated by the two methods.

23. The sample includes 80 countries for the last period of the panel.

24. See Sachs and Warner (1995); Gylfason, Herbertsson, and Zoega (1999); and Asea and Lahiri (1999).

References

Asea, Patrick, and Amartya Lahiri. 1999. "The Precious Bane." *Journal of Economic Dynamic and Control* 23 (5–6): 823–49.

Barro, Robert, and Jong-Wha Lee. 1994. Data Set for a Panel of 138 Countries. http://www.nber.org/pub/barro.lee/readme.txt

Barro, Robert, Gregory Mankiw, and Xavier Sala-i-Martin. 1995. "Capital Mobility in a Neoclassical Model of Growth." *American Economic Review* 85 (March): 103–15.

Benavot, Aaron, and Phyllis Riddle. 1988. "The Expansion of Primary Education, 1870–1940: Trends and Issues." *Sociology of Education* (July): 191–210.

Bernard, Andrew, and Charles Jones. 1996. "Comparing Apples to Oranges: Productivity Convergence and Measurement across Industries and Countries." *American Economic Review* 86 (5): 1216–38.

Blomström, Magnus, and Patricio Meller, eds. 1990. *Trayectorias Divergentes. Comparación de un siglo de desarrollo económico Latinoamericano y Escandinavo.* Santiago: Cieplan-Hachette.

Boughton, James. 1991. "Commodity and Manufactures Prices in the Long Run." Working Paper 91/47, International Monetary Fund, Washington, DC.

Caselli, Franceso, Gerardo Esquivel, and Fernando Lefort. 1996. "Reopening the Convergence Debate: A New Look at the Cross-County Growth Empirics." *Journal of Economic Growth* 1 (3): 363–89.

Chenery, Hollis B., and Moche Syrquin. 1975. *Patterns of Development, 1950–1970.* London: Oxford University Press.

Davis, Graham. 1995. "Learning to Love the Dutch Disease: Evidence from Mineral Economies." *World Development* 23 (10): 1765–79.

Easterly, William, Kremer Pritchett, Michael Lant, and Lawrence Summers. 1993. "Good Policy or Good Luck? Country Growth Performance and Temporary Shocks." *Journal of Monetary Economics* 32 (3): 459–83.

Edwards, Sebastian. 1997. "Openness, Productivity and Growth: What Do We Really Know?" NBER Working Paper 5978, Cambridge, MA.

Engerman, Stanley, Elisa Mariscal, and Kenneth Sokoloff. 1999. "The Persistence of Inequality in the Americas; Schooling and Suffrage, 1800–1945." Paper presented at the University of California Davis Center for History, Society, and Culture, and the All-U.C. Group in Economic History conference "On the Origins of the Modern World: Comparative Perspectives from the Edge of the Millennium," Davis, CA. October 15–17.

Feenstra, Robert, Dorsati Madani, Tzu-Han Yang, and Chi-Yuan Liang. 1997. "Testing Endogenous Growth in South Korea and Taiwan." NBER Working Paper 6028, Cambridge, MA.

Gylfason, Thorvaldur. 2001. "Natural Resources, Education, and Economic Development." *European Economic Review* 45: 847–59.

Gylfason, Thorvaldur, and Gylfi Zoega. 2002. "Natural Resources and Economic Growth: The Role of Investment." Paper presented at the Central Bank of Chile and World Bank Conference on Economic Growth and Natural Resources, Santiago, Chile, January.

Gylfason, Thorvaldur, Thor Herbertsson, and Gylfi Zoega. 1999. "A Mixed Blessing: Natural Resources and Economic Growth." *Macroeconomic Dynamics* 3 (2): 204–25.

Heckscher, Eli. 1968. *An Economic History of Sweden.* Cambridge, MA: Harvard University Press.

Lane, Philip, and Aaron Tornell. 1996. "Power, Growth, and the Voracity Effect." *Journal of Economic Growth* 1 (2): 213–41.

Lucas, Robert, Jr. 1988. "On the Mechanics of Economic Development," *Journal of Monetary Economics* 22 (July): 3–42.

Maddison, Angus 1995. *Monitoring the World Economy 1820–1992.* Paris: OECD.

Martin, William, and Devashish Mitra. 2001. "Productivity Growth and Convergence in Agriculture and Manufacturing." *Economic Development and Cultural Change* 49 (2): 403–22.

Matsuyama, Kiminori. 1992. "Agricultural Productivity, Comparative Advantage, and Economic Growth." *Journal of Economic Theory* 58, no. 2 (December): 317–34.

Mitchell, B. R. 1998a. *International Historical Statistics: Americas 1750–1993.* New York: Stockton Press.

———. 1998b. *International Historical Statistics: Europe 1750–1993.* New York: Stockton Press.

O'Rourke, Kevin, and Jeffrey Williamson. 1995. "Education, Globalization, and Catch-up: Scandinavia in the Swedish Mirror." *Scandinavian Economic History Review* 43 (3): 287–309.

Rodriguez, Francisco, and Jeffrey Sachs. 1999. "Why Do Resource Abundant Economies Grow More Slowly?" *Journal of Economic Growth* 4, no. 3 (September): 277–303.

Sachs, Jeffrey, and Joaquín Vial. 2001. "Can Latin America Compete?" In *The Latin American Competitiveness Report, 2001–2002,* ed. J. Vial and P. Cornelius. Cambridge, MA: Center for International Development and World Economic Forum.

Sachs, Jeffrey D., and Andrew Warner. 1995 (revised in 1997). "Natural Resource Abundance and Economic Growth." NBER Working Paper 5398, Cambridge, MA.

———. 1999. "The Big Push, Natural Resources Booms, and Economic Growth." *Journal of Development Economics* 59 (1): 47–76.

———. 2001. "The Curse of Natural Resources." *European Economic Review* 45: 827–38.

Solow, Robert. 1974. "Intergenerational Equity and Exhaustible Resources." *Review of Economic Studies, Symposium* 0: 29–45.

Temple, Johnathan. 1999. "The New Growth Evidence." *Journal of Economic Literature,* 37, no. 1 (March): 112–56.

Vincent, Jeffrey. 1997. "Resource Depletion and Economic Sustaintability in Malaysia." *Environment and Development Economics* 2 (1): 19–37.

Wright, Gavin. 1990. "The Origins of American Industrial Success, 1879–1940." *The American Economic Review* 80, no. 4 (September): 651–68.

Part II

Are Natural Resources a Curse? Lessons from History

5

Prebisch-Singer Redux

John T. Cuddington, Rodney Ludema,
Shamila A. Jayasuriya*

Motivation

DEVELOPMENT ECONOMISTS HAVE LONG DEBATED whether developing countries should be as specialized as they are in the production and export of primary commodities. Nowhere has this question been debated more hotly than in Latin America. Indeed, it was Latin America that provided the motivation for the seminal contribution of Prebisch (1950) on this topic. He, along with Singer (1950), argued that specialization in primary commodities, combined with a relatively slow rate of technical progress in the primary sector and an adverse trend in the commodity terms of trade, had caused developing economies to lag behind the industrialized world. Prebisch concluded that, "since prices do not keep pace with productivity, industrialization is the only means by which the Latin American countries may fully obtain the advantages of technical progress." Debate over the validity of Prebisch and Singer's claims, as well as the appropriate policy response, has occupied the literature ever since.

While much has happened in Latin America since 1950, the concern about specialization remains as topical as ever. According to noted economic historian and political economist Rosemary Thorp of Oxford University, "The 1990s already saw a return to a primary-exporting role for Latin America. All the signals are that the world economy will push Latin America even more strongly in this direction in the new century, especially in the fields of oil and mining. It behooves us to look very coldly at the political economy and social dimensions of such a model, with more than half an eye on the past. We need to be alert to what will need to change if primary-resource-based growth is to be compatible with long-term economic and social development."

In light of this ongoing concern about commodity specialization in Latin America, we believe it is important to revisit Prebisch's concern of more than 50 years ago that, over the long term, declining terms of trade would frustrate the development goals of the region. This paper has two main objectives. The first is to clarify the issues raised by Prebisch and Singer as they relate to the commodity specialization of developing countries (and Latin America in particular). The second is to reconsider empirically the issue of trends in commodity prices, using recent data and techniques.

The Prebisch-Singer Hypothesis

The Prebisch-Singer hypothesis normally refers to the claim that the relative price of primary commodities in terms of manufactures shows a downward trend.[1] However, as noted earlier, Prebisch and Singer were concerned about the more general issue of a rising per capita income gap between industrialized and developing countries and its relationship to international trade. They argued that international specialization along the lines of "static" comparative advantage had excluded developing countries from the fruits of technical progress that had so enriched the industrialized world.

They rested their case on three stylized facts: first, that developing countries were indeed highly specialized in the production and export of primary commodities; second, that technical progress was concentrated mainly in industry; and third, that the relative price of primary commodities in terms of manufactures had fallen steadily since the late 19th century. Together, these facts suggested that, because of their specialization in primary commodities, developing countries had obtained little benefit from industrial technical progress, either directly, through higher productivity, or indirectly, through improved terms of trade.[2]

To see this point more clearly, consider figure 5.1, which offers a simple model of the world market for two goods, primary commodities and manufactures. The vertical axis measures the relative price of primary commodities in terms of manufactures, $P_c P_m$, while the horizontal axis measures relative quantities, the total quantity of commodities sold on the world market divided by the total quantity of manufactures. The intersection of the relative demand (RD) and relative supply (RS) schedules determines the world market equilibrium.

If technical progress in the manufacturing sector exceeds that of the primary sector (as Prebisch and Singer supposed), then we should see the supply of manufactures growing faster than the supply of commodities. This would correspond to a declining relative supply of commodities, and this would be represented by a shift to the left of the RS schedule to RS'. The result would be a shift in the equilibrium from point A to point B and an increase in the relative price of primary commodities. This relative price

Figure 5.1 World Market for Primary Commodities Relative
to Manufactures

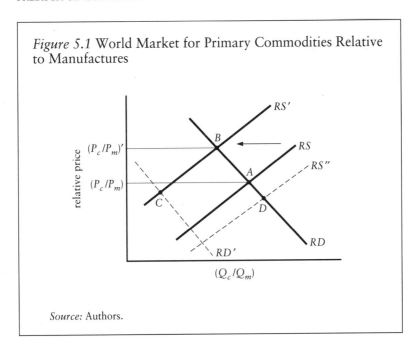

Source: Authors.

change would constitute an improvement in the terms of trade of commodity exporters (whom Prebisch and Singer supposed were developing
countries). What we have then is a mechanism, essentially Ricardian in
origin, by which technical progress in industrialized countries translates
into welfare gains for developing countries.

The main point of Prebisch and Singer was that this mechanism didn't
work: instead of rising, the relative price of commodities in terms of manufactures had actually fallen. They based this conclusion on a visual
inspection of the net barter terms of trade—the relative price of exports to
imports—of the United Kingdom from 1876 to 1947. The inverse of this
was taken to be a proxy for the relative price of primary commodities to
manufactures.

Prebisch and Singer also offered theories as to why the downward trend
had occurred and why it was likely to continue. These can be understood by
way of figure 5.1 as well. There are essentially two reasons why commodities might experience declining relative prices, despite their lagging technology. One is that something else may prevent the relative supply schedule
from shifting to the left or even cause it to shift to the right, like *RS"*. The
latter would result in an equilibrium at point *D*, with a lower relative commodity price. The second possibility is that something causes the relative
demand schedule to shift to the left (*RD'*) along with relative supply. If the

shift from *RD* to *RD'* is greater than that from *RS* to *RS'*, the result would be an equilibrium like point *C*, again with a lower relative commodity price. Over these two alternative explanations for the decline in commodity prices, one involving supply, the other demand, Prebisch and Singer parted company.

Prebisch offered a supply-side theory, based on asymmetries between industrial and developing countries and Keynesian nominal rigidities. The idea was that strong labor unions in industrialized countries caused wages in manufacturing to ratchet upwards with each business cycle, because wages rise during upswings but are sticky during downswings. This, in turn, ratchets up the cost of manufactures. In developing countries, Prebisch argued, weak unions fail to obtain the same wage increases during upswings and cannot prevent wage cuts during downswings. Thus, the cost of primary commodities rises by less than manufactures during upswings and falls by more during downswings, creating a continuous decline in the relative cost of primary commodities, that is, rightward movement in the relative supply schedule.

Singer focused more on the demand side, considering mainly price and income elasticities. Singer argued that monopoly power in manufactures prevented technical progress in that sector from lowering prices, that is, prevented the leftward shift in RS, much like the argument of Prebisch. However, Singer also argued that the demand for primary commodities showed relatively low income elasticity, so income growth tended to lower the relative demand for, and hence relative price of, primary commodities. Moreover, he argued that technical progress in manufacturing tended to be raw-material saving (for example, through the use of synthetics), thereby causing the demand for primary products to grow slower than for manufactures. Both of these arguments would be reflected in a leftward shift in *RD* in figure 5.1.

Finally, Prebisch and Singer drew policy implications from what they had found. Both argued that, as the way out of their dilemma, developing countries should foster industrialization. While they stopped short of advocating protectionism, it is clear that they had in mind changing the pattern of comparative advantage. Thus, whether intentionally or not, Prebisch and Singer provided intellectual support for the import substitution policies that prevailed in many developing countries through the 1970s.

The Prebisch-Singer thesis raises a number of questions that we plan to address in this chapter. First, is it reasonable to equate the relative price of commodities with the terms of trade of developing countries in general, and Latin American countries in particular? Second, has the relative price of commodities really declined over the years? Third, are the theories of commodity price determination that Prebisch and Singer put forth plausible? Finally, what policy measures, if any, should developing countries consider toward commodities?

In answering these questions, we shall draw mainly from the literature, although a complete review would be a huge task. For more extensive literature reviews, see Spraos (1980), Diakosavvas and Scandizzo (1991), and Hadass and Williamson (2001). The next two sections discuss the importance of commodity prices for developing countries and some of the factors that determine commodity prices, respectively. This is followed by a brief summary of some new empirical results on the time trend in the commodity terms of trade.[3]

How Important Are Commodity Prices for Developing Countries?

Prebisch and Singer assumed that developing countries were specialized in primary commodities and industrialized countries were specialized in manufactures. This generalization led them to treat the relative price of commodities in terms of manufactures as equivalent to the terms of trade of developing countries (and its inverse, terms of trade of industrialized countries). Of course, developing countries do not export only primary commodities, nor do industrialized countries export only manufactures, and thus commodity prices are distinct from the terms of trade. In this section, we consider the relevance of this distinction.

The fact that industrialized countries do not export only manufactures was addressed early on by Meier and Baldwin (1957) who pointed out that many primary commodities, such as wheat, beef, wool, cotton, and sugar, are heavily exported by industrialized countries. Indeed, Diakosavvas and Scandizzo (1991) note that the developing-country share of agricultural primary commodities was only 30 percent in 1983, down from 40 percent in 1955. Yet Spraos (1980) argues that this fact is immaterial, because the same trends that are observed in the broad index of primary commodity prices are found in a narrower index that includes only developing-country products.

How specialized are developing countries in primary commodities? One way to get at this is to measure the share of commodities in developing-country exports. This is not a perfect measure, however, because it will tend to fluctuate along with relative commodity prices. In particular, if commodity prices are declining, then the value share of commodities in a country's exports may fall, even without any changes in that country's export volume. Bearing in mind this limitation, we look at export shares to get a sense of the degree of specialization and the products in question.

Table 5.1 from Cashin, Liang, and McDermott (2000) shows the commodities that account for a large share of the export earnings for various developing countries. The countries that derive 50 percent or more of their export earnings from a single commodity tend to be in the Middle East and Africa, and the commodity is usually oil. Venezuela is the only such country in Latin America. Several countries receive 20–49 percent of export earnings from a single primary commodity. In Latin America, this includes Chile

Table 5.1 Commodities with a Large Share of Export Earnings in a Given Country (based on annual average export shares, 1992–97)

	50 percent or more of export earnings	20–49 percent of export earnings	10–19 percent of export earnings
Middle East			
Crude petroleum	Bahrain; Iran, Islamic Rep. of; Iraq; Kuwait; Libya; Oman; Qatar; Saudi Arabia; Yemen, Republic of	Syrian Arab Rep., United Arab Emirates	Egypt, Arab Rep. of
Aluminum			Bahrain
Africa			
Crude petroleum	Angola; Congo, Dem. Rep. of; Gabon; Nigeria	Cameroon, Equatorial Guinea	Algeria
Natural gas		Algeria	
Iron ore		Mauritania	
Copper	Zambia		Congo, Dem. Rep. of
Gold		Ghana, South Africa	Mali, Zimbabwe
Timber (African hardwood)		Equatorial Guinea	Central African Republic, Gabon, Ghana, Swaziland
Cotton		Benin, Chad, Mali, Sudan	Burkina Faso
Tobacco	Malawi	Zimbabwe	
Arabica coffee	Burundi, Ethiopia	Rwanda	
Robusta coffee	Uganda		Cameroon
Cocoa	São Tempe and Principe	Côte d'Ivoire, Ghana	Cameroon
Tea			Kenya, Rwanda
Sugar		Mauritius	Swaziland
Western Hemisphere			
Crude petroleum	Venezuela, R. B. de	Ecuador, Trinidad and Tobago	Colombia, Mexico
Copper		Chile	Peru

(continued)

Table 5.1 Commodities with a Large Share of Export Earnings in a Given Country (*continued*)
(based on annual average export shares, 1992–97)

	50 percent or more of export earnings	20–49 percent of export earnings	10–19 percent of export earnings
Western Hemisphere (continued)			
Gold			Guyana
Cotton			Paraguay
Arabica coffee			Colombia, El Salvador, Guatemala, Honduras, Nicaragua
Sugar		Guyana, St. Kitts and Nevis	Belize
Bananas		Honduras, St. Vincent	Costa Rica, Ecuador, St. Lucia
Fishmeal			Peru
Rice			Guyana
Europe, Asia, and Pacific			
Crude petroleum		Azerbaijan, Brunei Darussalam, Norway, Papua New Guinea, Russian Federation	Indonesia, Kazakhstan, Vietnam
Natural gas	Turkmenistan		
Aluminum		Tajikistan	
Copper		Mongolia	Kazakhstan, Papua New Guinea
Gold		Papua New Guinea	Uzbekistan
Timber (Asian hardwood)		Lao PDR, Solomon Islands	Cambodia, Indonesia, Myanmar, Papua New Guinea
Timber (softwood)			Latvia, New Zealand
Copra and coconut oil	Kiribati		
Cotton		Pakistan, Uzbekistan	Azerbaijan, Tajikistan, Turkmenistan

Source: Cashin, Liang, and McDermott 2000.

in copper, and several others in bananas and sugar. Still more countries have primary-export-revenue shares in the 10–19 percent range.

Table 5.2 shows the top two exported primary commodities (along with the export shares of these commodities) for several Latin American countries over the past century. Since 1900, the export share of the top two primary commodities has fallen in every country except República Bolivariana de Venezuela. Even in República Bolivariana de Venezuela, it has fallen since 1950. Today only three countries, Chile, Cuba, and República Bolivariana de Venezuela have commodity export shares above 40 percent. This decline may be simply because of declining commodity prices, but more likely it reflects changing comparative advantage: developing countries are competitive in certain areas of manufacturing, while industrialized countries have moved into the production of services. It may also reflect the effect of import-substitution policies in developing countries over the latter half of the century.

Several studies have taken a more rigorous approach to measuring the importance of commodity prices for the terms of trade of developing countries. Bleaney and Greenaway (1993), for example, estimate a cointegrating regression for nonoil developing countries from 1955–89, in which terms of trade of the developing countries (from IMF data) is expressed as a log-linear function of an index of commodity prices and real oil prices. The results show that the series are cointegrated, and that for every 1 percent decline in the relative price of commodities there is a 0.3 percent decline in the terms of trade of nonoil developing countries. These results are similar to those of Grilli and Yang (1988) and Powell (1991).

By far the most comprehensive study on this topic is Bidarkota and Crucini (2000). They take a disaggregated approach, examining the relationship between the terms of trade of 65 countries and the relative prices of their major commodity exports. Bidarkota and Crucini find that at least 50 percent of the annual variation in national terms of trade of a typical developing country can be accounted for by variation in the international prices of three or fewer primary commodity exports.

In the final analysis, the importance of commodities in developing countries depends on the precise question one wishes to address. Commodity price trends and fluctuations are clearly important to any policy designed to stabilize commodity prices or the income of commodity producers, such as a stabilization fund or commodity agreement. As noted by Cuddington and Urzúa (1989) and Deaton and Laroque (1992), the effectiveness of a stabilization fund depends crucially on whether shocks to commodity prices are temporary or permanent. Further, an understanding of commodity price trends should also inform longer-term policies affecting the allocation of productive factors across sectors, as was the original intent of Prebisch and Singer.[4] In both of these instances, however, the more disaggregated the data, the better.

Beyond informing policy, Prebisch and Singer sought to use their theory to explain the performance gap between developing and industrialized

Table 5.2 Top Two Commodities Exported by Latin American Countries, 1900–95 (share of each commodity (%) in total exports)

	1900	1910	1920	1930	1940	1950	1960	1970	1980	1990	1995
Argentina	wool (24)	wheat (23)	wheat (24)	wheat (19)	meat (23)	wheat (17)	meat (22)	meat (25)	meat (13)	meat (7)	oil (8)
	wheat (19)	wool (15)	meat (18)	meat (18)	wheat (16)	meat (15)	wool (14)	wheat (6)	wheat (10)	wheat (6)	wheat (5)
Bolivia	silver (39)	tin (54)	tin (68)	tin (84)	tin (80)	tin (67)	tin (66)	tin (50)	tin (43)	gas (26)	zinc (11)
	tin (27)	rubber (16)	silver (11)	copper (4)	silver (6)	lead (9)	lead (7)	gas (16)	gas (25)	zinc (16)	gas (10)
Brazil	coffee (57)	coffee (51)	coffee (55)	coffee (68)	coffee (34)	coffee (62)	coffee (55)	coffee (32)	soya (12)	soya (9)	soya (8)
	rubber (20)	rubber (31)	cocoa (4)	cotton (3)	cotton (18)	cocoa (7)	cocoa (6)	iron (7)	coffee (10)	iron (8)	iron (6)
Chile	nitrate (65)	nitrate (67)	nitrate (54)	nitrate (43)	copper (57)	copper (52)	copper (67)	copper (79)	copper (46)	copper (46)	copper (39)
	copper (14)	copper (7)	copper (12)	copper (37)	nitrate (19)	nitrate (22)	nitrate (7)	iron (6)	iron (4)	fish (4)	wood (6)
Colombia	coffee (49)	coffee (39)	coffee (62)	coffee (64)	coffee (62)	coffee (72)	coffee (75)	coffee (59)	coffee (54)	oil (23)	coffee (20)
	gold (17)	gold (16)	gold (13)	oil (13)	oil (13)	oil (13)	oil (13)	oil (13)	oil (13)	coffee (21)	oil (19)
Costa Rica	coffee (60)	banana (53)	coffee (51)	coffee (67)	coffee (54)	coffee (56)	coffee (53)	coffee (29)	coffee (27)	banana (24)	banana (24)
	banana (31)	coffee (32)	banana (33)	banana (25)	banana (28)	banana (30)	banana (24)	banana (29)	banana (22)	coffee (17)	coffee (14)

(continued)

Table 5.2 Top Two Commodities Exported by Latin American Countries, 1900–95 *(continued)* (share of each commodity (%) in total exports)

	1900	1910	1920	1930	1940	1950	1960	1970	1980	1990	1995
Cuba	sugar (61)	sugar (70)	sugar (87)	sugar (68)	sugar (70)	sugar (82)	sugar (73)	sugar (75)	sugar (82)	sugar (74)	sugar (50)
	tobacco (23)	tobacco (24)	tobacco (10)	tobacco (17)	tobacco (8)	tobacco (5)	tobacco (8)	tobacco (4)	nickel (5)	nickel (7)	nickel (22)
Mexico	silver (44)	silver (28)	oil (67)	silver (15)	silver (14)	cotton (17)	cotton (23)	cotton (8)	oil (65)	oil (32)	oil (10)
	copper (8)	gold (16)	silver (17)	oil (14)	zinc (13)	lead (12)	coffee (9)	coffee (5)	coffee (4)	coffee (2)	—
Peru	sugar (25)	copper (20)	sugar (35)	oil (33)	oil (26)	cotton (34)	cotton (18)	fish (27)	oil (20)	copper (18)	copper (19)
	silver (18)	sugar (19)	cotton (26)	copper (21)	cotton (21)	sugar (15)	copper (17)	copper (25)	copper (18)	fish (13)	fish (15)
Uruguay	wool (29)	wool (40)	wool (40)	meat (37)	wool (45)	wool (48)	wool (57)	wool (32)	wool (17)	wool (16)	meat (14)
	hides (28)	hides (23)	meat (30)	wool (27)	meat (22)	meat (19)	meat (20)	meat (32)	meat (17)	meat (11)	wool (9)
Venezuela, R. B. de	coffee (43)	coffee (53)	coffee (42)	oil (82)	oil (88)	oil (94)	oil (88)	oil (87)	oil (90)	oil (79)	oil (75)
	cacao (20)	cacao (18)	cacao (18)	coffee (10)	coffee (3)	coffee (1)	iron (6)	iron (6)	iron (2)	aluminum (4)	aluminum (4)

Source: Thorp 1998, 347.

Note: — = not available.

countries. For this purpose, it is more important to understand the terms of trade of developing countries than to understand commodity prices. This is the approach taken by Hadass and Williamson (2001). They bypass the question of the relationship between the terms of trade and commodity prices altogether and simply reexamine evidence on the Prebisch-Singer hypothesis, using country-specific terms of trade data, instead of commodity-price data. They construct estimates of the terms of trade for 19 countries, developing and industrialized, and aggregate these into four regions: land-scarce Europe, land-scarce Third World, land-abundant New World, and land-abundant Third World. Simply by comparing averages, they find that the terms of trade improved for all regions except the land-scarce Third World. They argue that this is due in part to rapidly declining transport costs during the sample period, which is consistent with Ellsworth's (1956) criticism of Prebisch and Singer.

Determinants of Commodity Prices: What Explains the Relative Price of Primary Commodities?

While most of the literature on the Prebisch-Singer hypothesis has focused on testing the claim of declining relative commodity prices, several papers attempt direct tests of the theories put forth by Prebisch and Singer. Diakosavvas and Scandizzo (1991) examine Prebisch's theory of asymmetrical nominal rigidities. In particular, they examine the implication that during upswings, the prices of primary products and manufactures should move roughly in tandem, while in downswings, prices of primary products should fall much more than do those of manufactures. They test this by looking at whether the elasticity of primary product prices with respect to manufactures prices is higher on downswings than on upswings. It turns out that the data reject the hypothesis for all but five commodities (nonfood, rice, cotton, rubber, and copper).

Bloch and Sapsford (1997, 2000) estimate a structural model to assess the contribution to commodity prices of a number of factors described by Prebisch and Singer. They build a model that assumes marginal cost pricing in the primary sector and markup pricing in manufactures. Wages are explicitly introduced to try and pick up the effects of unions in manufactures. The model also allows for biased technical change in á la Singer.

Recognizing the potential nonstationarity of the series, Bloch and Sapsford first difference the entire model and apply a two-stage least squares procedure. (While this has the intended effect of producing stationarity, it also has the unfortunate effect of sweeping out long-run relationships between the variables.) Bloch and Sapsford (1997) find that the main contributing factor to declining commodity prices is raw-material-saving technical change. There is also some contribution from faster wage growth in manufactures and a steadily increasing manufacturing markup.

The manufacturing markup interpretation is suspect, however, as the markup is based on price minus labor and intermediate input costs, leaving out rents to other factors, such as capital and land.

Whereas Bloch and Sapsford focus on microeconomic factors affecting commodity prices, Borensztein and Reinhart (1994) and Hua (1998) focus on macroeconomic determinants. Borensztein and Reinhart (1994) construct a simple model where commodities are used as inputs in the production of manufactures, and their prices are quoted in U.S. dollars on world markets. Global commodity demand, therefore, depends positively on world production of manufactures and negatively on the U.S. dollar real exchange rate. As the dollar appreciates in real terms, the relative price of commodities in non-U.S. industrial countries rises, thereby choking off their demand for commodity inputs. The authors assume market clearing where commodity demand is equated to an exogenous commodity supply, and they proceed to estimate both supply and demand effects.

As in Bloch and Sapsford, the model is first differenced before estimation by generalized least squares (GLS). When estimated without the supply component, the model fits well until the mid-1980s, after which it vastly overpredicts the relative price of commodities. The fit is restored, however, once supply shocks are introduced, and it is improved still further after account is taken of the fall in industrial production in Eastern Europe and the former Soviet Union in the late 1980s.

Hua (1998) estimates a demand-side model of commodity prices, similar to that of Borensztein and Reinhart, but he adds in the real interest rate (to capture the opportunity cost of holding commodities) and lagged oil prices. He estimates the model using a reduced-form error-correction specification. He finds that the hypothesis of a stationary long-run relationship between commodity prices and the levels of industrial output and real exchange rate cannot be rejected.

Empirical Evidence on Trends in Primary Commodity Prices: Is There a Downward Trend in the Relative Price of Commodities?

Evidence Up through Grilli-Yang (1988)

The bulk of the empirical literature on the Prebisch-Singer hypothesis looks for a secular decline in the relative price of primary commodities in terms of manufactures, rather than directly at the terms of trade of developing countries. Until fairly recently, the largest single obstacle to this search was a lack of good data. Prebisch and Singer had based their conclusions on the net barter terms of the United Kingdom from 1876 to 1947. Subsequent authors criticized the use of these data on several grounds, and various attempts were made to correct for data inadequacies.

Spraos (1980) discusses these criticisms in detail (see box 5.1 for a summary) and also provides estimates based on data that are marginally better than those used by other authors up to that point. Spraos concluded that over the period 1871–1938 a deteriorating trend was still detectable in the data, but its magnitude was smaller than suggested by Prebisch and Singer. When the data was extended to 1970, however, the trend became statistically insignificant. Implicit in this conclusion is the notion that the parameters of the simple time-trend model have not remained constant over time. We return to this point later.

Sapsford (1985) extended the Spraos data and considered the possibility of a once-and-for-all (or "structural") break in the time trend of relative commodity prices. He showed there to be a significant overall downward trend of 1.3 percent per year with a large, upward, nearly parallel, shift in the trend line around 1950.

Many of the data issues raised by early authors were put to rest by Grilli and Yang (1988), who carefully constructed a price index of 24 internationally traded nonfuel commodities spanning the period 1900–86. The nominal prices are drawn from a World Bank database consisting of annual observations on the 24 nonfuel commodities, as well as two energy commodities: oil and coal. The latter are not included in the Grilli and Yang (hereafter referred to as "GY") index. The nonfuel group includes 11 food commodities: bananas, beef, cocoa, coffee, lamb, maize, palm oil,

---

Box 5.1: Bad Data?

Numerous authors criticized Prebisch and Singer's use of British terms of trade data to proxy for relative commodity prices. Here are the four main problems, according to Spraos (1980) and references therein:

1) Britain's terms of trade were not representative of the terms of trade of industrialized countries on the whole.
2) Industrialized countries export primary commodities, too, so the inverse of their terms of trade is a bad measure of relative commodity prices.
3) British exports were valued without transport costs, while its imports were valued inclusive of transport costs. Thus, declining transport costs alone could improve the British terms of trade, thereby overstating the drop in commodity prices.
4) Introducing new manufactured goods and improving the quality of existing ones may push up the price index of manufactures, giving the impression of a decline in the relative price of commodities.

rice, sugar, tea, and wheat; seven nonfood agricultural commodities: cotton, hides, jute, rubber, timber, tobacco, and wool; and six metals: aluminum, copper, lead, silver, tin, and zinc. Based on 1977–79 shares, these products account for about 54 percent of the world's nonfuel commodity trade (49 percent of all food products, 83 percent of all nonfood agricultural products, and 45 percent of all metals).

To construct their nominal commodity-price index, Grilli and Yang weighted the 24 nominal prices by their respective shares in 1977–79 world commodity trade. To get a real index, GY divided their nominal commodity-price index by a manufacturing-unit-value (MUV) index, which reflects the unit values of manufactured goods exported from industrial countries to developing countries.[5] This is a natural choice of deflators, given Prebisch and Singer's (hereafter referred to as "PS") concern about the possibility of a secular deterioration in the relative price of primary commodity exports from developing countries in terms of manufacturing goods from the industrial world.

The MUV-deflated GY series, which has recently been extended through 1998 by IMF staff economists, is shown in figure 5.2.[6]

Using their newly constructed index, which covered the 1900–86 period, Grilli and Yang estimated a log-linear time trend and found a significant downward trend of –0.6 percent per year, after allowing for the presence of a downward break in the level of the series in 1921. They, therefore, concluded that their findings supported the PS hypothesis.

Post Grilli-Yang Work: Econometric Issues

Since the publication of the GY paper and associated long-span dataset in late 1980s, there has been a resurgence in empirical work on long-term trends in commodity prices. The search for a secular trend has shifted from the issue of data quality to econometric issues involved in estimated growth rates or trends in nonstationary time series. Most authors have used the GY dataset, extended to include more recent data in many cases. In a recent paper, Cashin and McDermott (2002) use The Economist's index of industrial commodity prices covering an even longer time span: 1862–1999 or 140 years! They find a downward trend of –1.3 percent per year.

Visual inspection of the MUV-deflated GY series in figure 5.2, as well as its 10-year moving average, leaves one with the strong impression that it has trended downward over time, as PS conjectured. Modern time-series econometrics, however, has taught us that it is potentially misleading to assess long-term trends by inspecting time plots or estimating simple log-linear time trend models (see box 5.2). Although the GY series in figure 5.2 does *not* appear to be mean stationary, it is critical to determine the source of

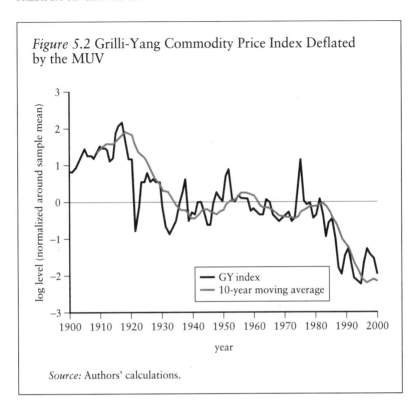

Figure 5.2 Grilli-Yang Commodity Price Index Deflated by the MUV

Source: Authors' calculations.

nonstationarity before attempting to make inferences about the presence of any trend. Possible sources of nonstationarity are:

- A deterministic time trend
- A unit root process, with or without drift[7]
- One or more structural breaks in the mean or trend of the univariate process
- General parameter instability in the underlying univariate model

The key econometric issues are, in short, the possible presence of *unit roots* and *parameter instability* in the univariate models being estimated. To facilitate a discussion of these issues and to put the existing literature into context, we first specify a general log-linear time trend model that may or may not have a unit root. Second, we describe three types of structural breaks in this framework, where there are sudden shifts in model

Box 5.2: Unit Root Perils

It is now well known in the time series econometrics literature that attempting to assess long-run trends and detect structural breaks based on graphical evidence and time series models is a highly misleading exercise, especially if the time series are, in fact, unit root process. To illustrate, consider the 10 series shown in the following box figures. Which series exhibit clear positive or negative trends? Which series show structural breaks? Which series have pronounced cyclical behavior?

Reviewing your answers to these three questions, you may find it somewhat surprising to learn that each of the 10 series is a driftless random walk. So, despite appearances, none of these series has any deterministic trend, cyclical component, or structural break(s)!

Even though these series are really driftless random walks, if you regress each of the series on a constant and a time trend (and correct for apparent first-order serial correlation in the residuals), you will (incorrectly) conclude that 9 of the 10 series have statistically significant time trends—6 are significantly negative; 3 are significantly positive. This is an example of the *spurious regression* phenomenon highlighted by Granger and Newbold (1974). There is also spurious cyclicity, reflected in the form of spuriously "significant" serial correlation coefficients (see Nelson and Kang (1981)). Finally, if you eyeball the data to identify dates when there have apparently been structural breaks, then add dummy variables (at the point where visual inspection suggests that the series "breaks") to your log-linear trend models, you will undoubtedly find spuriously significant structural breaks as well.

It is true that visual inspection of the deflated GY series in the box figures leaves little doubt that it is nonstationary in the mean, but this need not be the result of a deterministic time trend like (5.1). The random walk process above is the simplest example of a time series that is nonstationary in the mean due to the presence of a unit root. Unit root processes, with or without drift, are also nonstationary. The time series and unit root possibilities are nested neatly within the specification in (5.1)–(5.2). If $\rho < 0$, and $\beta \neq 0$, we have a deterministic time trend model. PS predicts $\beta < 0$. If $\rho = 1$ and $\beta \neq 0$, we have a unit root process with drift. Again, if $\beta < 0$, this is consistent with the PS hypothesis. If $\rho = 1$ and $\beta = 0$, we have a driftless unit root process. If real commodity prices are characterized by a unit root, this might be of concern to developing countries or to others who specialize or are contemplating greater specialization in primary commodities, but not for the reasons PS articulated. The concern would have to be refocused on managing risk, rather than on coping with secular deterioration.

Box 5.2: Unit Root Perils *(continued)*

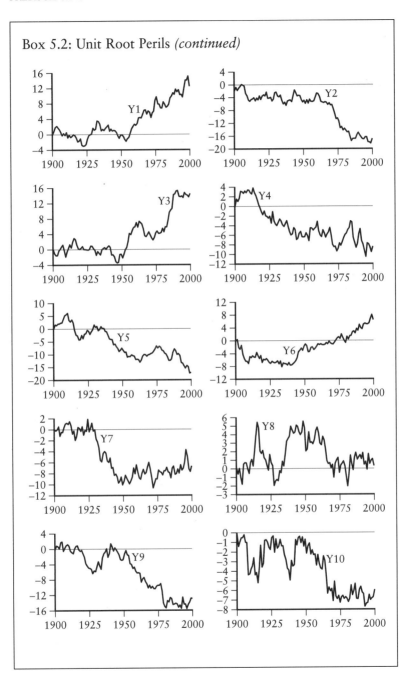

parameters. A more general type of parameter instability, where parameters are hypothesized to follow random walks, is briefly summarized.

Trend Stationary vs. Difference Stationary Models: Unit Roots

Attempts to estimate the long-term growth rate or trend in an economic time series typically begin with a log-linear time trend model:

$$\ln(y_t) = \alpha + \beta \cdot t + \varepsilon_t \tag{5.1}$$

In the PS literature, $y = P_C P_M$ is the ratio of the aggregate commodity price index to the manufacturing goods unit value. The coefficient β of the time index t is the (exponential) growth rate; it indicates the rate of improvement ($\beta > 0$) or deterioration ($\beta < 0$) in the relative commodity price y_t. It is important to allow for possible serial correlation in the error term ε_t in (5.1). Econometrically, this improves the efficiency of the parameter estimation; economically, it captures the often-pronounced cyclical fluctuations of commodity prices around their long-run trend.

The error process in (5.1) is assumed to be a general autoregressive, moving average (ARMA) process:

$$(1 - \rho L)A(L)\varepsilon_t = B(L)u_t \tag{5.2}$$

It will be convenient in what follows to factor the autoregressive component of the error process in a way that isolates the largest root in the AR part of the error process; this root is denoted ρ. The terms $(1 - \rho L)A(L)$ and $B(L)$ are AR and MA lag polynomials, respectively. The innovations u_t in (5.2) are assumed to be white noise.

A critical issue will be whether $|\rho| < 1$, indicating that the error process is stationary, or whether $\rho = 1$, indicating nonstationarity due to the presence of a unit root over time. In the former case, (1)-(2) is referred to as the *trend stationary (TS) model,* indicating that fluctuations of y_t around its deterministic trend line are stationary. y_t itself, however, is nonstationary unless $\beta = 0$.

If, however, y_t (or equivalently the error process in (5.2)) contains a unit root, estimating the TS model—with or without allowance for (supposed) structural breaks—will produce spurious estimates of the trend (as well as spurious cycles). An appropriate strategy for estimating the trend β in this case is to first-difference the model (5.1)–(5.2) to achieve stationarity. The result is the so-called *difference stationary (DS) model,* a specification in terms of growth rates rather than log-levels of the y_t series:

$$(1 - L)\ln(y_t) \equiv D\ln(y_t) = \beta + v_t \qquad (5.3)$$

where L and D are the lag and difference operators, respectively. The error term in (5.3) follows an ARMA process:

$$A(L)v_t = B(L)u_t \qquad (5.4)$$

In the DS model, a significant negative estimate of the constant term, β, would be support for the PS hypothesis.

Using the extended GY dataset (1900–98), suppose we ignore the possibilities of unit roots and structural breaks and simply estimate the TS model. The following results are obtained:

$$y_t = 2.19 - 0.003t + \varepsilon_t$$
$$\text{where } \varepsilon_t = 0.74\,\varepsilon_{t-1} + u_t$$

The error process is adequately modeled as a first-order AR process. There is a statistically significant trend coefficient equal to –0.3 percent per year ($t = -5.23$). Fitted values from the TS model, the long-term trend estimate, and the regression residuals are shown in figure 5.3. The figure reveals some potential problems. First, the fitted regression line does not fit the data especially well. Note that the fitted line consistently lags the turning points in the actual data.

Moreover, the residuals have possible outliers at 1921 and to a lesser extent in 1974 (or 1973). Reexamining the GY series itself in light of these observations, one might speculate that there have been structural breaks in 1921 and 1974. More formal methods for identifying the timing of a possible break (or two) are considered next. These methods indicate clear evidence of a break in 1921, with a second, but statistically insignificant, break in the early 1970s or mid-1980s.

One way to assess the structural stability of the TS-AR(1) model is to calculate recursive residuals and the two-standard error bands for the hypothesis that the recursive residuals come from the same distribution as those from the estimated model. As seen in figure 5.4, the recursive residuals in 1921 and 1974 are "large," suggesting structural breaks. Figure 5.4 also shows p-values for an N-step forecast test for each possible forecast sample. To calculate the p-value for 1920, for example, one would use data from 1900 through 1920 to estimate a TS-AR(1) model. This model is then used to forecast $y(t)$ for the remaining N years of the sample: 1921–98. A test statistic that incorporates the forecast errors, comparing the forecast with the actual value, for the N-steps ahead can be constructed to test the null hypothesis that such forecast errors could have been obtained from the underlying TS-AR(1) model with no structural

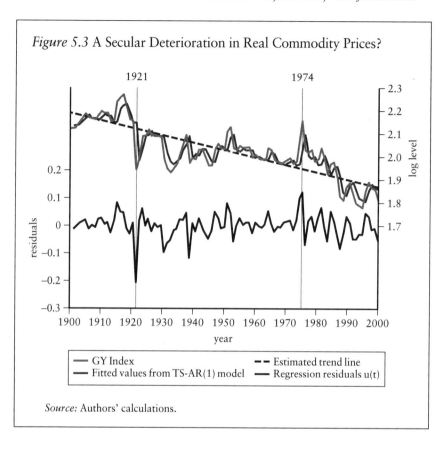

Figure 5.3 A Secular Deterioration in Real Commodity Prices?

Legend:
— GY Index   – – Estimated trend line
— Fitted values from TS-AR(1) model — Regression residuals u(t)

Source: Authors' calculations.

break. The p-value for the null hypothesis of no structural break gives the probability of finding an even larger test statistic if the null is, in fact, true. If the p-value is smaller than the size of the test, typically 0.01 or 0.05, then one should reject the null hypothesis of no structural breaks.

As seen in figure 5.4, the p-values very near 0.4 in the 1910–20 period indicate that the test statistic is so large that the probability of finding a larger one under the null is virtually zero. That is, this graph clearly shows that if the model is fitted with pre-1921 data and used to forecast into the future, there is clear rejection of parameter stability. If, instead, one uses data up through the 1940s or 1950s or 1960s, on the other hand, parameter stability is not rejected. If one uses data through the early 1970s to forecast commodity prices through the end of the 1990s, there is again instability—albeit somewhat less severe (judging from the p-values on the left-hand scale of the graph).

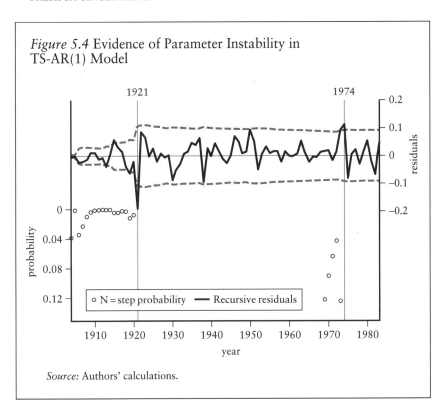

Figure 5.4 Evidence of Parameter Instability in TS-AR(1) Model

Source: Authors' calculations.

This evidence indicates that the issue of structural breaks or parameter instability must be taken seriously if one chooses the TS model for analyzing the long-term trends in primary commodity prices.

Consider now the DS model, which uses first-differences of the logged real commodity price series shown in figure 5.5, to estimate the growth rate in commodity prices. This specification is appropriate if one believes that the GY series is a unit root process.

Note that the $D(y)$ series is very volatile. The 10-year moving average is, not surprisingly, much smoother. It also "goes through the data" much better than it did the 10-year moving average of the log-levels in figure 5.2. This is consistent with the presumption that $D(y)$ is stationary, but y is not. The average value of $D(y)$ is small and negative, −0.3 percent per year (including the huge −22.0 percent outlier in 1921). Given the high variance of the series, however, it is not surprising that the null hypothesis of a zero growth rate cannot be rejected.

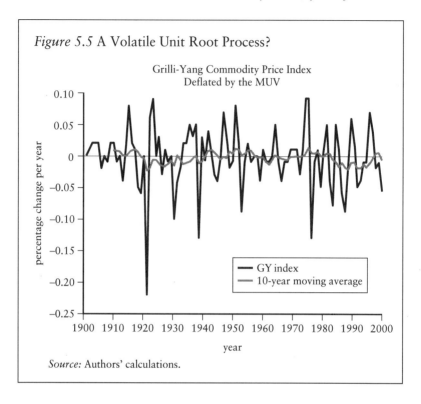

Figure 5.5 A Volatile Unit Root Process?

Source: Authors' calculations.

The regression results presented in table 5.3 are for a DS model, with two lags of DGY being sufficient to eliminate serial correlation in the residuals.

The recursive residual and N-step ahead forecast analysis, shown in figure 5.6, again suggests that there is a structural break in 1921. With the DS model, however, 1921 appears to be the only troublesome episode.

What is clear up to this point? In sum, the possibility of finding statistical significance for the trend in the real GY commodity price index depends critically on whether one believes *a priori*, or concludes, on the basis of unit root tests, that Grilli-Yang is trend stationary, or whether it contains a unit root. Regardless of whether the TS or DS specification is chosen, there is evidence that one or two breaks or parameter instability may be a problem.

Structural Breaks and Parameter Instability

It has long been recognized that estimated parameters in models like the TS and DS models earlier will be biased, or even meaningless, if the true

Table 5.3 Estimation Results for a Difference Stationary Model
for the GY Series

Dependent variable: DGY	
Sample (adjusted): 1903–98	
Constant	–0.004
	(0.005)
DGY(-1)	0.004
	(0.101)
DGY(-2)	–0.259
	(0.101)
R^2	0.066
Observations	96

Source: Authors' calculations.
Note: Standard errors are given within parentheses.

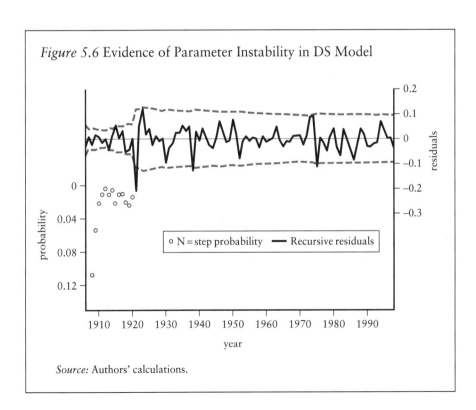

Figure 5.6 Evidence of Parameter Instability in DS Model

Source: Authors' calculations.

parameters do not remain constant over time. Suppose, for example, that the true growth rate was −4.0 percent in the first half of the sample, but 2.0 percent in the second half. An econometrician who ignored the shift in parameters might incorrectly conclude that the growth rate was a uniform −2.0 percent over the entire sample.

To consider the possibility of a change in parameters (α, β) in the TS model or β in the DS model,[8] one typically constructs a dummy variable: $DUM_{TB} = 0$ for all $t < TB$ and $DUM_{TB} = 1$ for all $t \geq TB$ where TB is the hypothesized break date. Using this "level-shift" dummy, as well as its first difference (a "spike" dummy) and a dummy-time trend interaction term, yields the "TS with break" model and the "DS with break" model, respectively:

TS with break model

$$\ln(y_t) = \alpha_1 + \alpha_2 DUM_{TB} + \beta_1 t + \beta_2 (t - TB) \cdot DUM_{TB} + \varepsilon_t \qquad (5.5)$$

DS with break model

$$D(\ln(y_t)) = \alpha_2 D(DUM_{TB}) + \beta_1 + \beta_2 \cdot DUM_{TB} + \nu_t \qquad (5.6)$$

These specifications are general enough to encompass the three types of breaks described in Perron's (1989) classic paper on testing for unit roots in the presence of structural breaks (which will be discussed later). His model A ("crash" model) involves only an abrupt shift in the level of the series; that is, $\alpha_2 \neq 0$, $\beta_2 = 0$. In model B ("breaking trend" model), there is a change in the growth rate, but no abrupt level shift: $\alpha_2 = 0$, $\beta_2 \neq 0$. Finally, model C ("combined" model) has change in both the level and growth rate: $\alpha_2 \neq 0$, $\beta_2 \neq 0$.

Suppose that one knows *a priori*, or decides on the basis of unit root testing, whether the TS or DS specification is appropriate. Then, if the break date, TB, is assumed to be known, it is straightforward to test for the presence of structural breaks by examining the T-statistics on α_2 and β_2. A test for a break of type C could be carried out using a $\chi^2(2)$ test for the joint hypothesis that $\alpha_2 = 0$ and $\beta_2 = 0$.

The latter is equivalent to (one variant of) the well-known Chow test for a structural break. More recent work on tests for parameter stability warns against arguing that the break date TB is known. Andrews (1993); Ploberger, Kramer, and Kontrus (1989); and Hansen (1992, 2001), for example, develop methods for testing for the presence of a possible structural break at an unknown date using algorithms that search over all possible break dates.

Recently, there have been attempts in the macroeconomics literature to extend the unknown break date literature to consider *two* break points at unknown dates (see, for example, Lumsdaine and Papell (1997) and Mehl

(2000)). An obvious issue that this extension raises is: why only two breaks rather than, say, three or four?

Authors developing parameter stability tests have also considered the alternative hypothesis where the parameters are assumed to follow a random walk. In this case, the model parameters are generally unstable, in a way that cannot be captured by a one-time shift at any particular date. This test of general parameter stability is a good diagnostic test when assessing the adequacy of a particular model specification.

Hansen (1992, 321) provides an excellent overview of the issue and possible approaches to dealing with it:

> One potential problem with time series regression models is that the estimated parameters may change over time. A form of model misspecification, parameter nonconstancy, may have severe consequences on inference if left undetected. In consequence, many applied econometricians routinely apply tests for parameter change. The most common test is the sample split or Chow test (Chow 1960). This test is simple to apply, and the distribution theory is well developed. The test is crippled, however, by the need to specify *a priori* the timing of the (one-time) structural change that occurs under the alternative. It is hard to see how any non-arbitrary choice can be made independently of the data. In practice, the selection of the breakpoint is chosen either with historical events in mind or after time series plots have been examined. This implies that the breakpoint is selected conditional on the data and therefore conventional critical values are invalid. One can only conclude that inferences may be misleading.

An alternative testing procedure was proposed by Quandt (1960), who suggested specifying the alternative hypothesis as a single structural break of unknown timing. Until recently, a difficulty with Quandt's test was that the distributional theory for the test statistic was unknown. This problem, however, was independently solved by Andrews (1993), Chu (1989), and Hansen (1990).

In situations where one is tempted to argue that there are several structural breaks, it probably makes sense to ask whether the situation might be better described as one of general parameter instability.

A Selective Review of Post Grilli-Yang Empirical Work

As mentioned earlier, the literature through Grilli-Yang (1988) used the TS model—as indicated by model 1 in figure 5.7, which summarizes approaches taken in the literature—to estimate the long-term trend in real commodity prices. A number of these authors recognized the possibility of structural changes in the form of one-time shifts in the level or trend in the

Figure 5.7 Alternative Specifications

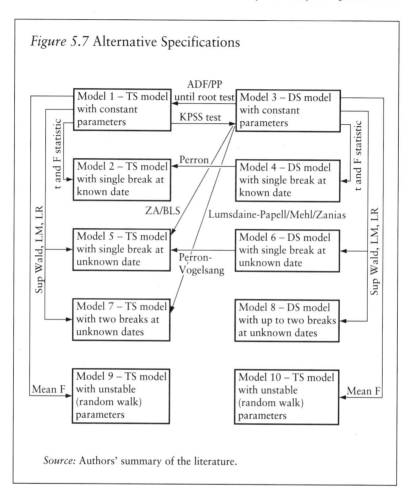

Source: Authors' summary of the literature.

real commodity price series. That is, they compared models 1 and 2. For example, Sapsford (1985) found a break in 1950 using pre-Grilli-Yang data, as mentioned earlier. Grilli and Yang (1988) and Cuddington and Urzúa (hereafter referred to as "CU") (1989) both identified a breakpoint in 1921 using the Grilli-Yang dataset for the period 1900–83. Contrary to Grilli-Yang, CU argued that, after accounting for the highly significant downward shift in the level of the real Grilli-Yang price index in 1921, the trends on either side of the break were not significantly different from zero in the TS specification. Not surprisingly, if one ignored the one-time downward step in the data, the estimated trend coefficient β appears to be negative and significant. This illustrates the potential for incorrect statistical inferences if structural shifts are ignored.

CU also demonstrated that the structural break in 1950 detected by Sapsford (1985) using the trend stationary model on pre-Grilli-Yang data was not significant when using the Grilli-Yang data once the 1921 break was included.

CU (1989) were the first to carry out unit root tests on the Grilli-Yang commodity price index. They were unable to reject the unit root hypothesis, and they, therefore, stated a preference for DS models rather than TS models when estimating the long-term trend in real commodity prices. Using data from 1900–83, they were unable to reject the null hypothesis that $\beta = 0$ in the DS model in (3)-(4), where β is the long-term drift in real commodity prices. This finding was robust to the inclusion or exclusion of the one-time drop in the level of the Grilli-Yang series in 1921. In terms of figure 5.7, CU (1989) considered models 3 and 4, and they formally tested model 3 against model 1 (assuming no unit root) and model 3 against model 4 (assuming there is a unit root). By carrying out augmented Dickey-Fuller (ADF) tests (1979), they compared model 3 to model 1, and using a new unit root test in Perron (1989), they tested model 4 against model 2.

Applying ADF unit root tests as well as Perron-ADF tests that allow for a possible structural break at a predetermined break date, CU (1989) showed that the unit root hypothesis cannot be rejected for the Grilli-Yang index. When CU estimated the DS model using Grilli-Yang data from 1900–83, the estimated long-term growth rate was statistically insignificant, regardless of whether one included a spike dummy to account for the downward shift in the level of the real Grilli-Yang series in 1921.

The DS specification, therefore, leads to the conclusion that real commodity prices follow a driftless unit root process. The policy implications from this specification are quite different from those based on the CU's TS model with a one-time level shift in 1921. The risk entailed for commodity producers, exporters, and commodity stabilization fund managers is considerably greater if one believes that the true model is the DS specification. The CU unit root tests failed to reject the null hypothesis of a unit root, but such tests have notoriously low power, so no definitive conclusion is warranted.

Note that the DS model with a one-time level shift in 1921 is a very plausible candidate model for the Grilli-Yang series. In fact, it is the specification preferred by Cuddington and Urzúa (1989). The year 1921, moreover, occurs early in the sample, precisely the situation where Leybourne, Mills, and Newbold (1998) warn that DF tests are likely to lead to false rejections of the unit root hypothesis when the true data-generating process is unit root with a structural break! In spite of this bias, CU did not reject the unit root when they assumed a known break date. Assuming an unknown break date implies smaller (that is, more negative) critical values for the resulting Zivot-Andrews-Perron (ZAP)-ADF test. So, again, one would not expect to reject the unit root hypothesis.

Cuddington (1992) repeated the exercise of testing for unit roots (with or without breaks at possible break dates determined by visual inspection) for each of the 24 component commodities in the Grilli-Yang index (1900–83). Some commodities had unit roots; others did not. Some commodities had negative price trends, while others had positive trends. Surprisingly, not a single commodity had a structural break in 1921![9] This led Cuddington and Wei (hereafter referred to as "CW") (1992) to conjecture that there was some aggregation issue involved in the construction of the Grilli-Yang index, as theirs was an arithmetic index. Cuddington and Wei constructed a geometric index, so that the results from the individual commodities should be reflected in the geometric index, as it was just a simple weighted average of the logs of the individual commodity prices that comprise the index. Using the CW index (over the slightly extended period 1900–88), they found that unit root tests are inconclusive. The estimated trend in the real commodity price index, however, turned out to be statistically insignificant regardless of whether one used the TS or DS model specification.

Subsequent work has reconsidered Cuddington and Urzúa's claim of a trendless series with a break in 1921. Powell (1991), for example, found three downward jumps, in 1921, 1938, and 1975, and no continuous trend. Ardeni and Wright (1992) used a "trend plus cycle model" and extend the Grilli-Yang data to 1988 to find a continuous trend between –0.14 percent and –1.06 percent, depending on the exact model specification. Moreover, this trend survives with or without a structural break in 1921. Bleaney and Greenaway (1993) avoided the issue of a structural break in 1921 by considering 1925–91 data, and they instead found a downward jump in 1980, with no continuous trend.

León and Soto (1997) and Zanias (2005) applied the Zivot-Andrews/Banerjee, Lumsdaine, and Stock (ZA/BLS) method for testing for unit roots in the presence of a single break at an unknown break point. Zanias, in particular, found that this method identifies 1984 as the primary break point. It is, however, difficult to know how to interpret a break point in a portion of the sample that Andrews and others recommend should be trimmed off, because it is too close to the end of the sample. Zanias went on to reapply the ZA/BLS approach to find a second break, conditional on the presence of the first break in 1984. This sequential procedure chose 1921 as the second break point

Although the PS literature has extensively explored the possibility of structural breaks, the more general phenomenon of parameter instability has only recently been explored. See Cuddington, Ludema, and Jayasuriya (2002) (hereafter referred to as "CLJ"), who apply Hansen's approach to the Grilli-Yang commodity index. Apart from the econometric issues raised by, for example, Hansen's quote earlier, parameter instability has interesting implications for testing the PS hypothesis. PS did not claim that the long-run trend would necessarily remain constant over time, only that it would be negative!

A New Look at Growth Rates, Possible Breaks, and Unit Root Tests

In testing the PS hypothesis, our primary interest is in the growth rate β in the deflated Grilli-Yang index. Has it been negative as PS predicted? Has it been relatively stable over time? Or has this parameter shifted or drifted over time, or exhibited a sharp structural break or breaks? In our particular application, we are less interested in the presence or absence of unit roots per se than was the applied macroeconometric literature. Unfortunately, it is difficult to estimate the growth rate β without making a decision on the presence or absence of a unit root first. Ideally, we would also like to formally test for the presence of structural breaks without prejudging the case of whether the series has a unit root. This objective, however, appears to be beyond our reach at this time.

The strategy in CLJ (2002) is the following. First estimate augmented ZAP-ADF-like regressions allowing for, at most, two structural breaks at unknown dates. Having searched for the two most plausible break dates, test whether each break is statistically significant. If both breaks are significant, assume two breaks in what follows. If only one break is statistically significant, reestimate the ZAP-ADF equation with a single break at an unknown date and test to see whether the remaining break is statistically significant. The results of this exhaustive unit root in the presence of two possible breaks at unknown dates is, alas, rather inconclusive—not in identifying the likely break points, but in resolving the issue of whether there is a unit root in the real commodity price index.

Given the uncertainty surrounding the question of unit roots, CLJ estimate both TS and DS models with one or two breaks. The diagnostic tests suggest that if the TS model is adopted, two break points are detected—in 1921 and 1985. With the DS specification, however, only a single break—in 1921—appears statistically significant. These specifications are chosen by carrying out a grid search over all possible pairs of break dates.

Estimated TS and DS Models with Two Breaks

Next, we consider the TS and DS models in turn, using our search algorithm to choose the dating of two break points.[10] As discussed earlier, we need to include only the level-shift and time-interaction dummies to allow for breaks of type A, B, and C in the TS model. Thus the criterion for choosing the break dates (TB1, TB2) is the $\sup\chi^2(4)$ statistic from the set of all $\chi^2(4)$ statistics testing the joint significance of the two dummies associated with all possible pairs of break dates. Analogously, in the DS specification, we need to include only the spike and level-shift dummies. The criterion is again a $\sup\chi^2(4)$ statistic.

Once the two most plausible break points have been identified in the TS and DS specifications, respectively, there are three subsamples of the

Grilli-Yang index to consider. It is necessary to estimate the growth rates for each segment: pre-TB1, TB1 through TB2, and post-TB2. Estimates of the trend segments for both the TS and DS specifications are shown in table 5.4. Also reported is the Wald test of the null hypothesis that each trend coefficient is equal to zero. A rejection of the hypothesis indicates the presence of a significant trend in the respective subperiod.

Examining the table, we find that $\sup\chi^2(4)$ statistics for both the TS and DS specifications are "large" (relative to the standard 1 percent critical value for $\chi^2(4)$ of 13.28). The mean$\chi^2(4)$ statistic for the DS model is very small, suggesting no issue of general parameter instability. The mean$\chi^2(4)$ statistic for the TS model is close enough to the standard critical value that it is impossible to guess the outcome of a formal parameter stability test based on simulated critical values.

The TS model estimation places the two breaks in 1921 and 1985. Moreover, the $\chi^2(2)\_TB1$ and $\chi^2(2)\_TB2$ stats for 1921 and 1985, respectively, are similar in magnitude, with 1985 being slightly larger (14.36 vs. 13.25, whereas the 1 percent critical value for $\chi^2(2)$ = 9.21).

The resulting calculations for the TS model growth rates and their χ^2 statistics (conventional p values noted) indicate that the trend in all three subperiods are not statistically different from zero. In conclusion, therefore, if one rejects the unit root hypothesis and accepts the TS model, the Grilli-Yang series is best characterized as a zero-growth series that has experienced two significant downward level shifts (type A breaks), first in 1921 and then again in 1985.

Table 5.5 shows the estimation results for the best-fitting TS model with two breaks. Figure 5.8 shows the actual logged GY series, the fitted values and residuals from the best-fitting TS specification with two breaks, and the forecasted values starting in 1900 in order to show the long-run trend segments more clearly. The tests summarized in table 5.4, indicate that the trend is insignificantly different from zero in each of the three segments of the TS model: pre-1920, 1921–84, and post-1984.

In contrast to the TS model, the DS model identifies the two break years as 1921 and 1974, rather than 1985. Note that for the DS model, the $\sup\chi^2(4)$ is very large, while the mean$\chi^2(4)$ statistic is quite small. (For comparison, the standard $\chi^2(4)$ = 13.28.) Also, the 1921 break has a much higher $\chi^2(2)$ stat than the 1974 break. Together, these χ^2 statistics suggest that, if one uses the DS specification, the Grilli-Yang series is well characterized by one (1921) or possibly two (1921 and 1974) structural breaks rather than general parameter instability. Examining the $\chi^2(2)\_TB1$ (= 19.32) and the $\chi^2(2)\_TB2$ (= 4.77) statistics, it is clear that the 1921 break is significant, while the 1974 break is not statistically significant.[11] Thus, the DS specification requires only a single break in 1921.[12]

Table 5.4 Grid Search Results for Two Possible Breaks at
Unknown Dates (TB1, TB2)[a]

Type of model	TS model	DS model
Type of structural break dummies	level and time interaction	level and spike
Chosen break points		
TB1 and TB2	**1921 and 1985**	**1921 and 1974**
Supχ²(4)	34.43	47.40
Meanχ²(4)	8.07	3.35
(Segmented) trend[b]		
1. pre_TB1	0.003 (0.184)	0.003 (0.656)
2. TB1 through TB2	–0.001 (0.130)	0.000 (0.970)
3. post_TB2	–0.002 (0.587)	–0.011 (0.031)
χ² stat(2)_TB1	13.25	19.32
χ² stat(2)_TB2	14.36	4.77

Source: Authors' calculations.

Note: a. On a Pentium III processor, the grid search program to consider all break date pairs runs for approximately 20 minutes each for the TS and DS models. In both cases, the maximum number of lags of the dependent variable considered (k) was six.

b. The p-value for the hypothesis that the trend coefficient is equal to zero is given in parentheses. P-values that are higher than your chosen test size (say .05) indicate failure to reject the null hypothesis of a zero trend for the given segment of the data. These p-values ignore the fact that TB1 and TB2 were chosen so as to maximize supχ²(4). Thus the p-values on the trend segments are possibly inaccurate.

Estimated DS Models with a Single Break

We now search for a single break in the Grilli-Yang series using the DS model. In this case, we include only the level and spike dummies in the estimation. We now use the supχ²(2) statistic to test the hypothesis that these two dummies are zero. Figure 5.9 graphs the χ²(2) for the DS model.

Here, the maximum supχ²(2) has a value of 32.26 and occurs in 1921. The second highest supχ²(2) has a value of 6.28 and occurs in 1975. In addition, the meanχ²(2) statistic is 1.58, a contrastingly low value compared to either the supχ² or the 1 percent critical value of 9.21 from the standard χ²(2) distribution. Therefore, with the DS specification, a single downward level shift in 1921 but with no ongoing (stochastic) trend fits the data well.

Table 5.5 Estimation Results for a Trend Stationary Model with Two Breaks for the Grilli-Yang Series

Dependent variable: GY
Sample (adjusted): 1902–98

Constant	1.489
	(0.203)
GY(–1)	0.622
	(0.098)
GY(–2)	–0.314
	(0.096)
TREND	0.002
	(0.002)
DUM1921	–0.069
	(0.026)
DUM1921*TREND	–0.003
	(0.002)
DUM1985	–0.012
	(0.244)
DUM1985*TREND	–0.001
	(0.003)
R^2	0.881
Observations	97

Source: Authors' calculations.
Note: Standard errors are in parentheses.

Conclusions

Despite 50 years of empirical testing of the Prebisch-Singer hypothesis, a long-run downward trend in real commodity prices remains elusive. Previous studies have generated a range of conclusions, due in part to differences in data but mainly due to differences in specification, as to the stationarity of the error process and the number, timing, and nature of structural breaks. In this chapter, we have attempted to allow the data to tell us the proper specification. In our most general specification (model 8, in figure 5.7), which allows for a unit root and searches for two structural breaks of any kind, we find the most likely pair of breaks to be in 1921 and 1974, but the 1974 break is statistically insignificant. Moreover, we cannot reject the hypothesis of a unit root. If we search for only one structural break, we find one very clearly in 1921, again, with no rejection of

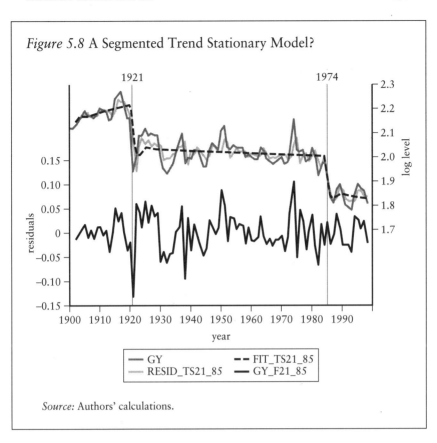

Figure 5.8 A Segmented Trend Stationary Model?

Source: Authors' calculations.

the unit root hypothesis. This model indicates also that there is no drift, either positive or negative, before or after 1921.

If we assume the Grilli-Yang series is trend stationary, we find much fuzzier results. The two-break model (model 7, in figure 5.7) puts the breaks in 1921 and 1985, with both breaks borderline significant. The three segments in this case (before, between, and after the breaks), show no trend. The model with one break puts the break in 1946, but is rejected in favor of model 1 (TS with no break). Only in the case of model 1—the model studied by researchers since the beginning of Prebisch-Singer testing—can one find a significant negative trend. Yet model 1 is inconsistent with our results in N-step ahead forecasting.

We conclude that the preponderance of evidence suggests that the series is well characterized as a unit root process with a single level-shift break (type A) in 1921.

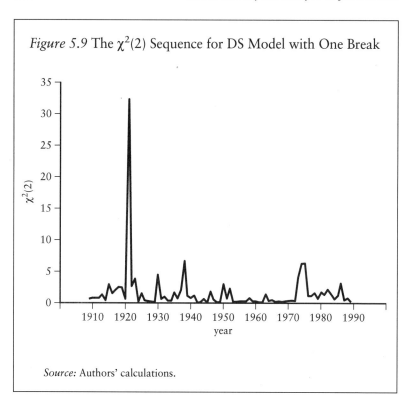

Figure 5.9 The $\chi^2(2)$ Sequence for DS Model with One Break

Source: Authors' calculations.

Notes

*The authors would like to thank Shuichiro Nishioka and two anonymous reviewers for helpful comments.
1. There is some debate as to whether the Prebisch-Singer hypothesis refers narrowly to a prediction about relative commodity prices or more generally to the idea that commodity specialization is inimical to development. We take the narrower view, mainly because Prebisch and Singer's argument hinges so crucially on their prediction about commodity prices. Furthermore, there are other arguments against commodity specialization in the literature that are unrelated to the terms of trade. It would be misleading to group all of them under the banner of the Prebisch-Singer hypothesis. That said, we strive in this chapter to give Prebisch and Singer their due, for their hypothesis, their reasoning, and what they perceived as its broader implications.
2. Singer (1950) went further to argue that foreign direct investment had also failed to spread the benefits of technical progress, because it tended to be isolated into enclaves with developing countries and, thus, have few spillovers.
3. These results, and the underlying methodology, are discussed in more detail in Cuddington, Ludema, and Jayasuriya (2002).
4. It is not at all clear that a policy of this kind is called for. The point is that, if a policy is to be considered, it should be done based on the information about commodity price trends.

5. GY also considered a U.S. manufacturing price index as a deflator and concluded that their results were not much affected by the choice of deflator.

6. We thank Paul Cashin of the International Monetary Fund Research Department for providing these data.

7. In principle, a series could contain both a deterministic trend and a unit root or more than one unit root; we ignore these cases here.

8. It is also possible to allow for shifts in the model parameters that describe the error process, as well as its serial correlation and variance, but we do not consider this extension here.

9. Cuddington found breaks for only coffee (1950) and oil (1974); the latter is not in the GY index.

10. Each specification requires the inclusion of two dummies for each break date. It can be shown that the break dates must be separated by at least one period to avoid perfect multicollinearity.

11. What about the calculated growth rates for each segment in the DS specification if we assume there are *two* breaks? Results for the DS model are slightly different from those obtained from the TS model. In spite of a statistically insignificant trend in each of the first two subperiods, the DS model identifies the existence of a "possibly significant" *negative* trend of 1.09 percent in the post-1974 period.

12. This is consistent with the ZAP-ADF tests reported in CLJ (2002), which found a single break and were unable to reject the null hypothesis of a unit root.

References

Andrews, Donald W. K. 1993. "Tests for Parameter Instability and Structural Change with Unknown Change Point." *Econometrica* 61 (4): 821–56.

Ardeni, Pier Giorgio, and Brian Wright. 1992. "The Prebisch-Singer Hypothesis: A Reappraisal Independent of Stationarity Hypothesis." *The Economic Journal* 102 (413): 803–12.

Banerjee, A., R. L. Lumsdaine, and J. H. Stock. 1992. "Recursive and Sequential Tests of the Unit-Root and Trend-Break Hypotheses: Theory and International Evidence." *Journal of Business and Economic Statistics* 10 (3): 271–87.

Bidarkota, Prasad, and Mario J. Crucini. 2000. "Commodity Prices and the Terms of Trade." *Review of International Economics* 8 (4): 647–66.

Bleaney, Michael, and David Greenaway. 1993. "Long-Run Trends in the Relative Price of Primary Commodities and in the Terms of Trade of Developing Countries." *Oxford Economic Papers* 45: 349–63.

Bloch, H., and D. Sapsford. 1997. "Some Estimates of the Prebisch and Singer Effects on the Terms of Trade between Primary Producers and Manufactures." *World Development* 25 (11): 1873–84.

———. 2000. "Whither the Terms of Trade? An Elaboration of the Prebisch-Singer Hypothesis." *Cambridge Journal of Economics* 24: 461–81.

Borensztein, E., and C. M. Reinhart. 1994. "The Macroeconomic Determinants of Commodity Prices." *IMF Staff Papers* 41 (2): 236–61.

Cashin, Paul, and C. John McDermott. 2002. "The Long-Run Behavior of Commodity Prices: Small Trends and Big Variability." *IMF Staff Papers* 49 (2): 175–99.

Cashin, Paul, Hong Liang, and C. John McDermott. 2000. "How Persistent Are Shocks to World Commodity Prices?" *IMF Staff Papers* 47 (2): 177–217.

Chambers, Marcus J., and Roy E. Bailey. 1996. "A Theory of Commodity Price Fluctuations." *Journal of Political Economy* 104 (5): 924–57.

Christiano, Lawrence J. 1992. "Searching for a Break in GNP." *Journal of Business and Economic Statistics* 10 (3): 237–50.

Chow, Gregory. 1960. "Tests of Equality between Sets of Coefficients in Two Linear Regressions." *Econometrica* 28 (3): 591–605.

Chu, C.-S. J. 1989. "New Tests for Parameter Constancy in Stationary and Nonstationary Regression Models." Working Paper, University of California at San Diego.

Cuddington, John T. 1992. "Long-Run Trends in 26 Primary Commodity Prices: A Disaggregated Look at the Prebisch-Singer Hypothesis." *Journal of Development Economics* 39: 207–27.

Cuddington, John T., and Carlos Urzúa. 1989. "Trends and Cycles in the Net Barter Terms of Trade: A New Approach." *The Economic Journal* 99 (396): 426–42.

Cuddington, John T., and H. Wei. 1992. "An Empirical Analysis of Real Commodity Price Trends: Aggregation, Model Selection, and Implications." *Estudios Economicos* 7 (2): 159–79.

Cuddington, John T., Rodney Ludema, and Shamila A. Jayasuriya. 2002. "Reassessing the Prebisch-Singer Hypothesis: Long-Run Trends with Possible Structural Breaks at Unknown Dates." Working Paper, Georgetown University, Washington, DC.

Deaton, Angus, and Guy Laroque. 1992. "On the Behavior of Commodity Prices." *Review of Economic Studies* 59: 1–23.

Diakosavvas, Dimitis, and Pasquale L. Scandizzo. 1991. "Trends in the Terms of Trade of Primary Commodities, 1900–1982: The Controversy and Its Origins." *Economic Development and Cultural Change* 39 (2): 231–64.

Dixit, Avinash. 1984. "Growth and the Terms of Trade under Imperfect Competition." In *Monopolistic Competition in International Trade,* ed. H. Kierzkowski. Oxford: Oxford University Press.

Ellsworth, P. T. 1956. "The Terms of Trade between Primary Producing and Industrial Countries." *Inter-American Economic Affairs* 10: 47–65.

Enders, Walter. 1995. *Applied Econometric Time Series.* New York: John Wiley.

Granger, Clive W. J., and Paul Newbold. 1974. "Spurious Regressions in Econometrics." *Journal of Econometrics* 2: 111–20.

Grilli, Enzo R., and M. C. Yang. 1988. "Primary Commodity Prices, Manufactured Goods Prices, and the Terms of Trade of Developing Countries: What the Long Run Shows." *The World Bank Economic Review* 2 (1): 1–47.

Hadass, Yael, and Jeffrey Williamson. 2001. "Terms of Trade Shocks and Economic Performance 1870–1940: Prebisch and Singer Revisited." NBER Working Paper 8188, Cambridge, MA.

Hansen, Bruce E. 1990. "Lagrange Multiplier Tests for Parameter Instability in Non-Linear Models." Working Paper, University of Rochester, Rochester, NY.

———. 1992. "Tests for Parameter Instability in Regressions with I (1) Processes." *Journal of Business and Economic Statistics* 10 (3): 321–35.

———. 2001. "The New Econometrics of Structural Change: Dating Breaks in U.S. Labor Productivity." *The Journal of Economic Perspectives* 15 (4): 117–28.

Hua, Ping. 1998. "On Primary Commodity Prices: The Impact of Macroeconomic Monetary Shocks." *Journal of Policy Modeling* 20 (6): 767–90.

León, Javier, and Raimundo Soto. 1997. "Structural Breaks and Long-Run Trends in Commodity Prices." *Journal of International Development* 3: 44–57.

Leybourne, Stephen J., Terence C. Mills, and Paul Newbold. 1998. "Spurious Rejections by Dickey-Fuller Tests in the Presence of a Break under the Null." *Journal of Econometrics* 87: 191–203.

Lumsdaine Robin L., and David Papell. 1997. "Multiple Trend Breaks and the Unit-Root Hypothesis." *Review of Economics and Statistics* 79 (2): 212–18.

Mehl, Arnaud. 2000. "Unit Root Tests with Double Trend Breaks and the 1990s Recession in Japan." *Japan and the World Economy* 12: 363–79.

Meier, G. M., and R. E. Baldwin. 1957. *Economic Development: Theory, History, Policy*. New York: John Wiley.

Nelson, C. R., and H. Kang. 1981. "Spurious Periodicity in Inappropriately Detrended Time Series." *Econometrica* 49: 741–51.

Perron, Pierre. 1989. "The Great Crash, the Oil Price Shock, and the Unit Root Hypothesis." *Econometrica* 57 (6): 1361–1401.

———. 1993. "The Great Crash, the Oil Price Shock, and the Unit Root Hypothesis: Erratum." *Econometrica* 61 (2): 248–49.

———. 1994. "Trend, Unit Root, and Structural Change in Macroeconomic Time Series." In *Cointegration for the Applied Economist*, ed. B. B. Rao, 113–46. New York: Macmillan.

Perron, Pierre, and T. J. Vogelsang. 1992. "Nonstationarity and Level Shifts with an Application to Purchasing Power Parity." *Journal of Business and Economic Statistics* 10 (3): 301–20.

Phillips, Peter C. B., and Pierre Perron. 1988. "Testing for a Unit Root in Time Series Regression." *Biometrika* 75: 335–46.

Ploberger, Werner, W. Kramer, and K. Kontrus. 1989. "A New Test for Structural Stability in the Linear Regression Model." *Journal of Econometrics* 40: 307–18.

Plosser, Charles I., and G. William Schwert. 1978. "Money, Income, and Sunspots: Measuring Economic Relationships and the Effects of Differencing." *Journal of Monetary Economics* 4: 637–60.

Powell, A. 1991. "Commodity and Developing Countries Terms of Trade: What Does the Long-Run Show?" *The Economic Journal* 101: 1485–96.

Prebisch, Raúl. 1950. "The Economic Development of Latin America and its Principal Problems." Reprinted in *Economic Bulletin for Latin America* 7 (1): 1–22, 1962.

Quandt, Richard. 1960. "Tests of the Hypothesis that a Linear Regression System Obeys Two Separate Regimes." *Journal of the American Statistical Association* 55 (290): 324–30.

Reinhart, Carmen M., and Peter Wickham. 1994. "Commodity Prices: Cyclical Weakness or Secular Decline?" *IMF Staff Papers* 41 (2): 175–213.

Sapsford, D. 1985. "The Statistical Debate on the Net Barter Terms of Trade between Primary Commodities and Manufactures: A Comment and Some Additional Evidence." *Economic Journal* 95: 781–88.

Singer, H. W. 1950. "U.S. Foreign Investment in Underdeveloped Areas: The Distribution of Gains between Investing and Borrowing Countries." *American Economic Review, Papers and Proceedings* 40: 473–85.

Spraos, John. 1980. "The Statistical Debate on the Net Barter Terms of Trade between Primary Commodities and Manufactures." *The Economic Journal* 90 (357): 107–28.

Thorp, Rosemary. 1998. *Progress, Poverty, and Exclusion: An Economic History of Latin America in the Twentieth Century*. Washington, DC: Inter-American Development Bank; distributed by Johns Hopkins University Press, Baltimore.

Zanias, George P. 2005. "Testing for Trends in the Terms of Trade between Primary Commodities and Manufactured Goods." *Journal of Development Economics* 78 (1): 49–59.

Zivot, Eric, and D. W. K. Andrews. 1992. "Further Evidence on the Great Crash, the Oil-Price Shock, and the Unit Root Hypothesis." *Journal of Business and Economic Statistics* 10 (3): 251–70.

6

Missed Opportunities: Innovation and Resource-Based Growth in Latin America

*William F. Maloney**

Introduction

THE 20TH CENTURY OFFERED MANY opportunities for rapid natural resource-based growth that Latin America systematically missed. Even if it were clear that, on average, resource-abundant countries have experienced relatively slow growth, the more interesting question is why some—Australia and Scandinavia, for example—successfully and rapidly developed while others did not.[1] Latin America's underperformance and its particularly virulent strain of dependency are in substantial measure due to impediments to technological adoption and to innovation arising from weak national "learning" capacity, as well as the perverse incentives of the protectionist era.

Concerns that resource-based sectors intrinsically lack dynamism have probably been exaggerated.[2] Even in Prebisch's era, future Nobel Prize winner Douglass North (1955, 252) argued that "the contention that regions must industrialize in order to continue to grow . . . [is] based on some fundamental misconceptions." The pioneer trade economist Jacob Viner argued that "there are no inherent advantages of manufacturing over agriculture" (Viner 1952, 72). His claim is supported by estimates that total factor productivity growth, the dominant explanation of differences in the growth of gross domestic product (GDP) per capita,[3] was roughly twice as high in agriculture as in manufacturing globally from 1967 to 1992.[4] Blomström and Kokko (chapter 8) argue that forestry will remain a dynamic sector in Sweden and Finland, where rapid productivity growth ensures competitiveness relative to emerging low-wage producers. Wright and Czelusta (chapter 7),

142   MALONEY

drawing on the early U.S. and Australian cases, argue that the stock of
minerals is, to an important degree, endogenous, and that major increases
in productivity can be realized in discovery and exploitation. More generally, the literature is clear that these development successes based their
growth on natural resources and, by Leamer's measure of resource abundance, several still do (see figure 6.1).[5]
    Latin America seemed unable to follow their lead. As a crude summary,
regressing Maddison's (1994) well-known growth data from 1820–1989
(table 6.1) on Leamer's measure of resource abundance suggests a *positive*
growth impact of resources from 1820–1950, but that Latin America's
especially poor performance in the post-war period is responsible for the
apparent "resource curse" afflicting that era.[6] This underperformance is
illustrated more starkly by several examples at the micro level. Despite
being far from the innovation frontier, and, hence, having the potential to
play "catch-up," the growth of total factor productivity in Latin America
in both agriculture *and* manufacturing perversely lags that of the countries
at the technological frontier (Martin and Mitra 2001, and figure 6.2). The

Figure 6.1 Natural Resource Endowments and Level of
Development

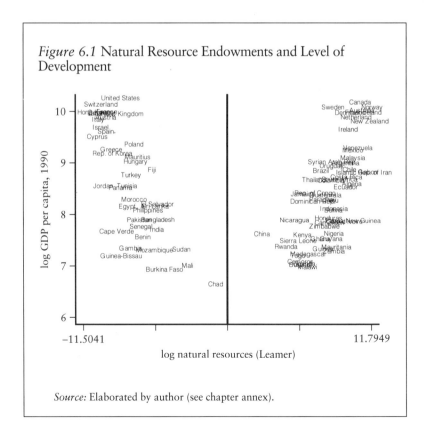

Source: Elaborated by author (see chapter annex).

Table 6.1 Growth Correlates: Maddison Data, 1820–1989

Growth summary regressions	Period					
	1820–1989		1820–1950		1950–89	
	a	*b*	*a*	*b*	*a*	*b*
Convergence measure[a]	–0.265**	–0.265	–0.51**	–0.52**	–0.19	–0.206
	–(2.25)	–(2.26)	–(5.31)	–(5.44)	–(1.05)	–(1.15)
Net primary per exports worker	–0.076	–0.048	0.107*	0.090	–0.34*	–0.270
	–(0.75)	–(0.46)	(1.89)	(1.56)	–(1.64)	–(1.30)
Latin America		–0.38		0.23		–0.86*
		–(1.29)		(1.30)		–(1.64)
1870–1913	0.612	0.618	0.721**	0.722		
	(1.54)	(1.56)	(4.16)	(4.19)		
1913–50	0.406	0.434	0.528**	0.517		
	(1.09)	(1.16)	(3.22)	(3.16)		
1950–73	2.64**	2.66**		1.43**	1.43**	
	(7.00)	(7.07)		(3.72)	(3.78)	
1973–89	1.19**	1.21**				
	(3.22)	(3.28)				
Constant	0.82	0.857**	0.935**	0.92**	1.96	2.11
	(2.69)	(2.80)	(6.73)	(6.63)	(5.25)	(5.55)
Observations	147	147	73	73	74	74
R^2	0.35	0.36	0.38	0.40	0.19	0.22

Source: Author's estimations using Maddison 1994 and World Bank, World Development Indicators.
Note: a. Difference in GDP per capita to the most advanced country.
(*t*-statistic values.) * significant at 10 percent level, ** significant at 5 percent level.

1944 Haig technical assistance mission to Chile revealed the "indisputable truth that an adequate management of our forests could become the basis for a great industry of forest products," yet nothing remotely similar to the dynamic Scandinavian experience appeared in this country until the late 1970s.[7] In chapter 7 of this volume, Wright and Czelusta categorize Latin American countries as traditional mineral "underachievers," and massive discoveries of deposits throughout the region in recent years confirm their view.[8] More emblematically, we could ask why a small antipodal dependency, Australia, would discover *La Escondida*, Chile's largest copper mine, a century after Chile's once-dominant native industry had all but vanished.

Central to every example are the foregone opportunities to exploit the global stock of knowledge to increase productivity growth and to create or perpetuate dynamic industries, as the Nordic and the East Asian miracles

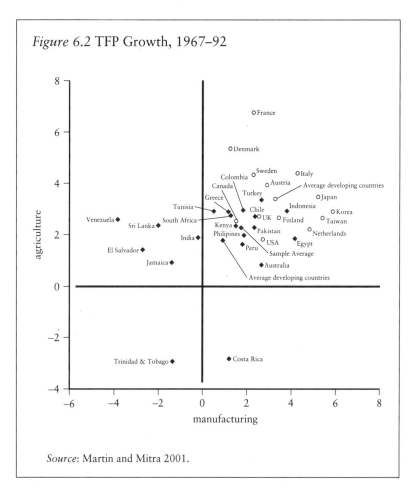

Figure 6.2 TFP Growth, 1967–92

Source: Martin and Mitra 2001.

have done (Baumol, Nelson, and Wolff 1994; Amsden and Hikino 1994). Or, to paraphrase Di Tella's (1985) broader historical view, the region proved unable to move beyond a state of exploiting the pure rents of a frontier or extraction of mineral riches, and beyond "collusive rents" offered by state-sanctioned or otherwise imposed monopoly, to tap the "unlimited source of growth" found in exploiting the quasirents of innovation.[9]

This article argues that this failure has two central, although by no means exhaustive, explanations. The first is a deficient national "innovative" or "learning" capacity: the human capital and networks of institutions that facilitate the adoption and creation of new technologies.[10] Wright (1999, 308) argues that the Unites States' success in mining "was fundamentally a collective learning phenomenon" incarnated in intellectual networks linking world-class mining universities, and both government and private research, features also undergirding Australia's current success and absent in the underachievers. In chapter 8, Blomström and Kokko argue that knowledge networks, or clusters of universities and private and public think tanks, are the key to further growth in productivity and the development of new products and are "perhaps the main strategic and competitive asset of the Swedish forest industry." Such knowledge clusters, by virtue of preparing firms to identify and to exploit unforeseeable technological opportunities, also make possible apparently discontinuous jumps such as the one Nokia made from excellence in forestry (Nokia was the site of Finland's earliest pulp mill) to leadership in telecommunications.

The second consists of the myriad barriers to technological adoption usually associated with artificially created monopoly power. Hirschman (1958, 57) argued early on that in an uncompetitive situation, such as the one posed by the guild system, "an innovation in producing a given commodity could only be introduced by someone who was already engaged in its production by the old process. . . . [T]his fact would, in itself, militate against many innovations that might render painfully acquired skills useless and valuable equipment obsolete. . . ." Parente and Prescott's (2000) simulations suggest that costs in a dynamic context of such barriers to new entry far exceed the few percentage point differences in GDP accounted for by the Harberger triangles of traditional static models. Anticompetitive forces that discourage innovation or inhibit entry can take the form of guilds, labor unions, concentrated credit markets that only lend to insiders, explicit trade barriers that impede knowledge spillovers from trade interactions (Barro and Sala-i-Martin 1997; Grossman and Helpman 1991), or barriers to foreign direct investment (FDI). All of these were exacerbated by the prolonged turning inward of the import substitution industrialization (ISI) period.

The impact of both factors can be formalized by hijacking Howitt and Mayer's (2005) "convergence club" model, which offers an explanation for how the scientific revolution led to large, global income inequalities, and applying it to the present question of why similarly endowed countries perform so differently. In the face of new technological shocks, countries with high "innovation-effective" (relative to the current level of technological advance) human capital, which I construe broadly to include knowledge clusters, will be able to create further new technologies; those with lower stocks of human capital will "implement" or adopt; and those with even lower levels of human capital will not be able to adopt and will stagnate. Though in the steady state the first two groups of countries grow at the same rate, driven by the arrival of new technological advance, the progress to their higher steady-state income levels will cause innovators to appear to grow faster.

Three additional findings of Howitt and Mayer's model are salient to the discussion of the rest of the article. First, once a leading economy introduces institutions that support science, lagging economies have only a finite window of opportunity in which to do so as well, after which they remain trapped in an implementation equilibrium or worse. Second, countries can slip out of the better equilibria if their innovation-effective knowledge infrastructure does not keep pace with technological progress.

Third, policies that either promote or impede innovation are influential in determining in which equilibrium the country finds itself. The inward-looking policies of the postwar period merit special focus in this respect. On the one hand, the extreme negative rates of protection found in many traditional sectors during the ISI period were a clear disincentive to innovation. On the other hand, the excessive protection in the manufacturing sectors may have the same effect by reducing the need to innovate to compete.[11]

As a crude test of the plausibility of this view, table 6.2 adds to the post-World War II regressions a "knowledge index" (see the technical annex to this chapter) comprising measures of scientists per capita, research and development (R&D) expenditure and patent applications, Sachs and Warner's (2001) measure of trade openness, and the investment rate. The first two columns use the two pooled cohorts of the post-1950 Maddison data, and the last two columns use the single cross-section of Sachs and Warner's data. Both data tell very similar stories. The new variables appear to capture the effect of the Latin America dummy appearing in columns 1a and 2a and contribute in the predicted ways: more open economies and those with a more developed "knowledge infrastructure" grow faster. In neither dataset does the measure of resource abundance enter significantly.

The next sections attempt to complement such overworked cross-country regressions by a historical comparison of several Latin American countries with a group of "beta" countries that have had more success with resource-based growth. This approach has two attractions. First, it presents what students of these countries have identified as critical elements of success or failure. Second, it establishes that Latin America was not *sui generis* in its concerns about dependency, its degree of suffering during the Great Depression, or, in fact, in adopting the inward-looking policies it did. But the region's response lies at the extreme end of a continuum that extends through Canada and Australia to Sweden at the most successful terminus. Acknowledging the similarities with more successful countries is vital since it prevents us from isolating the region as some sort of rare and unredeemable case operating under separate economic laws. Indeed, the persistent Australian interest in Argentina stems precisely from a perceived kinship and a desire to avoid its fate. By the same logic, there was probably nothing preordained about Latin America's disappointments of the last half of the 20th century—different policies could have led to better outcomes.

Deficient National Learning/Innovation Capacity?

Harvard historian David Landes, in his encyclopedic *Wealth and Poverty of Nations,* sees the divergence of the two paths of Latin America and

Table 6.2 Growth Correlates including Measures of Openness, Knowledge, Maddison, and Sachs and Warner Data

Dependent variable: Average annual growth rate	1a	1b	2a	2b
Initial level of income[a]	−0.215	0.975 **	0.335	−1.284 **
	−(1.17)	(3.31)	(1.62)	−(4.78)
Net primary exports per worker	−0.258	−0.088	−0.259 *	−0.106
	−(1.26)	−(0.46)	−(1.66)	−(0.89)
Latin America	−0.890 *	0.703	−1.483 **	−0.547
	−(1.67)	(1.29)	−(3.30)	−(1.35)
1950–73	1.411 **	1.908 **		
	(3.61)	(5.21)		
Openness		2.203 **		2.140 **
		(3.46)		(4.74)
Investment		5.848 *		1.224 **
		(1.71)		(5.06)
Knowledge index[b]		0.390 **		0.184 *
		(3.24)		(1.68)
Constant	2.149 **	−3.009 **	−1.375	7.848 **
	(5.47)	−(2.85)	−(0.80)	(3.70)
Observations	72	72	91	91
R^2	0.22	0.47	0.15	0.57

Sources: Author's estimations for 1a and 1b use Maddison 1994 database; 2a and 2b use Sachs and Warner 1997.
Note: a. For 1a and 1b relative to the maximum GDP per capita of each period.
b. Missing values were imputed using factor analysis (see chapter annex).
(*t*-statistic values). * significant at 10 percent level, ** significant at 5 percent level.

Scandinavia as stemming from the differing reactions of northern and southern Europe to the phenomenon of British industrialization. The literature is uniform that Scandinavia was poor at the beginning of the 19th century, but had laid the groundwork for rapid growth. Scandinavians enjoyed high levels of literacy and excellent higher education, and Landes argues that they were "equal partners in Europe's intellectual and scientific community. . . . They also operated in an atmosphere of political stability and public order. . . . Property rights were secure; the peasantry was largely free; and life was a long stretch of somber hard work broken intermittently by huge bouts of drinking and seasonal sunshine. . ." (Landes 1998, 248–52).

To this depiction Landes offers the dramatic counterexample of Mediterranean Europe, in particular of Italy, Portugal, and Spain, hurt by

political instability and a religious and intellectual intolerance with roots
in the reconquista and counter-reformation. Further, Spain in the 18th
century was a resource-rich nation that used its fantastic returns from silver and gold mines in the New World to purchase all that was needed, thus
developing a rentier mentality rather than that of a nation of hands-on tin-
kerers such as appeared in Britain, Scandinavia, and the United States.
This cultural Dutch disease was exported wholesale to the New World.

There is no shortage of Latin American observers disposed to self-
flagellation far more severe than Landes' critique. As examples, Encina
(1911) in *Nuestra Inferioridad Economica* and Pinto Santa Cruz (1959) in
Chile, Un Caso de Dessarollo Frustrado are only the best read of a line of
critics of aristocratic dandyism and indolence at the root of Chile's stagnation and dependence on foreigners.[12] Nor, in the light of extraordinary
expenditures on luxury goods, are they receptive to savings shortfalls as
unavoidable binding constraints on growth.[13]

But there must be some tempering of the condemnation of the entrepreneurial mettle of the Chilean elite, and that of the region more generally.
Pinto Santa Cruz is also clear that the elimination of Spanish restrictions on
trade caused Chilean exports to boom immediately after, and this was the
case throughout the continent. Chilean entrepreneurs were the second-
largest presence in Peru's nitrate fields, ahead of the British, and they pioneered copper mining in their home country. When the price of copper rose
in the mid-19th century, production by Chileans increased four-fold
between 1844 and 1860. In response to increased demand rising from the
Gold rushes in California and Australia, Chilean wheat exports rose 10-fold
in value during the period 1848–50.[14] Southern hacendados borrowed
heavily to clear lands to expand acreage three-fold from 1850 to 1870 (Conning 2002). Cariola and Sunkel (1985) argue that the early nitrate economy
was not merely an enclave in the Norte Grande, but elicited strong response
from Chilean entrepreneurs throughout the economy. In general, local talent proved very responsive in certain nontechnical sectors and would earn
global acclaim across history: two Nobel prizes in literature, a major surre-
alist/abstract expressionist painter, and first-class musicians.

In fact, Encina's lament was precisely that Chile was losing the
dynamism that it once had, which he partly attributes to a dearth of technical education that would permit staying at the forefront of development. Or, to borrow Howitt and Mayer's (2005) formalization, Chile's
innovation-effective human capital (relative to the technological frontier)
depreciated below the critical level for innovation and even for effective
adoption. The disappointing growth of Latin America had more to do
with a lack of supporting infrastructure for learning and innovation that
would enable local entrepreneurs to innovate and, hence, stay abreast of
competition than any *rentier* temperament inherited from Spain.[15] The
next sections focus on weaknesses in literacy and technical education as
particularly important.

The Foundation of Technical Absorptive Capacity: Literacy

Recent thinking suggests that Latin America's persistent wealth inequality may have had a role to play in slowing the region's ability to adopt foreign technologies.[16] Engerman, Haber, and Sokoloff (2000) argue that the period of sustained economic growth during the 18th and early 19th centuries that distinguished the United States and Canada from the other New World economies was fundamentally due to the patterns of settlement and crops that led to a relatively unequal distribution of income in the slower-growing areas. This concentration preserved the political influence of the advantaged elites and led to the marginalization of much of the population as measured by lower access to the franchise, natural resources, financial institutions, and property rights, as well as primary schooling.

The marginalization in education may have been particularly important. The concerns with social control, extreme inequality of income, weak public finance, and perhaps an intellectual commitment to a small state, all led to dramatically smaller efforts in Latin America toward universal education than the successful natural-resource exporters made. As figure 6.3 suggests, by 1870 more than 70 percent of the population age 10 or above in Australia, Canada, Sweden, and the United States were literate; this was three times the percentage in Argentina, Chile, Costa Rica, and Cuba, and four times the percentage in Brazil and Mexico. Latin America progressed unevenly toward these levels over the next half century. By 1925, Argentina, Chile, Costa Rica, and Uruguay would attain literacy rates of more than 66 percent, while Bolivia, Brazil, Colombia, Guatemala, Honduras, Mexico, Peru, and República de Bolivariana de Venezuela would hover at 30 percent until much later (Mariscal and Sokoloff 2000).

As Engerman and Sokoloff (1997, 287) note that this is particularly important given that early industrialization reflected the cumulative impact of incremental advances made by individuals throughout the economy, rather than being driven by progress in a single industry or the actions of a narrow elite. As one manifestation critical to the development of innovation, they note that the greater equality in human capital accounted partially for the high rates of invention in the United States overall. They also argue that "the more general concern with the opportunities for extracting returns from inventions contributed to a patent system which was probably, at the time, the most favorable in the world to common people. This stands in stark contrast to Mexico and Brazil, where patents were restricted by costs and procedures to the wealthy or influential, and where the rights to organize corporations and financial institutions were granted sparingly, largely to protect the value of rights already held by powerful interests."

In chapter 8, Blomström and Kokko argue that in Sweden, the introduction of a mandatory school system in 1842 and emphasis on literacy and

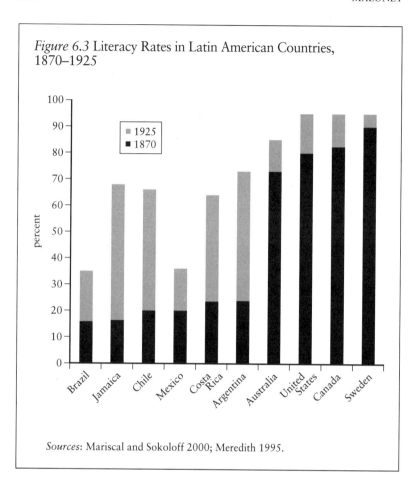

Figure 6.3 Literacy Rates in Latin American Countries, 1870–1925

Sources: Mariscal and Sokoloff 2000; Meredith 1995.

numeracy was essential for the ability of individuals and firms to learn and to adopt new technologies: much elementary learning and technology transfer were based on written instructions like blueprints and handbooks. This also suggests that the extensive literature comparing Argentina and Australia may be missing a critical point: despite a strong feeling of "there but for the grace of God go we" on the part of Australian authors, it is very clear that, in the mid-19th century, Australia was far closer to the industrialized countries in levels of literacy—and this in a country that until the 1840s was a penal colony of the United Kingdom! The story of the global conglomerate Broken Hill Proprietary Company, Ltd., started by a boundary rider on a sheep station, suggests the importance of a broad base of literate everymen to run with ideas and to enjoy supporting institutions.

Technical Education: The Critical Lag

A central theme of Blomström and Kokko's account of the Swedish growth experience is the early abundance of high-level human capital—the "impoverished sophisticate" Sandberg (1979) called it. The universities in Uppsala and Lund date from the 15th and 17th centuries and technical schools were established in the early 1820s. Examples of other institutions are the Swedish Academy of Science, founded in 1739, and the Swedish Ironmaster's Association, founded in 1747, which published a mining science journal beginning in 1817 and financed foreign-study trips for Swedish engineers and scientists. New engineering workshops, established for construction of iron bridges and lock gates for the Göta canal, served as training centers. Sweden possessed the fundamentals of a modern engineering industry by about 1850 (Ahlström 1992) and was exporting engineers by 1900. In the same year, serious research in chemistry was undertaken at the University of Oslo that would lay the foundation for the dominant fertilizer, electrochemical, and electrometallurgical industries in Norway.[17] As in Britain and the United States, Scandinavian mechanization was a slow process that implied ongoing accumulation of know-how, continuous interaction with the outside world, and extraordinary contributions at the technological frontier.[18] The exceptional long-run performance of Swedish firms established during this period, as Blomström and Kokko note in chapter 8, "has been based on the ability of Swedish industry to create, adapt, and disseminate new technologies."

By contrast, the colonial period in Latin America enforced in many ways a negative intellectual bias that specifically discouraged the adoption of foreign innovations. Many countries had a local franchise of the Inquisition, which in Colombia is memorialized for, among other things, having contributed to the "suffocation of the spirit of creativity and investigation."[19] Largely for reasons of political control, the icon of intellectual discourse, the printing press, was banned in Brazil until 1809 (Baer 2001). The Spanish crown kept out non-Spanish and non-Catholic businessmen, traders, and craftsmen and thus deprived the New World of important skills and knowledge.

Further, the nature of education in Latin America was less technical than that found in Scandinavia or the former English colonies. Spanish higher education was largely religiously based and focused on law, philosophy, and theology, and somewhat less respectably, medicine, and this pattern was replicated in the colonies. The Spanish enlightenment after 1750 saw the establishment of groups of autonomous *sociedaded economicas* that sought to diffuse technology from abroad and establish libraries throughout the country, as well as some royal societies emphasizing applied science. But Spain began training engineers seriously only in the 1850s, and by 1867 had only one functioning *Escuela de Ingenieros Industriales*, located in Barcelona.[20]

Latin America for the most part lagged behind Spain and Portugal in developing a technical class. In both Chile and Colombia, specific royal initiatives gave the initial impetus to scientific inquiry in the last decades of colonization.[21] However, as Will (1957, 17) documents for Chile, "With the exception of the inadequate facilities provided by a few religious organizations, there did not exist . . . before the middle of the eighteenth century an institution capable of furnishing the youth of the colony with the barest essentials of a secular education." Similar stories for developments in the 19th century are found throughout the region:[22] recurring political instability silenced prominent scientists and undermined fledgling universities; fiscal weakness prevented consistent financing of the sciences; and the unreliable demand for local engineers prevented the career from being lucrative, let alone socially respectable. An important exception appears in Mexico, where the precursor to the *Universidad Nacional*, the *Real Seminario de Mineria*, was founded in 1792 and taught higher mathematics, physics, chemistry, topography, dynamics, and hydraulics. Mexico was the primary exporter of technical knowledge on the continent, and it occupied the Vice Presidency of the World Mining Association at the turn of the 19th century.[23] Unfortunately, as Cárdenas (1997) makes clear, Mexico was not completely exceptional. The struggle for independence had devastating effects on the mining sector—martyred scientist-patriots, capital flight, flooding of mines, and a roughly 50 percent fall in output that took almost 70 years to reverse—causing a lost half-century of Mexican growth.

The low supply of engineers was in part driven by the limited and unstable demand for them, and, arguably, resource-based industries were catalysts pushing countries to reach better innovation equilibria. In Australia, Chile, Colombia, Mexico, and the United States, mining institutes were the kernels of technical schools and later important universities. Interestingly, railroads may have played a similar role. As Safford (1976) makes clear, troubled politics and public finances that frequently stalled railway construction undermined the momentum of the engineering profession in Colombia.

A corps of locally trained engineers emerged by the end of the 19th century in many countries, but this may have been too little and too late. As table 6.3 suggests, Australia had at least five times the numbers of Chile or Colombia in 1920, and Meredith (1995) argues that by 1926, Australia had 27 times more graduates of technical schools per capita than Argentina, perhaps the most educated country in Latin America. Sweden had almost 10 times the density of engineers as Colombia or Chile and, to repeat, by this time, Scandinavia was exporting engineers innovating at the technological frontier. The persistence of this deficit, measured as the percentage of architects and engineers per worker continued into the 1960s: Sweden (5.03), Finland (2.52), and Denmark (1.03) had the highest densities, compared to the lows of Argentina (0.55), Chile (0.7), Ecuador (0.18), and Uruguay (0.42).[24] Further, it is not clear how good the quality of the Latin American product was. At the end of the 19th century in both Colombia and Chile, local engineers complained that the government and private firms preferred to import engineers from France or the United States even for fairly straightforward tasks.

Table 6.3 Density of Engineers at the Turn of the 20th Century

Country	Year	Engineers per 100,000 workers
Australia	1920	47
Chile	1930	6
Colombia	1887	8
Sweden	1890	84
United States	1920	128

Sources: Australia, United States: Meredith 1995; Chile: Villalobos 1990; Colombia: Safford 1976; Sweden: Ahlstrom 1992. Elaborated by author.

Does Technological Capacity Matter?

Australian, Scandinavian, and U.S. literature strongly support the idea that such technical capacity, and more generally the ability to learn from abroad, were critical to accessing technological progress in more advanced countries and, in the long run, to establishing knowledge clusters. To support this contention, there are some provocative examples from Latin America.

Perhaps the first bit of evidence is the extraordinary dependence of Latin American countries on immigrants as innovators and entrepreneurs in new sectors. Industrialization in Mexico in the late 19th century would be almost entirely undertaken by the resident foreigners (Hansen 1971). Using machinery from their homeland, the French started the textile industries in Veracruz and Puebla (Buffington and French 1999), and foreigners also started Mexico's first iron and steel plant, the *Fundidora de Fierro y Acero de Monterrey*, in 1903; this plant would build on the region's ore deposits and anchor its industrial development. Hansen argues that, while there were entrepreneurial spillover effects that drew many Mexicans into the capitalist ranks, the initial impulse came from foreigners.

Collier and Sater (1996) also note the influence of immigrants in introducing new industry and technologies in Chile. Immigrants set up many of the industrial enterprises of the 1860s and 1870s: 36 of the 46 dressmakers counted in 1854 were French; Americans installed the flourmills; and Americans and British built the railroads. Loveman (1979, 193) notes that the list of officers and members of the executive committee of Sociedad de Fomento Fabril (SOFOFA), the principal organization of industrialists, showed the disproportionate influence of immigrants: "Only three Spanish surnames accompanied those of the other members of the directorate: Edwards, Subercasseaux, Hillman, Tupper, Tiffou, Mitchell, Gabler, Lanz, Klein, Muzard, Lyon, Bernstein, Crichton, Osthous, Stuven."

Fogarty (1985) tells a similar story for the development of beef, Argentina's "super staple," wherein a small group of *hacendados*, recently arrived from Europe, formed the *Sociedad Rural Argentina* in 1866. This group spearheaded the transformation of the pampas, improving the quality of livestock, pastures, and methods of animal husbandry necessary to take over the U.S. position as principal exporter of cattle to Europe by World War I, with dramatic forward and backward linkages throughout the economy. Fogarty also notes that, while in the Australia, Canada, and United States railroads were sponsored, financed, and constructed largely by nationals. In Argentina, Europeans were the prime movers. In each of these major sectors in the three countries, it was not locals who saw the possibilities for technological arbitrage, as was the case in Scandinavia, but those embodying the knowledge from abroad.

Just as important is the emphasis observers both present and contemporary put on the impact of engineering schools, such as the Antioquia *Escuela de Minas,* as critical providers of talent for emerging industry (see, among others, Safford 1976). In Brazil, Baer (1969) argues that, despite a tradition of iron smelting dating from the mid-16th century, the techniques used at the end of the 19th century were primitive. Of the 30 ironworks in the headwater region of the Rio Doce in 1879, only 7 used Italian forge methods and the rest used the old African *cadinho* (crucible) technique. Baer sees the critical event for the development of the native steel industry as the foundation in 1879 of the *Escola de Minas* at Ouro Preto, Minas Gerais, which led to the establishment of the first new blast furnace since the failures at the beginning of the century. Graduates of the *Escola de Engenharia do Exercito* established in 1930 would lead the steel industry as it developed through the 1960s.

Australian observers also put great emphasis on the role of nonuniversity innovation infrastructure in explaining the disparate evolution of the wheat industry in Argentina, Australia, and Canada. In all three countries, wheat had an early and firm toehold, but it became the super staple in Canada, largely due to government assistance to prairie agriculture in the form of experiment stations, seed-testing services, and technical assistance. Again, this assistance also came on top of determined efforts in Australia and Canada to achieve widespread literacy in the prairies; these have no analogue in Latin America. There was also provision of other important public goods that were less knowledge-related. For instance, public granaries and a wheat-grading system provided quality control that gave Canada an edge over Argentina's wheat, which had the reputation for inferior quality and lack of uniformity.[25] The provision of an extensive institutional and scientific infrastructure was recognized as key to Canada's success by contemporary Argentines, and it compared poorly with the lackluster efforts of the Argentine government.

Case Study 1. Convergence Clubs in Mining in Chile and Australia: Innovation versus Adoption Equilibria, or Worse? Howitt and Mayer's (2005) view of multiple convergence clubs offers insight into the differing trajec-

tories followed by Chile and Australia in copper mining. Arguably, the initially deficient local technical capacity, exacerbated by technological
progress elsewhere, led to Chile's loss of leadership in copper over the
course of the past two centuries. It also helps explain why Australia's Broken Hill Proprietary Company, hailing from an antipodal dependency of
similarly small size, would discover *la Escondida* and be the major force
in expanding Chilean production in the 1980s and 1990s. Chile saw its
world share fall from one-third to under 4 percent by 1911; as early as
1884, the *Sociedad de Mineria* openly wondered whether Chile's copper
mines would survive at all (Collier and Sater 1996, 139). This trajectory
casts some doubt on theories that argue that market scale is the key complementary factor in explaining why some resource-abundant countries,
the United States in particular, became technological leaders (Romer
1996). Chile once had the world market for copper and presumably an
advantage of scale.

Instead, the missing complementarity is likely to be technologically literate human capital. Collier and Sater attribute Chile's loss in market
share to a failure to update technology in the face of declining ore quality
and excessive reliance on the wasteful *piriquen* system. Chilean historians
date this technological slippage to the beginning of the 19th century when,
they note, there was little diffusion of European technologies and "the
work of mining was not very systematic" (Villalobos 1990, 95). With the
disappearance of the Academy of San Luis, there was no technical teaching of mining in the country and the "receipt of industrial innovations was
slow and without visible influence" (Villalobos 1990, 96). Charles Lam-
bert, representative of a British mining company in La Serena and trained
in the Politechnique in Paris, noted the primitive mining practice, scarce
knowledge of minerals, and inefficient smelting, all of which represented
poor technique relative to that employed in Europe. The Polish mining
engineer, Ignaci Domeyko, in 1841 helped establish a small school, and in
1847 the *Universidad de Chile* would begin to teach engineering. But Chile
was at this point 80 years behind the first mining school in Europe, and 50
years behind Mexico.

Chilean historians note the dominance of foreigners in applying new
technologies[26] and Pinto Santa Cruz spectacularly underlines how Chile
tragically passed up the power that gradual accumulation of know-how
offered to maintain competitiveness and dynamism:

The technological demands of the period, in contrast to what is occurring today in some areas of mining or industry, were relatively modest and thus not too costly. What could and had to be done in the
national mining companies and in agriculture, except in certain exceptions . . . was perfectly compatible with the resources accumulated in
the long periods of bonanza. If the process had been initiated and

maintained adequately, without doubt, it would have created the means to confront more challenging tasks, such as those posed by copper mining when it was necessary to exploit less rich veins. However, faced with the technological revolution, the local mining companies had behind them neither sufficient accumulated resources, nor the organizational or administrative capacity that were indispensable. In these circumstances, there was no other option but the introduction of foreign capital and expertise at a cost, without doubt of a considerable retribution. (Pinto Santa Cruz 1959, 71)

We can imagine a bad feedback loop where inability to innovate leads to lower profits and to less innovation-effective human capital arising from experience and, hence, further inability to innovate or even transfer technology, all of which eventually pushes local entrepreneurs out of the market. Perhaps this accumulated deficiency of technical facility was what led to a self-perception that Chileans were perhaps "unfit for the modern era" (Monteon 1982, 62). Tancredo Pinochet Le-Brun, granting that Chileans were inferior to Europeans, still wondered, "don't we have minds in this country that can go to Europe to learn what professors, whom we have imported and continue importing, have studied? Are we truly incapable of steering our own ship?"[27] As mentioned earlier, Encina answered pessimistically in 1911 for a variety of reasons, one of which was the dearth of applied technical education essential to progress in all fields.[28] One can imagine a sense of frustration among concerned Chileans that the big and visible advances were in the Guggenheim mines at el Teniente and Chuquicamata; a French steel mill, "El Tofo," in Coquimbo; and experiments in fishing by foreign capitalists (Monteon 1982, 75).

Chile would continue to slip in its technical capacity in copper. Meller (1991, 44) argues that "in the 1950s one could have learned more about Chilean copper in foreign libraries than in Chilean ones. . . . [Nor] was there training of Chilean engineers and technicians specializing in copper." The fact that, in 1952, the Controller General admitted that he had no idea of what went on in the companies (Moran 1974) suggests that part of the feeling of vulnerability and dependency must be attributed to the lack of technical capacity to monitor and to confidently critique the actions of the *Gran Minería*. It was not until 1955 that a government agency was created to oversee U.S. firms' operations, and a bureaucracy of Chilean professionals, engineers, and economists was created. "In short, it took about forty years, from 1925–1965, to develop a domestic capacity to analyze the role of copper and to educate Chilean professionals and technicians in the management of the [large copper firms]" (Meller 1991, 45). This is a striking statement about a country that began exporting copper long before the U.S. or Australian firms that would dominate the Chilean industry. Even today, there is relatively little interaction between the copper companies and universities or other think tanks. Such a knowledge cluster, Lagos

(1997) argues, may be necessary to transform the north into a regional service center after the inevitable decline in mining production over the next decades. Australia's trajectory was very different. While most mining was begun by Cornishmen who had a high degree of applied skill, in 1886, Australia recruited highly paid engineers and metallurgists from the United States, which firmly linked the country to U.S.-generated innovations (Wright 1999). Diaz Alejandro (1985) would note that Australia's mining exports provided a general interest in scientific and technical research absent in Argentina. Duncan and Fogarty (1984, 129) argue that "geological knowledge and mining expertise became part of the Australian heritage enriched by schools of mines of world class and the industry has been in the forefront in the development and application of mining and treatment technology." Although far ahead of Chile, Australia lagged behind the United States (until after 1920) in engineers per 100,000 population—47 versus 128—but Australia would reach 163 per 100,000 by 1955. Several important universities offered local beachheads for foreign research. The Sydney Mechanics Institute was established in 1843 and the Sydney Technical College in 1878, both with the goal of the diffusion of scientific knowledge. The University of New South Wales (UNSW) was founded in 1949 on the campus of the Technical College, with MIT and the Berlin University of Technology as models and a core focus on research and teaching in science and technology. The UNSW School of Mining Engineering now ranks as one of the largest educators of mining engineers in the world.[29]

In this context, one of Australia's most influential mining companies and industrial conglomerates emerged in 1883: Broken Hill Proprietary Company. Called by those of the region "the cradle of Australian industrialization,"[30] Broken Hill oversaw the expansion of mines and smelters and, in 1893, the establishment of the Australasian Institute of Mining and Metallurgy. When the easily accessed oxide zone was exhausted, Broken Hill metallurgists and engineers, among others, introduced the flotation process, which, as a residual, allowed the expansion of zinc production by new firms. During World War II, Australia, as the principal member of the Allies in the Pacific, benefited from the demand for iron-based goods and the transfer of technology. Industrial production rose by 45 percent in the war period, and technological acquisition jumped, a gain that subsequent Australian governments would seek to continue. Broken Hill and similar conglomerates became modern corporations, with vertical control from mining to blast furnaces to wire rope factories to shipping lines, as well as with links to foreign capital through joint ventures. Inverting the traditional center/periphery dichotomy, Broken Hill attained a global reach, acquiring mines in Canada, Chile, and the United States (in Utah). Australia now exports more in mining expertise—environmentally friendly techniques, mine closure methods, and mineral detection technologies, among others—than it does wine.

ISI as a Double Disincentive to Innovation: A Continuum of Experiences

The barriers to trade and investment that comprised the inward-looking policies implemented after the Great Depression stand as the second impediment to the transition to an innovation-based economy and offer a rationale for the negative post-1950 Latin American dummy in the growth regressions. Di Tella's (1985) distinction between entrepreneurs being driven to appropriate the quasirents arising from innovations abroad versus exploitation of artificially contrived rents is not new. It does, however, highlight why the natural resources/manufacturing debate probably misses the point. It is not that a manufacturing sector has been created, but whether what has been created is a source of innovation, or a brake on the dynamism of the traditional sectors that are forced to subsidize it. Blomström and Meller capture much of the ISI critique when they argue the following:

> When Latin America decided to force industrialization by import substitution, it was not an industrialization based on the countries' endowments that was supported. While the Scandinavian countries slowly and gradually filled in the empty slots in their input-output tables, the Latin American countries filled in all the numbers at the same time; and even worse, they tried to fill in the U.S. numbers! Suddenly there were several small Latin American economies with production structures similar to that of the United States (Blomström and Meller 1991b, 9).

Not only were these sectors out of line with comparative advantage and walled off from competition and the sources of innovation, they would also need to be subsidized, or at least would divert attention from sectors that had the potential for innovation.

Latin America's turn inward and suspicion of resource dependency is at one end of a continuum that passes through Australia and Canada and then to Sweden. As a crude proxy, figures 6.4–6.5 suggest that virtually all of the sample countries saw an increase in average effective tariffs after the Great Depression. Latin America's average jumps from 0.22 to 0.34, while those of our beta countries move from 0.10 to 0.16. Within the latter, however, Australia is as dramatic as Brazil, Mexico, or even Argentina, and even Canada could pass for Latin America across much of the period.

The usual battery of protectionist measures appeared, and from observers in these countries we hear exactly the critiques of inward strategies so familiar in Latin America. Dehem's citing of the Hirschman quote above (1962, 5) about barriers to innovation was employed, not in the developing countries context, but to explain Canada's "stunted growth" of the 1950s. This theme

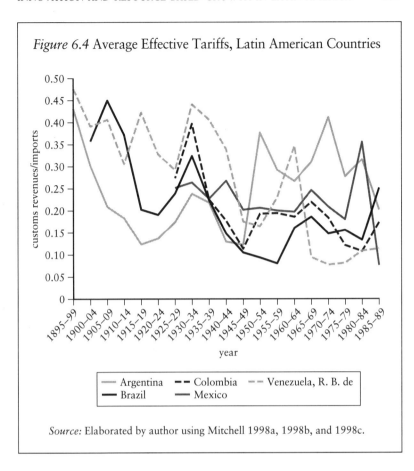

Figure 6.4 Average Effective Tariffs, Latin American Countries

Source: Elaborated by author using Mitchell 1998a, 1998b, and 1998c.

was picked up by Stykolt and Eastman (1960) seeking to explain the 30–35 percent differential in U.S. and Canadian incomes, as well as low labor productivity. One of the deans of Canadian economic history, Melville Watkins (1963, 158), ended one of his better known articles by noting "the emphasis increasingly placed by economists on the link between the inefficiency of Canadian secondary manufacturing industry and the Canadian tariff."

Prolonged Australian protection also remains the general culprit in most analyses of that country's lackluster industrial growth in this century (Anderson 1987; Maddock and McLean 1987). Fogarty (1985) argues that Australia's tariffs probably were responsible for the stagnation of the industrial sector in the late 1920s, precisely when Argentine manufacturing was growing well. Although it did have an indigenous automobile industry of some promise, and Broken Hill–type conglomerates with solid

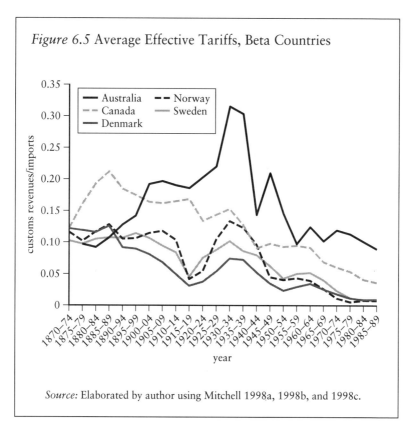

Figure 6.5 Average Effective Tariffs, Beta Countries

Source: Elaborated by author using Mitchell 1998a, 1998b, and 1998c.

roots, Australia and New Zealand would also nurture import-substituting industries that were neither of efficient scale or appropriate, given comparative advantage. McLean (1987, 22), summarizing the extensive Australian literature, concludes that ongoing protection of the manufacturing sector (into the 1970s) "led to a stifling, rather than promotion of desired structural change, no reduction in the dependence on natural resource-intensive exports, and to lower growth and living standards."

Differing Reactions to a Common Dependency

That the policy of other natural resource–abundant countries would parallel that of Latin America is not so surprising. Many of the factors cited in the canonical recounting of the reasons for the region's turn inward are found elsewhere.

The Great Depression, the watershed period for inward-looking policies, appears to have affected the beta countries as hard as it did Latin America.[31] Figures 6.6–6.7 and 6.8–6.9 show that the beta countries were

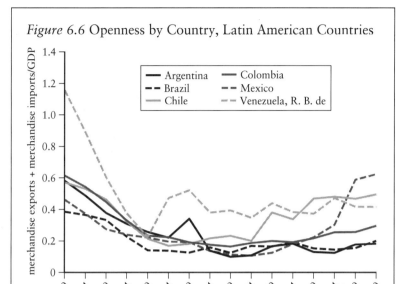

Figure 6.6 Openness by Country, Latin American Countries

Legend:
— Argentina   — Colombia
– – Brazil   – – Mexico
▨▨▨ Chile   ▨▨▨ Venezuela, R. B. de

y-axis: merchandise exports + merchandise imports/GDP
x-axis: year (1925–29, 1930–34, 1935–39, 1940–44, 1945–49, 1950–54, 1955–59, 1960–64, 1965–69, 1970–74, 1975–79, 1980–84, 1985–89, 1990–94, 1995–99, 2000)

Source: Elaborated by author using Mitchell 1998a, 1998b, and 1998c.

Figure 6.7 Openness by Country, Beta Countries

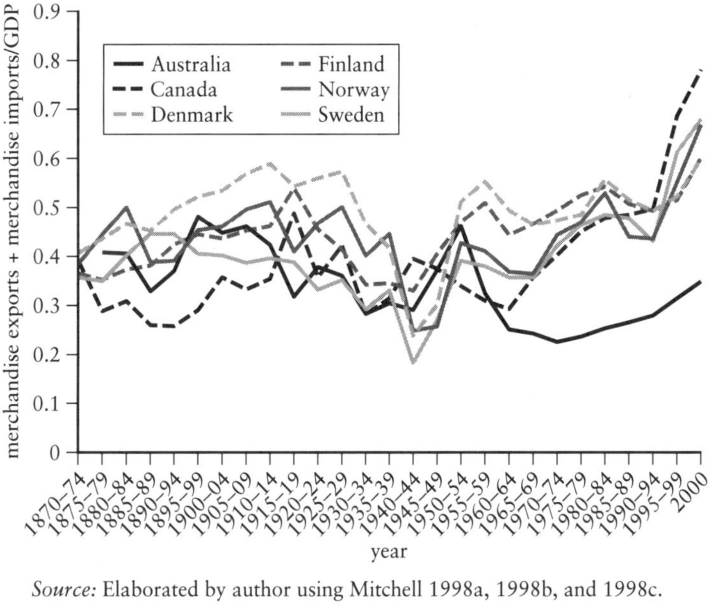

Legend:
— Australia   – – Finland
– – Canada   — Norway
– – Denmark   — Sweden

y-axis: merchandise exports + merchandise imports/GDP
x-axis: year (1870–74, 1875–79, 1880–84, 1885–89, 1890–94, 1895–99, 1900–04, 1905–09, 1910–14, 1915–19, 1920–24, 1925–29, 1930–34, 1935–39, 1940–44, 1945–49, 1950–54, 1955–59, 1960–64, 1965–69, 1970–74, 1975–79, 1980–84, 1985–89, 1990–94, 1995–99, 2000)

Source: Elaborated by author using Mitchell 1998a, 1998b, and 1998c.

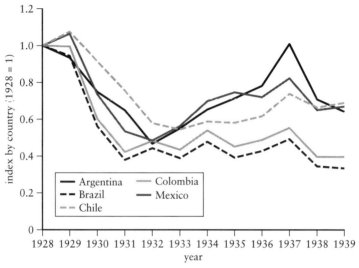

Figure 6.8 Impact of the Great Depression through Commodity Prices, Latin American Countries

Source: Elaborated by author using Mitchell 1998a, 1998b, and 1998c.

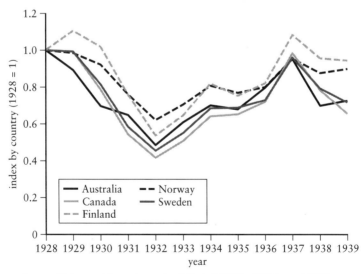

Figure 6.9 Impact of the Great Depression through Commodity Prices, Beta Countries

Source: Elaborated by author using Mitchell 1998a, 1998b, and 1998c.

far more open than Latin America; most were exporters of raw materials and most showed falls in export earnings as large as those seen in Latin America. Latin America appeared to recover more slowly; this is especially true of Brazil and Colombia, which suffered most by the fall in coffee prices. However, some countries in the region, such as Argentina, are not distinguishable from the other sample.

Table 6.4 suggests somewhat conflicting measures of actual impact. On the one hand, the reported falls in per capita output follow the continuum: Latin America hit hardest, then Canada and Australia, and least affected, the Scandinavian countries. On the other hand, the resulting unemployment rates, although notoriously incomparable, suggest that even the impact on Scandinavian countries was very high, roughly doubling during the Depression to levels between 20 and 30 percent. Meanwhile Argentina remained relatively unscathed at under 5.6 percent unemployment. Supporting evidence suggests that the general picture is broadly correct. Alhadeff (1985) cites the *Review of the River Plate* as arguing that Argentina was one of the least—if not the least—hard-hit countries to be found anywhere in the world, an impression confirmed by Alejandro Bunge, a prominent industrialist, in 1932 to London's Argentine Club.[32] Further, that both the lower need for "safety-net" expenditures and the fact that the British carried the railway debt implied that Argentina would have far fewer fiscal problems than either Australia or Canada.[33]

Table 6.4 Impact of the Great Depression (percent)

Country	Changes in terms of trade of commodities exports 1928–32	Maximum unemployment	Maximum negative change in GDP compared with 1929
Argentina	−45.0	5.6/7	−14.0
Brazil	−61.1	—	−6.0
Chile	−45.6	7.0	−27.0
Colombia	−56.5	—	−2.0
México	−51.5	6.0	−17.6
Beta Countries			
Australia	−51.5	20.0	−9.7
Canada	−58.3	19.0	−25.1
Denmark	—	32.0	positive
Finland	−46.3	—	−4.0
Norway	−38.0	33.0	−2.6
Sweden	−55	24.0	−4.0

Sources: Mitchell 1998a, 1998b, 1998c; Sadie 1969. Elaborated by author.
Note: — = not available.

At a deeper level, the region's concern with asymmetrical power relations in the world economy can be heard elsewhere. As Love (1996)
argued, the Romanian economist Mihail Manoilescu independently developed a dependency theory that strikingly parallels that of Prebisch to
explain the evolution of Central and Eastern Europe. Foreign control over
the economy emerges as a theme in even the most successful economies.
In 1909, 80 percent of Norway's mining, 85 percent of its chemical,
44 percent of its paper and textile, and 33 percent of its metal industries
were foreign-owned, and foreign control of almost 75 percent of all water-
falls essential to power generation generated widespread protests (Hveem
1991). Finland's extraordinary dependence on Russia as a Grand Duchy
and the extraordinary debt service repayments from 1945 to 1948—
5–6 percent of GDP—are high by even 1980s Latin standards (Haavisto
and Kokko 1991). At Australia's centennial in 1880, a sizable fraction of
the population, many the descendents of imported convict labor,
expressed resentment about dependence on the United Kingdom. The
Republican newspaper *Bulletin* argued that the convict "chains of iron are
merely exchanged for chains of gold." Citing the exploitative nature of
British capital investment, the editorial argued that it was better to be poor
and independent, referring to Chile and Mexico as enviable examples
(Hughes 1987, 509).[34] Canada surely can share Mexico's traditional
lament about being so close to the United States and so far from God. The
percentage of the value of production that was produced by U.S.–controlled and affiliated companies in 1932 ranged from 39 percent in iron
and products to 63 percent in nonferrous metals including electrical appa-
ratus (Marshall, Southard, and Taylor 1936, cited in Wylie 1990). Some
observers cited the "satellitic" nature of tariff-jumping U.S. industries as
responsible for their low rate of innovation.

Clearly, important differences are being elided here. But the fact is that,
in many ways, these economies were similar, and they would react to perceived dependency in the same way Latin America did. Wynia (1990) sees
far more similarities than differences in his article "Opening Late-Industrializing Economies: Lessons from Argentina and Australia." Analyzing
the difficulties of shifting away from a "rent-seeking" approach, he sees
both economies as attempting more merciful and less costly industrial rev-
olutions by relying heavily on government regulations and controls, as
well as contrived economic rents. He is careful to note the following:

None of this is confined to Latin America. Rent-seeking economics
is not derived from that region's patrimonial political traditions or
Hispanic affection for corporatist ways of doing politics. . . . Rather
it was a strategy chosen by authorities in nations that were, at the
time that economic modernization was accelerated, already too acti-
vated socially and politically to permit less politically self-conscious

approaches to economic renovation. . . . The Australians were not radically different from the Argentines in their approach to the protection of industry and labor. . . . They were guided by sentiments of nationalism and nativism, stressing the nation's defense against competition from cheaper labor and/or more powerful foreign economies (Wynia, 1990, 187–88).

The reaction was one of dependent countries seeking to diversify away from the natural resources that maintained the dependent relationship and that appeared to have taken them down during the Great Depression. Locating the region along a continuum is important, since it shows precisely that the Latin American countries are not rare species operating under special economic conditions or laws, but are firmly members of the "late modernizing resource-rich countries" phylum. They share similar liabilities, but also similar possibilities for growth.

However, figures 6.4 through 6.9 also suggest some critical differences. First, the Scandinavian experiment with protection reached levels attained by the Latin Americans only at their most open periods. Second, most of the beta countries reduced tariffs below 0.1 by 1950. By contrast, the Latin series are far more volatile and show no consistent trend toward decrease through the end of the 1980s. The average openness series suggest a similar pattern: the beta countries also became more closed in the 1930s and 1940s, but by 1950 had retained their previous levels. Even at their most closed they were far more open than their Latin counterparts, which by 1989 still had not recovered their 1895 levels.

Indeed, the greatest departure from the ISI trajectory is Sweden, which maintained low tariffs and an aggressive outward orientation throughout the postwar period. Sweden's labor dynamics are highly suggestive of the importance of resolving distributional issues early and bringing labor onboard to a country's position along the policy continuum. Hjalmarsson (1991), in "The Scandinavian Model of Industrial Policy," finds the anchor of the outward-looking policy in the attitude of Swedish trade unions who, "as early as the 1920s, strongly promoted a productivity enhancing industrial policy, emphasizing the rationalization of firms" that placed a premium on continual renewal of technology, plant organization, and machinery. He notes that the 1951 policy document of the Confederation of Trade Unions stressed competition to increase productivity and to force less-efficient firms out of the market, combined with active labor-market policies to reallocate displaced workers. In the 1950s, the confederation was resolutely free trade, strongly criticized government protectionist measures, and "argued that tariffs would decrease productivity growth since it would protect stagnating and less competitive industries." The importance of this case is precisely that it shows that there were alternative strategies for managing resource-abundant economies than the one that Latin America chose.

Industrial Drag on Natural Resource Development

Broadly speaking, the same continuum of effects is found surrounding the second innovation-impeding effect of ISI: industrialization policies, to a greater or lesser extent, were implemented on the backs of the traditional exporting sectors. Possible productivity gains and growth more generally were stymied than encouraged by price incentives. These disincentives and a general inattention to the primary sectors undercut their dynamism.

At one extreme, the Scandinavian and U.S. cases testify to the possibilities of sustained development building on resource endowments. Australian observers again see their country as an intermediate case, where the lesser degree of their turning away from traditional exports constitutes the critical difference from the Argentine case at the other extreme. As Australia encouraged investment in petroleum, refining, and electrical equipment in the postwar period, it initially neglected the rural sector, which grew at only half the rate of population growth. This led to debates about the logic of stimulating secondary industry in which the country had no comparative advantage and whose lagging performance, it was argued, had led to the country's periodic balance-of-payments crises. Agricultural policy was reversed in 1952 with the granting of investment subsidies, extension of credit, price stabilization programs, and extension of research and extension programs, which led to a doubling of production over the next decade.

Argentina, across the same inward-looking period of the 1940s–50s, inflicted permanent damage on its traditional leading sector, driving output growth to 0.2 percent per year and leaving the country perilously close to ceasing to export foodstuffs. This combination of inefficient industrialization with the demise of its traditional export sectors left it exceptionally vulnerable and prey to the cycles of boom and bust characterizing the region. Australia would continue to suffer from mild cycles of boom and balance-of-payments crises (and required International Monetary Fund assistance in 1952). However, a rebirth of interest in traditional mining sectors in the 1960s led to increased dynamism in the resources sector that may lead Australia to fourth in per capita income in the near future, despite inattention to the continuing inefficiencies of the ISI strategy that would not be addressed until the 1980s.

Case Study 2: Chile Redux: Fruit Redevivus Lest the magnitude of the impact of the disincentives to innovation and growth of the traditional sectors be underappreciated, it is worth going into some detail again on one case—resource exports in Chile, particularly those involving fruit. Chile aggressively undertook the public good and pro-innovation policies found in the successful natural resource exporters, but would find them undermined by policies toward the industrial sector. The Promethean efforts of the state development corporation (CORFO), founded in 1939 and growing to control 30 percent of total investment, laid the foundations for the dynamic export industries of the next half-century. Similar to what Wright (1999) documents in the United States case, CORFO financed and promoted prospecting for gold, silver, manganese, and iron. To develop the fishing industry, CORFO contracted technical assistance missions, established a marine biology station near Valparaíso in 1945, granted sizable tax exemptions in 1952, and joined the army and the University of Chile in surveying the coastal waters in 1954. It took the first inventories of forest stocks and contracted the 1944 Haig technical assistance mission to examine the forestry sector. In 1953 it financed processing plants for cellulose and newsprint. In the fruit industry as well, CORFO financed technical assistance missions, extended credit for cultivation and experimental plots, and invested in supporting infrastructure, and, in 1941, it financed efforts to promote exports of wood products and wine. Throughout the 1950s and early 1960s, CORFO established an experimental fishing station in Arauco, financed construction of modern boats and dock facilities in Tarapaca and Valivia, and founded fish canneries and fishmeal mills. The World Bank-financed Paper and Carton Manufacturing Company in Bio-Bio stimulated paper and cellulose-related forestry activities after 1957. There appears to be no want of state support for the fledgling resource sectors.

However, the overall context of incentives worked against them. CORFO may have been correct in boasting on its 20th birthday of Chilean history being divided in two eras: that before the construction of the Huachipato iron works near Concepción in 1947 and that after, which transformed the region into an important center of manufacturing. But even early on, local observers wondered at the costs. A compilation of seminars given in the business community in 1954 entitled *Negative Aspects of Economic Intervention: Failures of an Experiment* praised CORFO's irreplaceable role in creating the electricity and fishing industries, but derided the gross inefficiency of Huachipato and the National Petroleum Company and recognized the capriciousness of exchange controls as the overriding disincentive to needed foreign investment. The halving of export volume over the previous decade, the stagnation of agriculture, and the frustration of Chile's tremendous potential in vegetable and fruit exports were laid at the feet of irrational intervention in the price mechanisms and the persistently overvalued exchange rate (Correa Prieto 1954 cited in Maloney 1997).

In the 1960s, recurrent balance-of-payments crises would lead the Christian Democratic government of Eduardo Frei in Chile to seek to promote nontraditional and traditional exports. Yet Chile's areas of natural comparative advantage were stymied by the gross protection and inefficiencies that were the logical culmination of a system of protection and incentives that had mutated into literally incomprehensible degrees of distortion. Jeanneret (1972, 95), a researcher at the *Centro de Estudios de*

Planificación Nacional at the *Universidad Catolica*, noted that, in 1965, "the multiplicity of instruments used, and the frequency with which they were modified, had arrived at such extremes that it was humanly impossible to have a clear vision of their final impact by sector or for the economy as a whole." She found effective rates of protection extreme by global standards, ranging from –100 to 650 compared to –50 to 500 for Brazil, –25 to 200 for Malaysia, and –17 to 106 for Norway. These heavy negative rates of protection implied that 10 of 21 industries studied could export only at a loss and that "some of these sectors, principally wood, paper, paper products, fish and other minerals, would have become, perhaps, significant exporters." A contemporary observer, Marko Mamalakis, also wondered at the inability of the agro-export industry to grow, given that "export demand for raw or processed Chilean fruit, seafood, oils, wine and so forth [was] almost unlimited" (Mamalakis 1976, 151).

That these disincentives to invest and innovate were critical is borne out by subsequent history. As is well known, the history of the Chilean economy since 1975 has been one of relentless pursuit of integration with the world economy and a correction of the distortions accumulated in the previous decades. In the 20 years following 1975, noncopper exports increased by a factor of 10, essentially eliminating the traditional foreign exchange bottleneck to industry. The most dramatic story, however, occurs in the fruit sector, where exports grew at a rate of 20 percent annually in the first 20 years after the reforms of 1974. Areas planted to commercial orchard almost tripled, and fruit production and the number of entrepreneurs quadrupled.

Jarvis (1994) attributes this success to the rapidity with which Chileans were able to transfer, to adapt, and to extend fruit technologies initially developed for California and other fruit-growing regions to Chile. CORFO again had played an important role in the early 1960s in laying the foundations for this boom,[35] as did the 10-year program for cooperation with the University of California and the University of Chile, established in 1965 to permit technical cooperation and improve graduate training. This helped the University of Chile to develop first-rate faculty in fruit-related sciences and to begin modern fruit research. However, Jarvis is also clear that most of the post-liberalization initiatives in these areas were privately funded and driven by changes in price relationships and industry structure that increased returns to private R&D. Further down the innovation chain, the number of university theses on fruit submitted in Departments of Agricultural Engineering from 1976–80 to 1986–90 increased by a factor of 2.5. Although Jarvis expresses concern that private provision of a nonexcludable good might not be as likely as profits to the industry are eroded, there can be no question that the story of the renaissance of Chilean fruit is one of innovation made profitable by eliminating a bias against the sector.

Conclusion

The logical question is why Latin America occupies the extreme of the continuum sketched here. Though beyond the scope of this chapter, much of the explanation lies in political and economic dynamics—timing of the mobilization of urban classes, modernization of the rural areas, the form of integrating new actors into traditional power structures, and so forth— and these dynamics receive attention, particularly among Australian observers. Further, if the data in table 6.4 are to be trusted, Latin America may have suffered a greater fall in income.

However, in keeping with the general focus on national learning capacity and adoption of knowledge from abroad, three ideas suggest themselves.

First, the necessary degree of protection to preserve or jump-start industries is likely to be a function of their ability to innovate as fast as their foreign competitors. The Swedish forestry industry does not seek protection from Brazilian and Chilean exporters. But it is perhaps not surprising that 19th-century Brazilian iron smelters using archaic *cadinho* technologies complained of competition from more modern producers abroad, despite the high shipping costs. A lower national learning capacity would dictate higher necessary levels of protection to have a comparable stimulative effect.

Second, the same deficiency in national learning capacity may have implied reliance on technological know-how of foreign actors, which conferred a greater sense of dependency and additional suspicion of natural resources. It is likely that had Chile had the capacity to monitor the *Gran Mineria* in the 1950s, it would have enjoyed a stronger bargaining position, a greater confidence in copper as a continuing growth industry, a less distortive experiment with ISI, and potentially less divisive politics. Together, these two factors suggest that Latin America's poor postwar performance, and extreme inward-looking policies that contributed to it, reflect the cumulative impact of deficiencies with very deep historical roots.

Finally, innovation in economic knowledge may depend on the same factors. Between low levels of general literacy and the same weakness in tapping into foreign advances, Latin America may have been less familiar with the laws of economics and sound management than the beta countries. Duncan and Fogerty (1984) argue that Australia emerged from its traumatic period of Depression unemployment with a renewed commitment to economic management and state intervention. However, it retained the professionals from business and the universities who had successfully managed war production and directed them toward maintaining postwar prosperity. There was a fundamental belief in the need for a technically sound basis for economic management and a commitment to remaining engaged in the world economy. In Sweden, Jonung (1992) notes how unusually involved professors of economics were and remain in public life. Globally renowned figures like Cassel, Heckscher, Ohlin, and Wicksell were frequent government advisors, promoters of public debate, and even parliamentarians. This was, however, the same era as when Peron dismissed *tecnicos* like Raúl Prebisch, arguing that "there can be nothing more elastic than the economy" and that economists' alarmist warnings should be ignored. The latter suggests that this point should probably not be overstressed. Often in Latin American history, the macro-basics were firmly understood by key actors, but the political circumstances overrode their advice. Nonetheless, it is remarkable to hear many of the current Latin American leaders, in the face of vast international evidence, again reverting to policies that will guarantee that over the long run the region will remain far from the innovation frontier.

Annex

Variables:
Initial Level of Income: For the Maddison dataset, GDP per capita was calculated using the average growth rates per period and the GDP per capita (GDPpc) of 1989 in 1995 constant U.S. dollars. In order to control for different convergence across periods, the variable was calculated relative to the maximum GDPpc in the period. Thus, Initial GDPpc = Max (log GDPpc in t) – log GDPpc in t. For Sachs and Warner we use their variable LGDPEA70.
Net Primary Exports per Worker: Leamer's (1995) measure of Natural Resource (the sum of the exports minus imports of the categories divided by number of workers).
  1. Petroleum and Derivatives (SITC 33)
  2. Raw Materials (SITC 27, 28, 32, 34, 35, and 68)
  3. Forest Products (SITC 24, 25, 63, and 64)
  4. Tropical Agriculture (SITC 5, 6, 7, 11, and 23)
  5. Animal Products (SITC 0 to 3, 21, 29, 43, and 94)
  6. Cereals, Oil, Textile Fibers, Tobacco, and others (SITC 4, 8, 9, 12, 22, 26, 41, and 42) divided by total labor force. Data was taken from the database used for de Ferranti and others (2002).

Openness: This variable was taken from Sachs and Warner (1995). It contains a dummy per country and year indicating if the country was open or not.
Investment: For the Maddison database, it is the average of gross domestic fixed investment/GDP. It is taken from Nehru and Dhareshwa Physical Capital Stock dataset (World Bank, 1995). For Sachs and Warner, we use their variable LINV7089.
Knowledge Index: The index was taken from the database used for Lederman and Xu (2001) and de Ferranti and others (2002). It was constructed using R&D expenditures as a share of gross national product; persons in R&D per million people, patent applications by residents and nonresidents as share of worldwide patents applications; and patent applications in the United States by origin of the applicant as share of total patent applications in the United States. Missing values were imputed using factor analysis with regional and yearly dummies, GDP per capita, and general level of education.

Notes

*This paper originally appeared in Economia (Fall 2002, Volume 3, Number 1). The author is grateful to Particio Aroca, Magnus Blomström, Marcos Cueto, Jesse Czelusta, Pablo Fajnzybler, Rodrigo Garcia Verdu, Steven Kamin, Daniel Lederman, Osmel Manzano, David Mayer, Suzanne Meehan, Patricio Meller, Guillermo Perry, Roberto Rigobón, Andres Rodriguez-Clare, Elena Serrano, Sol Serrano, Luis Servén, Andrew Warner and Gavin Wright for helpful discussions. He is especially grateful to Gabriel Montes Rojas for inspired research assistance.

1. A now larger literature (see, for example Sachs and Warner 2001) has argued that resource abundance is associated with slower growth on average. Though this chapter will not attempt to resolve this debate, a couple of cautionary points are worth making. First, the time period where the data permit reasonable analysis covers 25 years at the end of the 20th century. This is probably not a representative period, including as it does the debt crisis (see Rigobón and Manzano's discussion in chapter 3) and structural reforms, and as suggested by the regressions here, probably cannot be extrapolated to earlier eras. Second, as Stijns (2005) and Lederman and Maloney show in this volume, the finding is not robust to using different measures of resource abundance, including the Leamer measure used here. Third, it is important to know whether underperformance is intrinsic to natural resources-based sectors, or a nonessential correlate, such as destructive political economy issues (see Auty 2001). See also endnote 6.

2. See, of course, Prebisch, but also more recently Matsuyama (1991), Sachs and Warner (2001), and Rodriguez and Rodrik (1999). Offsetting this literature is another stressing the importance of natural resources as a stimulus to growth in North America (see Findlay and Lundahl 1994).

3. See Parente and Prescott (2000), Dollar and Wolff (1997), Klenow and Rodriguez-Clare (1996).

4. Martin and Mitra (2001). See also Bernard and Jones (1996); Lewis, Martin, and Savage (1988); Martin and Warr (1993).

5. See Irwin (2000) for the United States; Innis (1933) and Watkins (1963) for Canada; Wright and Czelusta (chapter 7) and Czelusta (2001) for Australia; Blomström and Kokko (chapter 8) and Blomström and Meller (1991b) for Scandinavia. Latin America also offers its success stories: Monterrey, Mexico; Medallin, Colombia; and São Paolo, Brazil; all grew to become dynamic industrial centers based on mining and in the latter two cases, coffee.

6. Leamer's measure of resource abundance, net exports per worker, is broadly supported by the Heckscher-Ohlin framework. The greater temporal scope comes at a high cost in terms of available control variables used in other studies and the regressions must be treated as suggestive only. Further, both the lack of any temporal variation in our natural resource and the knowledge variables proscribe any meaningful panel treatment of the data. This implies that more sophisticated approaches, such as suggested by Arellano and Bond (1991), that would address important issues of unobserved heterogeneity correlated with regressors or the endogeneity of both the initial income or investment variables cannot be employed. (See Lederman and Maloney (2002) for a partial review).

7. Cited in Maloney (1997, 25).

8. Baer (2001) notes how the recent application of satellite technology has led to vastly expanded estimates of mining potential in Brazil relative to the stock, confidently seen as fixed in the 1960s. Mining exports doubled between 1992 and 1999 in Peru, making it the world's second-largest silver, bismuth, and tin producer, sixth in copper, and eighth in gold; however, Wright and Czelusta (chapter 7) argue that this is still far below potential.

9. Referring to the closing of the Argentine frontier, he argues, "This kind of area of new settlement was bound to see its rates of growth falter after initial colonization. Argentina behaved, to some extent, in this fairly predictable fashion. But the same was not true for the other countries. It must be acknowledged that the ability of the United States, Canada, and Australia to continue a process of vigorous growth even at the end of the expansion of the frontier has been a most extraordinary feat, and one that could not be taken for granted. . . . At that point the successful cases were able to move to a quasi-rent based stage—early for the most successful of all, the United States, less so for Canada and Australia, and rather later for Argentina; further development for the United States and Canada was more clearly based on innovation and less so in Australia. For Argentina it arose exclusively from collusive quasi-rents. To the extent that development was based on innovation, these countries were switching to an alternative and unlimited source of growth. To the extent that it was based on collusion, it opened up a limited, alternative path" (Di Tella 1985, 51).

10. See Stern, Porter, and Furman (2000), Romer (1990), Nelson and Wright (1992).

11. Recent literature by Aghion et al. (2005) stresses that for low levels of competition, the traditional Schumpeterian effect that reducing rents decreases innovation is outweighed by the incentive to innovate to escape competition from rivals.

12. Monteon (1982) summarizes the underlying critique that "the economic ideal of the nineteenth century remained that of a rentier—someone who makes his fortune in one quick speculation and thereafter lives on land rents or some other long-term yield. Domingo Sarmiento in 1842 referred to the effect of this ideal on native entrepreneurs: southern hacendados and northern mine-owners left their "affaires" in the hands of supervisors and moved to Santiago where they "tried to imitate or rather parody the European Aristocracy" (Monteon 1982, 14). This critique finds an even earlier expression in Juan Jose Santa Cruz, who in his *Reflections on the Economic State of Chile in 1791*, saw the potential with a small outlay of displacing the British fishing and whaling activity off the Chilean coast. But he lamented the introduction into the colony of "luxury, ostentation, and expensive tastes" and saw no permanent improvement in the economic conditions of Chile as possible as long as the population remained improvident and susceptible to sumptuous living (Will 1957, 57). The theme again recurs in Marcial Gonzalez' 1874 speech "Luxury our Enemy," where he argued that the clothes, jewels, coaches, and statues exceed those found anywhere else in America (reference in Monteon 1982). Pinto Santa Cruz (1959, 75) cites the historian Francisco Encina: "'if half of what we have wasted in the last 40 years or invested in luxury we had applied to buying Nitrate mining machinery or to setting up the copper industry, to irrigating our fields . . . the position of Chile in America would today be different. The propensity to save and invest was not, then, the most striking virtue of our community."

13. Though Pinto Santa Cruz (1959, 57) acknowledges some, although almost certainly not enough, of a role for corruption, "what was decisive was the absence of local individuals and groups interested in developing, on their own, the nitrate riches." In fact, although Chilean capital finance was very important, the British had dominated the nitrates industry in Peru and Bolivia and had substantial marketing networks. This made them the natural agents to continue mining once these lands were taken by Chile. Monteon (1982) also argues that the global condemnation of Chile's imperialism may have induced a strategy of dividing the world community by offering Britain a sweet deal. In any case, it appears that the British were aware of a government plan to allocate ownership on the basis of who owned the Peruvian titles. This inside information allowed them to purchase shares at a discount and emerge as owners. A question does emerge as to why Chilean capital was

so willing to sell and to why it did not protest more after the fact. One of the earlier Chilean nitrate pioneers, Jose Santos Ossa, petitioned that, given this dearth of local entrepreneurship, the government take over the job of mining. But the minister of the interior replied that the state would be corrupted by such an undertaking and that it was better to leave it to private interests, implying, foreign capital. This may have been due as much to an embrace of classical liberal economic values during the period as much as any Spanish *rentier* hangover, but Pinto seems less convinced. "The decision of the managing groups of the country to 'live from the rents' of the industry"(Monteon 1982, 56) and not play the Schumpeterian entrepreneurial midwife would cost the country, not only in income foregone, but also in expertise and dynamism that Pinto Santa Cruz argues let foreigners dominate in every field of domestic endeavor.

14. Encina, *Historia de Chile* XIII, p. 486, cited in Will (1957).

15. Pushing the argument further, if investment was constrained by human capital, it may have been rational to be purely *rentiers*.

16. The Scandinavian countries did not start with an egalitarian *tabula rasa*. In the 18th century, Danish land was in the hands of a few thousand families on large estates tilled by serfs, and only 23 percent of rural households owned land in Finland. But as Blomström and Meller (1991a, 6) argue, "what laid the foundation for the Scandinavian transformation to modern wealthy societies were the agrarian reforms" that created small and medium-size privately owned farms and which ranged in timing from Denmark's precocious beginnings in 1788 to Norway and Sweden's efforts in the 1850s and Finland's of the 1920s. As with the relatively equal distribution of land in Canada (Watkins 1963 and Armstrong 1985) and the United States, Blomström and Kokko (chapter 8) argue that "it is hardly possible to over-emphasize the importance of the improvement in agricultural productivity for Swedish industrialization, which facilitated transfer of labor and made possible exports that generated capital for investment in forestry and manufacturing in addition to providing a local market."

17. Hveem (1991).

18. Very early on, for example, Scandinavia was exporting know-how in the form of its own émigrés toward tsarist Russia, where Alfred Nobel was one of the pioneers of the infant petroleum industry. To a significant extent the expansion of manufacturing during the first decades of the 20th century was based on Swedish innovations: steam turbines, centrifugal separators, ball bearings, the adjustable spanner, the safety match, air compressors, automatic lighthouse technique, various types of precision instruments, techniques for precision measurements, and so forth (Lindbeck 1974, 5). The great companies known today were built on innovations in these areas. Ericsson (founded in 1876) thrived on the telephone; Alfa Laval (1879) on the separator; ASEA (1890) on electrical equipment; and SKF (1907) on bearings (Amsden and Hikino 1994).

19. Memorial plaque at the *Casa de la Inquisicion* in Cartegena de las Indias, Colombia.

20. Riera i Tuébols (1993).

21. See Will (1957) for Chile; Safford (1976) for Colombia; and López Soria (1999) for Peru. Despite having one of the oldest universities in Latin America, Peru would fail twice, once in 1852–53 with the Escuela Central de Ingenieros Civiles and again in 1875 with the Escuela de Minas, in establishing technical education. They would succeed in 1876 by creating the Escuela de Ingenieros Civiles.

22. See Safford (1976) for Colombia; Villalobos (1990) and Greve (1938) for Chile; and Baer (1969) for Brazil.

23. I'm grateful to Rodrigo García Verdú of the Banco de México for calling the Mexican case to my attention. http://ingenieria/unam.mx/historia/historia11b.html.

24. OECD (1969).

25. As an illustrative pseudo-experiment, Fogarty (1985) cites that fact that the same year that Spanish Merino sheep were introduced into New South Wales, Australia, a flock was introduced to the River Plate region. European capital was available for sheep breeding in both areas, and both suffered the ups and downs of the world wool market. In 1885, the two countries had the same number of sheep, but the average "clip" was getting almost twice as much on the world market in Australia as in Argentina, due not only to differences in wool types and quality, but to inferior yields per sheep. He attributes the differences to the innovation and visions of individual figures, rather than any structural features of the economy.

26. "It is worth noting that the empresarial spirit united with the motivation to apply new techniques was almost always the result of initiatives of foreigners who came to Chile and saw opportunities to develop or solutions to problems with practical experience. They brought and had a greater tradition of information, spirit of action, attention to detail and urgency to capitalize on the results or resources generated, which was not a common trait of the average inhabitant of the country whose nature of work was little developed beyond the artesanal level" (Villalobos 1990, 99).

27. Cited in Moran (1974).

28. See Encina (1911, 45). He notes that "from the point of view of capital and of technical and administrative aptitude, the copper industry is as demanding as the most complicated manufacturing industry." His studies reveal "an extraordinary economic ineptitude in the national population . . . consequence of an education completely inadequate to meet the demands of contemporary life. . ." (1911, 17).

29. http://www.mines.unsw.edu.au/school.htm; http://unsw.edu.au/about/about_history.html.

30. New South Wales Department of Mineral Resources (2001). http://www.minerals.nsw.gov.au/silver.htm. This section also draws on http://www.bhpbilliton.com/.

31. See Lederman (2001) for an excellent summary of the literature on determinants of trade liberalization. He also argues that in the Chilean case, trade protection arose before the Great Depression.

32. Södersten (1991) testifies to the traumatic levels in Sweden as well.

33. This also implied that fiscal problems during the Great Depression would be minor in Argentina compared with Canada or Australia. Both the lower demands of supporting the unemployed, and the fact that the railways, which ran major losses in all three countries, were largely in private hands in Argentina (whereas in both Canada and Australia they had far larger public participation), lessened the impact on some Latin states. Aldaheff (1985) suggests that half of Canada's budget deficit in 1932–33 and 1934–35 were dedicated to financing. Real expenditures between 1928–29 and 1933–34 rose 66 percent in Canada, 46 percent in Australia, and only 10 percent in Argentina. Further, in terms of managing external debt, debt service was calculated at 17, 22, and 23 percent for Argentina, Australia, and Canada, respectively, and per capita indebtedness was 167 pesos versus 863 and 224. Argentina's repayment record was excellent across the period and it was Australia, who had overborrowed in the 1920s, which had the most trouble servicing the debt. In sum, all three countries showed conservative and reasonable fiscal management in the face of shocks, but the Latin American entrant was relatively better off.

34. These same themes would continue through history and would surface over American ownership of Australian mines (which had risen to 41 percent by 1967) and agriculture in the 1960s and 1970s. Protests against perceived dependency would peak in virulent objection to the war in Vietnam and as a reaction against Yankee Imperialism that featured prominently in the 1972 labor campaign.

35. CORFO's interventions included analysis of potential demand; surveying existing fruit orchards; analysis of potential demand in foreign markets; elaboration of production goals; introduction and screening of new varieties; establishment of nurseries to propagate disease-free plants; construction of cold-storage facilities at strategic locations to promote post-harvest care; phytosanitary inspection of exported fruit; and establishment of favorable credit lines and working capital, as well as "drawback" payments for fruit exports. In 1964 Chile established the National Institute of Agricultural Research (INIA), which paid relatively higher salaries and attracted more skilled researchers, and INIA initiated a fruit research program. By these means, Chile developed the scientific personnel and knowledge to achieve technological transfer, identified and began to plant new varieties suitable for foreign markets, improved orchard and post-harvest management, upgraded fruit research and teaching, and developed the infrastructure necessary to export fruit to foreign markets. Several export companies emerged that gained experience with foreign markets.

References

Aghion, Philippe, Christopher Harris, Peter Howitt, and John Vickers. 2001. "Competition, Imitation, and Growth with Step-by–Step Innovation." *Review of Economic Studies* 68: 467–92.

Aghion, Philippe, Nicholas Bloom, Richard Blundell, Rachel Griffith, and Peter Howitt. 2005. "Competition and Innovation: An Inverted U Relationship." *Quarterly Journal of Economics* 120 (2): 701–28.

Ahlström, G. 1992. "Technical Competence and Industrial Performance: Sweden in the 19th and Early 20th Centuries." Lund Papers in Economic History 14. Lund, Sweden: Lund University.

Alhadeff, Peter. 1985. "Public Finance and the Economy in Argentina, Australia, and Canada during the Depression of the 1930s." In *Argentina, Australia, and Canada: Studies in Comparative Development, 1870–1965*, ed. D. C. M. Platt and Guido di Tella, 161–176. London: Macmillan Press.

Amsden, Alice H., and Takashi Hikino. 1994. "Staying Behind, Stumbling Back, Sneaking Up, Soaring Ahead: Late Industrialization in Historical Perspective." In *The Convergence of Productivity, Its Significance, and Its Varied Connotations,* ed. William J. Baumol, Richard R. Nelson, and Edward N. Wolff. Oxford and New York: Oxford University Press.

Anderson, Kym. 1987. "Tariffs and the Manufacturing Sector." In *The Australian Economy in the Long Run,* ed. Rodney Maddock and Ian McLean, 181. New York: Cambridge University Press.

Arellano, Manuel, and Stephen Bond. 1991. "Some Test of Specification for Panel Data: Monte Carlo Evidence and an Application to Employment Equations." *The Review of Economic Studies* 58 (2): 277–97.

Armstrong, Warwick. 1985. "The Social Origins of Industrial Growth: Canada, Argentina, and Australia, 1870–1930." In *Argentina, Australia, and Canada: Studies in Comparative Development, 1870–1965,* ed. D. C. M. Platt and Guido di Tella. London: Macmillan Press

Auty, Richard M. 2001. "The Political Economy of Resource-Driven Growth," *European Economic Review* 45: 839–46.

Baer, Werner. 1969. *The Development of the Brazilian Steel Industry.* Nashville, TN: Vanderbilt University Press.

———. 2001. *The Brazilian Economy. Growth and Development.* 5th ed. Westport, CT: Praeger Publishers.

Barro, Robert, and Xavier Sala-i-Martin. 1997. "Technological Diffusion, Convergence, and Growth." *Journal of Economic Growth* 2: 1–26.

Baumol, William J., Richard R. Nelson, and Edward N. Wolff, eds. 1994. *The Convergence of Productivity, Its Significance, and Its Varied Connotations.* Oxford and New York: Oxford University Press.

Bernard, Andrew, and Charles Jones. 1996. "Productivity across Industries and Countries: Time Series Theory and Evidence." *Review of Economics and Statistics* 78 (1): 135–46.

Bethell, L. 1998. *Latin American Economy and Society since 1930.* Cambridge, United Kingdom: Cambridge University Press.

Blomström, Magnus, and Patricio Meller, eds. 1991a. *Diverging Paths: Comparing a Century of Scandinavian and Latin American Development.* Washington, DC: Inter-American Development Bank.

———. 1991b. "Issues for Development: Lessons from Scandaniavia-Latin Comparisons." In *Diverging Paths: Comparing a Century of Scandinavian and Latin American Development,* ed. Magnus Blomström and Patricio Meller. Washington DC: Inter-American Development Bank.

Buffington, Robert M., and William French. 1999. "The Culture of Modernity." In *The Oxford History of Mexico,* ed. Michael C. Meyer and William Beezley. Oxford: Oxford University Press.

Cárdenas, Enrique. 1997. "A Macroeconomic Interpretation of Nineteenth Century Mexico." In *How Latin America Fell Behind: Essays on the Economic Histories of Brazil and Mexico, 1800–1914,* ed. Stephen Haber. Palo Alto, CA: Stanford University Press.

Cariola, Carmen, and Osvaldo Sunkel. 1985. "The Growth of the Nitrate Industry and Socioeconomic Change in Chile, 1880–1930." In *The Latin American Economies,* ed. Roberto Cortes Condre and Shan J. Hunt. New York: Holmes and Meier.

Collier, Simon, and William F. Sater. 1996. *A History of Chile, 1808–1994.* Cambridge, United Kingdom: Cambridge University Press.

Conning, Jonathan. 2002. "Latifundia Economics." Working Paper 02/1, Department of Economics, Hunter College, City University of New York.

Czelusta, Jesse W. 2001. "Natural Resources, Economic Growth, and Technical Change: Lessons from Australia and the United States." Processed. Stanford University, Palo Alto, CA.

de Ferranti, David, Guillermo Perry, Daniel Lederman, and William F. Maloney. 2002. *From Natural Resources to the Knowledge Economy.* Washington, DC: World Bank.

Dehem, Roger. 1962. "The Economics of Stunted Growth." *Canadian Journal of Economics and Political Science* 27: 502–10.

Diaz Alejandro, Carlos F. 1985. "Argentina, Australia, and Brazil before 1929." In *Argentina, Australia, and Canada: Studies in Comparative Development, 1870–1965,* ed. D. C. M. Platt and Guido di Tella, 95–109. London: Macmillan Press.

Di Tella, Guido. 1985. "Rents, Quasi Rents, Normal Profits and Growth: Argentina and the Areas of Recent Settlement." In *Argentina, Australia, and Canada: Studies in Comparative Development, 1870–1965,* ed. D. C. M. Platt and Guido di Tella, 19–37. London: Macmillan Press.

Dollar, David, and Edward N. Wolff. 1997. "Convergence of Industry Labor Productivity among Advanced Economies, 1963–1982." In *The Economics of Productivity*, ed. Edward N. Wolff, 39–48. Cheltenham, United Kingdom: Elgar Reference Collection.

Duncan, Tim, and John Fogarty. 1984. *Australia and Argentina: On Parallel Paths.* Carlton, Victoria, Australia: Melbourne University Press.

Encina, Francisco Antonio. 1911. *Nuestra Inferioridad Económica, Sus Causas, Sus Consequencias.* Santiago, Chile: Coleccion Imagen de Chile.

Engerman, Stanley I., and Kenneth Sokoloff. 1997. "Factor Endowments, Institutions, and Differentials Paths of Growth among New World Economies: A View from Economic Historians of the United States." In *How Latin America Fall Behind: Essays on the Economic Histories of Brazil and Mexico, 1800–1914*, ed. Stephen Haber. Palo Alto, CA: Stanford University Press.

Engerman, Stanley L., Stephen H. Haber, and Kenneth L. Sokoloff. 2000. "Inequality, Institutions, and Differential Paths of Growth." In *Institutions, Contracts, and Organizations,* ed. Claude Menard. Northampton, MA: Edward Elgar.

Findlay, Ronal, and Mats Lundahl. 1994. "Natural Resources, 'Vent for Surplus' and the Staples Theory." In *From Classical Economics to Development Economics,* ed. Gerald M. Meir, 68–93. New York: St. Martin's Press.

Fogarty, John. 1985. "Staples, Super-Staples, and the Limits of Staple Theory: The Experiences of Argentina, Australia, and Canada Compared." In *Argentina, Australia, and Canada: Studies in Comparative Development, 1870–1965,* ed. D. C. M. Platt and Guido di Tella, 1–18. London: Macmillan Press.

Greve, Ernesto. 1938. *Historia de la Ingeniería en Chile.* Tomo I. Santiago de Chile: Imprenta Universitaria.

Grossman, Gene M., and Elhanan Helpman. 1991. *Innovation and Growth in the Global Economy.* Cambridge, MA: MIT Press.

Haavisto, Tarmo, and Ari Kokko. 1991. "Politics as a Determinant of Economic Performance: The Case of Finland." In *Diverging Paths: Comparing a Century of Scandinavian and Latin American Development,* ed. Magnus Blomström and Patricio Meller. Washington, DC: Inter-American Development Bank.

Hansen, Roger D. 1971. *The Politics of Mexican Development.* Baltimore, MD: Johns Hopkins University Press.

Hirschman, Albert O. 1958. *The Strategy of Economic Development.* New Haven, CT: Yale University Press.

Hjalmarsson, Lennart. 1991. "The Scandinavian Model of Industrial Policy." In *Diverging Paths: Comparing a Century of Scandinavian and Latin American Development,* ed. Magnus Blomström and Patricio Meller. Washington, DC: Inter-American Development Bank.

Howitt, Peter, and David Mayer. 2005. "R&D, Implementation and Stagnation: A Schumpeterian Theory of Convergence Clubs." *Journal of Money, Credit, and Banking* 37: 144–77.

Hughes, Robert. 1987. *The Fatal Shore.* London: Pan Books.

Hveem, Helge. 1991. "Developing an Open Economy: Norway's Transformation 1845–1975." In *Diverging Paths: Comparing a Century of Scandinavian and Latin American Development,* ed. Magnus Blomström and Patricio Meller. Washington, DC: Inter-American Development Bank.

Innis, Harold. 1933. *Problems of Staple Production in Canada.* Toronto: University of Toronto Press.

Irwin, Douglas A. 2000. "How Did the United States Become a Net Exporter of Manufactured Goods?" Working Paper 7638, Cambridge, MA: National Bureau of Economic Research.

Jarvis, Lovell S. 1994. "Changing Private and Public Sector Roles in Technological Development: Lessons from the Chilean Fruit Sector." In *Agricultural Technology, Policy Issues for the International Community*, ed. J. Anderson. Wallingford, CT: CAB International.

Jeanneret, Teresa. 1972. "El sistema de protección a la industria chilena." In *Proceso a la industrialización chilena*. Centro de Estudios de Planificación Nacional. Santiago, Chile: Ediciones Nueva Universidad.

Jonung, Lars. 1992. "Economics the Swedish Way, 1889–1989." In *Economics in Sweden*, ed. Lars Engwalled. New York: Rutledge.

Klenow, Peter J., and Andres Rodriguez-Clare. 1996. "The Neoclassical Revival in Growth Economics: Has it Gone Too Far?" In *1997 Macroeconomics Annual*, Cambridge, MA: National Bureau of Economic Research.

Lagos, Gustavo. 1997. "Developing National Mining Policies in Chile: 1974–96." *Resources Policy* 23: 51–69.

Landes, David S. 1998. *The Wealth and Poverty of Nations*. New York: W. W. Norton.

Leamer, Edward. 1984. *Sources of International Comparative Advantage: Theory and Evidence*. Cambridge, MA: MIT Press.

Leamer, Edward. 1995 "the Heckscher-Ohlin Model in Theory and Practice." Princeton Studies in International Finance 77. Princeton University, Department of Economics, Princeton, NJ.

Lederman, Daniel. 2001. "The Political Economy of Protection: Theory and the Chilean Experience." Doctoral dissertation. Johns Hopkins University, Baltimore, MD.

Lederman, Daniel, and William F. Maloney. 2002. "Open Questions about the Link between Natural Resources and Economic Growth: Sachs and Warner Revisited." Processed. World Bank, Washington, DC.

Lederman, Daniel, and Colin Xu. 2001. "Comparative Advantage and Trade Intensity: Are Traditional Endowments Destiny?" Processed. World Bank, Washington, DC.

Lewis, P., W. Martin, and C. Savage. 1988. "Capital and Investment in the Agricultural Economy." *Quarterly Review of Rural Economy* 10 (1): 48–53.

Lindbeck, Assar. 1974. *Swedish Economic Policy*. Berkeley and Los Angeles: University of California Press.

López Soria, Ignacio. 1999. *Historia de la Universidad Nacional de Ingeniería, Los Años Fundamentales, 1876–1909*. Tomo 1. Lima, Peru: Universidad Nacional de Ingenieria, Proyecto Historia UNI. http://quiu.uni.edu.pe/OtrosWWW.webproff/historia/liberira.html.

Love, Joseph L. 1996. *Crafting the Third World: Theorizing Underdevelopment in Rumania and Brazil*. Palo Alto, CA: Stanford University Press.

Loveman, Brian. 1979. *Chile, the Legacy of Hispanic Capitalism*. New York: Oxford University Press.

Maddison, Angus. 1994. "Explaining the Economic Performance of Nations, 1820–1989." In *The Convergence of Productivity, Its Significance, and Its Varied Connotations*, ed. William J. Baumol, Richard R. Nelson, and Edward N. Wolff, 20–60. Oxford and New York: Oxford University Press.

Maddock, Rodney, and Ian McLean, eds. 1987. *The Australian Economy in the Long Run.* New York: Cambridge University Press.

Maloney, William F. 1997. "Chile." In *The Political Economy of Latin America in the Post-War Period,* ed. Laura Randall. Austin, TX: University of Texas Press.

Mamalakis, Markos. 1976. "The Growth and Structure of the Chilean Economy: from Independence to Allende." New Haven, CT: Yale University Press.

Manzano, Osmel, and Roberto Rigobon. 2001. "Resource Curse or Debt Overhang." NBER Working Paper 8390, Cambridge, MA.

Mariscal, Elisa, and Kenneth Sokoloff. 2000. "Schooling, Suffrage, and the Persistence of Inequality in the Americas, 1800–1945." In *Political Institutions and Economic Growth in Latin America: Essays in Policy, History, and Political Economy,* ed. Stephen Haber. Palo Alto, CA: Stanford University, Hoover Institution Press.

Martin, Will, and Devashish Mitra. 2001. "Productivity Growth and Convergence in Agriculture and Manufacturing." *Economic Development and Cultural Change* 49 (2): 403–22.

Martin, Will, and Peter Warr. 1993. "Explaining the Relative Decline of Agriculture: A Supply-Side Analysis for Indonesia." *World Bank Economic Review (International)* 7: 381–401.

Matsuyama, Kiminori. 1991. "Agricultural Productivity, Comparative Advantage, and Economic Growth." *Journal of Economic Theory* 58 (2): 317–34.

McLean, Ian. 1987. "Growth in a Small Open Economy: An Historical View." In *Australian Economic Growth: Essays in Honour of Fred H. Gruen,* ed. Bruce Chapman. Canberra, Australia: Centre for Economic Policy Research and Australian National University.

Meller, Patricio 1991. "Chilean Economic Development, 1880–1990." In *Diverging Paths: Comparing a Century of Scandinavian and Latin American Development,* ed. Magnus Blomström and Patricio Meller. Washington, DC: Inter-American Development Bank.

Meredith, David. 1995. "The Role of Education and Health Services in the Economic Development of Australia and Argentina 1880–1940." School of Economics Discussion Paper. Sydney, Australia: University of New South Wales.

Mitchell, Brian R. 1998a. *International Historical Statistics, Europe, 1750–1993.* London: Macmillan Reference; New York, NY: Stockton Press.

———. 1998b. *International Historical Statistics, The Americas, 1750–1993.* London: Macmillan Reference; New York, NY: Stockton Press.

———. 1998c. *International Historical Statistics, Africa, Asia & Oceania, 1750–1988.* London: Macmillan Reference; New York, NY: Stockton Press.

Monteon, Michael. 1982. *Chile in the Nitrate Era: The Evolution of Economic Dependence, 1880–1930.* Madison: University of Wisconsin Press.

Moran, Theodore H. 1974. *Multinational Corporations and the Politics of Dependence: Copper in Chile.* Princeton, NJ: Princeton University Press.

Nehru, Vikram, and Ashok M. Dhareshwa. 1995. *A New Database on Physical Capital Stock: Sources, Methodology and Results.* World Bank, Washington, DC. http://www.worldbank.org/research/growth/ddnehdha.htm.

Nelson, R. R., and G. Wright. 1992. "The Rise and Fall of American Technological Leadership: The Postwar Era in Historical Perspective." *Journal of Economic Literature* 30 (4): 1931–64.

New South Wales Department of Mineral Resources. 2001. http://www.minerals .nsw.gov.au/silver.htm.

North, Douglass. 1955. "Location Theory and Regional Economic Growth." *Journal of Political Economy* 63 (3): 243–58.

OECD (Organisation for Economic Co-operation and Development). 1969. *Statistics of the Occupational and Educational Structure of the Labour Force in 53 Countries*. Paris: OECD.

Parente, Stephen L., and Edward C. Prescott. 2000. *Barriers to Riches*. Cambridge, MA: MIT Press.

Pinto Santa Cruz, Anibal. 1959. *Chile, Un Caso de Desarrollo Frustrado*. Santiago de Chile: Editorial Universitaria.

Platt, D. C. M., and Guildo di Tella, eds. 1985. *Argentina, Australia and Canada: Studies in Comparative Development, 1870–1965*. London: Macmillan Press.

Ramos, Joseph. 1998. "A Development Strategy Founded on Natural Resource-Based Clusters." *CEPAL Review* 66: 105–27.

Riera i Tuébols, Santiago. 1993. "Industrialization and Technical Education in Spain, 1850–1914." In *Education, Technology, and Industrial Performance in Europe, 1850–1939*, ed. Robert Fox and Anna Guagnini. Cambridge, United Kingdom: Cambridge University Press.

Rodriguez, Francisco, and Dani Rodrik. 1999. "Trade Policy and Economic Growth: A Skeptic's Guide to the Cross-National Evidence." International Monetary Fund Seminar Series 2000-11, Washington, DC.

Romer, Paul M. 1990. "Endogenous Technological Change." *Journal of Political Economy* 98: 71–102.

———. 1996. "Why, Indeed, in America? Theory, History, and the Origins of Modern Economic Growth." *American Economic Review* 86 (2): 202–06.

Sachs, Jeffrey, and Andrew Warner. 1995. "Economic Reform and the Process of Global Integration." *Brookings Papers on Economic Activity*, 25th Anniversary Issue, 1–118. Washington, DC: The Brookings Institution.

———. 1997. "Natural Resources and Economic Growth." Revised Version, Harvard Institute for International Development, Cambridge, MA.

———. 2001. "The Curse of Natural Resources." *European Economic Review* 45: 827–38.

Sadie, J. L. 1969. "Chile, Población Económicamente Activa 1930–1975." In *Chile: población económicamente activa, migración, seguridad social, fecundidad, mortalidad, fuentes de datos demográficos*. Serie I, No. 1. Santiago, Chile: Centro Latinoamericano de Demografía.

Safford, Frank. 1976. *The Ideal of the Practical: Colombia's Struggle to Form a Technical Elite*. Austin, TX and London: University of Texas Press.

Sandberg, Lars G. 1979. "The Case of the Impoverished Sophisticated: Human Capital and Swedish Economic Growth before World War I." *The Journal of Economic History* 29 (1): 225–41.

Södersten, B. 1991. "One Hundred Years of Swedish Economy Development." In *Diverging Paths: Comparing a Century of Scandinavian and Latin American Development*, ed. Magnus Blomström and Patricio Meller. Washington, DC: Inter-American Development Bank.

Stern, Scott, Michael E. Porter, and Jeffrey L. Furman. 2000. "The Determinants of National Innovative Capacity." NBER Working Paper 7876, Cambridge, MA.

Stijns, Jean-Philippe. 2005. "Natural Resource Abundance and Economic Growth Revisited. *Resources Policy* 30: 107–30.

Stykolt, Stefan, and Harry C. Eastman. 1960. "A Model of the Study of Protected Oligopolies." *Economic Journal* 70: 336–47.

Villalobos, Sergio R. 1990. *Historia de la Ingeniería en Chile.* Santiago, Chile: Hachette.

Viner, Jacob. 1952. *International Trade and Economic Development.* Glencoe, IL: Free Press.

Watkins, Melville. 1963. "A Staple Theory of Economic Growth." *The Canadian Journal of Economics and Political Science* 29: 141–58.

Will, Robert Milton. 1957. "Some Aspects of the Development of Economic Thought in Chile (ca. 1775–1878)." Unpublished doctoral dissertation, Duke University, Durham, NC.

Wright, Gavin. 1999. "Can a Nation Learn? American Technology as a Network Phenomenon." In *Learning by Doing in Markets, Firms, and Countries,* ed. Naoomi R. Lamoureax, Daniel M.G. Raff, and Peter Temin. Chicago: National Bureau of Economic Research and University of Chicago Press.

Wylie, Peter J. 1990. "Indigenous Technological Adaptation in Canadian Manufacturing, 1900–1929." *Canadian Journal of Economics* 23 (4): 856–72.

Wynia, Gary W. 1990. "Opening Late-Industrializing Economies: Lessons from Argentina and Australia." *Policy Sciences* 23 (3): 185–204.

7

Resource-Based Growth
Past and Present

Gavin Wright and Jesse Czelusta*

RESOURCE-BASED ECONOMIC GROWTH has had a bad press for some time.
Adam Smith wrote the following:

> Projects of mining, instead of replacing the capital employed in
> them, together with the ordinary profits of stock, commonly absorb
> both capital and stock. They are the projects, therefore, to which of
> all others a prudent law-giver, who desired to increase the capital of
> his nation, would least chuse [sic] to give any extraordinary encour-
> agement . . . (1776, 562).

Perhaps abetted by the intuition associating "primary" products with
"primitive" modes of production, coupled with the Ricardian-Malthusian
premise that nonrenewable resources are fated to diminish over time
(since, as gifts of nature, they cannot be replenished), the impression has
been prevalent for at least two centuries that economic progress entails
moving away from natural resources into sectors based on knowledge,
skills, capital, and technology.

Recent studies in development economics seem to add quantitative
rigor to this impression. Richard M. Auty writes, "Since the 1960s the
resource-rich developing countries have underperformed compared with
the resource-deficient economies" (1998, viii). Sachs and Warner (1997)
report that the adverse effect of a natural resource environment on per
capita GDP growth is robust in the face of controls for institutional quality, the share of investment in GDP, changes in relative prices, and other
variables. The inverse association between resource abundance and
growth has been widely accepted as one of the stylized facts of our times
(Auty and Mikesell 1998, 6.) Although dissenting studies (such as Davis

1995) have appeared, recent restatements by Sachs and Warner (2001) and Auty (2001) are virtually unchanged from the original. This "resource curse" hypothesis is often encountered and uncritically accepted in the popular press (see, for example, James Surowiecki's 2001 *New Yorker* article, "The Real Price of Oil").

Can it really be true that less equals more, that, like King Midas, developing countries would be better off with smaller endowments of natural resources? There are good reasons to question whether these reported associations are true structural relationships inherent in resource-based activity. Cross-country regressions are notoriously subject to bias. If countries fail to build productively upon their resource base, then measures of "resource dependence" (such as the share of resources in exports) may serve primarily as proxies for development failure, for any number of reasons having little to do with the resources themselves.[1] When greater care is given to defining and measuring "resource abundance," the purported "curse" results typically disappear.[2]

The literature occasionally recognizes that there are exceptions to the general rule—countries well endowed with minerals whose economies have, in fact, performed successfully in recent decades. If there are prominent exceptions, can it then be true that "the problems of mineral economies [are] inherent to the production function of mining . . ." (Auty 1998, 46)? Since most treatments of the phenomenon culminate sooner or later in a discussion of politics, it would seem that (to quote the same author) "the staple trap is a less deterministic outcome than Sachs assumes and owes more to policy choice" (Auty 1998, 40). What we may have, in other words, is a set of countries whose political structures and institutions have failed to support sustained economic development. One can well imagine that in a setting of fragile institutions and factionalized politics, windfall resource gains may be a mixed blessing. But on this reading, the underlying problems are not inherent in resource-based development, and the successfully managed resource economies surveyed in this chapter are the exceptions that prove this rule.

The chapter highlights several cases of successful resource-based development. The first is historical: the United States from the mid-19th century to the mid-20th. Not only was the United States the world's leading mineral economy in the very historical period during which the country became the world leader in manufacturing (roughly from 1890 to 1910), but linkages and complementarities to the resource sector were vital in the broader story of American economic success. Subsequent sections describe successful modern development of the minerals sector in South American countries, leading up to a more detailed look at the remarkable rejuvenation of minerals in Australia—a country that had earlier consigned the resource-based phase of its development to history. The broad lesson is that what matters for resource-based development is not the inherent character of resources, but the nature of the learning process through which their economic potential is achieved. The main failing of the recent literature is to regard natural resources as "endowments" whose economic essence is fixed by nature. This characterization does not fit U.S. history, and it is no more appropriate for the resource-based economies of today.

The United States as a Resource-Based Economy

According to the figures of Angus Maddison, the United States overtook the United Kingdom in gross domestic product (GDP) per worker-hour as of 1890, and it moved into a decisive position of world productivity leadership by 1913 (Maddison 1991, chapter 2 and table C.11). Perhaps surprisingly, in the same historical phase the United States also overtook the previous world leader in GDP per worker-hour—Australia. In a neglected footnote, Maddison writes, "In defining productivity leadership, I have ignored the special case of Australia, whose impressive achievements before the First World War were due largely to natural resource advantages rather than to technical achievements and the stock of man-made capital" (p. 45, note 1). Resource-based leadership, it seems, is a second-class variety, not to be confused with the real thing.

How unexpected it is, therefore, to find that in 1913 the United States was the world's dominant producer of virtually every one of the major industrial minerals of that era. Here and there a country rivaled the United States in one or another mineral—France in bauxite, for example—but no other nation was remotely close to the United States in the depth and range of its overall mineral abundance. Furthermore, there is reason to believe that the condition of abundant resources was a significant factor in shaping, if not propelling, the U.S. path to world leadership in manufacturing. The coefficient of relative mineral intensity in U.S. manufacturing exports actually increased sharply between 1879 and 1914, the very period in which the country became the manufacturing leader (Wright 1990, 464–68). Cain and Paterson (1986) find a significant materials-using bias in technological change in 9 of 20 U.S. manufacturing industries between 1850 and 1919, including many of the largest and most successful cases. A study of the world steel industry in 1907–09 put the United States on a par with Germany in total factor productivity (15 percent ahead of Britain), but the ratio of horsepower to worker was twice as large in America as in either of the other two contenders (Allen 1979, 919). Resource abundance was evidently a distinguishing feature of the American economy, yet economists do not seem inclined to downgrade U.S. performance on this account.

There are good reasons not to. The American economy may have been resource abundant, but Americans were not renters living passively off of their mineral royalties. Clearly the American economy *made* something of its abundant resources. Nearly all major U.S. manufactured goods were closely linked to the resource economy in one way or another: petroleum products, primary copper, meat and poultry packing, steel works and rolling mills, coal mining, vegetable oils, grain mill products, sawmill products, and so on. The only items not conspicuously resource-oriented were various categories of machinery. Even here, however, some types of machinery (such as farm equipment) serviced the resource economy, while virtually all were beneficiaries in that they were made of American metal. These observations by no means diminish the country's industrial achievement, but they confirm that American industrialization was built upon natural resources.

The Endogeneity of American Mineral Resources

There is a deeper reason to reject the notion that American industrialization should be somehow downgraded because it emerged from a setting of unique resource abundance: on closer examination, the abundance of American mineral resources should not be seen as merely a fortunate natural endowment, but rather as a form of collective learning, a return on large-scale investments in exploration, transportation, geological knowledge, and the technologies of mineral extraction, refining, and utilization. This case is set out in detail by David and Wright (1997), and it may be briefly summarized here.

For one thing, the United States was not always considered minerals-rich. Writing in 1790, Benjamin Franklin (as quoted in Rickard 1932, 2) declared: "Gold and silver are not the produce of North America, which has no mines." (In the 18th century, "mine" referred to an outcropping or deposit of a mineral.) Harvey and Press note that before 1870, Britain was self-sufficient in iron ore, copper, lead, and tin, and "Britain was easily the most important mining nation in the world" (1990, 65). U.S. lead mine production did not surpass that of Britain until the late 1870s. Leadership in coal came even later. Despite a vastly larger area, U.S. coal production did not pass Germany's until 1880, and Britain's only in 1900. Leadership or near-leadership in copper, iron ore, antimony, magnesite, mercury, nickel, silver, and zinc all occurred between 1870 and 1910. Surely this correspondence in timing among so many different minerals cannot have been coincidental.

In direct contrast to the notion of mineral deposits as a nonrenewable "resource endowment" in fixed supply, new deposits were continually discovered, and production of nearly all major minerals continued to rise well into the 20th century—for the country as a whole, if not for every mining area considered separately. To be sure, this growth was to some extent a function of the size of the country and its relatively unexplored condition before the westward migration of the 19th century. But mineral discoveries were not mere byproducts of territorial expansion. Some of the most dramatic production growth occurred not in the Far West but in older parts of the country: copper in Michigan, coal in Pennsylvania and Illinois, and oil in Pennsylvania and Indiana. Many other countries of the world were large, and (as we now know) well endowed with minerals. But no other country exploited its geological potential to the same extent. Using modern geological estimates, David and Wright show that the U.S. share of world mineral production in 1913 was far in excess of its share of world reserves (1997, 205–2). Mineral development was thus an integral part of the broader process of national development.

David and Wright identify the following elements in the rise of the American minerals economy: (i) an accommodating legal environment; (ii) investment in the infrastructure of public knowledge; and (iii) education in mining, minerals, and metallurgy.

U.S. mineral law was novel in that the government claimed no ultimate legal title to the nation's minerals, not even in the public domain. All other mining systems retained the influence of the ancient tradition whereby minerals were the personal property of the lord or ruler, who granted users rights as concessions if he so chose. This liberality was not entirely intentional, but emerged from the collapse of federal leasing efforts in lead mines between 1807 and 1846 and from the de facto nonintervention policy during the great California gold rush that began in 1848. The federal mining laws of 1866, 1870, and 1872 codified what was by then an established tradition of minimal federal engagement: open access for exploration, exclusive rights to mine a specific site upon proof of discovery, and the requirement that the claim be worked at some frequency or be subject to forfeit. Although the fuel minerals coal and oil have received separate treatment in the 20th century, most U.S. mining activity has been governed by the Mining Law of 1872, among the most liberal in the world.

It would be a mistake to view the encouragement to mining as flowing exclusively from a simple well-specified system of rights and incentives, because much of the best U.S. mineral land was transferred into private hands outside of the procedures set down by federal law. Nearly 6 million acres of coal lands were privatized between 1873 and 1906, for example, mostly disguised as farmland. Most of the iron lands of northern Minnesota and Wisconsin were fraudulently acquired under the provisions of the Homestead Act. Nevertheless, whether through official or unofficial procedures, the posture of American legal authority toward mining was permissive and even encouraging well into the 20th century.

This discussion may convey the impression that the rise of U.S. mineral production was primarily an exercise in rapid exhaustion of a nonrenewable resource in a common-property setting. Although elements of such a scenario were sometimes on display during periodic mineral "rushes," resource extraction in the United States was more fundamentally associated with ongoing processes of learning, investment, technological progress, and cost reduction, generating a manyfold expansion rather than depletion of the nation's resource base. A prime illustration is the United

States Geological Survey (USGS). Established in 1879, the USGS was the most ambitious and productive governmental science project of the 19th century. The agency was the successor to numerous state-sponsored surveys and to a number of more narrowly focused federal efforts. It proved to be highly responsive to the concerns of western mining interests, and the practical value of its detailed mineral maps gave the USGS, in turn, a powerful constituency in support of its scientific research. The early 20th-century successes of the USGS in petroleum were instrumental in transforming attitudes within the oil industry toward trained geologists and applied geological science.

The third factor was education. By the late 19th century, the U.S. emerged as the world's leading educator in mining engineering and metallurgy. The early leader was the Columbia School of Mines, opened in 1864; some 20 schools granted degrees in mining by 1890. After a surge in enrollment during the decades bracketing the turn of the 20th century, the University of California at Berkeley became the largest mining college in the world. The most famous American mining engineer, Herbert Hoover—an early graduate of Cal's cross-bay arch-rival, Stanford—maintained that the increasing assignment of trained engineers to positions of combined financial and managerial, as well as technical, responsibility, was a distinctive contributing factor to U.S. leadership in this sector. A manpower survey for military purposes in 1917 identified 7,500 mining engineers in the country, with a remarkably broad range of professional experience, domestic and foreign.

Technology and Increasing Returns: The Case of Copper

The net effect of these developments was that the United States produced far more minerals than one might have expected purely on the basis of geological potential. The case of copper is illustrative and is outlined in David and Wright (1997). Between 1900 and 1914, copper mines in the United States produced more than 10 times as much copper as did the mines of Chile, but this vast differential was not based on superior geological endowment. Figure 7.1 shows that Chilean copper production exceeded that of the United States until the 1880s, and it nearly recovered its relative standing by the 1930s. During the 1880–1920 era of U.S. ascendancy, however, there was no comparison. The rapid growth of U.S. copper production illustrates the ways in which investment and technology can expand a country's resource base, effectively creating new natural resources from an economic standpoint.

The pure native coppers of the Great Lakes region were indeed a remarkable gift of nature, but the capital requirements for profitable exploitation of this potential were immense. Along with the railroads, the copper companies of Michigan pioneered in the organization of the giant integrated business enterprise. Advances in the 1870s and 1880s reflected

Figure 7.1 Copper Mine Production, United States and
Chile, and Real U.S. Price of Copper, 1845–1976

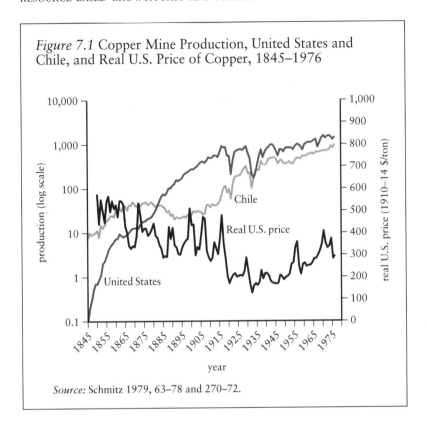

Source: Schmitz 1979, 63–78 and 270–72.

technological developments in drilling and blasting such as the use of
nitroglycerine dynamite and rock-drilling machines powered by com-
pressed air. Steam engines were adapted to hoist ore from the deepest
mines in the country, as well as for use in stamping and other surface operations. Beginning in the 1870s, national totals were augmented by production from newly discovered deposits in Arizona and Montana, but
Michigan copper continued to grow absolutely until the 1920s.

What truly propelled the copper industry into the 20th century was a
revolution in metallurgy, overwhelmingly an American technological
achievement. In the 1880s and 1890s, the major breakthroughs were the
adaptation of the Bessemer process to copper converting and the introduction of electrolysis on a commercial scale for the final refining of copper. These advances made possible a nearly complete recovery of metal
content from the ore. The dramatic new development of the first decade
of the 20th century was the successful application of the Jackling method
of large-scale, nonselective mining using highly mechanized techniques
to remove all material from the mineralized area—waste as well as

metal-bearing ore. Complementary to these techniques—indeed essential to their commercial success—was the use of the oil flotation process in concentrating the ore. Oil floatation called for and made possible extremely fine grinding, which reduced milling losses sufficiently to make exploitation of low-grade "porphyry" coppers commercially feasible.[3]

Together, these technological developments made possible a steady reduction in the average grade of American copper ore, as shown in table 7.1. By contrast, in copper-rich Chile—where output was stagnant—yields (the amount of metal recovered from a given quantity of ore) averaged 10–13 percent between 1890 and 1910 (Przeworski 1980, 26, 183, 197). From these facts alone, one might infer that the United States had simply pressed its internal margin of extraction further than Chile, into higher-cost ores. But figure 7.1 makes it evident that the real price of copper was *declining* during this period, confirming that the fall in yields was an indicator of technological progress. Indeed, the linkage between yield reduction and the expansion of ore reserves was exponential, because of the inverse relationship between the grade of ore and the size of deposits (Lasky 1950). Advances in technology thus led directly to an expansion of American mineral wealth.

Capital requirements and the need for long time horizons made copper an industry for corporate giants, an organizational form in which the United States may also have had a comparative advantage. Large enterprises internalized many of the complementarities and spillovers in copper technology, but they also drew extensively on the national infrastructure of geological knowledge and on the training of mining engineers and metallurgists. Although the initial impact was primarily within U.S. territory,

Table 7.1 Average Yields of Copper Ore (percent)

1800	English	9.27
1850	English	7.84
1870–85	English	6.56
1880	American	3.00
1889	American	3.32
1902	American	2.73
1906	American	2.50
1907	American	2.11
1908	American	2.07
1909	American	1.98
1910	American	1.88
1911–20	American	1.66
1921–30	American	1.53

Sources: David and Wright 1997, using data from W. Y. Elliot et al. 1884, p. 374; Leong et al. 1940.

ultimately these techniques and organizations were transportable internationally, and, by the 1920s, Chile's copper production was on its way back to world leadership, largely through American technology, expertise, and corporate organization.

Historians differ on the reasons for the Chilean lag. In the mid-19th century, the Chilean industry was comparable to, and probably superior to, that of the United States in its technological sophistication. But the supply of high-grade ores began to decline in the 1880s, and, in contrast to the United States, Chile did not respond to this deterioration with either new discoveries or technological adaptation. Political historians stress the lack of national consensus in support of the industry and the predominance of revenue motives in government policy. Economists tend to emphasize the obstacles posed by large, fixed, capital requirements in transportation and other forms of infrastructure, as well as in mining and processing facilities. One might attribute the comparative performance to economies of scale at the national level, since the United States had a much larger territorial area, and American copper benefited from engineering skills, geological knowledge, and transport facilities that were developed to support many other resources besides copper. Scale economies were not independent of the legal and political regime, however; in Chile, for example, the mining code discouraged the consolidation of individual mining claims.[4]

Whatever the precise mixture of explanation, the important point is that Chile's problem was not its mineral endowment but, rather, delay in developing its resource potential. The barriers were real, but large U.S. companies found profitable what the Chileans did not, and investments by Guggenheim and Anaconda after the turn of the century began the long-term reversal of the industry's fortunes. Through massive investments in railroads, roads, steamships, water, and housing, these private firms in effect created their own infrastructure.

Resource-Rich Underachievers

What was true of Chilean copper was also true of other areas of the world that are now known to be richly endowed with mineral resources: Canada, Latin America, Russia, and even Australia—a country whose economic performance has been impugned for its excessive reliance on natural resources. Although European settlement of Latin America was largely motivated by the search for precious metals, the Spanish and Portuguese rulers had little interest in possible spillover benefits from gold and silver mining to broader mineral development. As of 1913, the countries of Latin America had barely made a beginning at exploiting their potential in zinc, lead, bauxite, iron ore, phosphate rock, and petroleum. While contemporaries and historians have found many rationalizations for this pattern of underachievement, the proximate impediment seems to have been a lack of accurate knowledge about the extent and distribution of mineral deposits. A 1913 report by Orville A. Darby, calling attention to enormous undeveloped deposits of high-grade iron ore in Brazil, attracted great interest in that country. Yet, even in the 1930s, experts cautioned that "a belief that South America is a vast reservoir of untouched mineral wealth is wholly illusory" (Bain and Read 1934, 358). Somehow the illusions metamorphosed into real resource endowments within 60 years, as mining investments blossomed throughout Latin America in the 1990s.

Australia was a leading gold-mining country in the 19th century but an underachiever in virtually every other mineral, particularly coal, iron ore, and bauxite, all of which are now known to be abundant. In a nation with a strong mining sector and a cultural heritage similar to that of the United States, why should this have been so?

Here, too, it is easy to identify adverse factors that may have discouraged resource exploitation. The population of Australia has been small relative to its area, and the harsh climate of the large desert areas has discouraged migration from the coast. But similar conditions prevailed in much of the western United States. States such as Arizona, Montana, and Utah are not famous for their gentle climates. Australia did invest in institutions of learning related to mining (such as geological surveys, mining schools, and museums), and indications are that "a viable and independent technological system did develop in the years approximately 1850 to 1914" (Inkster, 1990, 43). Yet Australia lagged well behind other developed countries in engineers per capita (Edelstein, 1988, 14) and was heavily dependent upon foreign science. Into the 1880s, most large Australian mines were managed by Cornishmen, who had much practical experience but were untrained in metallurgy and resistant to new technology. The emerging Australian technological system was distinctly informal, reliant upon outside science, and lacking in scale economies relative to the United States. In the early 20th century, as Britain fell behind in minerals education and research, and as protectionist policies inhibited inflows of knowledge embodied in goods and people, the relative pace of learning in the Australian minerals sector decreased substantially. In a 1977 lecture at the University of Queensland, Raymond J. Stalker, a professor of mechanical engineering, stated that "on the eve of the Second World War, the 'self-image' of Australia was that of a relatively unsophisticated and technologically dependent dominion of the British Empire" (as quoted in Magee 1996).

Above all, what seems to have been missing in Australia was an atmosphere of buoyant expectations about the prospects for major new discoveries. Arguably as a result of the above factors, in conjunction with low mineral prices, by the 1930s Australians had become pessimistic about the possibilities for further expansion of their natural resources. Sinclair (1976, 201) speaks of "a greatly reduced willingness to underwrite a process of development based primarily on the exploitation of natural resources." In parallel with growing concerns in other countries about the extent of natural resource supplies, Australians deemed it prudent to conserve minerals for domestic industries.

Pessimism led to misguided policies and lack of survey effort. In 1938, when Australia had recently begun to export iron ore on a small scale and gave promise of expanding this traffic, the government imposed an embargo on all iron ore shipments in an effort to conserve the remaining supply—effectively raising a barrier to exploration that remained in place for the next 25 years. The policy was justified by a report to the Commonwealth in May 1938: "It is certain that if the known supplies of high grade ore are not conserved Australia will in little more than a generation become an importer rather than a producer of iron ore" (quoted in Blainey 1993, 337). As late as the 1950s, the accepted view was that Australian minerals were fated to diminish over time. A 1951 report stated the following:

We have been utilizing several of our basic metals at an ever-increasing rate and, with the development of many of the so-called backward nations, it appears likely that that rate will not diminish in the future; demand is likely to increase. We have not an unlimited supply of these metals available to us by economic processes as known today, nor is there any indication that sources other than the kind of ore-deposits worked today will become available to us. The capacity for production of some metals cannot be increased indefinitely. . . . Periods of shortage such as we have experienced will recur more frequently (Dunn 1951, 93).

However, when the policy regime changed in the 1960s, lifting the embargo and offering state encouragement to exploration and construction of new ore terminals, a rapid series of new discoveries opened up previously unknown deposits, not only of iron ore but of copper, nickel, bauxite, uranium, phosphate rock, and petroleum. By 1967, proved reserves of high-grade iron ore were already more than 40 times the level of 10 years earlier (Warren 1973, 215).

Before the 1960s, Australians accepted any number of unscientific rationalizations for the absence of important minerals such as petroleum: oil could not be found south of the equator; Australia's rocks were too old to contain oil; the country had been so thoroughly scoured by prospectors that surely nothing valuable could remain to be found. But this very attitude could lead to lethargic and therefore self-confirming search behaviors. Geologist Harry Evans recalled his own classic "rational expectations" reaction when a search party from the Weipa mission on the Cape York Peninsula found extensive outbreaks of bauxite in 1955: "As the journey down the coast revealed miles of bauxite cliffs, I kept thinking that, if all this is bauxite, then there must be something the matter with it; otherwise it would have been discovered and appreciated long ago."

Indeed, there was nothing wrong with it: by 1964 Weipa held about one-quarter of the known potential bauxite in the world (Blainey 1993, 332)

Minerals and Economic Development:
˙ Modern Success Stories

Are mineral resources a sensible basis for economic development in today's world? One must acknowledge that certain things have changed over the past century. The rise of oil-based transportation was the first major crack in the breakup of the huge industrial concentrations that were dominant on the basis of locational economics, such as the "American Manufacturing Belt" in the northeast and midwest. Daniel Yergin portrays World War I as a metaphorical contest between the locomotive and the truck, the rigid technology of the past versus the high-mobility wave of the future (Yergin 1991, chapter 9). The process of geographic dispersion was further advanced by electrification, the chief advantages of which were the speed at which power could be transmitted over long distances and the flexibility with which it could be deployed. Indicators of geographic concentration in manufacturing within the United States show a steady decline since World War II from the peaks of the 1920–40 era, an indicator of underlying tendencies in a setting unconstrained by national boundaries (Kim 1995, figures I and II). With the liberalization of world trade and the decline in world transportation costs, international differences in the costs of industrial inputs such as iron ore and coking coal fell to insignificance by the 1960s. For all of these reasons, industrialization behind the "natural protective barrier of distance" ceased to be a viable strategy for resource-producing countries. On the whole, these trends are favorable from a global perspective, because they have expanded opportunities for successful industrialization in countries with few natural resources on which to build. But does this imply that countries should not develop the resources they do possess?

The operational question is not whether countries should attempt to reinvent themselves as entirely different historical and geographic entities than they are in actuality—such things are not matters of choice. The practical policy issue is whether countries with resource potential should encourage investment, exploration, and research for the purpose of developing that potential to its maximum. Even skeptics about resource-based development concede that policies to restrict exports in order to "conserve" nonrenewable resources have had disastrous consequences (Auty and Mikesell 1998, 47). But such writers continue to base their analysis on the erroneous assumption that "natural resources, in contrast to assets produced by capital and labor, represent an endowment to society" (Auty and Mikesell 1998, 45); or that natural resource industries, "which rely on exhaustible factors of production, cannot expand at the same rate as other industries" (Rodriguez and Sachs 1999, 278).

In reality, so-called natural resources require extensive investments before they are valuable—perhaps more so today than in the past—and the required investments include not just physical capital and transportation, but also the acquisition of knowledge about the resource base and the development of technologies that increase the value of that resource base. The fact that "information" can be disseminated costlessly and instantaneously around the world by no means implies that location-specific knowledge is no longer valuable. If anything, the opposite is true. Because extending the "knowledge frontier" can extend a country's effective resource base, it is entirely possible for resource sectors to lead an economy's growth for extended periods of time.

To be sure, there are risks associated with resource-based growth. Sudden windfalls or unexpected "natural resource booms" may disrupt otherwise healthy industries, calling for a level of policy restraint that may be difficult to achieve. Still worse, resource booms that channel profits directly to the state may constitute irresistible temptations for corruption and rent-seeking activity. It may even be, as Ascher (1999) has argued, that resource sectors are peculiarly vulnerable to such policy failures. The essence of the policy failures described by Ascher, however, is not excessive expansion of resource-based activity, but political interference with incentives to develop these resources more fully. At times of fiscal crisis, cash-poor governments in both Mexico and República Bolivariana de Venezuela chose to raid the investment budgets of the state-owned oil companies, crippling development programs for a decade if not longer (Ascher 1999, chapter 6). Statistical analysis of such episodes may tell us much about the pitfalls of resource management, but they do not justify a conclusion that resource development itself is mistaken as a national policy. By pointing instead to the successes of well-managed resource-based regimes, we can illustrate what is possible in today's world.

Latin America

Having neglected their resources for generations, and having stifled incipient expansion in more recent decades through misguided state policies, many Latin American countries turned the corner in the 1990s. The turnaround was fostered by reforms encouraging foreign investment in mining and increasing the security of mining investments—sometimes including privatization of mining companies, but also with strong roles for state geological agencies (World Bank 1996). Latin America is now the world's fastest-growing mining region, well ahead of Africa, Australia, Canada, and the United States in its share of spending on exploration (Project Survey 2002, 29). The business press regularly reports new discoveries, new investment projects to develop existing deposits, and new technological developments that extend the mining potential of particular areas. The leaders in this burgeoning new minerals growth are Chile, Peru, and Brazil. Argentina has yet to experience major minerals success, but maintains a high level of exploration activity, knowing that "the country as a whole is underexplored compared to its neighbors" (Exploration in South America 2001, 289).

Chile   During the 1990s, the Chilean economy grew at a remarkable 8.5 percent per year. The mining industry has been central to this growth, accounting for 8.5 percent of GDP and 47 percent of all exports during the decade. Copper is still Chile's most important mineral; Chilean mined copper accounted for 35 percent of world production and 40.5 percent of Chile's export earnings in 2000. Chile also produces and exports substantial quantities of potassium nitrate, sodium nitrate, lithium, iodine, and molybdenum.

The *Engineering and Mining Journal* notes that "investment plans are . . . coming into the pipeline at a higher-than-average rate in Chile"; planned mine projects rose to $10.7 billion in 2001 (January 2002, 29–30). As the *Engineering and Mining Journal* comments "Without successful exploration, many such projects would not have come to fruition." The state mineral development company (Codelco) has been very active in exploration activity. Typical reported projects include $7 million "to continue delineating the Gaby Sur porphyry copper deposit located in Region II"; "Codelco plans to spend $20 million during 2001 quantifying reserves at the Mina project in the north"; "Codelco was also active in a number of exploration joint ventures"; "Codelco is in talks to form a partnership with Ventanas, the copper smelter and refinery complex owned by another state body, Enami" (Chadwick 2001, 234). The relationship between ore grade and reserve quantity is illustrated by reports such as the one stating that "estimated resources at Escondida, which include resources used to define ore reserves, have increased significantly due to the release for the first time of low grade ore, which is below the current concentrator cut-off grade but above the *economic* cut-off grade" (Chadwick 2001, 234). Investments in exploration and processing continue to expand for an array of other minerals, even as production of almost every Chilean mineral continues to rise. In early 2002, Couer d'Alene Mines Corp. announced the discovery of high-grade gold and silver deposits on its Cerro Bayo property in southern Chile but noted that "only a small portion of the Cerro Bayo property has been explored" (Coeur Discovers More Gold at Cerro Bay 2002, 15).

Peru   Peruvian mining is considered the region's "greatest success story." After the privatization program started in 1992, mining exports doubled to $3.01 billion by 1999. As of the end of 2001, Peru ranked second in the world in production of silver and tin, fourth in zinc and lead, seventh in copper, and eighth in gold. As reported in *Mining Magazine*, "There is a determination that the mining sector should play an even larger role in the economy and a number of legal instruments are now in place aimed at promoting foreign investment. . . . As mining regimes go, Peru's can be fairly described as possessing an enabling environment" (Chadwick 2001, 234). The president of Codelco, Juan Villarzu, "liken(s) the country to Chile in the early 1990s" (Exploration 2002, 12). That present development is far below potential is confirmed by such reports as: "Iscaycruz is one of the world's highest-grade zinc mines, but at present operates on only 1,000 ha of the 52,000 ha it holds in concessions" (Chadwick 2002, 234).

Yet Peru appears to be on its way to reaching this potential. For instance, "Roque Benavides, chief executive of Compania de Minas Buenaventura, . . . is forecasting that by 2008, output will have climbed to 1.38 Mt for copper, 1.16 Mt for zinc, and 146 Mt for gold" (Potts 2002, 6); these figures represent increases relative to 2000 of 145, 28, and 11 percent, respectively. (Note that this prediction was made before the Barrick gold discovery, discussed later). A $3.2 billion project that began production at Antamina in 2001 is expected to yield 675 million pounds of copper over the first 10 years (Yernberg 2001, 21). In Yanacocha, "exploration efforts (by Minera Yanacocha, Latin America's largest gold producer) indicated major copper sulfide deposits under the gold deposits . . . Yanacocha may someday become a major copper producer in addition to gold" (Yernberg 2001, 21). In May of 2002, Barrick Gold Corp. announced the discovery of an estimated 3.5 million ounces of gold at its Alta Chicama property in southern Peru (*Skillings Mining Review* 2002, 8). Substantial investments in mineral processing facilities are also underway (Yernberg 2001, 21).

Brazil Brazil is the leading industrial nation of the region, though the share of the mining sector is low relative to its neighbors. Following an intensive government investment program in prospecting, exploration, and basic geologic research (highlighted by the Radar Survey of the Amazon Region Project), mineral production grew at more than 10 percent per year in the 1980s. Exploration was interrupted between 1988 and 1994, because of restrictions imposed by the Constitution of 1988 on foreign participation in mining. These restrictions were lifted in 1995, and the government mining company (Compania Vale de Rio Doce) was privatized in 1997 (USGS 1999). Mineral exploration activities expanded significantly in the 1990s, increasing both production and Brazil's reserves of most minerals. Currently, Brazil produces more than 60 mineral commodities and is the world's largest exporter of iron ore.

At present, Brazil has only one copper mine and imports substantial amounts of copper. Because of a number of major discoveries in the Carajas region in Para State, however, Brazil expects "to occupy a prominent

position in world copper production beginning in the period 2003–2005"
(Exploration in South America 2001, 289). Production capacity for bauxite, which has already risen dramatically over the past two decades, is
expected to increase further, with Brazil's largest bauxite producer plan-
ning to finish a $200 million expansion by the end of 2002 (Industry
Newswatch 2002, 10).

Botswana

In 1963, the USGS *Minerals Yearbook* joint entry for the British protec-
torates of Swaziland, Bechuanaland (now Botswana), and Basutoland
(now Lesotho) paints a geologic picture that is somewhat surprising given
subsequent history. Of the three, the mineral sector of Swaziland was the
most developed and appeared to have the best future prospects:

SWAZILAND: Mineral industry has had a major role in the Swaziland economy for many years and is becoming increasingly important. In 1961 the industry contributed 40 percent of the total value
of exports, and by 1965 its contribution may be of the order of 50
percent. Mineral exports were valued at R4.1 million in 1963 and in
1959–63 averaged R4.8 million with no sharp fluctuations from
year to year. While some 10 minerals generally were mined during
the period, asbestos each year contributed more than 90 percent of
total value. Large-scale iron mining to begin in 1964 is expected to
increase the value of the Swaziland mineral exports by 100 percent
(USGS 1963, 857).

The depiction of Bechuanaland, while hopeful, is less certain:

BECHUANALAND: Considerable mineral exploration by large
companies was in progress in Bechuanaland in 1963, but as for several previous years, production was limited to chrysotile asbestos,
manganese ore, and gold with minor associated silver. Mineral
exports were valued at R368,397, of which asbestos contributed
59.4 percent and manganese ore 39.6 percent. Gold and silver
exports amounted to 142 ounces and 21 ounces. The 1963 export
value compares with R616,129 in 1961, when minerals contributed
about 10 percent of the total value of exports (USGS 1963, 856).

Notably, Basutoland is the only country of the three that, at the time,
produced diamonds, a supposed "high-rent" commodity:

BASUTOLAND: Mineral surveys conducted in recent years (by
DeBeers and Mr. Jack Scott) in this mountainous territory have
resulted in discovery both of diamonds and of kimberlite rock from

which diamonds derive. No other economic minerals have been found in workable deposits. Recorded exports of Basutoland diamonds were 5,110 carats valued at R153,423 (USGS 1963, 855).

These assessments were made just a few years before independence in each country. Today, this picture is distinctly inverted. Swaziland and Lesotho have largely become dependents of South Africa, with each nation growing more slowly than Botswana and mining as an economic activity dwindling in both countries. Meanwhile, Botswana has become a relatively stable, thriving economy, noted for its "good institutions" (Acemoglu, Johnson, and Robinson 2003, 88) and rapid growth. Minerals, especially diamonds, have been the major engine of this growth, with mining accounting for 36 percent of GDP and 70–80 percent of exports in 2003 (Central Intelligence Agency 2005).

One might argue that Swaziland's minerals sector had peaked in the 1960s, and that impending declines in demand for asbestos sealed its fate. Yet asbestos was important in both Swaziland and Botswana, both countries were producers of other minerals, and exploration was ongoing in both countries. Botswana's advantage may have been its larger land area. According to a "resource curse" interpretation, however, the sum of these factors should have favored Swaziland, not Botswana. Likewise, the fact that Lesotho did not develop its minerals sector to the same degree as Botswana should have augmented its long-run growth. Almost four decades later, however, Botswana has far surpassed Swaziland and Lesotho with respect to per capita GDP and the state of its institutions.

As Good (2003) highlights, Botswana is not free from repression or civic strife. Still, "there is almost complete agreement that Botswana achieved this spectacular growth performance because it adopted good policies" (Acemoglu, Johnson, and Robinson 2003, 83). Less certainty exists, however, with respect to the role played by minerals in the economic success of Botswana. Acemoglu, Johnson, and Robinson note at the outset that Botswana's growth is a puzzle in light of the fact that "in many other countries, natural-resource abundance appears to be a curse rather than a blessing," and ask "how did Botswana do it?" (2003, 83). Some pages later, the authors appear to have dismissed the notion of an institutional "resource curse": "by the time the diamonds came on stream, the country had already started to build a relatively democratic polity and efficient institutions. The surge of wealth likely reinforced this" (Acemoglu, Johnson, and Robinson 2003, 105). Such a treatment suggests but does not make explicit the idea that path dependence, along with associated positive and negative feedback loops, should be a consideration in theories of institutions and resources.

In addition, this interpretation might be augmented by attention to at least two crucial aspects of Botswanan resource abundance. First, as evidenced by its large land area and the significant exploration that had been conducted by the time of Botswana's independence, economic actors must have guessed that Botswana's resource base was potentially quite large, even if the magnitude of kimberlitic diamond deposits was unknown. Botswana already produced the other minerals noted earlier as of 1966, and DeBeers had begun prospecting for diamonds after a small discovery in 1955 (Jefferis 1998, 301). The case of Botswana thus poses an even deeper puzzle for institutional "resource curse" advocates, since political players knew of Botswana's minerals potential even before postindependence institutions were established. Second, Botswana's resource abundance was as much an effect as a cause of institutions. Although Botswanan mineral rights belong to the government, private companies made many of the investments needed to locate and develop mineral deposits. These investments took place in the context of relatively stable property rights. Thus, the story of Botswana's remarkable growth has at its center a virtuous cycle in which resource abundance and institutions are complementary.

Minerals did not always have a large presence, as Modise notes:

It is often believed that minerals have been a feature of Botswana's development right from independence in 1966. This is not true, however. Mineral development was in fact phased over a number of years, the first few years being largely insignificant. (2003, 79)

In contrast to the notion that resources represent "booms" or "windfalls," expansion of the minerals sector in Botswana has been incremental and steady. The Botswanan minerals sector has grown both as a percentage of GDP—from 12.3 percent in 1975–76 (derived from Modise 2003, table 5.1) to 36 percent in 2003—and in absolute terms, with production of diamonds increasing from 2.36 million carats in 1976 to 30.4 millions carats in 2003 (USGS 2003). Notably, this growth does not appear to have occurred at the expense of other sectors.

Despite earlier predictions that Botswana's diamond sector had peaked (see, for instance, Jefferis 1998, 315), Botswana's production of diamonds has continued to grow. In addition, there is no evidence that this trend will soon be reversed. As the USGS *Minerals Yearbook 2003* notes:

Revenues from diamond mining and cutting are expected to continue to be the mainstay of the economy for the foreseeable future; Debswana's (the joint venture of DeBeers and the Botswanan government that controls diamond exploration and production) identified diamond resources will be sufficient to maintain 2003 production levels for at least 25 to 30 years. . . . The country's favorable geologic environment, mineral investment climate, low tax rates, and political stability are expected to continue to make Botswana a target for foreign mineral investment. Exploration was ongoing for diamond and base and precious metals (Coakley 2003, 5.2)

Botswana stands out as a modern example of an underdeveloped country growing on a sustainable basis through development of its minerals potential.

Australia

The most striking success story is Australia. Beginning in the 1960s, Australia witnessed a simultaneous resurgence of successful minerals search and economic growth. Figure 7.2 showcases a few of the dramatic increases in Australian minerals production that have occurred in recent decades. Contrary to earlier fears, increased production has not diminished mineral reserves. From 1989 to 1999, Australian mineral reserves expanded alongside production for 22 out of 32 minerals and for all but one (bauxite) of the seven major minerals in figure 7.2. As the *Mining Journal* reports,

> There have been 136 gold discoveries since 1970. . . . In other mineral sectors and against a background of difficult commodity prices, (more) recent Australian successes include an entirely new mineral sands province, the Murray Basin; the development of lateritic nickel deposits such as Murrin Murrin, Cawse and Bulong, and sulphide nickel deposits such as Black Swan, Cosmos and RAV 8; and major zinc and copper discoveries such as Century, Cannington, and Ernst Henry (April 5, 2002, 244).

Expansion of gold has been especially rapid after 1975, making Australia (after South Africa) the second-leading producer in the world, as the yellow metal has become the country's third-largest commodity export. Gold reserves were extended by intensive use of exploration geochemistry, while the frontier of economically viable yields was steadily lowered by innovations in gold-processing technologies, specifically carbon-based gold extraction methods that allowed commercial treatment of low-grade ores (Huleatt and Jaques 2005, 30–34).

The case of Australia demonstrates that expansion of a country's minerals base can go hand-in-hand with economic growth *and* technological progress. The Australian minerals sector's share of GDP expanded through the mid-1980s as Australia reversed more than a century of relatively slow GDP growth in reaching its current rank as the sixth-wealthiest country. The surge in production of mineral inputs has carried a number of new and old industries along in its wake. In the decades following the onset of Australia's most recent minerals boom, leading manufacturing industries had obvious connections to minerals: metal and steel products, autos, industrial equipment, petroleum products, ships, and chemicals.

The Australian minerals sector is knowledge-intensive. In the past 10 years, income from Australian intellectual property in mining has grown

Figure 7.2 Australian Mine Production, Selected Minerals, 1844–1998

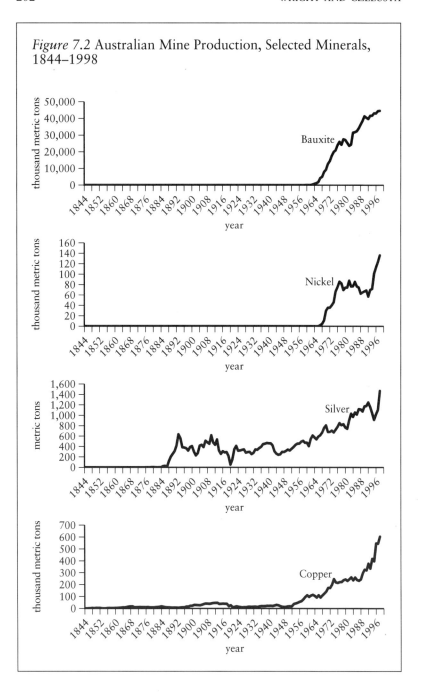

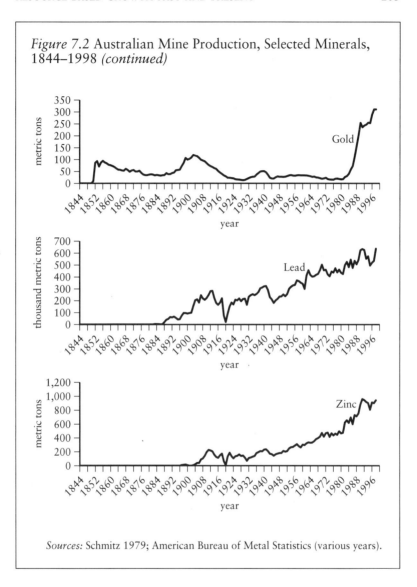

Figure 7.2 Australian Mine Production, Selected Minerals, 1844–1998 *(continued)*

Sources: Schmitz 1979; American Bureau of Metal Statistics (various years).

from $40 million a year to $1.9 billion a year, a larger sum than that earned by the wine export industry. Research and Development (R&D) expenditures by the mining sector accounted for almost 20 percent of R&D expenditure by all industries in 1995–96, a disproportionate contribution relative to the sector's share of GDP. The mining sector's contributions to Australia's human capital are also relatively large. From July to September 1996, the mining sector spent an average of $896 per employee on training, while the average for all industries was $185; over the same period, the proportion of payroll spent on training was 5.8 percent for mining and 2.5 percent for all industries (Stoeckel 1999, 17–18).

As Australia's mineral production has flourished since the abandonment of the passive conservation policies of the 1930s, the country has emerged as one of the world's leaders in mineral exploration and development technology. "Australia leads the world in mining software and now supplies 60 to 70 percent of mining software worldwide" (Stoeckel 1999, 25). Australia's unique geology calls for unique science; for example, World Geoscience, an Australian company, is a leader in the development of airborne geophysical survey techniques. Industry leaders have put forward an ambitious technological vision known as the "glass Earth project," a complex of six new technologies that would allow analysts to peer into the top kilometer of the earth's crust to locate valuable mineral deposits. One executive stated: "The discovery of another Mt. Isa or Broken Hill—and we think they are out there—would lift us to fifth [place in the world]" (Cave 2001). Yet many of the technologies coming out of Australia's particular geological conditions find applications in other parts of the world, and "Australian mining companies search the world for minerals, (with) the bigger Australian companies now spending 30–40 percent of their exploration budgets offshore" (Stoeckel 1999, 31).

As environmental concerns increase, Australians also see promising opportunities to market the country's know-how and technology in cleaning up air, water, and soil; recycling waste; and eliminating pollution. According to the CEO of an environmental-industry "venture catalyst," "It is lovely that the environment benefits, but I'm really more interested in the business case and how it either saves costs or generates revenue. This field isn't recognized as a sector yet and Australia is well placed to take up a leading position" (Cave 2001).

The Development Potential of Minerals

Economists have known for some time that Harold Hotelling's theoretical prediction that the scarcity and relative prices of nonrenewable resources would rise inexorably over time has not been borne out by the facts of history. Jeffrey Krautkraemer's recent comprehensive survey of the evidence reaches the following conclusions:

> For the most part, the implications of this basic Hotelling model have not been consistent with empirical studies of nonrenewable resource prices and in situ values. There has not been a persistent increase in nonrenewable resource prices over the past 125 years. . . . Economic indicators of nonrenewable resource scarcity do not provide evidence that nonrenewable resources are becoming significantly more scarce.

Instead, they suggest that other factors of nonrenewable resource supply, particularly the discovery of new deposits, technological progress in extraction technology, and the development of resource substitutes, have mitigated the scarcity effect of depleting existing deposits (1998, 2066, 2091).

Krautkraemer's analysis, like most economic writing on this subject, is conducted at the level of the entire market for a commodity, which is to say the world as a whole. Although this may be appropriate for testing the Hotelling thesis, these conclusions leave open the possibility that the specter of depletion has only been staved off at the global level, that is, in large part through the opening up of new or previously underexplored territories. What has not been appreciated is that the process of ongoing renewal of nonrenewable resources has operated within individual countries as well as across continents.

Table 7.2 displays average annual growth rates of mine production for eight major minerals in six relatively well-managed mineral-producing nations. The strong positive growth rates for the world as a whole reinforce Krautkraemer's point. Equally striking, however, is the vigorous production growth of nearly every mineral in nearly every country. The one notable exception (among the minerals displayed in table 7.2) is lead mining, for which production has declined in the world as a whole. This decline is presumably related to lead's unique position as a recyclable: two-thirds of consumption consists of scrap recovery, thus reducing demand for the newly mined mineral. For a true mineral-economic success story like Australia's, however, production growth has continued for every one of the minerals on the list, lead included. For the group taken as a whole, it is remarkable that

Table 7.2 Average Annual Percentage Growth Rates of Mine Production for Selected Mineral/Country Pairs, 1978–2001

	Australia	Brazil	Canada	Chile	Mexico	Peru	World
Bauxite	3.41	7.72	—	—	—	—	2.18
Cobalt	5.30	—	6.43	—	—	—	0.20
Copper	5.77	16.89	−0.22	6.93	9.02	1.96	2.91
Gold	14.04	4.45	5.14	9.49	9.02	16.39	2.38
Lead	2.08	−6.32	−3.54	−0.67	−0.63	1.83	−1.09
Nickel	3.03	8.93	1.69	—	—	—	2.61
Silver	3.73	5.47	1.03	8.12	2.16	2.90	2.55
Zinc	4.17	2.98	−0.62	13.17	2.63	2.96	1.08

Sources: USGS, *Minerals Yearbook* (selected years from 1978 to 2001).
Note: Growth rates are coefficients from a semi-log trend regression. Brazilian copper production in 1979 set equal to that of 1978 (100 metric tons).
— = not available.

production has expanded country-by-country across a 20-year period during which real minerals prices drifted steadily downward.

The error in most of the "resource-curse" literature is not just the assumption that nonrenewables are fixed in quantity and therefore cannot grow, but also the failure to differentiate between demand-side fluctuations and the determinants of long-run supply. Typical titles feature keywords such as "windfall" or "boom," and the analysis concerns itself with optimal resource allocation in the presence of (to cite one recent work) "mineral deposits that could reasonably be expected to run out in the not too distant future" (Hannesson 2001, 6). Despite its hopeful title (*Investing for Sustainability: The Management of Mineral Wealth*), Hannesson's book presents time graphs of mineral revenues (in various countries and in Alaska) that do not separate price from quantity effects, and thus convey a misleading impression that the declines since the 1970s are associated with resource exhaustion. The book never considers the possibility that a country's resource base might be extended by investments in knowledge and relevant technology.

Many economists are aware of the global historical evidence but remain in the grip of the intuition that because minerals are nonrenewable, eventually they must grow scarcer; these forms of advance serve only to "mitigate" the Hotelling forecast, so that "finite availability . . . has not *yet* led to increasing economic scarcity of nonrenewable resources" (Krautkraemer 1998, 2103, emphasis added). But if examples of successful country-specific mineral development are so numerous, the question arises whether common underlying processes in such countries may exist, and this possibility, in turn, leads to reconsideration of the sustainability of nonrenewable resources as a base for economic development.

We are not qualified to make pronouncements about the geographical distribution of minerals in the earth's crust, much less within particular countries. But a cursory reading of the geological literature on mineral stocks convinces us that most geologists would not be surprised by the patterns we have described. DeVerle P. Harris, for example, notes in a recent survey article that "ore deposits of a specific kind, for example, massive sulfide copper, are created from common crustal material by earth processes that are characteristic of that deposit type. Consequently, such deposits exhibit some common characteristics irrespective of where they occur, for example, in the African or North American continents" (1993, 1035).

Among these characteristics are deposit size, average grade, intra-deposit grade variation and depth to deposit. Mapping the statistical properties of these distributions is now the object of sophisticated, large-scale computer modeling, such as the Minerals Availability System of the U.S. Bureau of Mines. The broad picture that emerges from such investigations is that the underlying elasticities of mineral supply are very high with respect to any number of physical and economic margins. The more that is learned about the effects of deposit features on "discoverability," and the information gain that occurs from continued exploration within regions, the more it is evident that the potential for expansion of the resource base—the economically meaningful concept of mineral-resource endowment—is vast if not unlimited.

From the standpoint of development policy, a crucial aspect of the process is the role of country-specific knowledge. Although the deep scientific bases for progress in minerals are undoubtedly global, it is in the nature of geology that location-specific knowledge continues to be important. Sometimes this has to do with unique features of the terrain, affecting the challenge of extraction. At other times, heterogeneity in the mineral itself calls for country-specific investments in the technologies of manufacture and consumption. The petroleum industries of Norway and República Bolivariana de Venezuela, respectively, provide examples of these two possibilities. More generally, in virtually all of the countries we have examined, the public-good aspects of the infrastructure of geologic knowledge have justified state-sponsored or subsidized exploration activities, often with significant payoffs to provincial or national economies.

Perhaps the clearest recent example of the importance of country-specific knowledge comes from the United States, a country that has extracted more minerals for a longer time period than any other nation on earth, and yet it is still among the world's mining leaders. Tilton and Landsberg (1999) recount the technological breakthroughs that served to revive American copper mining in the 1980s and 1990s, after it had been pronounced dead by observers in the mid-1980s. The primary vehicle was not new discoveries and newly opened mines, but development and application of the solvent extraction-electrowinnowing (SX-EW) process, which separates the mineral from the ore more effectively and is especially useful for the leaching of mine dumps from past operations. Although this technology will ultimately become global, its near-term impact has been most significant in countries like the United States, which have substantial accumulated waste piles of oxide copper minerals and where copper deposits are located largely in arid regions. The SX-EW process is also best suited for countries with stringent environmental regulations, which require recovery of sulfur emissions from smelting operations, thus providing a low-cost source of sulfuric acid for the SX-EW process. Thus, there is a symbiotic relationship between the new SX-EW process and traditional technology (Tilton and Landsberg 1999, 131).

Conclusion

This chapter argues that the mineral abundance of the United States was an endogenous historical phenomenon, a forerunner for the many modern examples of successful resource-based growth. Contrary to long-entrenched intuition, so-called nonrenewables can be progressively extended through exploration, technological progress, and investments in appropriate knowledge. We suggest that such processes operate within countries as well as for the world as a whole. The countries we have reviewed are by no means representative, but they are far from homogeneous, and together they refute the allegation that resource-based development is "cursed."

The resource price escalation of the 1970s did indeed constitute an exogenous unanticipated windfall boom from the perspective of many minerals-based economies. It is obvious in retrospect that those boom times were destined to end, and perhaps one can make the case that even in the midst of those turbulent times, countries should have been more aware of the ephemeral character of the boom and planned accordingly. Without doubt, many countries made poor use of these one-time gains. Nothing in this chapter offers any guarantees against corruption, rent-seeking, and mismanagement of mineral and other natural resources. Our point is, however, that the experience of the 1970s stands in marked contrast to the 1990s, when mineral production steadily expanded primarily as a result of purposeful exploration and ongoing advances in the technologies of search, extraction, refining, and utilization—in other words, by a process of learning. It would be a major error to take the decade of the 1970s as the prototype for minerals-based development.

To state the obvious, we have no way of knowing ex ante whether all of the major minerals-based economies have comparable potential. But surely investing in such knowledge should be seen as a legitimate component of a forward-looking economic development program. The danger of the resource-curse thesis is that countries may be discouraged from pursuing this reasonable and potentially fruitful avenue for economic progress.

Notes

*For helpful advice on earlier drafts, the authors thank Kenneth Arrow, Paul David, Lawrence Goulder, Stephen Haber, Gary Libecap, William Maloney, and Jeffrey Vincent.

1. Parts of this essay first appeared as "The Myth of the Resource Curse," *Challenge* 47 (March/April 2004): 6–38.

2. See particularly Stijns (2005).

3. This account of copper technology draws upon Parsons (1933), Schmitz (1986, 403–5), and Lankton (1991, chapters 2–4).

4. Accounts of the contrasting histories of the Chilean and U.S. copper industries include Przeworksi (1980) and Culver and Reinhart (1985, 1989).

References

Acemoglu, D., S. Johnson, and J. A. Robinson. 2003. "An African Success Story." In *In Search of Prosperity*, ed. D. Rodrik. Princeton, NJ: Princeton University Press, 80–119.

Allen, Robert. 1979. "International Competition in Iron and Steel, 1850–1913." *Journal of Economic History* 39: 911–37.

American Bureau of Metal Statistics. (various years). *Non-Ferrous Metal Yearbook*.

Ascher, William. 1999. *Why Governments Waste Natural Resources*. Baltimore, MD: Johns Hopkins University Press.

Auty, Richard M. 1998. *Resource Abundance and Economic Development*. World Institute for Development Economics Research. New York: Oxford University Press.

———. 2001. "The Political Economy of Resource-Driven Growth." *European Economic Review* 45: 839–946.

Auty, Richard M., and Raymond F. Mikesell. 1998. *Sustainable Development in Mineral Economies*. Oxford: Clarendon Press.

Bain, H. F., and T. T. Read. 1934. *Ores and Industry in South America*. New York: Harper & Brothers.

Blainey, Geoffrey. 1993. *The Rush That Never Ended: A History of Australian Mining*, 4th ed. Melbourne, Australia: Melbourne University Press.

Cain, Louis P., and Donald G. Paterson. 1986. "Biased Technical Change: Scale and Factor Substitution in American Industry, 1850–1919." *Journal of Economic History* 41: 153–64.

Cave, Michael. 2001. "Technology: How Well Australia Performs." *Australian Financial Review* (March).

Central Intelligence Agency. 2005. *The World Factbook 2005*. Washington, DC. http://www.cia.gov/cia/publications/factbook/.

Chadwick, John. 2001. "Andean Action." *Mining Magazine* (May): 234.

Coakley, George J. 2003. "The Mineral Industry of Botswana." In *USGS Minerals Yearbook*. Reston, VA: United States Geological Survey, 5.1–5.4.

Culver, W. W., and C. J. Reinhart. 1985. "The Decline of a Mining Region and Mining Policy: Chilean Copper in the Nineteenth Century." In *Miners and Mining in the Nineteenth Century*, ed. T. Greaves and W. Culver. Manchester, United Kingdom: Manchester University Press.

———. 1989. "Capitalist Dreams: Chile's Response to Nineteenth Century World Copper Competition." *Comparative Studies in Society and History* 31: 722–44.

David, Paul A., and Gavin Wright. 1997. "The Genesis of American Resource Abundance." *Industrial and Corporate Change* 6: 203–45.

Davis, Graham A. 1995. "Learning to Love the Dutch Disease: Evidence from the Mineral Economies." *World Development* 23: 1765–79.

Dunn, J. A. 1951. "The Base Metals in Australia." In *The Australian Mineral Industry: Economic Notes and Statistics*, vol. 4. Melbourne, Australia: Australian Bureau of Mineral Resources, Geology, and Geophysics.

Edelstein, Michael. 1988. "Professional Engineers in Australia: Institutional Response in a Developing Economy, 1860–1980." *Australian Economic History Review* 28(2) (September): 8–32.

Elliott, William Yandell, Elizabeth S. May, J. W. F. Rowe, Alex Skelton, and Donald H. Wallace. 1937. *International Control in the Non-Ferrous Metals*. New York: Macmillan.

"Exploration in South America." 2001. *Mining Journal* (April 20): 289.

Good, K. 2003. "Bushmen and Diamonds: (Un)civil Society in Botswana." Nordiska Afrikainstitutet Discussion Paper 23.

Hanneson, Rögnvaldur. 2001. *Investing for Sustainability: The Management of Mineral Wealth*. Boston: Kluwer Academic.

Harris, DeVerle P. 1993. "Mineral Resource Stocks and Information." In *Handbook of Natural Resource and Energy Economics*, Vol. 3, ed. Allen V. Kneese and James L. Sweeney. Amsterdam: North-Holland.

Harvey, C., and J. Press. 1990. *International Competition and Industrial Change: Essays in the History of Mining and Metallurgy, 1800–1950*. London: Frank Cass.

Huleatt, M. B., and A. L. Jaques. 2005. "Australian Gold Exploration 1976–2003." *Resources Policy* 30: 29–37.

"Industry Newswatch: Brazilian Bauxite Producer Expands Capacity." 2002. *Mining Engineering* 54, no. 3 (March): 10.

Inkster, Ian. 1990. "Intellectual Dependency and the Sources of Invention: Britain and the Australian Technological System in the Nineteenth Century." In *History of Technology*, Vol. 12, ed. Graham Hollister-Short and Frank A. J. L. James. London and New York: Mansell.

Jefferis, K. 1998. "Botswana and Diamond-Dependent Development." In *Botswana: Politics and Society*, ed. W. Edget and M. Lekorwe, 300–18. Pretoria: J. L. van Schaik Publishers.

Kim, Sukkoo. 1995. "Expansion of Markets and the Geographic Distribution of Economic Activities." *Quarterly Journal of Economics* 110: 881–908.

Krautkraemer, Jeffrey A. 1998. "Nonrenewable Resource Scarcity." *Journal of Economic Literature* 36 (December 1998): 2065–107.

Lankton, L. 1991. *Cradle to Grave: Life, Work, and Death at the Lake Superior Copper Mines*. New York: Oxford University Press.

Lasky, S.G. 1950. "How Tonnage and Grade Relations Help Predict Ore Reserves." *Engineering and Mining Journal* 151: 81–85.

Leong, Y.S., Emil Erdreich, J. C. Burritt, O. E. Kiessling, C. E. Nighman, and George C. Heikes. 1940. "Technology, Employment, and Output per Man in Copper Mining." Works Project Administration National Research Project E-12. Philadelphia.

Maddison, Angus. 1991. *Dynamic Forces in Capitalist Development*. New York: Oxford University Press.

Magee, Gary B. 1996. "Patenting and the Supply of Inventive Ideas in Colonial Australia: Evidence from Victorian Patent Data." *Australian Economic History Review* 36, no. 2 (September): 30–58.

Modise, M. D. 2003. "Managing Mineral Revenues in Botswana." In *Development Policies in Natural Resource Economies*, ed. J. Mayer, B. Chambers, and A. Faroq. Cheltenham, United Kingdom: Edward Elgar, 78–97.

Parsons, G. W. 1933. *The Porphyry Coppers*. New York: American Institute of Mining and Metallurgical Engineers.

Potts, Adrianna. 2002. "Peru's Comeback." *Mining Magazine* (January): 6.

"Project Survey." 2002. *Engineering and Mining Journal*. 203 (January): 28–39.

Przeworski, J. F. 1980. *The Decline of the Copper Industry in Chile and the Entry of North American Capital*. New York: Arno Press.

Rickard, T. A. 1932. *A History of American Mining*. New York: McGraw Hill.

Rodriguez, Francisco, and Jeffrey D. Sachs. 1999. "Why Do Resource-Abundant Economies Grow More Slowly?" *Journal of Economic Growth* 4: 277–303.

Sachs, Jeffrey D., and Andrew M. Warner. 1995. "Natural Resources and Economic Growth." Discussion Paper 517a. Harvard Institute for International Development, Cambridge, MA.

———. 1997. "Natural Resource Abundance and Economic Growth," revised from 1995. NBER Working Paper 5398. National Bureau of Economic Research, Cambridge, MA.

———. 1999. "The Big Push, Natural Resource Booms, and Growth." *Journal of Development Economics* 59: 43–76.

———. 2001. "The Curse of Natural Resources." *European Economic Review* 45: 827–38.

Schmitz, C. J, 1979. *World Non-Ferrous Metal Production and Prices, 1700–1976.* London: Frank Cass.

———. 1986. "The Rise of Big Business in the World Copper Industry, 1870–1930." *Economic History Review* 39: 392–410.

Sinclair, W. A. 1976. *The Process of Economic Development in Australia.* Melbourne, Australia: Cheshire Publishing.

Skillings Mining Review. 2002. "Coeur Discovers More Gold at Cerro Bay." 91, no. 3.

Smith, Adam. [1776] 1976. *An Inquiry into the Nature and Causes of the Wealth of Nations.* Oxford: Clarendon Press.

Stijns, Jean-Phillipe C. 2005. "Natural Resource Abundance and Economic Growth Revisited." *Resources Policy* 30 (2): 107–30.

Stoeckel, Andrew. 1999. *Minerals: Our Wealth Down Under.* Canberra, Australia: Centre for International Economics.

Surowiecki, James. 2001. "The Real Price of Oil." *The New Yorker*, December 3.

Tilton, John E., and Hans H. Landsberg. 1999. "Innovation, Productivity Growth, and the Survival of the U.S. Copper Industry." In *Productivity in Natural Resource Industries,* ed. R. David Simpson. Washington, DC: Resources for the Future.

USGS (United States Geological Survey). 1999. *The Mineral Economy of Brazil.* In Cooperation with Departamento Nacional de Producão Mineral, Digital Data Series 53.

———. 1963–2003. *Minerals Yearbook.* Reston, VA.

Warren, Kenneth. 1973. *Mineral Resources.* Newton Abbott: David and Charles.

World Bank. 1996. "A Mining Strategy for Latin America and the Caribbean." Technical Paper 345, Washington, DC.

Wright, Gavin. 1990. "The Origins of American Industrial Success, 1879–1940." *American Economic Review* 80: 651–68.

Yergin, Daniel. 1991. *The Prize.* New York: Simon and Schuster.

Yernberg, William R. 2001. "Peruvian Mining Convention Highlights Mining's Development and Potential." *Mining Engineering* 53, no. 12 (December): 22–24.

8

From Natural Resources to High-Tech Production: The Evolution of Industrial Competitiveness in Sweden and Finland

Magnus Blomström and Ari Kokko

Introduction

WHILE SWEDEN AND FINLAND ARE AMONG the world's richest and most highly developed economies today, it is often forgotten that the Nordic region was still one of Europe's poorest and most backward corners around the middle of the 19th century. The remarkable transformation that commenced around 1850 in Sweden and some decades later in Finland has gradually changed both countries from underdeveloped agricultural economies to advanced industrial welfare states. This process is interesting not only from a historical perspective, but also from the point of view of today's developing economies.

One of the distinguishing features of the Nordic development history is that growth was fuelled by the expansion of industries based on domestic raw materials, such as timber and iron ore. From a position as suppliers of simple intermediate products to more advanced economies in Western Europe, Sweden and Finland were able to upgrade the technological level of their raw-material-based industries and to establish a foundation for a more diversified economic structure. Over time, both countries managed to successfully diversify into related activities, such as machinery, engineering products, transport equipment, and various types of services. Many of today's developing economies have abundant supplies of natural resources, but few countries seem to base their long-term development strategies on resource-intensive sectors. The reason is arguably the risk that they may never be able to move from production and exports of low-value-added commodities to more advanced industries. However, the Swedish and Finnish experiences suggest that development strategies based on raw materials may form a solid base for sustainable development and demonstrate some of the requirements for diversification and growth of more advanced industries.[1]

Another notable observation regarding the Nordic economies is that industries based on domestic raw materials still account for a significant share of manufacturing activity, although the export, production, and employment shares of more knowledge-intensive manufacturing and service sectors have increased rapidly during the past decades. The forest and metal industries together employ almost one-fifth of the industrial labor force in Sweden and supply about a quarter of total Swedish exports; in Finland, the corresponding shares are even higher. The continuing prominence of these sectors implies that raw-material-based production is not only a temporary stage in economic development, but can instead be a sustainable element of an advanced industrial structure. This kind of long-run success requires public policies and company strategies that preserve the raw material resources and create the skills and competence that are needed to remain competitive in the face of increasing labor costs and changing technologies.

A third point to note is the rapid change in industrial structure that has taken place in both Sweden and Finland during the past decade. Since the early 1990s, Sweden and Finland have taken leading roles in the development and application of information and communications technologies, and they have enjoyed remarkable success in knowledge-based sectors. For instance, the Swedish firm Ericsson and the Finnish Nokia are world leaders in the telecom industry, and they have accounted for a major share of the very significant export increases recorded in the two countries during the past decade. Table 8.1 shows how the world market shares of Sweden, Finland, and some other advanced countries in four broad industry groups have changed from 1980 to 1996. The industry groups are distinguished by their level of technological sophistication, ranging from high-tech industries like telecommunications and pharmaceuticals to low-tech sectors like wood and paper products. The most striking feature of the table is the rapid growth of the Swedish and Finnish world market shares in the high-tech sectors. It is also notable that the fastest changes occurred during the 1990s. As late as 1990, computer and telecom products accounted for less than 7 percent of Swedish and Finnish exports. By 2000, this share had increased to nearly 20 percent in Sweden and 30 percent in Finland. This development is very encouraging for small countries that are arguably in a relatively weak position in research and development (R&D)-intensive sectors where economies of scale are important; however, it raises many questions regarding the explanations for the Swedish and Finnish success in this field.

Table 8.1 Changes in World Market Shares in Broad Industrial Groups, 1985, 1990, and 1996 (index 1980 = 100)

	High			Medium high			Medium low			Low		
	1985	1990	1996	1980	1990	1996	1985	1990	1996	1985	1990	1996
Finland	100	167	321	94	82	93	87	103	121	86	79	69
Germany	86	88	76	111	140	138	127	113	139	104	115	97
Japan	143	122	107	93	107	91	95	112	95	107	66	53
Sweden	94	91	130	90	86	90	120	129	111	98	89	80
United Kingdom	80	87	91	135	115	113	115	79	86	85	88	91
United States	98	90	86	89	103	92	99	128	106	90	92	102

Source: Hultin 2000, based on the Organisation for Economic Co-operation and Development–STAN database 1998.
Note: Classification of industries:
High technology: pharmaceuticals, computers, telecommunications equipment, airplanes
Medium-high technology: chemicals, machinery, electronics, transport equipment, instruments
Medium-low technology: petroleum, plastics, stoneware, steel, metal products, shipbuilding
Low technology: food products, clothing and textiles, wood products, paper and pulp, printing

This chapter aims to describe and analyze the evolution of industrial competitiveness in Sweden and Finland in a long-term perspective, with some focus on lessons for growth and development strategies in today's developing countries. The chapter begins with a look at the foundations for industrial take-off in Sweden. The focus is on Sweden, for good reasons. Swedish economic development has progressed in a remarkably steady fashion during the past 100 or 150 years—the average annual gross domestic product (GDP) growth rate has been around 2 percent, with few booms and depression. The main explanations are that Sweden managed to stay out of the two world wars, and their political development has been very stable, with few (if any) dramatic changes in economic policies. Finnish development, by contrast, has been rocked not only by the Second World War, but also by a civil war, a long period as a Grand Duchy under Russian rule, and many decades under the shadow of the Soviet Union. This notwithstanding, most of the factors underlying Swedish industrialization are found in Finland as well.

The next section turns to a more detailed description of the development of the Swedish forest industry in a historical perspective. The focus in the first part of the section is on identifying the factors facilitating the initial take-off and the subsequent diversification from simple timber exports to more advanced products like pulp and paper. Some of the main findings are related to the successful transfer of foreign technology to Sweden, and the development of universities and other institutes for education and training of labor. The same conclusions apply also for Finland. The structure of the Swedish forest industry cluster in the early 1990s is outlined, with some emphasis on one aspect that has seldom received sufficient attention in the international debate: the institutions supplying knowledge and skills to the industry. We argue that the institutional network is one of the major determinants of the continuing success of the Swedish forest industry, and many of the problems in, for example, the sawn wood products industry are related to weaknesses in the industry's knowledge institutions. It is clear that the relative importance of the raw-material-based sectors diminished during this 1990s, while the "knowledge-based" industries have expanded. However, one of the conclusions of this chapter is that even seemingly simple activities like pulp and paper production need to be knowledge based in order to remain competitive in a changing international environment.

In the following section we discuss the factors underlying the success of the telecommunications industry in Finland, which has taken over as the strategically most important sector, at least in a short- and medium-run perspective. While it is clearly relevant that Nokia, the flagship of the industry, began as a forestry company, what we stress are the parallels with the discussions of technological advance in the previous sections, as well as the nature of the process of industrial evolution. The tentative conclusion from our analysis is that the industry's success is a mix of systematic knowledge creation and random technological innovation. Although it is impossible to plan major technological breakthroughs such as the digital telephone exchanges underlying the Groupe Speciale Mobile (GSM)[2] cellular phone systems, we argue that it is possible to create an environment where firms or entire industries are well positioned to adjust to changing conditions and to benefit from innovations and market opportunities. We close the chapter with a summary and conclusions.

Creating a Base for Industrialization: The Swedish Example

During the 100 years from 1870 to 1970, Sweden developed from one of the poorest countries in Europe to one of the richest and most advanced economies of the world. This development was fuelled by the growth of several raw-material-based industries: sawn wood, pulp and paper, iron ore, steel, and grains were the most important ones. We start this section by summarizing some of the factors contributing to the Swedish industrial breakthrough. The purpose is to highlight two central observations: first, much of Swedish growth and development have been determined by factors that have little to do with domestic policies, such as foreign demand for Swedish products. Second, when domestic policies or decisions have been important, they have typically influenced institutions, education, and learning. These observations are also relevant to the present debate on development strategies, since they suggest what type of policy interventions are possible and desirable.

We begin by pointing to some important prerequisites for the Swedish industrialization process, then go on to describe the industrial breakthrough, with some emphasis on the role of technology transfer and the creation of domestic competence.

The Prerequisites for Industrialization

Most studies of Swedish economic history suggest that industrialization commenced around the middle of the 19th century, and that the real take-off occurred some decades later, during the 1870s and 1880s. However, the Swedish economy had already begun to change at the beginning of the 19th century, and the transformation laid a necessary foundation for the subsequent industrialization process. This foundation was, to some extent, created through conscious policies in agriculture and education, but exogenous technical changes also played an important role.

Agriculture The most significant changes took place in the agricultural sector. Up to the end of the 18th century, Swedish agriculture had relied on archaic production techniques, and harvests were barely sufficient to feed the population. Famines were not uncommon: the last wide-spread famines occurred in the early 19th century. Three main changes contributed to a transformation of agriculture that began around 1800 and continued through the 19th century.

First, the structure of land ownership was reformed. Traditionally, the landholdings of rural families had been divided into several separate strips of land, dispersed around the village. The purpose was to make sure that farmland of different quality was distributed fairly among all families belonging to the village. However, the fragmented ownership pattern also contributed to inefficiency and slow diffusion of innovations, since all production decisions—including adoption of new technologies—had to be coordinated among the village members. To overcome these obstacles, land reforms were undertaken in most parts of the country during the first decades of the 19th century. The traditional ownership pattern was broken up, and land was redistributed so that each farm got one larger plot instead of the many separate pieces (for more information, see Carlsson (1980)). In some parts of the country (especially in the more fertile southern regions), this also meant that the villages were broken up: the peasant families moved their houses from the village to the center of their own plot of farmland.

Second, new production techniques were adopted, and agricultural productivity increased. This was partly a result of the land reforms—diffusion of new techniques became faster when it was not necessary to convince the village majority about adoption of new practices—but it was also related to technical progress in the machinery industry. The most important innovations during the early part of the century were better ploughs, and after the 1850s, machinery for sowing, harvesting, and threshing also became widely used. Furthermore, increasing use of fertilizers made more intensive cultivation possible.

Third, potatoes became the new staple crop. They had been introduced to Sweden several centuries earlier, but their breakthrough did not come until the end of the 18th century. Potato growing was well suited to Swedish conditions, and it yielded larger harvests than the traditional staple foods, beets and turnips.

One result of the changes in the agricultural sector was a marked improvement in food supplies. Together with improvements in medicine (and a long period of peace beginning in 1809), this led to rapid population growth. During the first 60 years of the 19th century, the Swedish population increased from 2.3 million to about 4 million. The area of farmland grew from 1.5 million hectares in 1800 to 2.6 million hectares in 1850 and 3.6 million hectares in 1900 (Larsson 1991, 28). Agricultural productivity grew continuously, and output sufficed to feed both the farmers and a growing urban population. In fact, Sweden became a significant exporter of cereals in the 1850s. This is remarkable, since the country had been a steady net importer of grains until the 1830s.

It is hardly possible to overemphasize the importance of the improvements in agricultural productivity for Swedish industrialization. The higher productivity facilitated the transfer of labor to urban occupations and made possible exports that generated capital for investments in forestry and manufacturing. The increasing rural incomes also translated into demand for the goods produced in the emerging manufacturing industries.

Education and Human Capital

Another important development that had commenced before the advent of industrialization was an improvement in the level of education and human capital. Like the institutional changes in agriculture, this was also a result of conscious policies. Both formal and informal types of education and training were supported by the state and some private institutions.

At the summit of the formal education system were the old universities in Uppsala and Lund, established already in the 15th and 17th centuries. These expanded throughout the 19th century, with heavier emphasis on the natural sciences than earlier, when law and theology had been the dominant subjects. Institutions for advanced technical education were founded during the first half of the 19th century: both the Technological Institute in Stockholm and the Chalmers Technical School in Gothenburg, which later became the country's first technical universities, were established in the 1820s. The universities and the technical schools played a central role for the creation of new technology. Many of the successful Swedish innovations that emerged toward the end of the 19th century were made by people educated in these institutions, as we will discuss in closer detail later.

The introduction of a mandatory school system in 1842 was also crucial for the creation of a skilled human-capital base and for the dissemination of technologies. The official ambition was to guarantee basic skills in reading, writing, and arithmetic to all citizens, and literacy rates reached nearly 100 percent within one generation. This was essential for the ability of individuals and firms to learn and to adopt new technologies: much elementary learning and technology transfer was based on written instructions, like blueprints and handbooks.

Parallel to the development of formal education, there also appeared other institutions that were involved in the development of technology and industry. The Royal Swedish Academy of Science dated back to 1739, and the Swedish Ironmasters' Association was established in 1747. The Ironmasters' Association, which was partly state financed, was particularly important for the transfer of foreign technology to Sweden. The association started the publication of the mining science journal *Annalerna* in 1817. It also financed a very large number of foreign-study trips made by Swedish engineers and scientists, requiring detailed written reports that were made available to the rest of Swedish industry. New engineering workshops, like Motala Verkstad, established for the construction of lock-gates and iron bridges for the Göta canal network in the early 19th century, were also indispensable as training centers. In addition, it is necessary to note the importance of labor migration. Swedish engineers were often trained and educated in Great Britain and Germany, and important contributions were made by several British engineers who immigrated to Sweden (Schön 1982). Ahlström (1992) argues that as a result of this development of technical skills and competence, Sweden already possessed the fundamentals of a modern engineering industry by about 1850.

Protoindustrialization

The industrialization process was also facilitated by the development of primitive manufacturing activities—a kind of protoindustrialization—that had begun several centuries earlier. Unlike the changes in agriculture and education, these activities were not part of any explicit policy to strengthen productivity or technical progress, but they provided valuable skills and expertise for the industrial era.

One type of industrial operation that existed before the 19th century had grown from the Swedish army's procurement of supplies and equipment. Cloth, uniforms, weapons, utensils, tobacco, and alcohol were produced by so called *manufaktur* companies, and these were relatively large, although their production methods were primarily based on handicrafts. Yet they provided some elements of industrial culture, and the towns where the manufaktur firms were located had an advantage over other locations after the advent of the industrial revolution.

Due to the highly seasonal nature of Nordic agriculture, the rural households had traditionally produced significant amounts of handicrafts during the winter months: leather goods, textiles, shoes, and simple tools were made by most families. After 1800, this production increased and became more specialized, both because of population growth and increases in agricultural productivity, as well as because demand was growing due to higher incomes. In some parts of the country, merchants purchased a large share of the output, and they sometimes commissioned the production of entire villages. The main significance of this type of activity may have been the development of commercial skills. As modern technologies for production of textiles became available after the middle of the 19th century, the Swedish textile factories were often established by merchants who had been involved in the trade with handicrafts.

A related development was apparent in mining and forestry. Swedish producers had strong positions in the European markets for copper, iron, and tar starting in the 17th century, and it has been argued that one of the most important skills learned during the early years was international marketing (Hallvarsson 1980, 13). Merchants and traders were involved in the establishment of many of the ironworks and sawmills that emerged because of good export opportunities during the 19th century. Hence, some important elements of industrial culture were already in place before the advent of industry itself.

The Industrial Breakthrough

The industrial breakthrough was largely based on the progress in agriculture, education and skills, and handicrafts discussed earlier, but it was triggered by several other events that occurred more or less simultaneously around 1850. These were related to increasing foreign demand for Swedish products, to technical innovations, to the continuing development of skills and competence in Sweden's emerging industrial sector, and to some important institutional changes.

Exports   The most important reason for the inception of Swedish industrialization in the 1850s was a boom in foreign demand for Swedish products. Export demand continued to be a major determinant of industrial development throughout the century, although the domestic market took the lead toward the 1890s. The early stages of the Swedish industry's growth was fuelled by exports of simple products like sawn wood (and cereals), whereas more advanced commodities like pulp and paper and iron ore became the main exports later on.

Exports of cereals were of tremendous importance for the industrialization process, although their origin was in the agricultural sector rather than in manufacturing and although the era of cereal exports lasted only from the 1850s to the 1880s. One reason was that the expansion of agriculture during these three decades provided employment for the increasing population at a time when industry was not sufficiently developed to absorb enough employment. Another reason was that exports brought in large amounts of capital, which was used to finance important parts of the early industrial expansion.

Sweden had been a net importer of cereals until the 1830s, as noted earlier, and exports were still limited during the late 1840s, reaching some 40,000 barrels annually. At the peak, 30 years later, exports had grown to 4 million barrels per year (Carlsson 1980, 212). The reasons for the cereal boom were largely to be found outside of Sweden. Demand was high, especially from England, where the industrialization process had taken off, and domestic cereal production was not sufficient to feed the growing urban population. Bad harvests in England and elsewhere on the European continent during the early 1850s increased demand further. At the same time, Swedish harvests were unusually plentiful. Moreover, the leading European cereal exporter, Russia, was hit by the Crimean War in 1853–56, and Russian exports ceased almost completely.

The successful Swedish response to these new export opportunities was a combination of the flexibility of the agricultural sector (that had been created by the institutional changes in the structure of land ownership) and the appearance of various technical innovations that increased productivity, such as machinery for sowing, harvesting, and threshing. Sweden managed to hold on to large shares of the English cereal imports until the 1880s, but the trade disappeared as suddenly as it had emerged after that. The reasons were that Russian exports resumed on a large scale, and the United States emerged as the new leader when the Great Plains had been taken into production.

From the middle of the 19th century, there was also an increase in the demand for forest products—mainly pit props and sawn wood—that was fed by the English urbanization. Before the 1840s, Swedish exports of sawn wood products had been insignificant for a number of reasons: Norway was a stronger exporter, both because of shorter transport costs and because the technical level of Norwegian sawmills was higher. In addition, the English *Navigation Acts* gave preferential treatment to Canadian producers (Carlsson 1980, 218). However, the situation changed very rapidly in the early 1850s. The English import protection was abolished, and the Norwegian forest resources were overexploited, which gave ample opportunities for Swedish wood exporters to step in. Other factors that facilitated the export success were of an institutional or technical nature. Most important, the Swedish state had restructured its forest holdings some years earlier. Large amounts of forest land had been distributed to private owners, especially in southern Sweden, and the structure of forest ownership had been registered. This meant that property rights were well defined, and the private owners were in a position to respond rapidly to the increasing export demand. There were also some technical improvements, as steam-powered saws were introduced, and the sawmills became more efficiently organized, after Norwegian models. In fact, several Norwegian firms moved to Sweden because of the dwindling forest supplies in Norway.

As a consequence, exports of sawn wood increased from less than 200,000 cubic meters in the 1830s to 4,800,000 cubic meters at the end of the century. In the 1870s, wood products had grown to make up 43 percent of Swedish exports (Hallvarsson 1980, 14).

Later on during the 19th century, there were new export booms for pulp and paper and iron ore. Exports of pulp and paper began growing toward the end of the 19th century, and Sweden had become the world's largest pulp exporter by 1913. However, this expansion differed from the sawn wood boom in several ways. Sawmilling had been an easy start, since the capital requirements were low and the technology was simple. Pulp and paper production was significantly more capital intensive and technology intensive, and it posed much stricter requirements on domestic institutions and technological competence than sawmilling had done.

Domestic policies were also much more important for the success of the industry. Thanks to the development of a relatively efficient banking system, profits from sawmills could be channeled to finance the expansion of pulp and paper mills. The development of domestic technological capability had also proceeded far enough to allow production and exports of more advanced goods. In fact, Swedish inventors had taken the lead in the development of pulp technologies, and the world's first chemical pulp factory was established in Bergvik, on the coast of Norrland, in 1872.

The mining industry that started expanding during the last decades of the century was also heavily dependent on modern technology. Table 8.2 illustrates the changes in the structure of Swedish exports between 1881–85 and 1911–13. The relative importance of sawn wood and cereals fell, whereas more advanced products, such as pulp and paper, engineering products, and iron ore, became more important.

Domestic Demand   The driving force behind the early stages of industrial development during the 1850s and 1860s was undoubtedly export demand. However, the domestic market became gradually more important, partly as a result of explicit policy intervention. One example was the development of the domestic infrastructure. The heavy investments in railroads (especially during the 1870s) and the introduction of electric energy (from the 1880s) made it possible to specialize production and to transport raw materials and finished goods across the country. The earliest industrial developments—in sawmills, for example—had relied on waterways, but now a more general industrialization, based on the domestic markets, was possible. The demand for metal and wood generated by the construction of infrastructure facilities, mainly railroads, also stimulated domestic demand.

Another reason for the heavier emphasis on the home market was more directly related to policy. The export booms during the early stages of the industrialization process took place at a time when economic liberalism

Table 8.2 The Structure of Swedish Exports 1881–85 and 1911–13

	1881–85 (percent)	1911–13 (percent)
Sawn wood	40	26
Iron and steel	16	9
Cereals	12	1
Butter	6	6
Pulp and paper	5	18
Engineering products	3	11
Iron ore	—	8
Other	18	21
Total	100	100

Source: Larsson and Olsson 1992, table 3.

and free trade ideologies reached a first peak. This meant not only that Sweden could freely sell primary products to the rest of Europe, but also that Sweden imported many advanced consumer and investment goods from the industrially more developed countries in Europe. These policies changed from the late 1880s, when a wave of protectionism swept over Europe. Both agricultural and industrial imports were restricted, and the average tariff level in Sweden before the First World War reached about 15 percent of value added. A further sign of the changing policy climate was the introduction of policies to limit foreign ownership of Swedish resources. Earlier, foreign participation and investment had been welcomed. This meant that domestic markets became more important, since similar developments occurred in the rest of Europe as well.

One can only speculate about the significance of the timing of policy regimes. It appears that Sweden was fortunate in that the inward-looking policies were not introduced until there was a firm base for domestic development. Agriculture had expanded and the increased productivity created incomes and demand for various types of consumer goods. Technological skills had been developed, which facilitated the creation of a variety of import-substituting industries. The export success had brought in foreign capital, and a foundation for a more comprehensive industrialization was in place. These elements were not in place in most of the developing countries where inward-looking policies failed during the 20th century.

Technical Innovations   In addition to the exogenous changes in foreign demand for Swedish products, there were exogenous changes in technology that had a heavy influence on the direction of Swedish industrialization.

In the metal industries, Sweden had held a strong position in the international market for several centuries. The main export product until the middle of the 19th century was bar iron. The production of iron was strictly controlled by the state, in order to avoid deforestation and degradation of forest resources, as the industry used a massive amount of timber, in the form of charcoal. It has been estimated that the mining industry's use of wood was four to five times larger than wood exports as late as 1854. Hence, exports of iron ore and pig iron (which were low-value-added products) were restricted.

The strict rules were liberalized in 1850s, when technological innovations—the Bessemer and Martin processes—made it possible to use coal and coke instead. However, Swedish production and exports of iron and iron ore stagnated during the decades after 1850 because the comparative advantage of the Swedish iron industry had been the abundant supply of charcoal. Instead, coke- and coal-based steel production in continental Europe increased rapidly. It was not until the so-called Thomas process was introduced that the industry started recovering. It had been known for centuries that there were rich iron ore deposits in northern Sweden (Lappland). These had not been exploited earlier because of their high content of phosphor, which made the steel weaker. Now it became economically viable to develop the industry, and new ironworks were established. Production of steel for domestic use increased rapidly, but exports of steel remained low. Instead, iron ore was exported directly to the main iron and steel plants in Germany and Great Britain.

The development of mechanical and engineering industries, which started during the latter part of the 19th century, was also driven by technological innovations, but these were more directly connected to domestic capabilities and skills. The 1880s especially proved to be a golden decade for Swedish industry, when several path-breaking innovations were presented and when industrialization really took off: the number of industrial workers increased by 66 percent between 1880 and 1889 (Hallvarsson 1980, 9).[3]

Examples of long-lived Swedish firms that were established during the late 19th century or the first years after the turn of the century are Ericsson, Alfa Laval, ASEA (today ABB), AGA, Nobel, and SKF. The exceptional performance of these firms has been based on the ability of Swedish industry to create, to adapt, and to disseminate new technologies. The development of institutions for science, technology, and education has established the foundation for this kind of success.

Science, Technology, and Education The first technical universities of Sweden date back to the early parts of the 19th century. The Technological Institute in Stockholm was founded in 1826 and became the Royal Institute of Technology in 1877. In Gothenburg, the Chalmers Technical School was established in 1829; it provided scientific and technical education at a university level from its inception, although it was not formally named a Technical University until 1937 (Ahlström 1992, 4). Concurrent with the development of specialized institutions for technical education, there was also an expansion of the natural sciences at the universities in Uppsala and Lund, and it has been argued that the great increase in the number of professorial chairs between 1870 and 1914 was of "immense importance" for Sweden's industrial breakthrough (Ahlström 1993, 38).

Technical colleges were established in several Swedish cities—Malmö, Borås, Örebro, and Norrköping—during the 1850s. From the middle of the century onward, numerous vocational training schools were also set up in various parts of the country; these numbered about 35 at the end of the 19th century and 66 in 1908–1909 (Ahlström 1992, 7). The guild system was abolished in 1846, and these schools quickly began to replace apprenticeships as the main form of vocational education. Most of the vocational schools depended on private initiatives, although some were financed by the state. Among the latter were nautical training schools (starting in 1842), forestry secondary schools (starting in 1860), and agricultural colleges (starting in 1887) (Nilsson and Svärd 1991, 5).

Among the institutions that were involved in the creation and dissemination of skills and knowledge, we have already mentioned—the Royal Swedish Academy of Science and the Swedish Ironmasters' Association. Several new organizations, including the Swedish Association of Engineers and Architects and the Stockholm Engineering Association, emerged during the 1860s. The Swedish Academy of Engineering Sciences, the Wood Pulp Association, and the Swedish Institute of Metal Research were added during the 1910s. These institutions were closely in touch with scientific research and technical education, and they played—and continue to play—a significant role for the diffusion and dissemination of technical skills.

It is difficult to find accurate measures of the importance of these different types of investment in skills and human capital. However, it is clear that the supply of skilled technical workers increased steadily from the 1850s. The number of engineers educated at the higher technical institutes reached approximately 700–800 in 1850 and about 2,000 in the late 1890s. The number of engineers with secondary education also reached about 2,000 at the end of the 19th century (Ahlström 1992, 9).

Moreover, the founders and leaders of several of the most successful Swedish companies were educated at the technical institutes and had received foreign training that was paid for by the state or some of the institutions discussed previously. For instance, Hans Tore Cedergren, who played a central role in the emergence of the Swedish telephone industry, and Gustav de Laval, founder of AB Separator in 1883 (known as Alfa-Laval after 1963), were educated at the Technological Institute of Stockholm. Gustav Dalén, manager and chief engineer of AGA, was a graduate of Chalmers, and Sven Winquist, founder of SKF, had been educated at the technical college of Örebro. Lars Magnus Ericsson, the founder of the telephone company still carrying his name, had received state grants for studying the electrical engineering industry in Germany and Switzerland, as had most other leading industrialists in the country.

Ahlström (1992, 1993) argues that the successful innovators and entrepreneurs illustrate that there already existed a network among the technical institutions, industry, and government by the middle of the 19th century, and this contributed significantly to the success of Swedish industrialization. The networks were of central importance for the development of industry, especially after the 1880s, when products became more differentiated and goods such as pulp, paper, and engineering products became more important. Until the period between the two world wars, these networks substituted for specialized R&D departments in many firms.

The importance of education and labor skills for industrial success has not diminished since the early era of Swedish industrialization. On the contrary, the increasing supply of skilled labor has generally been considered as one of Sweden's main comparative advantages during the last decades. Apart from a well-developed educational system of the classical type, the existence of large-scale vocational education programs is also noteworthy (Nilsson and Svärd 1991).

Swedish vocational education dates back to several schools started during the 19th century, as we have noted earlier. Yet the real growth in the area did not start until the 1920s, when the state became more engaged in the provision of vocational education. The number of people involved in vocational training programs increased rapidly during the 1920s and 1930s, partly because of persistent unemployment: special courses were arranged for unemployed youths. However, the system was criticized because the courses focused more on upholding the morale of unemployed people than on useful vocational skills (Nilsson and Svärd 1991, 6). Starting in the 1940s and 1950s, however, the system changed. There was a shift from manual to more intellectual skills, which meant that most courses included general education as well as specific training, and full-time courses became more common. The quantitative explosion of vocational education can easily be illustrated with some figures. In 1950, some 15,000 people graduated from full-time vocational courses lasting at least one semester. By the late 1960s, the number had increased to more than 100,000 (Nilsson and Svärd 1991, 18).

Institutional Change   Several of the institutional changes that contributed to the industrial revolution—including the establishment of property rights for forest land, trade policies, and the support for education and science—have already been discussed. Another notable reform was the introduction of limited company laws in 1848. These made it possible to raise more capital and to take risks, which were necessary as the rate of technical change increased during the second half of the century. Earlier, most firms had been owned or at least dominated by a single family, and the owners were personally responsible for the firm's debt (Larsson 1991, 32–33). Limited companies—where the owners' stake was limited to their share of the firm's initial capital—employed 45 percent of the industrial labor force in 1872 and 80 percent of the labor force in 1912 (Hallvarsson 1980, 19).

Moreover, credit markets and banks emerged during the second half of the 19th century. The development of the banking sector was supported both by the export booms and by the construction of the Swedish railroad network. The railroad system was largely financed with foreign capital, and several of the larger commercial banks were employed by the state to sell Swedish government bonds abroad. At the end of the 1870s, the Swedish financial system comprised 35 commercial banks with offices in 160 cities, which was comparable to the most highly developed nations in the world (Larsson and Olsson 1992). It is interesting to note that the foreign debt built up to finance the domestic infrastructure investments was comparable to the present debt burden of many developing countries. For instance, the interest payments to foreigners amounted to 10 percent of export value in 1908 (Hallvarsson 1980, 26). The eventual repayment of the debt also illustrates the importance of chance and luck for long-term development. Most of the debt stock was denominated in German marks and French francs, and the heavy depreciation of these currencies after the First World War reduced the value of the outstanding liabilities to very modest amounts.[4]

The Swedish Forest Industries

Although Swedish sawmills had already felt the increasing demand from England during the first half of the 19th century, the breakthrough for the wood industry did not come until the middle of the century, as noted earlier. Up to that time, Swedish exports had been hampered by the competition from Norwegian sawmills and by the British *Navigation Acts*, which favored Canadian producers. When British imports were liberalized around 1850, Sweden became the major supplier: Norwegian exporters were not able to expand production because of short supplies of raw materials, and Canadian producers were more expensive because of the longer transports.

The first steam-powered sawmills were established at this time. The early development of the industry benefited greatly from contacts with the international economy. Much of the industry's technological development was driven by relations with Norwegian firms and technicians, and a significant share of the investment capital was raised in England. Several of the individual entrepreneurs were also of foreign origin, and they established long-lived firms such as Ljusne and MoDo (Larsson 1991, 37). However, the new technologies did not change the overall structure of the sawmill industry very much. Most mills were small and remained water-powered until the 1880s, because few of the owners were willing to undertake the necessary investments. Moreover, there were no changes in the geographical distribution of sawmills, although the introduction of steam-powered saws would have made it possible to locate saw mills elsewhere than at the major rivers. The reason the mills were not moved was that the raw material, the timber, was still transported along the old waterways. The development of the Swedish railway network during the 1860s and 1870s had a stronger impact on the industry, since it facilitated the establishment of many new sawmills in the inner parts of the country.

However, growth in the sawmill industry slowed down during the 1890s due to competition from the pulp and paper industry for stagnant forest production. These problems led to the creation of a comprehensive legal structure for the forest sector. In 1903, laws were established to guarantee replanting and to ensure that fellings would not exceed the growth of the timber stock. The crisis of the 1920s resulted in some concentration of the industry, because few of the old-fashioned, family-based companies managed to generate the resources necessary to bring them through the Depression, so they went out of business or were bought by larger firms. Another important development during the late 1920s was an increasing emphasis on paper and pulp, motivated by weak productivity in simple sawmilling operations. This period saw the beginning of the "integrated forest firm," with operations in several of the forest industries—pulp and paper, timber, sawn wood, boards, and so forth. Overall, weak market development through the Second World War and through the mid-1960s mandated several changes for the industry. However, the main elements of the industry structure established during the interwar period—with a relatively small number of large integrated firms in sawmilling and pulp and paper—remained largely intact and continue to this day.

The improvement in the business climate for the forest industries during the mid-1960s led to large productivity gains through mechanization and rationalization of operations. However, the boom ended with the first oil crisis, and prices stagnated during the mid-1970s. The companies with their own small holdings of forest were hardest hit by the recession: forest owners were simply not willing to sell raw material, although timber prices did not fall at the same rate as prices for finished products. The situation did not improve until the early 1980s, with the upturn in the international business cycle. The 1980s also witnessed a new phenomenon, namely a comprehensive internationalization of the Swedish pulp and paper industry. The industry's strategies during the past couple of decades have aimed to increase the degree of processing and value added of the final products. This has required close contact with customers in the European market, and a large number of foreign firms manufacturing paper and paper products have been acquired. By the early 1990s, Swedish forest companies had established nearly 200 subsidiaries throughout Europe. The sawmill industry remains more domestic, although increased value added and more advanced products are also major strategic objectives.

By 1990, the forest industry—producing sawn wood, prefabricated houses and building joinery, wooden furniture, pulp and paper, paper products, and various other goods—accounted for some 15 percent of value added and employment in the Swedish manufacturing sector, as well as 20 percent of the sector's exports. In addition to the 107,000 people directly employed in the forest industry, suppliers of investment goods and inputs, transport companies, and service industries employed another 75,000 people, about 40,000 of whom were engaged in the forestry sector.

The Swedish Forestry Sector

More than 60 percent of Sweden is covered with forests. Timber supply is increasing continuously, and today it is more than twice as large as a decade ago: in fact, in debates with environmental organizations, forest companies seldom fail to point out that the growing stock is probably larger now than ever before. Though roughly 50 percent of total forest area is held in private holdings averaging 50 hectares, the steady growth of overall supply suggests that this has not proven a major problem. To balance the market power of the large pulp and paper firms and the forest owners' associations, sawmills and other wood manufacturers have been forced to establish cooperative purchasing organizations.

There were two main industry groups in the Swedish forest sector in 1990: sawn wood products and pulp and paper, accounting for 6.9 percent and 8.6 percent of manufacturing value added and 7.6 and 7.1 percent of manufacturing employment, respectively. The higher productivity in paper and pulp is explained by the industry's high capital intensity. The forest sector made a larger contribution to the Swedish balance of payments than any other industry. In aggregate terms, Sweden was the world's third-largest exporter of both pulp and paper in 1990 (with 12 percent of world trade) and sawn softwood products (with 9 percent of world trade). The major competitors were the Canada, Finland, United States, and although Brazil, Chile, Russia, and other developing countries have emerged as significant exporters in some product groups.

By 1990, most of the leading Swedish forest companies had integrated their operations, and owned and managed sawmills, paper mills, and various value-added activities: the largest Swedish firms—Stora, ASSI-Domän, SCA, and MoDo—were all involved in production of pulp, paper, and sawn wood products. In addition, the firms owned significant amounts of forest, which adds forestry as an important activity to these companies' operations. Figure 8.1 shows the core of the Swedish forest industry cluster and illustrates some of the connections between the different types of activities. The figure depicts the flow of goods from each of the major product groups to customers at home and abroad, as well as the flow of raw materials and intermediates within the cluster. The data on sales and resource flows (in million SEK) are for 1987, since information for more recent years is not conveniently available.

The pulp and paper industry produces a large assortment of pulp and paper grades, which are used for a variety of purposes ranging from writing paper and newsprint to packaging of liquids and hygienic tissues. Since the emergence of industrial technologies for mechanical pulp production in the 1860s, and the first chemical pulp mills in the 1870s, pulp and paper have grown to become the largest product groups in the forest industry. The technology for pulp and paper production has also developed over time, and today, the industry must be counted among the most R&D-intensive sectors of the Swedish economy, in spite of the seemingly simple end products. More than 4 percent of the industry's value added is devoted to R&D, in addition to the research efforts that take place in the industry's various research institutes.

Sawmills and plants manufacturing wooden houses and building joinery (doors, window frames, sashes, staircases, and so forth) accounted for

Figure 8.1 The Swedish Forest Industry Cluster

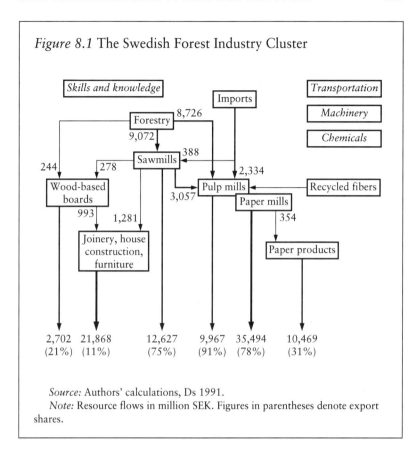

Source: Authors' calculations, Ds 1991.
Note: Resource flows in million SEK. Figures in parentheses denote export shares.

most of the activities in the sawn wood products industry. Between the 1970s and 1990s, nearly half of the work places and a third of the employees disappeared, at the same time as productivity and plant size increased. Moreover, there was a shift from sawmills to joinery and house production, that is, toward more advanced products with higher value added. It is worth noting here that the development of the sawmill sector is closely connected to the activities of the industry's marketing and research organizations. The explicit aim is to move into operations with higher value added, and the industry organizations are heavily involved in various types of ventures to facilitate this intention. For instance, the organizations provide advice and detailed instructions (including plans and blueprints) for various construction projects; they are currently making efforts to establish common European standards for building components and other wood products; and they are working continuously to disseminate information about the characteristics of wood as a construction material. The same applies also for other

wood product industries, as well as for paper and pulp, and we will return
later to a more detailed discussion about the organizations that create and
disseminate the skills and knowledge used in the forest industries. The
export success of the Swedish home-furniture industry owes much to the
remarkable international expansion of the furniture retailer IKEA. More
than 100 IKEA stores are now found throughout Europe, North America,
and Asia, and, despite its international character, IKEA still purchases a
large share of its furniture from Swedish suppliers.

The Knowledge Cluster

The forest sector is still often characterized as a mature low-technology
industry facing many difficult challenges and with bleak prospects for the
future. For instance, it is often pointed out that increasing competition
from the transition economies of Eastern Europe and emerging markets
like Chile, Brazil, and Indonesia will depress prices and reduce the profitability of Swedish production. Increases in Swedish costs for labor, capital, and energy will worsen the situation. The growing concern about the
environmental effects of forestry practices and production methods will
present other types of demands that will necessitate changes in both products and processes. The most pessimistic predictions have for a long time
suggested stagnation and decline of the kind seen in industries such as textiles, shipyards, or mining.

However, one of the main points of this chapter is that this is not an
appropriate description of the forest sector. Pulp, paper, and sawn wood
products have been among the most important Swedish exports for nearly
150 years, and it is likely that they will continue to be important in the
future, in spite of the many challenges facing the forest industry. A primary reason for this positive outlook is that most forecasts point to a continuing high demand for the industry's products, both at home and
abroad. The consumption of paper products is predicted to continue
growing with growing incomes and education levels in Western Europe
and other major markets for Swedish exporters, while the development
and growth in the transition economies of Eastern and Central Europe are
expected to generate demand for sawn wood products.

Another reason is that the knowledge and skills used by the industry are
continuously being updated, in response to changes in the competitive
environment. Swedish industry has managed to overcome the obstacles
created by high raw-material and labor costs by mechanizing production
processes and by moving into operations with higher value added. At the
same time, product development is generating new uses for forest
resources. For instance, wood is becoming an increasingly important input
in the construction industry as the use of laminated and finger-jointed
products spreads. Moreover, Sweden has become a leader in the development and implementation of environmentally correct forestry practices

and industrial processes. The forest industry is one of the few modern industrial activities that is inherently "green," in the sense that all products are biodegradable and can be recycled or used to generate energy, and even the most polluting processes, such as pulp production, can be made completely self-contained. Many of these opportunities are available because the forest industry has created dynamic networks of institutions and organizations involved in the production and dissemination of the knowledge and skills that are needed to remain competitive. *This network of organizations—or "institutional framework" or "knowledge cluster"— is perhaps the main strategic and competitive asset of the Swedish forest industry*, as we have already argued.

Since the forest industries and the related organizations are closely integrated, it is difficult to define separate institutional clusters for each industry group: new knowledge and technology may be developed by institutions that are intimately connected to one specific actor, but the innovations typically also affect the other industry groups. Nevertheless, it may be useful to look separately at the knowledge clusters in the sawn wood products group (including furniture) and in paper and pulp, because there are some differences in structure and performance. Most important, it appears that the cluster in the sawn wood products group is weaker than that in pulp and paper. This may be an important factor in explaining why the pulp and paper industry has been relatively more successful in recent decades.

Skills and Knowledge in Sawn Wood Products   For purposes of presentation, it is useful to distinguish between two essential elements of industrial technology and competence in its use: skills and knowledge (Ds 1991:62). Skills are embodied in people and generated through various types of education and training, whether on-the-job training or formal schooling. Knowledge is a public good that is generated by research and development activities, and it can be transferred from person to person through various means of communication, such as lectures, scientific articles, handbooks, manuals, and so forth. It is also convenient to distinguish between institutions and organizations that generate and disseminate skills and knowledge, although the distinction is seldom very sharp. For instance, most organizations involved in the generation of knowledge are also engaged in disseminating research results to potential users or the general public.

Table 8.3 identifies some of the participants in the network that supplied skills and knowledge to the sawn wood products industries in the early 1990s. Some forestry institutions are also included. The table covers the main actors in the knowledge and skill cluster, but it is not complete: there was a total of more than 100 different associations, institutions, and organizations in the forest sector at the time, and most of them were involved in the generation and dissemination of knowledge and skills.[5]

Table 8.3 Participants in the Knowledge and Skill Cluster in the
Swedish Sawn Wood Products Industry, 1990

	Generation	*Dissemination*
Skills (Education)	Royal Technical University University of Agricultural Sciences University of Luleå (School for Forest Engineering) (Forest Institutes)	—
Knowledge (Research)	Royal Technical University University of Agricultural Sciences University of Luleå Swedish Institute for Wood Technology Research Swedish Furniture Research Institute Chalmers Technical University Lund Technical University (School for Forest Engineering) (Institute for Forest Improvement) (Forest Operations Institute)	Swedish Institute for Wood Technology Research Swedish Furniture Research Institute University of Agricultural Sciences Swedish Building Material and Building Trade Federation Swedish Furniture Manufacturer's Association Swedish Sawmill Federation Swedish Wood Exporter's Association Swedish Timber Council

Sources: Ds 1991: 62, *Handbook of Northern Wood Industries* (1991/92).
Note: Institutes in parentheses are primarily involved in forestry.

Education at the university level was provided by several institutions. The University of Luleå and the Royal Technical University of Stockholm educated engineers specializing in wood technology. The number of graduates varied between 15 and 40 per year in the late 1980s and early 1990s. Forest officers and forest engineers were trained at the Swedish University of Agricultural Sciences (SUAS) in Uppsala and Umeå, the School for Forest Engineers, and several forest institutes. About 170 students per year graduated from the forestry programs in the early 1990s.[6] The wood products industry's own investments in education and training of labor were considered to be small (Ds 1991: 62, 26).

Except for the School for Forest Engineers, all the institutions mentioned also offered postgraduate training and managed extensive research programs in areas related to forestry and wood manufacturing. SUAS was particularly active, and it managed special research programs on wood construction technology, wood treatment and protection, and integration of forestry and sawmilling in various parts of the country. The research budget of the Faculty of Forestry at the University of Agricultural Sciences amounted to more than SEK 225 million in 1991. Forestry research was also found at the Institute for Forest Improvement, which employed 81 people and spent SEK 36 million per year, and the Forest Operations Institute, with 62 employees and a budget of SEK 62 million. Other universities, such as Chalmers in Gothenburg and Lund Technical University, were also involved in wood research, but at a more limited scale.

The main actor in the generation of knowledge directed toward the wood manufacturing sector was the Swedish Institute for Wood Technology Research, which is the sawmill industry's collective research institute. In the early 1990s, it employed some 80 people in three research divisions, and its annual budget amounted to around SEK 80 million. The research at the Stockholm branch was focused toward sawmills and wood construction. Building joinery was the main research area at the Skellefteå branch, which was also closely connected to and coordinated its research with the department for wood technology at the University of Luleå. Research on other wood products, for example, furniture, was concentrated to Jönköping. The institute was also involved in some research dealing with wood-based boards, although on a relatively limited scale. The Swedish Furniture Research Institute, located in Stockholm, was the locus for research, development, and testing of materials and products in the furniture industry. This was a smaller institute, with a staff of 20 people and a research budget of about SEK 8 million.

The Institute for Wood Technology Research, the Furniture Research Institute, and the University of Agricultural Sciences were all actively involved in the transfer and dissemination of research results. In addition, several other industry organizations focused on providing information and technical support to member companies, customers, and the general public. Some of these were the Swedish Building Material and Building Trade Federation, the Swedish Furniture Manufacturer's Association, the Swedish Sawmill Federation, and the Swedish Wood Exporter's Association.

However, the efficiency of the technology and knowledge transfers was sometimes questioned. One problem seemed to be that too few resources were spent on the dissemination phase, particularly taking into account the fragmented nature of the industry. Another problem was that many firms in the industry were unable to absorb the information provided by these organizations; this seemed to be the result of the failure of the institutions or organizations to focus on the transfer and dissemination of skills from the universities to the industry. In fact, it was claimed that the main structural weakness of the entire sawn wood products group was a shortage of academically educated university-educated staff in sawmills and other firms (Ds 1991: 62, 33). If the necessary skills are not available

within companies, it is difficult to keep pace with technological developments and changes in the competitive environment: even if the research
organization manages to generate product and process innovations, few
individual firms will recognize the opportunities and adopt the innovations. The lack of institutions promoting the transfer of skilled personnel
from the universities to the industry may also have explained the variability in interest for university education in wood technology.

The knowledge cluster in the pulp and paper industry had apparently
managed to overcome some of these problems, and improvements in the
institutional framework of the sawn wood products industry—presumably based on lessons that could be learned from pulp and paper—were
integral elements of the industry's growth strategy, as will be described
later on.

Skills and Knowledge in the Pulp and Paper Industry   Most companies in
the pulp and paper industry devote considerable resources to R&D activities, as well as to in-house education, which was contrary to the situation
in the sawn wood products industry. One explanation is, of course, that
the average size of pulp and paper companies is much larger than that of,
for example, sawmills. Firm-specific R&D has also become relatively
more important as the pulp and paper companies grew through mergers
and acquisitions during the past couple of decades. Yet, the network of
institutions permeating the industry is still essential for maintaining and
developing international competitiveness, not least concerning education
and dissemination of skills from universities and research organizations to
the industry.

Table 8.4 illustrates the institutional network connected to the pulp
and paper industry. University training of engineers specializing in pulp
and paper processing and related fields was provided by the Royal Technical University in Stockholm and the Chalmers Technical University in
Gothenburg. Degree programs in pulp and paper technology and biotechnology were also offered by the University of Karlstad. It is also notable
that the industry's leading research institution, the Swedish Pulp and
Paper Research Institute, was actively involved in academic education
through financing student research projects, arranging guest lectures, and
providing lecture rooms and equipment. About half of the graduate engineers recruited by the industry had this type of training, but the increasingly sophisticated production technology requires an increasing number
of specialists from other fields as well. In addition, most of the forestry
training programs mentioned in the section on sawn wood products were
equally relevant for the pulp and paper industry.

A major share of postgraduate education was managed jointly by the
Swedish Pulp and Paper Research Institute and the technical universities.
The Research Institute also accounted for a major share of the research and
development activities taking place in the cluster. With 250 employees, half

Table 8.4 Participants in the Knowledge and Skill Cluster in the Paper and Pulp Industry, 1990

	Generation	*Dissemination*
Skills (Education)	Royal Technical University Chalmers Technical University University of Karlstad Swedish Pulp and Paper Research Institute	Swedish Pulp and Paper Research Institute
Knowledge (Research)	Royal Technical University Chalmers Technical University University of Karlstad Swedish Pulp and Paper Research Institute Institute of Surface Chemistry Graphical Research Laboratory Swedish Packaging Research Institute Swedish Newspaper Mills' Research Laboratory	Swedish Pulp and Paper Research Institute Institute of Surface Chemistry Graphical Research Laboratory Swedish Packaging Research Institute Swedish Newspaper Mills' Research Laboratory

Sources: Ds 1991:62, Statistical Yearbook of Forestry 1993, Handbook of the Northern Wood Industries 1991/92.

of whom were qualified researchers, and a budget of almost SEK 200 million per year, it was one of the largest research institutions of any kind in Sweden, and it recognized as one of the internationally leading centers as well. However, during the early 1990s, the character of the institute's operations was changing somewhat, because of the growing level of competence in the industry's larger companies. Product development was gradually shifting to the industry's corporate research laboratories, while the Pulp and Paper Research Institute concentrated on basic and applied research (and advanced education) of common interest for the entire industry. Research was also conducted at the technical universities and at several of the industry's smaller collective research institutes, such as the Institute of Surface Chemistry, the Graphical Research Laboratory, the Swedish Packaging Research Institute, and the Swedish Newsprint Mills' Research Laboratory.

In addition to the activities that took place in each of the research institutes, there were collaborative research projects involving several of the industry's institutions. One example is a multidisciplinary research program entitled Paper-Color-Print (PCP), which aimed to develop Swedish competence in paper processing, paper coating, and printing technology. The project was conducted jointly by the Royal Technical University, the

Swedish Pulp and Paper Research Institute, the Institute of Surface Chemistry, the Graphical Research Laboratory, and the Swedish Newsprint Mills' Research Laboratory, with financing from the participating institutions, independent research foundations, and the government. Launched in 1993 and planned to run for six years, employing on average 40 full-time researchers, the project was estimated to result in five doctoral dissertations, 20 licentiate dissertations, 50 graduate engineering degrees, and 100–150 scientific publications and lectures.

Most of the industry's research institutions were involved in the dissemination of research results. Technology transfer was significantly more efficient in the pulp and paper industry than in sawn wood products because the industry's general level of education and skills was markedly higher. The explanation for this is probably that the Pulp and Paper Research Institute had been very active in transferring skills from the academic institutions to the industry. In fact, the Research Institute acted on two fronts. On the one hand, it attempted to stabilize the demand for engineers and researchers by recruiting skilled labor during slumps in the business cycle. These recruitment activities were financed directly by the pulp and paper industry. On the other hand, it encouraged the industry to employ skilled labor, both by providing information about various types of education to the industry and by influencing the content of higher education in the direction of the industry's demand.

Related Industries

The forest sector has also made up a firm base for the evolution of some related and supporting industries, and there are several examples of firms that have subsequently developed internationally competitive positions.

With the mechanization of forestry operations, Sweden built a leading position in several types of specialized machinery. Some examples are specially designed tractors, forwarders, log harvesters, and machines for thinning and planting. Many of the firms in these product groups have subsequently been merged with the two Finnish firms Repola and Valmet. The pulp and paper industry stimulated the manufacturing of various kinds of pulp and drying machinery, the production of fabrics and felts for paper machinery, and the production of systems for process automation, production control, and pump equipment. The Swedish producers of sawmill machinery, such as conveyors, drying kilns, and saw tools, have not been equally successful in the international market, and exports have stayed at around 20 percent of production, although they have managed to largely control the home market.

The forest sector is a major user of transportation services. Transportation is actually the second-largest variable cost for pulp and paper producers: only raw materials account for a larger cost share. Forest industry products have accounted for a third of domestic rail transports and a fifth of domestic road transports (excluding iron ore) in recent years. In fact, adopting a historical perspective, it is obvious that the transport needs of the forest sector have been major determinants of the construction of roads and railways in Sweden, especially in the less-populated areas. The forest industry's shares of the export industry's goods transports have been even higher than the domestic shares, with nearly half of sea transports, two-thirds of rail transports, and more than one-third of road transports involving forest products. The forest sector has also been important for the production of transport equipment. Part of the impetus for the production of heavy trucks by Volvo and Scania has been the demand for timber and paper transports, and both companies are world leaders in the industry. Earlier, the transport needs of the forest sector were also instrumental in the development of shipyards and production of railway equipment.

Strategies in the Swedish Forest Industries   The global consumption of wood has increased by about 50 percent over the past 25 years, as world population has grown and incomes have risen; hence, at an aggregate level, consumption of wood products is expected to continue increasing for the foreseeable future. In developing countries, the shift from agriculture to services and manufacturing boosts the demand for packaging materials, for example, in the food industry, while urbanization leads to an expansion of the construction sector, the main user of sawn wood products. Higher levels of education bring increasing demand for writing paper, newspapers, journals, and books. Hygiene products, such as various types of tissue paper, have become more widely used. The market for forest products in the established industrialized countries has also grown over time, in line with the rising level of income, although the structural changes that bring about growth are less explicit than in developing countries. One of the driving forces in the industrialized countries appears to be the growing importance of the service sector, which consumes more wood—in the form of paper—than many manufacturing industries. Contrary to forecasts from the 1970s and 1980s, there are no signs that the digitalization of the administrative services sector will reduce the consumption of paper.

The picture is less clear in the short run for individual industrialized countries, where differences in domestic supplies of wood resources and in environmental regulations, trade policies, and industry structure can have significant effects on the development of the market. How strong the connection between economic growth and increases in the consumption of forest products will be depends on how successfully the forest industry can supply the products that are demanded by the expanding sectors. Flexibility—that is, the ability to recognize and respond to new types of demand and competition—and active product and process development are therefore important key components of the strategies of Swedish forest companies, both in the pulp and paper and the sawn wood products industries.

One of the main challenges facing the Nordic forest industries in the early 1990s was the need to adapt forest management practices, production processes, and products to stricter environmental regulations and requirements, which have generally led to higher production costs. This, together with the increasing supply and demand for recycled paper, have induced some new strategies for the largest paper producers. Their main foreign investments have been directed to recycled newsprint mills in Continental Europe, which benefit both from the proximity to customers and the cheap supplies of raw material in the densely populated urban areas. The domestic operations are moving away from commodities, such as market pulp and newsprint, and are focusing more closely on specialized products requiring high proportions of virgin fibers. To this end, domestic investments have largely aimed to improve product quality and environmental safety. The strategies in other product groups, such as sawn goods, are also characterized by an emphasis on high-quality products, added value, and greater material processing. It can be expected that these trends will continue to be strong during the foreseeable future, not least because of the increasing competition in world markets for commodity products coming from countries such as Brazil, Chile, and Indonesia. The long-term ability of the Nordic forestry firms to adapt is closely related to their assets in terms of human capability and technological skills, which we have already discussed in some detail.

In the Swedish forestry companies, there are signs of several different development strategies focusing on different products and customers, as well as entailing slightly different requirements for skills and research and development efforts. In the pulp and paper industry, the **Fiber Strategy** departs from the traditional comparative advantage of the Swedish forest industry—the availability of high-quality raw material, that is, wood fiber—as well as ongoing comparative advantage due to technological progress. Both the Swedish pulp producers and the industry's research institutions are leading the international development in this area, and many of the industry's process innovations have been developed and introduced in Sweden.

The industry has also adopted a **Value Added Strategy** that implies phasing out sales of market pulp over time in favor of more refined products that embody higher value added. Some of the benefits of this strategy are that (i) adding more processing steps somewhat reduces the disadvantages of high raw material costs; (ii) more advanced products allow higher prices and profit margins; (iii) there are gains to be made from integrating pulp and paper mills with downstream production stages; and (iv) there is less volatility in more processed goods. The main drawback of the strategy is that it requires heavy investments in production facilities, distribution channels, and marketing operations, whether it is done from scratch or through acquisitions of existing firms. Foreign direct investment is also necessary in many cases, since sales of more advanced products to foreign customers require presence in the foreign market, and Sweden remains on the periphery of the European market. The way the strategy has been implemented in the major Swedish companies has essentially involved a shift from pulp to standardized grades of paper, mainly newsprint and kraft paper, where the main research requirements are related to surface chemistry and printing characteristics. This is also one of the fields where large collaborative research efforts (for example, the PCP-project) have been initiated by the organizations in the industry's knowledge cluster.

Finally, the **Specialization Strategy** places less emphasis on the gains from integration and more on the development of products that can carry high prices and allow acceptable profit margins through increased customization. A wide assortment of new products—cigarette paper, napkins, table cloths, and colored paper—and product variants have been introduced as the paper industry's technology has advanced. At the same time, changes in printing technologies have created demand for many different varieties and qualities of paper, and increasing environmental awareness has made it possible to market "green" products, which are manufactured using environment-friendly processes. While technological complexity is not a necessary requirement for the strategy, close customer contacts are. Consequently, the main problems faced by the Swedish producers focusing on the specialization strategy are related to their location, far from the center of the European market.

The strategies employed in the sawn wood products industry are more difficult to categorize, both because of the very heterogeneous structure of the industry and because most of the smaller firms seem to lack explicit strategies. The majority of Sweden's 2,500 sawmills concentrate on the production of simple sawn and planed wood products without much further processing. Developing alternatives would be a challenge to most of these businesses: the equipment of most sawmills is limited to saws, planing mills, debarkers, and chippers, and there is usually not enough skills or capital in the firm to invest in activities with higher value added. Many of the older sawmills are able to survive only because their overheads are low and their capital equipment was written off long ago.

Nevertheless, many of the larger firms in the industry can still be characterized in terms of the **Value Added Strategy** used in the pulp and paper industry—they could increase the value added of their output by refining the sawn wood in different ways or by diversifying into building joinery, prefabricated houses, or furniture. As with the pulp and paper industry, adding processing stages is seen as a way to overcome the disadvantages related to the high prices of Swedish raw materials, and diversification helps reduce the volatility of sales and earnings. And, again, the necessary investments are costly, although the main barriers are not related to financial strength, but rather to human capital. Diversification requires skilled labor, as the added production stages require competence in areas that are not familiar for most traditional sawmills. Hence, the success of the strategy is partly dependent on whether the transfer of skills from universities and research centers can be smoothly implemented: as noted in the discussion of the knowledge cluster of the sawn wood products industry, this was the main weakness in the present institutional structure. Further, establishing higher and consistent product quality (standards for most common pulp and paper qualities were established long ago) is essential for building marketing and distribution relations; this is one of the prioritized R&D areas also for the future. Finally, a few of the firms in the building joinery and furniture industries have managed to specialize in narrow product segments, such as wooden floors, kitchen and bathroom cabinets, and exclusive furniture. The requirements for customer contacts posed by this **Specialization Strategy** are more important and costly in terms of brand names, trademarks, and design than even those in the pulp and paper industry.

Strategies for the Knowledge and Skill Clusters

The strategic requirements for the knowledge and skill clusters in the paper and pulp and sawn wood products industries differ slightly because of differences in the structure of the industries and institutions. Yet both networks are affected by requirements in several different areas: education and recruitment, academic competence, research orientation, dissemination of research results, and financing of R&D.

Education and Recruitment

One of the main differences between the institutional structures in the sawn wood products and pulp and paper industries is that the former lacks organizations that are actively involved in the transfer of skilled personnel from universities and other research centers to the industry. As a consequence, the academic competence in sawmills and related activities is low, particularly considering the industry's objectives to diversify production and increase value added. The flow of students to higher education in wood technology is also low, and the supply of wood engineers is often scarce, largely due to the high cyclicality in hiring practices that make the three-to-five-year educational investment risky. In the paper and pulp industry, this problem is alleviated through the operations of the Pulp and Paper Research Institute, which recruits engineers as "trainees" during times when industry demand is low. This does not only stabilize the market for skilled labor, it also improves the connections between research organizations and pulp and paper companies. Consequently, a major challenge for the sawn wood products cluster is to set up a similar arrangement, with the Institute for Wood Technology Research filling the void identified in table 8.3.

Academic Competence

The company strategies in the forest industry are all dependent on the creation of new knowledge regarding materials, products, and processes. Much of the product development in the pulp and paper industry takes place in the research divisions of the larger companies, but basic research is done at the universities and the specialized research organizations. The firms in the wood products sector are smaller and have very limited resources for in-house R&D: the universities and research institutes account for almost all of the advanced research.

A general opinion in the forest industry is that the resources spent on forest-related research at the universities are much too small in relation to the industry's requirements. The industry has therefore lobbied successfully to increase the number of tenured professors at the main universities. During the 1990s, some 20 new full-professor positions in the forest sector— each with a connected assistant professor, graduate students, secretaries, and technical support—were established at the main research institutions. Part of the cost was financed by the forest industry.

In the pulp and paper sector, the Royal Institute of Technology presently employs tenured professors in pulp technology, paper technology, and wood chemistry, while the Chalmers Technical University has chairs in forest industrial chemistry. There are also chairs in paper surfacing, paper chemistry, and packaging technology (at the Royal Institute) and wood chemistry (at Chalmers). The newest positions focus mainly on paper and printing technologies, as well as environmentally oriented pulp production technologies.

In the sawn wood products field, there are presently tenured positions at the Royal Institute of Technology (wood technique) and the University of Luleå (wood technology). The Royal Institute also has professors in wood physics and wood drying, wood material research, and glue-laminated wood and composite materials. In addition, there are several tenured professors in wood and forestry-related areas at the University of Agricultural Sciences, focusing on issues like wood protection, biotechnology, and timber quality. The newest positions in the wood products field focus on wood substitutes, wood physics, and integrated production systems, and they are based in the southern part of the country, where most of the woodworking industry is located.

Another objective of the industry's research strategy is to improve the cooperation and coordination between the universities and the independent research organizations. To this end, there are attempts to concentrate the academic programs to two large research departments at the Royal Institute of Technology and Chalmers. This would not only facilitate the coordination of activities, but also allow the departments to benefit from economies of scale.

Research Orientation and Dissemination of Research Results

The large firms in the pulp and paper industry devote significant resources to commercial R&D (about 4 percent of value added, as noted earlier) and concentrate on the development of products and processes that are of immediate commercial value. The basic research is carried out in the industry's research institutes and at the universities. Presently, there is no clear division of responsibilities between the institutes and universities. Another part of the industry's strategy is to define more clearly the areas of responsibility for these two institutions.

Much of the university research takes the form of doctoral or licentiate dissertations, which implies that the projects involved are of a relatively long-term nature. It is often impossible to direct dissertations to focus on the issues that are of acute interest to the industry. The industry's research institutes, however, are much more flexible, and they can set up comprehensive research programs on relatively short notice. This distinction defines a natural division of responsibilities in research orientation. Regarding presentation and dissemination of research results, there are similar differences. The universities' research efforts are published in condensed form in academic publications that are not easily accessible to the industry. Hence, the Pulp and Paper Research Institute and other organizations make up a natural bridge between the academic institutions and the industry. In addition to presenting their own original research, these organizations are expected to take on greater responsibility for the dissemination of academic findings and to see to their being presented in a more operationally oriented manner.

A similar labor division applies for the relation between the sawn wood products industry, the research organizations, and the universities. The main difference is that the industry's expenditures for in-house R&D are very limited, meaning that the knowledge cluster will be responsible also for product and process development (not just basic research) in the short and medium run. Moreover, the task of disseminating research results is much more complicated, since the industry is so fragmented and there are few academically educated employees. Significant resources must therefore be spent on finding efficient channels for the transfer and dissemination of research findings. It is recommended that an intermediary between the research institutions and the individual companies must be created for this purpose, since most sawmills and related plants are too small to handle direct contacts with the research institutions. Some local and regional networks of small companies have already been created to manage the communication, with research results coming in one way and information about the companies' needs and problems going the other way. Although this is a costly way of creating the links, since the participating companies must employ a full-time administrator, but the results have apparently been positive. The success of these operations will not only influence the profitability of the sawmill industry, but will also have a profound impact on the industry's future demand for academically educated personnel. Sawmills and related plants will demand engineers and other highly skilled employees only if they understand the uses to which their skills can be applied.

Effects

While a detailed analysis of how these strategies affected the industry's performance during the 1990s is beyond the scope of the present study, some comments are still in order. First, the measures taken to strengthen the industry's competitiveness were moderately successful. The sector's aggregate production had increased by some 20 percent by the late 1990s, with higher increases in high-value added activities. Second, the structural changes in the forest sector continued. The production structure became more concentrated in both paper and pulp, sawmills, and sawn wood products. This is likely to be particularly beneficial for productivity in the sawmill and sawn wood products industry. In paper and pulp, the structural changes reached across national boundaries, as the European paper industry adjusted to the single European Market. For instance, Swedish Stora and Finnish Enso merged in the mid-1990s to achieve economies of scale in R&D and to coordinate their continental European production and distribution networks.

Third, the efforts to strengthen the industry's knowledge and skill cluster were reasonably successful. Several new programs in higher education and research were established during the 1990s, significantly raising the total investment in forest-related R&D. For instance, a new research center for pulp and paper technology was established at Mitthögskolan University in Sundsvall, with primary backing from the forest company SCA. New research projects focusing on sawn wood products, with financing from industry, government, and the European Union, were established in the Dalarna region in the central part of the country. Similarly, a broad program for wood product development was established at Luleå Technical University. Altogether, several hundred million SEK were invested in these ventures during the 1990s.

While the overall growth rate of the forest sector is likely to remain modest over the foreseeable future, it is likely that these investments will make it possible for the industry to maintain its competitive position. This is important, not least because the forest sector's net exports, amounting to some 75 billion SEK in 2000, are still as large as the aggregate net exports of telecommunications equipment and electronics, cars, and pharmaceuticals, which are at the core of the "modern" economy of Sweden. It is hardly possible to overestimate the importance of this source of hard currency and import capacity: Swedish economic development would undoubtedly be slower and more uncertain without these assets.

The Emergence of the Nordic Telecom Industry

Although the traditional raw-material-based industries have been able to maintain their strong positions in Sweden and the other Nordic countries over the years, the Nordic economies have been in a process of fundamental structural change since the early 1990s. At that time, the raw-material-based industries were quickly overtaken by the rapidly growing information and telecommunications sector. The frontrunners, companies like Nokia and Ericsson, not only become strategic actors in the Finnish and Swedish economies, but have also gained considerable international fame. For instance, in early 2000, Nokia joined the ranks of Microsoft, Cisco, and General Electric in the list of the world's top 10 most valuable companies.

The step from raw-material-based industry to high-tech activities like telecommunications and information technology may appear large, but there are important similarities between the two. In particular, knowledge and human resource development—in the form of well-developed knowledge clusters, as in the mature forest industry or in the form of in-house assets, as in the early stages of Nokia's and Ericsson's breakthrough in the mobile phone industry—were essential for success in both sectors. While it is not possible to systematically create innovations, like the NMT and GSM technologies that propelled Nokia's and Ericsson's breakthroughs, it is possible to systematically prepare for those commercial and technological opportunities and the challenges that will inevitably occur. Both Nokia and Ericsson were well prepared when the pivotal innovations emerged, and they could therefore exploit the opportunities when they opened up.

The following section outlines Nokia's development from a raw-material-based conglomerate to a high-tech telecom producer, with some focus on how the skills and knowledge needed for a high-tech breakthrough were acquired.

Nokia

Nokia is today best known for its mobile phones and telephone systems, but telecommunications has not been at the core of the company's business for more than about a decade. Yet, the history of Nokia reaches more than 100 years back in time. In 1865, the mining engineer Fredrik Idestam established a groundwood mill in Tampere in southwestern Finland, expanding it in 1869 to the nearby village of Nokia. There, the river Emäkoski provided the energy needed for Idestam's business venture, Nokia Ltd, which soon became Finland's largest pulp and paper mill. Some decades later, in 1898, the newly established Finnish Rubber Works also set up production at Nokia, attracted by the hydropower resources of the Emäkoski rapids. In 1912, Finnish Cable Works was established in Helsinki to supply the cables and wires needed for the electrification of the country's emerging industrial sector. In all three cases, much of the relevant technology was imported. Idestam had studied the pulp technology during his travels in Germany in the early 1860s. The engineer Antti Antero, long-time manager of the Finnish Rubber Works, had studied a Russo-French rubber factory in Riga, Latvia, and Arvid Wikström, founder of Finnish Cable Works, had studied Werner Siemens' innovations in cable production technology in Germany. Nokia, Finnish Rubber Works, and Finnish Cable Works rapidly managed to gain a strong position in the domestic Finnish market, as well as a foothold in the large Russian market. (Before independence in 1917, Finland was a Grand Duchy under Russian rule.)

These three companies are the predecessors of today's Nokia. In 1918, Finnish Rubber Works acquired the majority of shares in Nokia Ltd, to secure access to the hydropower resources at Nokia. Some years later, the new conglomerate also took control of Finnish Cable Works, although the three companies were allowed to successfully develop independently during the following decades. Nokia Ltd became a large conglomerate producing electric energy, pulp, and paper, mainly toilet paper. Finnish Rubber Works produced rubber boots and car and bicycle tires, with the development of the world's first winter tire as a particular success. Finnish Cable Works posted the most impressive performance of the three, partly as a result of Finland's war reparations to the Soviet Union after the Second World War. By the time the war reparations were completed, Cable Works had not only been forced to improve productivity, it had also secured a market in the Soviet Union that was able to absorb almost unlimited amounts of cable and wire. The existence of what seemed like a secure export market was a strong impetus to increase capacity as soon as the postwar currency restrictions were lifted. Diversification was also possible: an electronics department with a group of R&D engineers was established in 1960, which resulted in the development and production of a variety of electronic goods. For instance, in 1962, Finnish Cable Works developed a prototype radiotelephone at the request of the Finnish Army (in competition with the country's two other leading electrical engineering firms, Salora and Televa, and the Swedish producer, Sonab) (Pulkkinen 1997, 75).

By the mid-1960's, all three had outgrown the home market, but were hesitant to take on Western export markets on their own, so the three companies were merged in 1966. The new Nokia Corporation was organized into four divisions: paper, cable, rubber, and electronics. The electronics division was the smallest of these, with only 460 employees and 3 percent of the conglomerate's total turnover in 1967. The fastest growth during the 1960s and 1970s occurred in the cable division, but significant resources were also invested in the electronics division. In particular, the research department was given generous funding for product development, although its profitability was very low or even negative for a long time. Nevertheless, Nokia's CEO Bjorn Westerlund made sure that the

electronics workshops had access to the latest technology, and he protected the division's independence against criticism from the board of the
Cable division, which argued that the entire electronics division should be
closed down (Bruun and Wallén 2000, 22). The company took advantage
of the seemingly limitless demand for cable, radio telephones, and rubber
boots during the 1960s and 1970s (Haavisto and Kokko 1991), but to
avoid becoming dependent on the Soviet Union, it matched this with
increases in trade with the West, achieving parity by 1977. Many large
Finnish export companies that failed to implement similar restrictions in
favor of the lucrative dealings with the Soviet Union ended up in severe crisis in 1991, when Soviet trade collapsed.

To Become a High-Tech Company

When Kari Kairamo took over as CEO in 1977, Nokia was Finland's
largest private company, with around 16,000 employees (or about 2 percent of the country's industrial labor force). At that time, Nokia was still
primarily a producer of paper, tires, and cable, but Kairamo was committed to changing this and to transforming Nokia into a leading high-tech
company. The foundation was already in place, in the form of Nokia's
electronics division, which had managed to diversify significantly during
the preceding decade. The production of radiotelephones had expanded
when a nationwide public radiotelephone system had been established in
the early 1970s. The cellular NMT network that was to be launched in the
early 1980s in all the Nordic countries pushed Nokia to develop new
products for what was expected to be a rapidly growing market. Nokia
had also been marketing Siemens, Bull, Elliot, and Honeywell computers
in Finland since the late 1960s, and it had found a market for adapting foreign computer equipment into package solutions for domestic industrial
customers, for example, the nuclear power plants built in Finland during
the 1970s. By the late 1970s, the learning process had been successful
enough to allow Nokia to produce and to market its own computer terminals. However, the company was too small to take on the world market, and although the electronics division had been reasonably successful,
it still lacked the necessary skills and experience. It was therefore necessary
to focus on alliances and acquisitions to secure the strategic resources
needed to grow large enough to compete with the large European, Japanese, and American incumbents in the international electronics market.

Internally, Nokia allied and eventually purchased another Finnish telecom actor, Salora, which had televisions and other consumer electronics as
its core business. It was the market leader in radiotelephones and had a 30
percent market share in the Nordic region. Salora's principal attraction was
a technically advanced telephone that could operate on a larger number of
channels than those of the competitors. In the early phases, competition
with Salora, in particular, pressured Nokia to improve its radiotelephones

and prepared it to meet the competition from leading companies, including Siemens, Motorola, Hitachi, NEC, and Mitsubishi. Another competing player and future partner, the state-owned Televa, was stronger in telephone systems, and it possessed a beleaguered and underfunded research unit that had been experimenting with a digital telephone exchange—the DX 200.

In 1979, Nokia and Salora established a joint venture, Mobira, to pool their R&D resources, as well as Salora's formidable marketing skills. Nokia emerged as the dominant partner, and though the Nordic market accounted for half of the world's cellular phone sales until the mid-1980s, its CEO Kari Kairamo pushed for leadership in the European and world markets. After the first few years, the challenges increased. Nordic proposals to adopt the NMT as a European standard were rejected in favor of five analogue national and mutually incompatible standards that largely aimed to protect national producers. To become a global player, it was therefore necessary for Nokia to adapt to a multitude of standards. It was believed that the tough competition and the need to adapt to all the different mobile phone standards would force the company to acquire the skills needed to succeed on a global scale.

In the mid-1980s, Nokia also entered into several other alliances in phone production. The joint venture with the United States' Tandy Corporation gave Nokia phones a global marketing network through its Radio Shack outlets, as well as joint production of cell phones in South Korea. Nokia learned much from Tandy's competence in cost-efficient production design and from its sales and marketing skills (Pulkkinen 1997, 152). Increasing demand for computerized telephone exchanges, an area in which Nokia had little in-house capacity, forced Nokia to send a research team to Alcatel in France to learn all that was needed to start license production of Alcatel's new digital exchanges in Finland. This meant that Finland now had two digital exchanges in development, Televa's DX 200 and Nokia's French technology. The Finnish post and telecommunications authority argued that this was not feasible in such a small country and encouraged the two companies to work together. As a condition for increased collaboration, Nokia originally demanded discontinuation of the DX 200, and the project was kept alive only by a single contract with Houtskär, a small 700-person municipality in the archipelago of southwestern Finland. In the end, a strong preference by the Soviets (Finland's predominant market in light of the tightly regulated European market), tilted the balance toward DX 200, which eventually became a key component in Nokia's GSM technology, developed in collaboration with Alcatel, which took over in the 1990s.

The acquisitions and strategic alliances that were made during the late 1970s and 1980s were of central importance for Nokia's transformation from a raw-material-based to knowledge-based high-tech company. Another component was a broad push for human resource development within the company. One part of CEO Kairamo's internationalization program was to encourage as many as possible of Nokia's Finnish staff members to gain international experience by working in Nokia's foreign affiliates.[7] Another area was formal education. Kairamo was engaged in several ventures to improve the Finnish (and European) public education system, which he considered bureaucratic and old-fashioned. Among other ideas, Kairamo emphasized the need for broad international student exchange programs; stressed the need for continuous, life-long learning; and called for close collaboration between industry and academia. The most tangible result was the establishment of "Nokia University." This was a comprehensive and ambitious education program managed by several Finnish universities in collaboration with Nokia, with the aim to raise the formal competence of all Nokia employees by one level. Holders of bachelor's degrees were encouraged to obtain master's or licentiate degrees, and those who had master's and licentiates were expected to aim for doctoral degrees. This increase in the level of human resources was essential for Nokia's ability to absorb and to diffuse the skills and knowledge that were obtained through acquisitions and strategic alliances during this stage of Nokia's development.

Taken together, this meant that Nokia was well prepared for the future development of the global telecom market by the late 1980s: at that time, about a quarter of the world's NMT telephone systems were supplied by Nokia. The company had developed or acquired both the technical skills and the marketing, sales, and distribution skills needed for a global breakthrough. However, mobile phones and telephone systems accounted for less than 15 percent of Nokia's turnover.[8] Cables, rubber products, and forest products were more important. Further, and almost fatally, the largest part of the firm, and its strategic focus, was consumer electronics, in particular TV sets and information technology (for example, computers). Miscalculations about the potential size of this market given its saturation by existing producers nearly caused the collapse of the entire company.

Only the breakthrough of the digital GSM technology in 1991 and a simultaneous turnaround in Nokia's mobile phone design strategy saved the company. Nokia had begun the development of its first GSM network (largely on the basis of the DX 200 switchboard) in 1987, when it entered into an alliance with Alcatel and AEG. The first orders for the DX 200-based GSM technology came from France and Germany in 1988, with operators in Austria, Finland, and the Netherlands following the year thereafter. By 1990, new orders were flowing in from around the world, particularly from Europe, facilitated by deepening of European integration. Subsequent efforts in cellular phone design further consolidated Nokia's lead. From a simple raw-material-based company, Nokia has become a dynamic knowledge-based high-tech industry and one of the world's largest players in cellular technology.

Summary and Conclusions

Although the different sections of this chapter have examined industrial development at different levels of aggregation and at different points in time, it is still possible to point to some common findings and results, which include the following:

• Institutions and institutional reforms have played an important role for growth and development. Several examples have been highlighted throughout this chapter. For instance, the land reforms in the early 19th century were essential for the introduction of new technology in agriculture, and the subsequent increase in agricultural productivity was a prerequisite for industrialization. Similarly, the introduction of laws to guarantee replanting and to limit the concentration of forest ownership in the early 20th century were essential to creating a sustainable resource base. More recently, various environmental regulations have forced the Nordic corporate sector to take a leading role in the development of environmentally sustainable production technologies. The role of various public or semipublic institutions in promoting research and knowledge diffusion has also been emphasized repeatedly.

• The acquisition of relevant skills and knowledge has been an essential success factor. The Swedish industrialization process—as well as the early development of the forest industry—relied to a great extent on foreign technology and capital. Foreign direct investment in Sweden was important, but the international experience of Swedish entrepreneurs and innovators also contributed significantly. The foreign technologies that were transferred to Sweden were rapidly absorbed in domestic industry, since the level of education was relatively high. Over time, an increasing share of the forest industry's technology has been created in the sector's knowledge and skill cluster, which is made up of a multitude of institutions and organizations involved in the creation and dissemination of knowledge and skills. We have argued that this cluster is of essential importance for the Swedish forest industry's ability to adjust to a continuously changing competitive environment. In the telecommunication sector, the acquisition of knowledge has largely taken place at the firm level.

• Similarly, the acquisition of knowledge and skills has been of central importance for Nokia's breakthrough. Unlike the mature forest industry, where much of the skill and knowledge are created in the industry's knowledge clusters, the telecommunications industry has not yet developed any similar institutional structure. Nokia has therefore been forced to internalize these processes, systematically acquiring the skills needed for further stages in research and product development. At the same time as new knowledge has been brought into the corporation, there have also been comprehensive efforts to raise the educational level of existing staff members. The establishment of Nokia University in the 1980s and the emphasis on individual development and life-long learning during the past two decades have been essential for the diffusion of new technology throughout the company. It is not until the second half of the 1990s that the telecommunications industry in Finland began to develop the institutions for a knowledge cluster. Very substantial public investments in relevant higher education, the establishment of formal linkages between universities and industry, and industry-financed research organizations are contributing to the creation of a knowledge cluster.

• Internationalization has been essential at all levels of development. The first stages of Swedish industrialization were clearly export-led, driven by the demand for forest products in Great Britain and other parts of Western Europe. In the forest industry, in particular the large-scale paper and pulp industry, growth has been based on access to the European and international markets. Internationalization has also been essential for the Nordic telecom producers to finance the large fixed costs related to R&D. In addition, a relatively open trade regime has been necessary for the acquisition of modern technology, both at the early stages of industrialization and in today's high-tech industries: many of the core patents in the telecom sector are held by U.S., Japanese, and continental European producers. The need to adapt technologies to international standards and the continuous competitive pressure from other international producers have also been important driving forces in many industries, not least telecommunications.

• The technological innovations underlying both Nokia's (and Swedish Ericsson's) breakthroughs were possible only thanks to long-term investments in R&D programs. In Nokia's case, early orders from the Soviet Union were essential to securing financing for technology development. At the same time, it is clear that focused long-term research projects are high-risk ventures. Neither Nokia nor Ericsson prioritized the R&D programs that eventually generated the innovations necessary for the successful development of the GSM technology. For instance, Nokia's primary investment emphasis was on projects that eventually failed, such as the HDTV program. An essential success factor has therefore been flexibility: both companies were able to shift rapidly from other activities to the mobile phone industry when it took off in the early 1990s.

• While most of the industry's early development was based on in-house assets, it now appears that a knowledge and skill cluster is emerging in the telecommunication industry. It is possible that this suggests a general pattern in the development of new technologies or industry sectors. Intangible, firm-specific assets dominate the early stages of a technology's life cycle, whereas an increasing share of the essential knowledge and skills are of a "public good" character at later stages. Knowledge and skill clusters can arguably not emerge unless a large share of the essential knowledge and skills are available to most participants in the cluster. A central determinant of how "public" the knowledge and skills are may be the extent to which the public education system is involved in the industry. In the forest industry, it is obvious that the public higher education system plays a central role: this may be underway also in the telecom sector, as a result of the increased investments in relevant higher education.

A tentative conclusion from this chapter is that an industry's success is a mix of systematic knowledge creation and random technological innovation. It is not possible to systematically generate major technological breakthroughs, but it is possible to create an environment where firms or entire industries are well positioned to adjust to changing conditions and to benefit from innovations and market opportunities. In mature raw-material-based industries like paper or wood products the innovations are likely to be incremental, and a large share may be related to changes in demand or international competition, rather than to major changes in production technology. A solid knowledge base is, nevertheless, necessary to ensure the necessary flexibility and adaptability. In younger industries like telecommunications, fundamental changes in technology will be more common, and the main challenges are related to the ability to acquire the technical skills necessary to remain competitive. Although mergers and acquisitions as well as various kinds of strategic alliances are likely to be important in these sectors, a solid knowledge base at the company level is also essential to facilitating the dissemination and implementation of new technologies throughout the firm or industry.

These conclusions suggest an important role for public policy. The experiences discussed in this chapter suggest, in particular, that public policy should provide an appropriate institutional framework for facilitating the sustainable use of land, raw materials, and other resources, as well as promote learning and internationalization. While most successful companies invest heavily in in-house programs for knowledge creation and human resource development, it is essential that the public education system also provide graduates with appropriate skills and knowledge. This is not only a prerequisite for successful life-long learning in the business sector, but may also provide a common knowledge base for the development of various networks and clusters in industry. Support for the development of industry-level organizations, as outlined in the discussion of the Swedish forest industry's knowledge cluster, is also likely to be useful. Direct support to in-house commercial research, however, is more questionable. Although Ericsson's experience points to successful collaboration between the company and the Swedish public sector in the development of its NMT and GSM technologies, it is often a costly and inefficient way to promote a competitive business environment. One problem is that direct state intervention distorts competition. Another problem is the risk inherent in any long-term R&D project: failures are more likely than successes.

Internationalization is best supported through open and outward-oriented trade policies. It has repeatedly been noted that access to export markets is essential for small-country producers, but it should also be pointed out that access to imports at competitive cost is perhaps equally important. Few countries can rely exclusively on domestic resources for economic development. A significant share of the cheapest intermediates and best technologies for any industry, even in relatively simple raw-material-based sectors, is likely to be found abroad. Outward-oriented trade regimes will promote the flow of information about these resources, both through trade and foreign direct investment.

Notes

1. For a more comprehensive discussion about the relevance of the Scandinavian development model for today's developing countries, see Blomström and Meller (1991). This volume also points to the importance of political and demographic factors in long-run growth.
2. For an outline of the evolution of the GSM technology, see http://www.gsmworld.com/about/history.shtml
3. Yet agriculture was still the dominant activity. It was not until about 1900 that the GDP share of manufacturing equaled and eventually surpassed that of agriculture, and agricultural employment remained larger than manufacturing employment until the 1930s (Jörberg 1984, 9–10).
4. The importance of chance is also reflected by the sizable Swedish migration to America during the second half of the 19th century. This made it possible to urbanize at a rate that was consistent with industrial development. It is estimated that a quarter of the Swedish population (1.2 million people) emigrated between 1850 and 1910. As a result, Sweden avoided the worst problems related to rural poverty and mass unemployment: it is also likely that this helped avoid political problems caused by polarization between left and right. See further Haavisto and Kokko (1991).
5. The *Handbook of the Northern Wood Industries 1991/92* provides an incomplete list with 74 different associations at the national level.
6. In addition to university-level education, there were also upper secondary schools specializing in forestry, with more than 500 graduates per year. See National Board of Forestry (1993).
7. Kairamo argued that not only Nokia but all of Finland should become more outward oriented, which made him a strong proponent of Finnish membership in the European Community long before this was a politically correct view. In this context, Bruun and Wallén (2000, 37) report that Kairamo's vision was "to see a Finnish name in the passenger list every time an airplane crashes somewhere in the world."
8. Thanks to the very lucrative exports of DX 200 telephone exchanges to the Soviet Union, it is likely that the share of profits was significantly higher, but there are no detailed data on Nokia's earnings from Soviet trade.

References

Ahlström, G. 1992. "Technical Competence and Industrial Performance: Sweden in the 19th and Early 20th Centuries." Lund Papers in Economic History 14, Lund, Sweden: Lund University.

————. 1993. "Industrial Research and Technical Proficiency: Swedish Industry in the Early 20th Century." Lund Papers in Economic History 23, Lund, Sweden: Lund University.

Asgard, L., and C. Ellgren. 2000. *Ericsson: historien om ett svenskt företag*. Stockholm, Sweden: Nordstedt.

Blomström, M., and P. Meller, eds. 1991. *Diverging Paths: Comparing 100 Years of Scandinavian and Latin American Development*. Baltimore, MD: Johns Hopkins University Press.

Bruun, S., and M. Wallén. 2000. *Boken om Nokia*. Stockholm, Sweden: Fischer & Co.

Carlsson, B. 1980. "Jordbrukets roll vid Sveriges industrialisering." In *Industriell utveckling i Sverige*, ed. E. Dahmén and G. Eliasson. Stockholm, Sweden: Almqvist & Wicksell.

Ds 1991: 62, *Kunskap för konkurrenskraft–skogsindustrins kunskapsförsörjning,* Ministry of Industry, Stockholm.

Haavisto, T., and A. Kokko. 1991. "Finland." In *Diverging Paths: Comparing 100 Years of Scandinavian and Latin American Development*, ed. M. Blomström and P. Meller. Baltimore, MD: Johns Hopkins University Press.

Hallvarsson, M. 1980. *Industrialismens 100 år*. Stockholm: Sveriges Industriförbunds Förlag.

Handbook of Northern Wood Industries. 1991/92. Stockholm, Sweden: B. Svensk Travarutining Publishers.

Hultin, M. 2000. "Internationell handel, en möjlig tillväxtmotor!" In *Svenskt näringsliv och näringspolitik 2000,* Stockholm, Sweden: Nutek. Based on the OECD–STAN Database, 1998.

Jörberg, L. 1984. "Den svenska ekonomiska utvecklingen 1861–1983." Meddelande från Ekonomisk-historiska institutionen, Lunds universitet, Nr. 33. Lund, Sweden.

Larsson. M. 1991. *En svensk ekonomisk historia 1850–1985*. Stockholm, Sweden: SNS Förlag.

Larsson, M., and U. Olsson. 1992. "Industrialiseringens sekel." In *Sveriges Industri*. Stockholm, Sweden: Industriförbundet.

National Board of Forestry. 1993. *Statistical Yearbook of Forestry 1993*. Jönköping.

Nilsson, A., and B. Svärd. 1991. "The Quantitative Development of Vocational Education in Sweden 1950–1990." Lund Papers in Economic History 12. Lund, Sweden: Lund University.

Pulkkinen, M. 1997. *The Breakthrough of Nokia Mobile Phones.* Helsinki School of Economics and Business Administration, Acta Universitatis Oeconomicae Helsingiensis A-122.

Schön, L. 1982. *Industrialismens förutsättningar.* Malmö: Liber Förlag.

SIND 1986. *Möbelindustrin: Nuläge och framtids-möjligheter.* Stockholm, Sweden: SIND.

————. 1989. *De tropiska trädslagen: Hot eller nya möjligheter för svenskt snickerivirke.* Stockholm, Sweden: SIND.

————. 1990. *Japan. Ny marknad för svenska träprodukter.* Stockholm, Sweden: SIND.

Skogsindustrierna. 1994. *A Search for Sustainable Forestry: The Swedish View.* Stockholm, Sweden: Annual Publication 1993, Swedish Pulp and Paper Association.

Sölvell, Ö., I. Zander, and M. Porter. 1993. *Advantage Sweden,* 2nd ed. Stockholm: Norstedts Juridik.

Statistical Yearbook of Forestry 1993. National Board of Forestry, Jönköping, Sweden.

STFI. 1994. *STFI Annual Report 91/92.* Stockholm, Sweden: Swedish Pulp and Paper Research Institute.

Svensén, M. 1992. "Skogsindustri." In *Sveriges Industri.* Stockholm, Sweden: Industriförbundet.

United Nations. 1986. *European Timber Trends and Prospects to the Year 2000 and Beyond.* New York: United Nations.

Part III

Are Natural Resources Destiny?

9

Trade, Location, and Development: An Overview of Theory

Anthony Venables *

Introduction

THE THEORY OF INTERNATIONAL TRADE has been transformed in recent decades, moving beyond the stylized world of perfect markets and factor endowments to models that incorporate a variety of imperfections. Frictions to international trade and investment flows do not arise just because of tariff barriers, but also because of geography, institutions, and information barriers. Markets are not all perfectly competitive—rather, they contain firms with market power, and there are imperfections in labor and capital markets. Production often involves increasing returns to scale, which requires that focus be put on firms, rather than simply on the sectors of activity studied in competitive trade theory. Attention to firms has allowed the theory of foreign direct investment (FDI) to be brought into the mainstream of trade theory. Dynamics and the processes of technology development and transfer have been analyzed in this context.

Importantly, these new elements have been studied in combination with each other as well as with the previous general equilibrium models of trade and specialization, and the combination has brought results that are much greater than the sum of the parts. For example, understanding international differentials in wage rates is an inherently general equilibrium subject. We have to know about labor endowments (and how these change because of education or migration decisions) and about labor demands, which depend on the decisions of firms. Firms' profitability will be influenced not only by wage rates, but also by considerations of access to markets and to supplies of other inputs. Combining these elements can give outcomes where small initial differences between countries translate into large differences in outcomes. With increasing returns to scale, cumulative causation processes can operate, so both the economic structure and income levels of countries can follow divergent paths, thus making factor endowments, including natural resources, relatively unimportant as exogenous determinants of income levels and economic structure.

While these developments in international economics have been taking place, there has been relatively little work focusing on trade and development. This is in sharp contrast to the development economics literature of the 1960s and 1970s, where attention was directed to investigating the effects of alternative trade regimes. As will become clear in the course of this chapter, more work is needed in applying developments in trade theory (and in industrial organization) to issues of economic development, as well as to draw out policy conclusions. Above all, empirical work on trade, industry, and development is needed, establishing exactly what shape industrial development patterns take in a world of new technologies, regional integration, and generally liberal trade regimes.

The remainder of this chapter is organized into three main sections. The first section looks at the bases of comparative advantage and their implications for production structure and the international distribution of income. The analysis starts with traditional endowment-based trade theory, but widens it out to show how geography and market size can themselves be bases for comparative advantage. In the following section, we demonstrate how the bases of comparative advantage are themselves endogenous. We provide a brief review of the implications of capital mobility (through FDI) and of skill acquisition. More attention is devoted to "spatial externalities." We use this term to capture the idea that the productivity of firms in a location is influenced by the activities of other firms in the same location, through knowledge spillovers or linkages of some kind. Pursuing this approach gives new ways of thinking about some trade and development issues, while also connecting modern economic analysis to older ideas of development economics such as those developed by Hirschman (1958) and Myrdal (1957), as well as the ideas of business economists such as Porter (1990). Next, we draw out some policy applications of the approaches discussed in previous sections, focusing on sectoral policies, infrastructure investments, and regional integration. Throughout, the primary objective of the chapter is to provide an exposition of developments in theory. Connections are made with empirical work at various points, although much empirical work is needed on the issues addressed in this chapter.

Comparative Advantage, Trade, and Income

What determines the economic structure of an open economy, and how do openness and the ensuing structure influence factor prices and income levels?

To answer these questions we proceed in two stages, looking first at production structure and income given a country's comparative advantage, although we define comparative advantage more broadly than does the standard approach. We then look at some of the ways in which the basis of countries' comparative advantages can change, as well as at the implications of these changes.

The analytical approach of comparative advantage theory is to put a particular structure on the more general framework of competitive equilibrium theory. Competitive equilibrium theory is based on consumers and firms respectively maximizing their utility and profits and interacting only through perfectly competitive markets. The framework can encompass many locations (countries) as well as many dates (as in intertemporal competitive equilibrium). Equilibrium determines the market clearing prices and quantities of all goods, and at equilibrium, it will generally be the case that consumption and production are not equal for all goods in all locations, generating trade between locations. Trade theory puts a structure on this general framework by assuming that countries differ in certain well-defined ways, and goods (or industries) also differ systematically. It then asks, what is the relationship between the characteristics of countries and the characteristics of the goods that they export? We answer this question first for the traditional case, where the characteristics are factor endowments and factor intensities, and then show how the insights of this approach can be generalized.

Endowments

Much analysis is based on the assumption that the only difference between countries is in their endowments of primary factors, assumed to be internationally immobile. Correspondingly, commodities differ in their techniques of production, especially the intensities in which they use different primary factors. The Heckscher-Ohlin-Samuelson theorem tells us that economies that are relatively labor abundant will export relatively labor-intensive goods and so on.

This interaction between country characteristics and industry characteristics is illustrated in figure 9.1. Suppose that there are many countries that differ only in the ratio in which they are endowed with labor and capital, L_i, and one horizontal axis ranks countries according to this ratio (over the set of countries, with individual countries indexed by i). There are many industries (indexed by k), differing only in labor intensity, which we denote γ^k; industries are ranked along the other axis in the horizontal plane. The surface of the figure plots equilibrium output levels of each industry in each country, measured by the share of production of good k in country i.

As expected, L-abundant countries have high production in industries in which the share of this factor is large (high γ^k) and low production in

Figure 9.1 Cost Share and Endowment

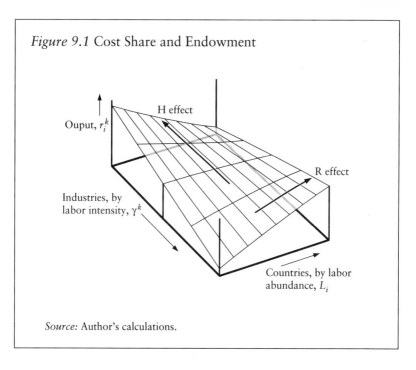

Source: Author's calculations.

industries where it is low, giving a saddle-shaped surface. The arrow marked R on the surface indicates how, in a particular industry, production varies with factor endowments; moving to more L-abundant countries increases output for products with high γ and decreases it for products with low γ. The arrow marked H shows how, for a particular country, the structure of production depends on its factor endowment: an L-scarce economy has relatively high production in low γ industries, while an L-abundant country has relatively low production in these industries. The effects illustrated by the R and H arrows can be thought of as generalizations of the Rybczynski and Heckscher-Ohlin-Samuelson effects, showing how output of each industry depends on factor endowments, and how the structure of production of each country depends on factor intensities

This example is constructed with countries and industries varying in just one dimension, L-abundance and L-intensity. In practice, they differ in many dimensions, each of which supports a surface like that in figure 9.1, although with countries and industries ordered differently (because the ranking of countries by land abundance may be quite different from the ranking by skilled labor abundance).[1] However, the general principles outlined here remain applicable. Comparative advantage is determined by

the interaction between an industry characteristic and a country characteristic. Furthermore, econometric analysis allows these surfaces to be identified from the data (see Ellison and Glaeser 1999 and Midelfart-Knarvik,
Overman, and Venables 2001).[2]

Discussion of "industries" or "goods," while standard, is perhaps misleading. In many activities the vertical production chain is now split, or
"fragmented," with different stages of production taking place in different
locations according to their input intensities. Heckscher-Ohlin trade theory applies at this level, so its predictions are that labor-intensive stages of
production should take place in labor-abundant economies. We return to
this issue in our discussion of production networks later on.

Finally, the model predicts that each country gains from trade (as must
any trade model set in perfect market conditions). There is also a tendency
for international equalization of prices of a particular factor, this implying
that each country's scarce factors may suffer a real income loss (as they
effectively come to compete with foreign factors) while abundant factors
experience real income gain (as they come to be exported, embodied in
goods that are intensive users of the factors).

Location

The insight that the pattern of production is determined by the interaction
of country characteristics and industry characteristics, according to a surface qualitatively like that of figure 9.1, is far more general than sometimes
appreciated. For example, country characteristics include a measure of
institutional quality, and industry characteristics might include the effect
of institutional quality on unit costs. Countries with good institutions
would then have production skewed toward sectors where institutional
quality was important.

The effects of geography on industrial structure can be analyzed using
the same approach. Suppose that countries differ only in their distance
from the world market, and commodities differ only in transport costs.
Then the insight of von Thunen (1826) was that countries (or land area)
close to markets would specialize in transport-intensive commodities, and
locations further out would produce goods with lower transport costs.
This approach is developed in a trade theory framework in Venables and
Limao (2002), and illustrated in figure 9.2a. The horizontal axis is the set
of countries, and point 0 is the center, representing developed countries
that export a good or composite of goods (good 0), while importing
goods 1 and 2. Points $z > 0$ are countries lying at increasing distances
from this center and potentially trading with it. The vertical axis gives the
value of production of good 0, good 1, and good 2 in each country. The
structure of production is, as before, determined by the interaction
between country characteristics and commodity characteristics, these

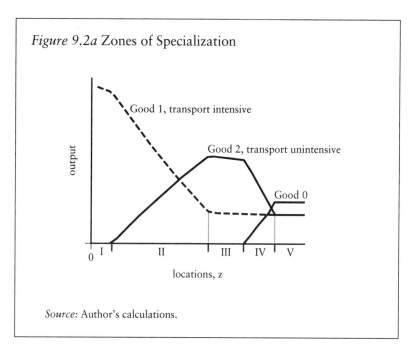

Figure 9.2a Zones of Specialization

Source: Author's calculations.

now being countries' distances from the center, and goods' transport intensity (transport intensity being high if transport costs are high or the commodity is dependent on imported intermediates).

The figure illustrates an example in which endowments are the same in all locations, and goods and factors are labeled such that good 1 has a higher transport intensity and higher labor intensity than good 2. The following structure emerges: countries at locations close to the center (zone I, at the left of the figure) specialize in the good with high transport intensity, good 1. Because they export this good, they import the other two goods, 0 and 2. Moving further out (zone II), production of the less transport intensive good (good 2) commences, and beyond some point, countries become exporters of good 2. Further out again is zone III, in which it is not profitable to export the high transport-intensity good (good 1) and countries become self sufficient in good 1, while continuing to export good 2 and import good 0. Thus, between zones I and III the pattern of production and trade has reversed, even though factor endowments are the same everywhere. Zone IV is one of import substitution—good 0 has become so expensive that it is profitable to produce it locally. Eventually, in zone V, there is autarchy.

Factor prices and real incomes corresponding to this example are given in figure 9.2b. More remote locations have progressively lower real

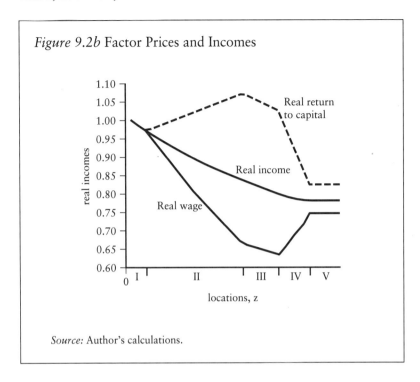

Figure 9.2b Factor Prices and Incomes

Source: Author's calculations.

incomes as they forego the gains from trade. The magnitude of this decline is determined by transport costs on final and intermediate goods and by the share of intermediates in output. If imported intermediates account for 50 percent of gross output and there are transport costs of just 10 percent on these and on exports of the final product, then value added is reduced by a full 30 percent. Prices of each of the factors can vary in a more complex way, depending on the factor intensities of the sectors. Thus, if the transport-intensive good (good 1) is also labor intensive (as assumed in this example), the wage falls rapidly.[3]

While this is just an example, it illustrates an important general point. In this example all activities have constant returns to scale and perfect competition, and all countries have identical technologies, yet considerations other than factor endowments determine (in a systematic way) production structure, factor prices, and income levels. Geography matters for what countries do and how well off they are. However, the basic insight is simply that of comparative advantage trade theory; production structure is determined by the interaction of country characteristics and product characteristics, applied in this example to the geography of countries and transport intensities of products.

Production Networks and Vertical Fragmentation

The factor intensities of different stages of the production process vary at least as widely as do the factor intensities of finished products as a whole. The scope for trade therefore depends on the extent to which it is worth "fragmenting" the vertical production process and undertaking different stages of production in different locations. While the benefits of fragmentation are input costs saved, the costs are those incurred in shipping goods (including the costs of time in transit) and managing remote operations or supply chains. Recent decades have seen reductions in shipping costs and times (Hummels 1999, 2000) and perhaps, more important, the development of information and communications technologies that have done much to reduce the costs of remote management. The consequent growth of "vertical specialization" is documented by a number of authors. Yeats (1998) estimates that 30 percent of world trade in manufactures is in components rather than final products. For Asian countries, Ng and Yeats (1999) report an overall pattern of assembly in lower-wage economies, with components production taking place in Japan, Singapore, and Taiwan (China). Hummels, Ishii, and Yi (2001) chart trade flows that cross borders multiple times, as when a country imports a component and then reexports it embodied in some downstream product. They find that (for 10 Organisation for Economic Co-operation and Development countries), the share of imported value added in exports rose by one-third between 1970 and 1990, reaching 21 percent of export value.

Analytically, the main basis of this trade is the interaction of factor abundance and factor intensity, as in Heckscher-Ohlin trade theory, but several comments are worth making. First, because products are likely to cross borders multiple times (as components are reexported embodied in downstream stages of production), transport costs are likely to be a particularly important obstacle to this type of trade. Security of supply will also be important, as delay will disrupt the entire production chain. Patterns of production and trade therefore depend on interactions of transport intensities and location, as well as factor intensities and endowments. Thus, proximity to other stages of the production process and final markets is likely to matter, particularly for bulky commodities. Fragmentation can affect middle-income countries if, for example, processing of primary products is relocated from them to low-wage countries.

Second, although this trade is based on factor price differences, an increase in the trade does not necessarily narrow international differences in these prices, as might be expected. The reason is that an activity relocating from a northern to a southern economy may be unskilled-labor intensive relative to other activities in the northern economy, but skilled-labor intensive relative to the endowment of the southern economy. Feenstra and Hanson (1996) develop this idea and argue that it may apply to many of the activities that have relocated from the United States to Mexico; these activities are unskilled-labor intensive compared to the U.S.

economy, but skilled-labor intensive compared to the Mexican economy. The effect is to increase wage inequality in the North (as unskilled-labor-intensive jobs leave) *and* in the South, as the new pattern of labor demand is more skilled-labor intensive than the previous southern employment structure.[4]

Increasing Returns, Market Access, and Supplier Access

The "new trade theory" that was developed starting in the late 1970s added to trade theory systematic treatments of increasing returns to scale (at the level of the firm) and imperfectly competitive market structures. A number of insights came from the analysis. On the welfare economics side, there is improved understanding of the sources of gains from trade. In addition to comparative advantage, trade increases product variety, and it is likely to have a procompetitive effect, reducing monopoly power while at the same time allowing firms to become larger and to better exploit economies of scale. On the policy side, there was extensive study of "strategic" industrial policy, although this came with a realization that the effects of policy were likely to be unpredictable, particularly given the limited information available to policymakers (see Brander 1995 for a survey).

In regard to the pattern of trade, the literature provides a theoretical explanation of the large volumes of intra-industry trade that are observed, and it also shows how market size can provide a basis for comparative advantage. The main result (sometimes known as the "home market effect") is that economies with large markets will get a disproportionately large share of increasing returns industries. The intuition is derived from thinking about the location decisions of potentially footloose firms, operating in the presence of some transport costs on their output. These firms will seek to locate in the large market to save transport costs and have lower marginal costs of supplying consumers, and this will create outcomes in which an economy with, say, twice the market size, will have more than twice as many firms as a smaller country. Obviously, in general equilibrium this will translate into higher factor prices in the larger economy, giving an outcome in which firms trade off benefits of market access against the higher wage costs of central locations. As in figure 9.1, general equilibrium will mean that economies with good market access will tend to specialize in industries where the home market effect is strong, and vice versa.

To make these ideas operational, they have to be generalized to a multicountry setting with a real geography of trade costs between locations, rather than just the linear world of figures 9.2a and 9.2b. This can be done both in theory (for example, Fujita, Krugman, and Venables 1999) and empirically. A measure of "market access" can be computed for each location and is a theoretically well-founded version of the old idea of market potential, measuring demand at each location, weighted by a decreasing function of distance. In addition, an analogous measure of "supplier access" can be constructed to measure proximity to suppliers of intermediate goods. Redding and Venables (2001) show how the market access and supplier access of each country can be computed from trade data, and they confirm empirically the importance of these variables in determining cross-country variations in income, as suggested by theory. Access to foreign markets and suppliers can explain one-third of the cross-country variation in per capita income, and the full measures of market access and supplier access explain up to two-thirds of the variation.

Changing the Basis of Comparative Advantage

The analysis outlined previously takes as given the endowments, technologies, and market and supplier access of countries and then shows how this generates cross-country patterns of production, trade, and income distribution. However, in a developing country or region all of these elements are subject to change, and analysis must be extended to handle this. We proceed in three stages. First, we look at FDI. Inflows of FDIs may bring capital into the country, although they are probably more important for bringing in technology and other firm-specific assets. We then look briefly at issues of labor supply, reviewing ideas on the interactions between trade and skill acquisition. The third stage is to look at the implications of externalities between firms in an economy. These may be either technological or pecuniary externalities. Either way, they make comparative advantage endogenous, so their presence requires a major rethinking of the basis of trade and of the effects of trade on incomes.

Capital and Foreign Direct Investment

Multinational corporations provide an important vehicle for providing countries with capital and, more importantly, technologies for production and for gaining access to export markets. Their importance in the world economy has been extensively documented, with the overseas production of affiliates of U.S. firms now three times larger than total U.S. exports and nearly half of U.S. exports going directly to U.S. affiliate companies.

The literature focuses on three motivations for foreign investment in developing countries. The first is to gain access to natural resources, and we devote no further attention to this. The second is to gain better access to host-country markets; this is known as horizontal FDI, since it typically involves duplicating a part of the production process that is already operating elsewhere (for example, undertaking vehicle assembly in several regions). The third motive is to benefit from factor price differences by, for example, moving unskilled-labor intensive activities to low-wage economies; this is known as vertical FDI, as it involves breaking up the vertical production structure. It underlies the formation of production networks or production chains.

The decision to undertake horizontal FDI is usually posed as a trade-off between supplying a market by exports or by local production.[5] If supply is through exports, then marginal costs of supply might be high because of transport costs, delivery lags, or failure to tailor the product to local circumstances. The alternative, supplying the market by local production, typically yields lower marginal costs, but higher fixed costs are incurred in operating a further production plant. This suggests several circumstances where FDI is more likely to occur. One is where transport costs or other trade barriers are high, as happens when "tariff-jumping" FDI is used to avoid the barriers created by import-substituting regimes. Another is where local markets are large: here, FDI allows the fixed costs of setting up an additional plant to be spread across a large volume of output. Thus, as with the "home market effect" mentioned earlier, increasing returns to scale activities are drawn into large markets. In addition, there is considerable evidence that FDI projects cluster together in particular countries. This may just be because of the underlying characteristics of the country, but is likely to also be because of "herding," where one FDI project has a demonstration effect, encouraging others.

For vertical investments, the trade-off is quite different. The advantage is access to cheap labor to undertake labor-intensive parts of the production process. The main costs are the additional costs incurred in managing an operation at a distance, and the transport costs (which include shipping costs as well as possible delay and increased uncertainty) involved. Thus, we expect production networks to form where lower-wage economies are close to, or have very good transport links with, higher-wage countries, as well as in commodities that are transport unintensive. Here too, there is evidence of the geographic clustering of investment projects.[6]

Turning to effects, there are once again important differences between horizontal and vertical FDI. Horizontal FDI is likely to be a substitute for trade, as firms use FDI instead of imports to supply the market. Of course, this statement needs some qualification as components are likely to be imported, total sales may increase, and a particular project may be used as a base from which to supply a larger regional market. Nevertheless, its basic function is to replace imports. By contrast, vertical FDI is a complement to trade, and it may even create trade flows that are much larger than the value of the final good produced as component parts cross borders repeatedly, embodied in the product being shipped.

Turning to employment and income-generation effects, horizontal inward FDI will generally increase labor demand, as local production replaces imports. However, if local firms are operating in the industry, then there are also likely to be competition effects, as the FDI project takes sales from these firms. In contrast, vertical FDI is typically export oriented, so it will not have competition effects in the local market. It can be viewed as a mechanism for achieving the effects predicted by factor-endowment trade theory, enabling countries to export their lower skilled labor embodied in firms' output.

Finally, it is often suggested that one of the main effects of FDI is to generate beneficial spillovers to the rest of the economy. The spillovers can arise through demonstration effects, direct linkages between FDI and local firms (for example, collaboration to improved input product and process quality), and labor-market turnover of trained workers. There is a good deal of case study evidence of the importance of all of these mechanisms, although the picture from econometric studies is more mixed (see Blomström, Kokko, and Zejan 2000 for a survey).

Labor and Skill Acquisition

The quantity and quality of labor are obviously the most important elements of a country's factor endowments, and these too are subject to change, particularly as education changes a country's skill mix. Analytical work on the interaction between trade and skills takes the Heckscher-Ohlin model as point of departure. In this model, a long established—although perhaps not as well known—result is that trade liberalization reduces the incentive for workers in unskilled-labor-abundant economies to acquire skills. For example, if the factors of production are skilled and unskilled workers then, under autarchy (or restricted trade), an economy with few skilled workers will tend to have a high wage for these workers, compared to the more abundant unskilled workers. This creates an incentive to become skilled. Trade liberalization, however, allows skill-intensive goods to be imported while expanding production of unskilled-intensive goods. This reduces the demand for skilled labor relative to unskilled labor, narrowing the wage gap between the two groups and reducing the return to education.

The relevance of this result can be questioned on several grounds. The first is that trade in new activities—as when a stage of production can be detached and relocated—can be unskilled intensive relative to northern endowments, but skilled intensive relative to southern endowments (as discussed earlier). Similarly, if nontraded activities are unskilled-labor intensive, then opening up the economy and expanding the share of activity in tradable sectors might increase demand for skilled labor. There may therefore be factor-endowment-based trade that increases the incentive for southern workers to acquire education. The dichotomy between skilled and unskilled labor is also too sharp, as there is evidently a continuum of skill levels. There is plenty of evidence (for example, from the Asian experience) that at least primary-level skills are at a premium in modern sector manufacturing export activities.

An alternative mechanism arises if trade liberalization allows movement of some factor (or knowledge) that is complementary to skilled labor. Tang and Wood (2000) suppose that globalization allows "knowledge workers" to gain better access to cheap, southern unskilled labor. If knowledge workers combine with relatively skilled labor in the South, then the effect will be to raise wages of skilled workers in the South and increase incentives for education. The same argument can be made for the movement of capital, for the package of activities embodied in FDI, and for transfer of new technologies. In addition, it may be the case that openness to trade changes the incentives for government to support education. A political-economy analysis of this is undertaken by Bourguignon and Verdier (2000).

Spatial Externalities and Cumulative Causation

Studies of cumulative causation processes have a long history in development economics. They were emphasized particularly in the writings of Hirschman (1958) and Myrdal (1957). In recent years they have come to attract renewed interest, both in policy circles (for example, Stern 2001) and in formal economic analysis (for example, Murphy, Shleifer, and Vishny 1989). The trade and geography literature has shown how the location of production can be subject to these processes and has drawn out implications for the spatial structure of activity and of incomes.

We have so far made the conventional assumption that firms can internalize the effects of their actions. What happens if externalities are—in some sectors at least—pervasive and the actions of one firm have a direct impact on the performance of others? If an externality were to be transmitted equally to all industries, or to a particular industry in all countries, then comparative advantage would be unaffected. Usually, however, externalities are limited in both sectoral and geographic scope. A new product or technique will only be used in some sectors, and the price of the product or availability of the technique will vary across countries. If externalities are sector- and location-specific in this way, they form a basis for comparative advantage, which now becomes endogenous.

Externalities between firms may be either technological or pecuniary, the former arising when actions of one firm affect another without going through a market and the latter when the interaction is through a market but firms are not able to capture the full benefits (or costs) of their actions. The main sort of technological externalities are knowledge spillovers of various types. These could take the form of demonstration effects, or spillovers of research and development, technical knowledge, or accumulated learning by doing. Early work modeling the international implications of these effects includes Krugman (1981, 1987). For example, Krugman (1981) assumes that labor input coefficients in manufacturing are decreasing functions of a region's capital stock. These increasing returns imply that any initial differences between regions will be amplified as one gets ahead of the other, creating one developed and one underdeveloped region. The problem with this approach is that the key mechanism—the source of the technical spillover—is left as a "black box." Subsequent research has sought to look inside this box to identify the sources of the market failure that generates the externalities.

In contrast to technological externalities, pecuniary externalities are transmitted through markets. The key feature is that firms are unable to fully capture the benefits of their actions. One example is the introduction of an improved intermediate good (or business service) that may carry with it a net benefit to purchasers, who become recipients of a forward linkage.[7] Thus, the benefits of the new product are not all appropriated by the suppliers, but are instead being transmitted to the downstream firms— a pecuniary externality.

Backward linkages arise if firms sell output at price greater than marginal cost. When price equals marginal cost, a small change in volume sold is of no value to the firm (since the extra revenue simply equals the extra cost). But if price is greater than marginal cost then a shift in the demand curve increases profits. Thus, increased activity by downstream firms will raise demand for upstream firms, and if there are transport costs or other trade frictions, the extra demand will be spatially concentrated. These backward linkages will therefore raise profits of local upstream firms, perhaps also attracting the entry of new firms.

The combination of forward and backward linkages creates a potential process of cumulative causation: expansion of downstream activity increases demand for upstream output, which attracts entry, improving the supply (price or varieties) of intermediates, attracting further downstream entry, and so on. Of course, this interaction of forward and backward linkages has been studied before in development economics.[8] However, the mechanism is dependent on market imperfections, and it is only quite recently—following the development of models of trade with increasing returns to scale and imperfectly competitive market structures—that the mechanisms have been analyzed formally, and their implications for trade and production have been drawn out in a rigorous manner.

Pecuniary externalities can arise in factor markets as well as product markets. For example, if one firm trains labor it may not be able to appropriate all the benefits, as workers can quit and work for other firms. There may also be labor market "pooling" effects, arising as firms and workers are better able to share random shocks in larger labor markets. Notice again that the range of the externality will typically be limited across industries (depending on the specificity of labor skills) and across space (depending on the mobility of workers).

To see the implications of these externalities, it is worth developing a simple example. Suppose that there are just two locations (countries) and an industry in which the total number of firms is fixed (at n). How is the distribution of firms between countries determined? Figures 9.3a and 9.3b give two alternative cases. The fixed number of firms is measured by the length of the horizontal axis, while the numbers in country 1 and country 2, n_1 and n_2, are measured by distance from the right- and left-hand ends of this axis, respectively; thus, a point on the horizontal axis measures a division of the industry between the two countries. The

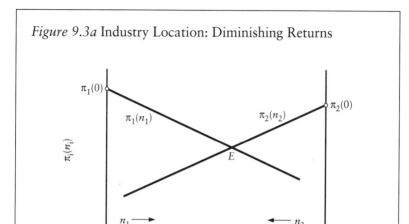

Figure 9.3a Industry Location: Diminishing Returns

Source: Author's calculations.

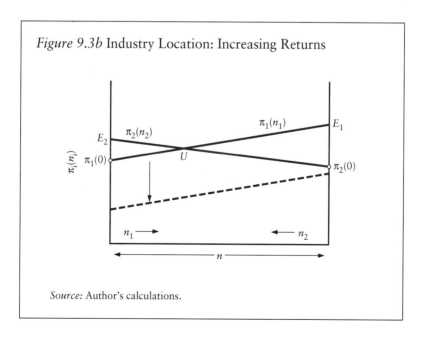

Figure 9.3b Industry Location: Increasing Returns

Source: Author's calculations.

vertical axis measures the profitability of a single firm in each location, assumed to depend only on the number of firms active in the location, $\pi_1(n_1)$ and $\pi_2(n_2)$.

Figure 9.3a indicates a standard "neoclassical" case. The functions $\pi_i(n_i)$ are downward sloping, indicating diminishing returns to the activity in each location (perhaps because expansion bids up the price of some scarce factor, or because it reduces the price of output). The equilibrium is at point E, where returns are the same in both countries, so it is not profitable for any firm to relocate. The figure is constructed under the assumption that country 1 has a comparative advantage, so the $\pi_1(n)$ line is higher than $\pi_2(n)$. Consequently, country 1 has more of the firms in the equilibrium.

Figure 9.3b gives the case where positive externalities are strong enough to overturn any forces for diminishing returns, making the $\pi_1(n_1)$ and $\pi_2(n_2)$ schedules upward sloping. The intersection of these curves is now an equilibrium, but it is unstable (if a firm relocated from country 2 to country 1, it would raise π_1 relative to π_2, so other firms would follow). There are two stable equilibria at the points on the axes labelled E_1 (where all firms are in country 1 and $\pi_1(n) > \pi_2(0)$), and E_2 (where the converse applies). These points are equilibria, as there is no incentive for any firm to relocate.

Several lessons can be drawn from this simple example. First, there are multiple equilibria. Activity agglomerates, but there is nothing in the theory to tell us in which country. We need to go outside the theory—to history, for example—to resolve this indeterminacy. Second, the equilibria are robust to parameter changes. Suppose that we reduce country 1's comparative advantage, pushing the $\pi_1(n_1)$ schedule downward. In figure 9.3a the equilibrium moves continuously to the left, but in figure 9.3b the equilibria might be unaffected. For example, if the equilibrium were at E_1, no firms relocate until $\pi_1(n_1)$ reaches the dashed line illustrated, at which point there is "catastrophic" change. Once it becomes worthwhile for a single firm to relocate (when $\pi_2(0) > \pi_1(n)$), other firms will follow. E_1 ceases to be an equilibrium, and all activity moves to country 2. These points demonstrate how there is a possible first-mover advantage. If a location becomes established in an activity, then it will be difficult for another center to become established. The cluster may well have a "deep" comparative advantage and be able to pay high wages or survive adverse shocks.

The example shows how activity may cluster in one location, but what implications does this have for real income in each location? The answer depends on the alternative uses of the factors employed in the industry. If the cluster is small, then factor supply curves may be horizontal (over the relevant range), so having the cluster does nothing to raise wages or other factor prices. Benefits are instead all passed on to consumers (worldwide and local, depending on the magnitude of any trade costs). But if the cluster is large enough for its presence to change factor prices, then the country with the cluster will, other things being equal, be better off: having the cluster raises labor demand and wages.

Agglomeration and North-South Inequalities

Models of clustering have been applied to a number of different trade and development issues, and we now review some of these applications. We base discussion on the Krugman-Venables (1995) model (see also Fujita, Krugman, and Venables 1999), in which there are two different types of economic activity. One is termed "agriculture," and it represents a composite of all of the perfectly competitive (and nonincreasing returns) sectors of the economy. The other is "manufacturing," and it has two key features. One is that firms operate under increasing returns to scale and are potentially footloose, choosing where to locate according to market access and production costs. The other is that these manufacturing firms use primary factors *and* manufactures, and they sell their output both to consumers *and* to other manufacturing firms. This input-output structure means that there are forward and backward linkages, and firms will tend to locate close to other firms, who supply some of their inputs and provide some of their market. The labelling "agriculture" and "manufacturing" is intended to capture these differences, although it is clearly very stylized.

Krugman and Venables (1995) showed how this model could give rise to large wage and income inequalities between countries that have the same underlying characteristics of endowments, technology, preferences, and location.[9] Their results are summarized in figure 9.4, in which w_i measures the real wage in country i, and there are just two countries in the world. The horizontal axis is a measure of trade barriers, and we see that when these are very high, the two countries are identical ($w_1 = w_2$). This is because firms have to locate near final consumers, which prevents clustering from occurring. At lower levels of trade costs, the need to be close to final consumers is reduced, so the clustering forces generated by linkages become relatively more powerful. Manufacturing then agglomerates in one country; theory does not say which, but in figure 9.4 it is assumed to be country 1, which, as a consequence, has higher labor demand and higher wages. This change is "catastrophic," as the model passes through a bifurcation point at which there is a qualitative change in the structure of equilibria.[10] The economic story is that, as transport costs are reduced, one region of the world "deindustrializes" the other, and the world necessarily develops a dichotomous "North-South" structure. Wages are much higher in the North, but no firm wants to move to the South as by so doing it would forego the advantages of proximity to a large market and large number of supplier firms.

In this model, further reductions in trade costs narrow the wage gap as the world enters the "globalization" phase. The reason is that at low trade

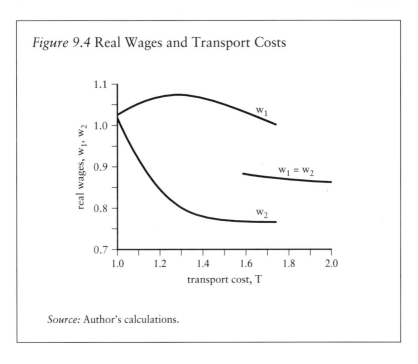

Figure 9.4 Real Wages and Transport Costs

Source: Author's calculations.

costs the pecuniary externality created by firms becomes less spatially concentrated—intermediate goods can be shipped more cheaply between countries. In the limit of perfectly free trade the model reduces to textbook international economics, with factor price equalization. Factor price equalization occurs as the limit of this model because at perfectly free trade we reach the "death of distance." However, other sorts of pecuniary or technological externalities might be less sensitive to trade costs (for example, externalities in the labor market), in which case factor price equalization is not reached.

The general message of figure 9.4 is, then, that at very high trade costs, location of manufacturing is determined by the need to be close to final consumers. At low trade costs, factor supply becomes important, and relocation of industry will narrow factor price differences. At intermediate trade costs, the potential for clustering and consequent income inequalities is greatest.

The Spread of Industry

The story just outlined is one of reductions in transport costs that, beyond some point, start to narrow international income differences by facilitating the spread of industry out from established clusters of activity. Thus, economic development occurs as concentrations of industrial activity start to disperse to new locations. In a world containing many countries, what form does this dispersion take?

A conventional view of growth and convergence would suggest that countries will all converge at a more or less similar rate to common steady-state values of capital and income per worker. The new economic geography view suggests, by contrast, that the world may consist of a rich club and a poor club, and development might take the form of selected countries, in turn, making a rather rapid transition from one group to the other. This is illustrated in figure 9.5, drawn from Puga and Venables (1996), who apply the preceding model in a multicountry framework. In the initial situation, illustrated at the left-hand edge of the diagram, manufacturing is concentrated in country 1, and other countries have only agriculture. Exogenous technical progress increases demand for manufactures in the world economy (moving to the right on the figure), and this increases the wage gap between country 1 and other countries. At some point, the wage gap becomes too large to be sustainable, and industry starts to relocate to other countries. However, it does not go to all other countries, because to do so would be an unstable equilibrium; if one country were to get just slightly ahead, the linkages generated would cause this country to become the preferred location for further manufacturing expansion. In the case illustrated, country 2 industrializes, while 3 and 4 are left behind.

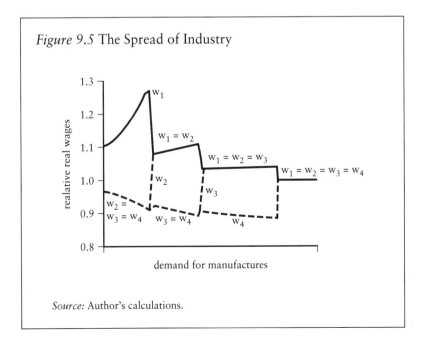

Figure 9.5 The Spread of Industry

Source: Author's calculations.

The process then repeats itself. Countries 1 and 2 have industry and a wage gap relative to the rest of the world. Continuing demand growth raises the wage gap until manufacturing once again spills over and spreads to a new location. Development is therefore the rapid transition of countries in sequence, from the poor club to an expanding rich club.

Puga and Venables argued that the model is suggestive of Asian development experience, although as theoretically modeled the structure is obviously too stark, particularly in its assumption that all candidate countries for industry are identical. Country differences that make a location an attractive host are the obvious ones of good institutions and low unit labor costs. Also important is proximity to established regions, so that intermediates can be imported and exports shipped at relatively low cost. Large market size is beneficial, providing a local market for developing industry. Combining some of these factors implies that a strong natural resource base has opposing effects: it increases local expenditures and market size, but by raising wages and unit costs is likely to deter industrialization.[11]

The theoretical model also suggests that—as long as there are some remaining benefits to clustering—there is no guarantee that all countries will eventually experience industrialization. World demand for manufactures may perfectly well be met by efficient size clusters in a subset of countries. There may then be continuing North-South disparities, the magnitude of which depends on the terms of trade between the different commodities they produce.

The discussion has so far been couched in terms of an aggregate manufacturing sector. In reality, this must be disaggregated, so that the linkages between sectors depend on the structure of the input-output matrix as well as the tradability of the product. What can then be said about the way in which the industrial structure evolves during the development process?

Activities that are most easily detached from existing centers are those with a high labor share (benefiting from low wages) and that receive few linkages, either forward or backward, from activities in existing centers. Receipt of backward linkages will be unimportant if the commodity is easily traded, or if it can be sold to a local market rather than being dependent on demand from existing centers. Receipt of forward linkages will be unimportant if intermediate manufactured inputs are a small share in production, or if intermediates are very easily traded. (Of course, in the case of primary processing industries, linkages may be available from local supplies of natural resources or primary products). Finally, transferability of labor skills and technologies may be important (see Sutton (2000) for investigation of the determinants of transferability of firm capabilities).

While linkages received by the sector are important for assessing which activities can be detached from existing centers, linkages transmitted by the sector are important for determining both the speed and the shape of the development path. Some preliminary investigations of these effects were undertaken in Puga and Venables (1999) and Fujita, Krugman, and

Venables (1999), who found that development was typically most rapid when upstream industries could be easily detached from existing centers, since these industries then created strong forward linkages, facilitating the movement of downstream industries.

These ideas are suggestive, but empirical work has not yet been undertaken to confirm them. We return to the policy implications of this approach later on.

External Trade and Internal Economic Geography

Discussion so far has been based at the national level, and it has been assumed that labor is not mobile between locations. What difference does it make if labor is mobile on a large scale, as is likely to be the case within a country and, in some circumstances, internationally?

Immobility of labor is a major force for dispersion of activity because as a cluster develops, it raises wages, choking off further growth. Removing this labor-supply constraint makes agglomeration more likely, and Krugman (1991a and 1991b) shows how falling transport costs could lead to agglomeration of manufacturing activity and population in a single region. Expansion of the region will continue until choked off by rising prices of immobile factors (land) or external diseconomies of scale, such as congestion. The approach has been developed to investigate the growth of cities in developing countries (Puga 1998). Although this is not the place for a review of the internal economic geography of developing countries, several points are worth making.[12]

Whether agglomeration forces will give rise to megacities depends on the breadth of activities over which clustering forces operate. In developed countries, clustering often takes quite a narrow sectoral form, arising because of externalities associated with particular sector-specific skills or sector-specific input requirements. This supports a number of sector-specific clusters, each of which may be quite small relative to the economy as a whole—vehicles in one region, electronics in another, financial services in a third, and so on. In contrast, it is possible that clustering in developing countries has a wider sectoral range, as externalities occur at the level of provision of basic business services, public sector services, or general (rather than sector-specific) labor skills. In this case, instead of multiple clusters, a single cluster—a megacity—is likely to develop, until further expansion is choked off by diseconomies of size.

Relatively closed and inward-looking economies are likely to be more prone to development of these megaclusters than are open ones (Krugman and Livas 1996). To the extent that clustering is driven by forward and backward linkages, the strength of clustering will be lower the more outward oriented are firms, purchasing inputs from and supplying outputs to the world rather than to local markets. Thus, it is suggested that an additional benefit of trade liberalization is that it promotes the restructuring of a country's internal economic geography, facilitating a deconcentration of activity from the prime city region.

Policy Issues

The benchmark for assessing policy is, as always, the first theorem of welfare economics, which establishes the efficiency of competitive equilibrium. Policy analysis is then based on the identification of market failures and the design of policies targeted at these failures. This methodology remains applicable in the presence of increasing returns, imperfect competition, and consequent pecuniary externalities, although policy design becomes more complex for two reasons. First, market failures may be pervasive throughout large sectors of the economy, in which case the usual second-best arguments apply with force. Second, we have seen how these failures can lead to multiple equilibria and corner solutions. The fact that there are multiple equilibria means that policy instruments do not map uniquely into outcomes. Policy might seek not just to make a marginal adjustment to an interior equilibrium, but to cause a nonmarginal change, shifting the economy to another equilibrium. Awareness of these difficulties, combined with awareness of the problems of policy capture and government failure, has made researchers reluctant to develop a theory of economic policy in this sort of environment. Nevertheless, some remarks are possible, and, in this section, we discuss a number of policy issues, looking first at sectoral policies, then at general infrastructure and trade promotion policies, and finally at preferential trade promotion policies—regional integration.

Sectoral Policies

Differential Rates of Demand Growth   Countries that are specialized in commodities with fast-growing demand will tend to do better through time than countries whose terms of trade are declining because of slow growth of export demand. The differential rates of demand growth could be due to a number of reasons—income effects or technical change—and slow growth will lead to larger terms of trade deterioration the less price elastic are demand and supply.[13]

These observations have led to the suggestion that countries should actively seek to specialize in faster-growing sectors. However, for this to constitute a valid reason for policy intervention, the case has to be made that the private sector is either failing to perceive demand conditions or failing to respond to them. The former is a hard case to make. There is no reason to believe that government has better information than the private sector in forecasting demand growth, and the record of governments in picking winners is not good.

The latter case—poor private sector response—provides a sounder basis for policy, but requires diagnosis of why the private sector response is lacking. The classic answer is to link poor response to capital market failure; the long-run investments required to profit from growing demand are not made because of credit market constraints or a price of capital exceeding its social marginal cost. This is not an industry-specific market failure, and the response should be in the capital market, not in the support of a particular sector.

Externalities   The presence of externalities provides a well-established case for the use of policy to expand activities that create positive externalities and to contract activities that create negative ones. Since much of the previous discussion turned on the presence of externalities, what are the policy implications?

The first issue is, can sectors or projects that create relatively large externalities be identified? Theoretically, the answer is yes, although it depends on a complex combination of factors. How will derived demands for inputs be split between local firms and imports, determining the extent of backward linkages? Is there imperfect competition in the upstream industry? What is the likely quantity response in the upstream industry? Will this quantity response create positive forward linkages? How firm-specific are labor skills created by the project? Empirically, we know little about how these effects vary across industries. There is an inherent unpredictably, in so far as the externalities create value only as they elicit positive quantity responses from other firms.

Second, the type of industrial linkages and externalities discussed earlier are generally reciprocal externalities—each firm creates them and also receives them from other firms. The market failure is therefore often described as a coordination failure, rather than simple externality, as the problem could be solved by the collective action of a group of firms. This is the logic behind policies such as business or science parks, and infrastructure, research, and education policy to facilitate the development of clusters. Such policies need not provide sectorally targeted assistance, but do create the environment in which coordination failures are minimized.

Finally, the record of government action in providing sectoral support is, with a few notable exceptions, generally poor. There is also the Catch-22 of this sort of policy. If we knew exactly what sort of sectoral policy worked, then it would be used by many governments, the price of output from these sectors would decline, and (at policy equilibrium) there would be no return to another government employing the policy.[14]

Infrastructure Investment and the Costs of Distance

We have argued that there can be substantial costs from being remote from economic centers and from having high trade and transport costs.

The theoretical arguments are confirmed in the work of Sachs and his coauthors (Gallup, Sachs, and Mellinger 1998, Radelet and Sachs 1998), who find that activity is concentrated in regions with geographical advantages, such as proximity to a coast.

These arguments suggest the benefits of open trade policy and point to the potentially high value of infrastructure investments or other measures that reduce the costs of international transactions.[15] The appraisal of such investments requires, of necessity, full cost-benefit analysis. In addition to direct benefits that can be captured by investors, a major infrastructure project changes prices, creating economic surplus that accrues elsewhere in the economy but should nevertheless be included in the calculation. The total surplus created by such a project will consist of the cost reduction times the existing quantity, plus an amount that is proportional to the elasticity of the quantity response with respect to the cost reduction. The message from theory is that this quantity response is potentially large, as the economy is drawn into fuller participation in the world trade. If production networks develop, then quantities of trade will be large and, as we have argued, cumulative causation processes might also cut in. Of course, infrastructure investments alone are not sufficient to ensure effective participation, but they are a necessary part of reducing the costs of peripherality.

Regional Integration

In the light of the overview of modern trade theory presented here, what are the likely effects of regional integration? Economic effects can be grouped into three main types, corresponding to some of the theory arguments.

First, costs and benefits depend on the comparative advantage of member countries relative to each other and relative to the rest of the world. This is the basis of the traditional trade creation and trade diversion argument, and it provides a strong argument for North-South rather than South-South agreements. South-South agreements are prone to trade diversion, as sectors develop in the member country that has comparative advantage in the sector relative to the partner country, but not relative to the world as a whole. Trade diversion occurs as members' imports come to be sourced according to this regional comparative advantage rather than to global comparative advantage.[16]

Second, benefits are potentially derived from fuller exploitation of economies of scale, combining with procompetitive effects as firms in member countries are brought into more direct competition with each other. To the extent that a regional integration agreement achieves a larger integrated market, it may be possible to have both more competition and larger firms. The home market effects discussed above might operate to strengthen manufacturing sectors as a whole.

Third, propensity to cluster brings both benefits and costs. Regional integration may create a larger integrated market, which will increase the scale of activities, allowing critical mass to develop. However, the development might be in just one of the member countries rather than in all of them. We have argued earlier that in developing countries clustering is likely to involve a relatively wide range of activities rather than simply occurring in particular sectors. This suggests a potential for divergence of economic structure and income between member states of developing-country regional-integration agreements. The unequal distribution of costs and benefits implied by trade creation and diversion can be amplified by these mechanisms.

Conclusions

There is now compelling evidence that full participation in the world economy is an inherent part of modern economic growth. In the words of Lindert and Williamson (2001), "the empty set contains those countries that chose to be less open to trade and factor flows in the 1990s than in the 1960s and rose in the global living-standard ranks at the same time. As far as we can tell there are no anti-global victories to report for the postwar Third World."

This conclusion is supported by the work of Dollar and Kraay (2004), who compare the economic performance of a set of developing countries they term the "globalizers" with the performance of all other developing countries. The globalizers are identified on the basis of the decline in their tariff rates between the 1980 and the late 1990s and the increase in their trade-to-gross domestic product ratio. The striking point is that, while these countries fared worse than others in the 1960s and 70s, their performance was dramatically better during the 1980s and 1990s, with per capita growth of 5.3 percent per year compared to –0.8 percent per year for the nonglobalizers.

While these findings establish an association between trade performance and growth, they do not establish a causal relationship, and still less do they identify particular trade policy instruments as determinants for causing growth. Cross-country regression studies endeavoring to establish the effect of trade policy on growth have not, in general, been successful.[17] This suggests that trade policy reforms, while perhaps necessary, are not sufficient for good economic performance. Institutional and geographical factors matter and theory tell us that, given cumulative causation, it is possible that very small differences in these initial conditions can translate into large differences in outcomes. It is worth noting that natural resource endowments are not an important part of the story in the context of the theoretical models discussed in this chapter. Theory also tells us that where successful growth performance is achieved, so too is strong export performance, as countries grow by developing and exploiting a comparative advantage in a range of activities.

Now that attention has been turned back to these issues of cumulative causation, much more work—empirical work in particular—is needed on the determinants of manufacturing success in developing countries, on the path that industrialization takes, and on the policy levers that are most conducive to it. In Stern's words, we need further research on how countries can "design credible investment reforms" to "hoist themselves onto a virtuous circle characterized by increasing returns" (Stern 2001).

Notes

*The author thanks Daniel Lederman and William Maloney for their helpful comments.

1. We choose not to get drawn into discussion of "dimensionality" issues in trade theory, but note that if there are few distinct types of primary factors, then there will be a greater degree of country specialization than suggested by the surface of figure 9.1. For implications of this, see Leamer's work on multiple cones (1987) and the more recent work of Schott (2000).

2. The model outlined here gives each country a slightly differentiated variety of each product. The limiting case of this more general model is one in which products are perfect substitutes, in which case dimensionality issues (numbers of goods versus numbers of factors) become important.

3. Although in this example good 0 is also assumed to be labor intensive, so the wage starts to rise in the import substitution region, zone IV.

4. The Feenstra and Hanson model is one of capital mobility, but the same possibility arises in a pure trade model; see Venables (1999).

5. See Brainard (1997) and Markusen (1995).

6. See Feenstra (1998).

7. Only if the seller were a perfectly discriminating monopolist could it extract all of the surplus from the new good.

8. Notably by Hirschman (1958) and Myrdal (1957).

9. Much of this literature constructs economies to be ex ante identical to demonstrate how, despite this extreme assumption, they can have different equilibrium economic structures and income levels.

10. At high trade costs, the symmetric equilibrium is unique. There is then a range of trade costs in which there are five equilibria; the symmetric equilibria is stable, as are equilibria with agglomeration in either country, and between these stable equilibria are two unstable equilibria. At lower trade costs, the symmetric equilibrium becomes unstable (the point on figure 9.4 where the $w_1 = w_2$ line ends), and there are three equilibria, the two agglomerated equilibria being stable.

11. Crafts and Venables (2001) argue that the sheer size of the 19th century U.S. economy, assisted by an import tariff, was sufficient to cause industrialization, reversing its endowment-based comparative advantage in primary products. For the ambiguous role of tariffs in smaller economies, see Puga and Venables (1999).

12. See Henderson, Shalizi, and Venables (2001) for a review of some of this material.

13. For a more modern statement of this view, see Matsuyama (2000).

14. See Norman and Venables (2001).

15. See Limao and Venables (2001).

16. See Venables (2001).

17. See Rodriguez and Rodrik (2001) for a critique of these studies.

References

Blomström, M., A. Kokko, and M. Zejan. 2000. *Foreign Direct Investment: Firm and Host Country Strategies.* London: Macmillan.

Bourguignon, F., and T. Verdier. 2000. "Globalization and Endogenous Educational Responses: The Main Economic Transmission Channels." Discussion Paper, Ecole Normale Superieure–Delta, Paris.

Brainard, S. L. 1997. "An Empirical Assessment of the Proximity Concentration Trade-off between Multinational Sales and Trade." *American Economic Review* 87: 520–44.

Brander, J. A. 1995. "Strategic Trade Policy." In *Handbook of International Economics,* volume 3, ed. G. Grossman and K. Rogoff. New York: North Holland.

Crafts, N. F. R, and A. J. Venables. 2001. "Globalization in History: A Geographical Perspective." London School of Economics. http://econ.lse.ac.uk/~ajv/craven4.pdf.

Dollar, D., and A. Kraay. 2004. "Trade, Growth, and Poverty." *Economic Journal* 114 (493): F22–F49.

Ellison, Glenn, and Edward L. Glaeser. 1999. "The Geographic Concentration of Industry: Does Natural Advantage Explain Agglomeration?" *American Economic Review, Papers and Proceedings* 89: 311–16.

Feenstra, R. C. 1998. "Integration of Trade and Disintegration of Production in the Global Economy." *Journal of Economic Perspectives* 12: 31–50.

Feenstra, R., and G. Hanson, 1996, "Foreign Investment, Outsourcing, and Relative Wages." In *Political Economy of Trade Policy: Essays in Honor of Jagdish Bhagwati,* ed. R. Feenstra, G. Grossman, and D. Irwin. Cambridge, MA: MIT Press.

Fujita, M., P. Krugman, and A. J. Venables. 1999. *The Spatial Economy: Cities, Regions, and International Trade.* Cambridge, MA: MIT Press.

Gallup, J., J. Sachs, and A. Mellinger. 1998. "Geography and Economic Development." *Proceedings of the World Bank Annual Conference on Development Economics.* World Bank, Washington, DC.

Henderson, V., Z. Shalizi, and A. J. Venables. 2001. "Geography and Development." *Journal of Economic Geography* 1 (1).

Hirschman, A. 1958. *The Strategy of Economic Development.* New Haven, CT: Yale University Press.

Hummels, D. 1999. "Have International Transportation Costs Declined?" http://ntl.bts.gov/lib/24000/24400/24443/hummels.pdf.

———. 2000. "Time as a Trade Barrier." http://www.mgmt.purdue.edu/centers/ciber/publications/pdf/00-007Hummels2.pdf.

Hummels, D., J. Ishii, and K-M Yi. 2001. "The Nature and Growth of Vertical Specialization in World Trade." *Journal of International Economics* 54 (1): 75–96.

Krugman, Paul. 1981. "Trade, Accumulation, and Uneven Development." *Journal of Development Economics* 8: 149–61.

———. 1987. "The Narrow Moving Band, the Dutch Disease, and the Competitive Consequences of Mrs. Thatcher." *Journal of Development Economics* 27: 41–55.

————. 1991a. "Increasing Returns and Economic Geography." *Journal of Political Economy* 99: 483–99.

————. 1991b. *Geography and Trade.* Gaston Eyskens Lecture Series, Cambridge, MA: MIT Press.

Krugman, P., and R. E. Livas. 1996. "Trade Policy and the Third World Metropolis." *Journal of Development Economics* 49: 137–50.

Krugman, Paul, and A. J. Venables. 1995. "Globalization and the Inequality of Nations." *Quarterly Journal of Economics* 110: 857–80.

Leamer, E. 1987. "Paths of Development in the Three-Factor, n-Good General Equilibrium Model." *Journal of Political Economy* 95 (5): 961–95.

Limao, N., and A. J. Venables. 2001. "Infrastructure, Geographical Disadvantage, Transport Costs, and Trade." *World Bank Economic Review* 15: 451–79.

Lindert, P., and J. Williamson. 2001. "Does Globalization Make the World More Unequal?" http://post.economics.harvard.edu/faculty/jwilliam/papers/GlobalUnequal_10_25.pdf.

Markusen, J. R. 1995. "The Boundaries of Multinational Firms and the Theory of International Trade." *Journal of Economic Perspectives* 9: 169–89.

Matsuyama, K. 2000. "A Ricardian Model with a Continuum of Goods under Nonhomothetic Preferences: Demand Complementarities, Income Distribution, and North-South Trade." *Journal of Political Economy* 108 (6): 1093–1120.

Midelfart-Knarvik, K. H, H. G. Overman, and A. J. Venables. 2001. "Comparative Advantage and Economic Geography: Estimating the Location of Production in the EU." CEPR Discussion Paper 2618.

Murphy, R., A. Shleifer, and R. Vishny. 1989. "Industrialization and the Big Push." *Journal of Political Economy* 97: 1003–26.

Myrdal, G. 1957. *Economic Theory and Under-Developed Regions.* London: Duckworth.

Ng, F., and A. Yeats. 1999. "Production Sharing in East Asia: Who Does What for Whom and Why." Policy Research Working Paper 2197, World Bank, Washington, DC.

Norman, V. D., and A. J. Venables. 2001. "Industrial Clusters: Equilibrium, Welfare, and Policy." CEPR Discussion Paper 3004. London.

Porter, M. E. 1990. *The Competitive Advantage of Nations.* London: Macmillan.

Puga, D. 1998. "Urbanization Patterns: European versus Less Developed Countries." *Journal of Regional Science* 38 (2): 231–52.

Puga, D., and A. J. Venables. 1996. "The Spread of Industry, Spatial Agglomeration, and Economic Development." *Journal of the Japanese and International Economies* 10 (4): 440–64.

————. 1999. "Agglomeration and Economic Development: Import Substitution versus Trade Liberalization." *Economic Journal* 109: 292–311.

Radelet, S., and J. Sachs. 1998. "Shipping Costs, Manufactured Exports, and Economic Growth." Paper presented at the American Economic Association Meetings, Harvard University.

Redding, S. J., and A. J. Venables. 2001. "Economic Geography and International Inequality." http://www.econ.lse.ac.uk/staff/ajv.

Rodriguez, F., and D. Rodrik. 2001. "Trade Policy and Economic Growth: A Sceptic's Guide to the Evidence." In *Macroeconomics Annual,* ed. B. Bernanke and K. Rogoff. Cambridge, MA: NBER.

Schott, P. 2000. "One Size Fits All. Heckscher-Ohlin Specialization in Global Production." http://www.som.yale.edu/Faculty/pks4/files/research/papers/cones_ 1100.pdf.

Stern, N. H. 2001. "A Strategy for Development." ABCDE Paper, World Bank, Washington, DC. http://www.econ.worldbank.org/files/1732_stern1.pdf.

Sutton, J. 2000. "Rich Trades, Scarce Capabilities: Industrial Development Revisited." STICERD Discussion Paper EI28, London School of Economics and Political Science, London.

Tang, P., and A. Wood. 2000. "Globalization, Cooperation Costs, and Wage Inequalities." Institute of Development Studies, Brighton. http://www.ids .ac.uk/ids/global/ttint.html.

Venables, A. J., 1999. "Fragmentation and Multinational Production." *European Economic Review* 43: 935–45.

———. 2001. "Geography and International Inequalities: The Impact of New Technologies." Paper prepared for ABCDE, World Bank, Washington, DC. http://www.econ.lse.ac.uk/staff/ajv.

Venables, A. J., and N. Limao. 2002. "Geographical Disadvantage: A Heckscher-Ohlin-von Thünen Model of International Specialization." *Journal of International Economics* 58: 239–63.

von Thünen, J. H. 1826. "*Der Isolierte Staaat in Beziehung auf Landtschaft und Nationalokonomie*, Hamburg. (English translation by C. M. Wartenburg. *von Thünen*'s Isolated State. Oxford: Pergamon Press).

Yeats, A. 1998. "Just How Big is Global Production Sharing?" Policy Research Working Paper 1871, World Bank, Washington, DC.

10

Comparative Advantage and Trade Intensity: Are Traditional Endowments Destiny?

*Daniel Lederman and L. Colin Xu**

Introduction and Motivation

FOR VARIOUS REASONS, ECONOMISTS AND POLICYMAKERS alike worry about economic structure. Researchers have a long tradition of studying the determinants of patterns of international trade within and across countries (see the literature reviews by Deardorff 1984, and Leamer and Levinsohn 1995).[1] Generally speaking, the literature on the empirical determinants of trade structure has been controversial because the existing econometric estimates have tended to yield only weak evidence linking factor endowments to trade flows, both across countries and within countries across industries. These weak results have led some (Leamer 1984; Leamer and Levinsohn 1995; Wood 1994) to criticize the existing literature along various dimensions, including model misspecification, collinearity of explanatory variables, and the lack of consideration of nonlinear effects. Hence, Wood (1994) calls for giving "Heckscher and Ohlin a chance," arguing that existing studies do not adequately test the endowments-driven theory of international trade.

More recently, Harrigan and Zakrajsek (2000) found that production patterns (not trade patterns) across countries can, indeed, be explained by traditional notions of factor endowments, but these authors did not consider alternative, observable, explanatory variables of country characteristics. Based on very disaggregated U.S. import data, Schott (2000) found that rich and poor countries surprisingly tend to export similar products to the U.S. market, but that poor countries receive significantly lower unit prices for their products. This last finding suggests that countries do specialize, since the price data show that even similar products exported by rich and poor countries alike are quite different.

Policymakers have historically been concerned about the determinants of trade patterns because of the perception that policy should aim to change such patterns by promoting sectors with "higher value added." Indeed, these types of concerns have been at the center of intellectual threats to the free-trade bias of most professional economists over history (see Irwin 1996), including the well-known infant-industry argument and the concerns related to the secular deterioration of the terms of trade of countries that specialize in primary commodities. More recently, researchers have again become concerned about the patterns of specialization in developing countries because of the perception that trade patterns affect economic performance, especially economic volatility (de Ferranti et al. 2000; Kraay and Ventura 2001).

In Latin American countries, which experimented with protectionist regimes in the period roughly since between the two world wars until the early 1980s, the move to trade liberalization aimed to bring about a change in the structure of trade in favor of labor-intensive sectors. However, the region's average pattern of international trade, as reflected in the net exports per worker across Leamer's (1984 and 1995) clusters of commodities, has remained dependent on and even increased the net exports of land- and natural-resource-intensive commodities, as shown in figure 10.1. The hopes of structural change were perhaps misguided, because neoclassical trade theory predicts that countries with abundant land and natural resources will specialize even more in these sectors after liberalization. Nevertheless, the increased dependence on such products has again raised eyebrows and instigated recent calls for reevaluating the structural effects of development strategies based on liberal trade policies (see, for example, Katz 2000 and Ramos 1998).

This chapter presents new econometric results about the determinants of trade structure and trade intensity. It contributes to the existing literature along several dimensions. First, we provide new estimates of the determinants of trade patterns using panel data. Most existing estimates rely on pure cross-country data. Second, our panel-data estimates rely on nonlinear models of comparative advantage and trade intensity, an improvement suggested by Leamer (1984) and Leamer and Levinsohn (1995). These estimates control for the simultaneous determination of intensity of trade (that is, the level of net exports per worker) and comparative advantage. Specifically, we model export intensity as a Heckman selection model, where country characteristics or factor endowments determine comparative advantage, and the size of domestic markets, the macroeconomic environment, and trade policy determine export intensity. Third, we allow the estimates of trade intensity for net-importer and the net-exporter subsamples to differ. Fourth, several explanatory vari-

Figure 10.1 Average Net Exports per Worker by
Commodity Groups, 1982–97

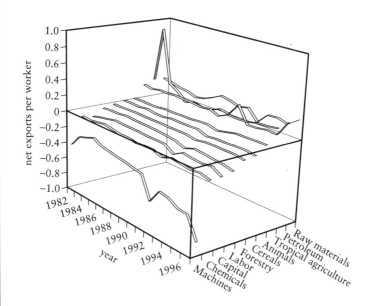

Source: Authors' calculations based on data from the World Bank.
Note: Sample of 22 countries: Argentina, Barbados, Belize, Bolivia, Brazil,
Chile, Colombia, Costa Rica, Ecuador, El Salvador, Guatemala, Honduras,
Jamaica, Mexico, Nicaragua, Panama, Paraguay, Peru, Suriname, Trinidad and
Tobago, Uruguay, and República Bolivariana de Venezuela.

ables are grouped into composite indexes so as to reduce the problems
caused by the collinearity of explanatory variables. Fifth, the explanatory
variables are limited to several groups of variables that tend to be country specific, or at least seem to be variables that are not highly mobile
across countries, including domestic infrastructure (roads, railroads),
knowledge (patents, domestic expenditures in research and development,
and the number of technical workers).

In brief, our results show that the traditional concepts of factor
endowments, such as land and capital per worker, do help explains patterns of trade across countries, but they are by no means the whole story.
For some industrial clusters, comparative advantage is also determined by
domestic infrastructure, domestic institutions, knowledge and schooling,

and macroeconomic volatility. We find notable asymmetries in the determination of trade intensity across countries with and without comparative advantages in manufactured goods. For example, scale effects (or "home-biases" in consumption) related to the size of the domestic market (represented by the gross domestic product [GDP] per capita and the national population) are only important for countries that already have an observed comparative advantage (that is, positive net exporters) in some industries. Macroeconomic instability has notable differential effects across commodity (industrial) clusters. Finally, institutional development is associated with higher levels of trade intensity across countries and over time, especially in agricultural commodities.

The following section reviews Leamer's (1984) representation of the Heckscher-Ohlin-Vanek (HOV) model, which serves as the building block for our econometric models. Next, we present the econometric model of comparative advantage and trade intensity. As is common in the literature, the results of these types of models need to be interpreted with care, because cross-country regressions estimated separately for each commodity cluster must be interpreted in a general equilibrium setting. This is followed by a presentation of the data used in the econometric models: the discussion is organized by groups of explanatory variables, including traditional endowments, knowledge and schooling, infrastructure and transport costs, transaction costs and institutions, an indicator of trade orientation, macroeconomic variables that might affect trade intensity, and the level of development as a control variable. Following the discussion, we present the empirical results and summarize the main conclusions.

Leamer's HOV Model and Some Extensions

In this section we first present a basic model derived from Leamer's (1984) exposition, which justifies the link between net exports and endowments. We then discuss several extensions and complications that add some nuances to the basic model, and we discuss their implications for our model specifications.

The Basic Model

Perhaps the most basic proposition of Leamer (1984) is that the pattern of net exports across countries is determined by the Heckscher-Ohlin theorem, which states that a country with balanced trade will export the commodity that uses intensively its relatively abundant factor and will import the commodity that uses intensively its relatively scarce factor. While this proposition is very familiar among students of international economics, the empirical implementation of this argument is not necessarily straightforward. In particular, it is not clear what exactly should be the dependent variable to be explained.

Assuming Leontieff technology, the framework in Leamer (1984) begins with the system of equations that relate factor supplies to factor demands as follows:

$$K = a_{K1}Y_1 + a_{K2}Y_2 \text{ and} \qquad (10.1)$$

$$L = a_{L1}Y_1 + a_{L2}Y_2 \qquad (10.2)$$

K and L are the amounts of two factors of production—call them capital and labor—available in a given country. These amounts are country-specific and are assumed to be internationally immobile. The Y's denote the quantity produced in the given country of two commodities (labeled by the subscripts 1 and 2). The a's are the traditional factor intensities determined by the available production technologies in each sector, and they represent the units of each factor required to produce a unit of output. Equations (10.1) and (10.2) represent a system that can be solved for outputs Y as a function of the inputs K and L and the factor intensities.

In matrix notation, this setup can be generalized to a model with multiple products and multiple factors of production as long as the latter do not exceed the number of products or as long as the model is just identified or underidentified. Then

$$Y = A^{-1}V \qquad (10.3)$$

where Y is the vector of product outputs and V is the vector of endowments. The A is the vector of factor intensities, which is invertible as long as the production technologies are different across sectors so that the ratios of factor intensities across sectors are not identical.

Still following Leamer (1984), the production of the world economy as a whole can also be written in the same format:

$$Y_W = A^{-1}V_W \qquad (10.4)$$

Assuming that countries consume commodities in the same proportions, the country consumption levels can be expressed as follows:

$$C = sY_W \qquad (10.5)$$

where Y_W is the world's output vector and s is the proportion consumed by each country.[2] Hence, the vector of net exports is simply the product of the inverse of the vector of factor intensities across product clusters and the difference between each country's vector of endowments and the world's vector of endowments. An often forgotten step in the derivation of testable hypotheses is that the key dependent variable is net exports, not gross exports or gross imports. This is clear after considering the fact that net exports are the difference between domestic production and consumption:

$$NX = Y - C = A^{-1}(V - sV_W) \qquad (10.6)$$

In principle, empirical models of the neoclassical trade theory should be estimated with net exports as the dependent variable and excess factor endowments as the explanatory variables. In turn, the signs of the estimated coefficients on the endowment variables, or the values inside the inverted A matrix, reflect the factor intensities of production.

At this point, it is important to note that the inverted vector A contains factor intensities across product clusters, not relative factor abundances across countries. However, each country's consumption share (relative to the world) is a weighted average of its factor shares (also relative to the world's endowments), so that s is as follows:

$$K / K_W > s > L / L_W, \text{ or, } K / K_W < s < L / L_W \qquad (10.7)$$

That is, a capital-abundant country will have $K/K_W > s > L/L_W$, while a labor-abundant country will have $K/K_W < s < L/L_W$.

Extensions

This simple model can be extended in several directions to make it more realistic (Leamer 1984; Deardorff 1994). A particularly important one is the demonstration that perfectly internationally mobile factors of production should not affect the structure of net exports across countries, but rather enter into the model indirectly by being determined by both the domestic abundance of the immobile factors and internationally determined relative factor prices. Wood (1994) argues that cross-country trade models should not include the domestic capital stock as an explanatory variable for this reason. However, the extent of international capital mobility is still debatable (Feldstein and Horioka 1980; Lewis 1999; Kraay et al. 2000), hence Wood (1994) suggests that domestic real interest rates should be used instead of the capital stock. This and other data issues will be discussed further. The main point to keep in mind at this point is that mobility considerations should guide the design of the empirical model analogs of equation (10.6).

Another extension to consider, especially when using panel data with annual observations, is the relaxation of the balanced-trade assumption, which underlies equation (10.6). Deardorff (1994, 6) points out that this model holds in multiple periods as long as trade is balanced over all periods together. However, it can easily be unbalanced in single periods, especially in annual data. The condition of unbalanced trade can indeed change observed patterns of net exports. Following Deardorff (1994), consider the two-tradable-goods economy depicted in figure 10.2. The balanced trade consumption and production points, denoted C_{BT} and Y_T, respectively, lie on the same relative price line. The unbalanced-trade consumption point is denoted by C_{UT}, which is to the right of the balanced-trade constraint, thus showing the situation with a trade deficit. In this case, the production point remains at Y_T. Note that net exports of both Y_1 and Y_2 are lower than under the balanced-trade condition. It is an empirical question whether factors leading to unbalanced trade can produce "HOV-inconsistent" results due to the fact that point C_{UT} can be located so far out that net exports of Y_2 become negative. Nevertheless, factors that determine the domestic absorption of tradable goods, including the relative price between tradable goods and nontradable goods (although the nontradable sector is not explicitly depicted in figure 10.2), clearly affect the observed value of net exports. Hence, estimates of the determinants of net exports across countries based on panel data need to consider variables other than factor endowments that might determine the value of net exports per worker (or "trade intensity").

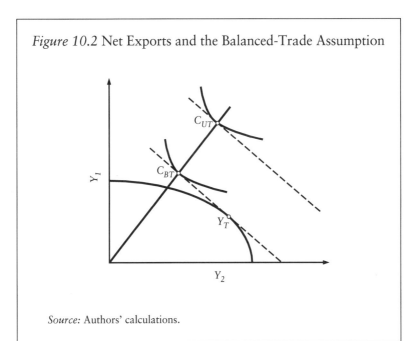

Figure 10.2 Net Exports and the Balanced-Trade Assumption

Source: Authors' calculations.

Homothetic preferences are also a limiting assumption of the traditional HOV model, due to Vanek's (1968) emphasis on this aspect of the
theory. However, Leamer (1984, 39–41) shows that income-dependent
consumption preferences can be easily accommodated into an expanded
version of this model by allowing a portion of consumption to be dependent on total expenditures, which in turn are dependent on income. This
point can be seen clearly in figure 10.3. It shows two production possibility frontiers, with the one closer to the origin representing the poorer economy. Also note that a shift from the lower production frontier to the
higher one could be interpreted as either growth of an economy over time
or a static comparison between a rich and a poor country. The two
straight vectors emanating from the origin represent the income expansion
paths for consumption and production at constant relative prices for
goods Y_1 and Y_2. The one going through production points Y_a and Y_b is
the production path; the one going through consumption points C_{BT} and
C_b corresponds to the consumption path.

C_b is the consumption point for the richer economy if the composition
of consumption does not depend on the level of income.[3] When the composition of consumption depends on the level of income, the higher consumption point will not necessarily be C_b, but it could be a point such as
C_d in figure 10.3. The upward-bending curve that goes through points

Figure 10.3 Nonhomothetic Tastes and Net Exports

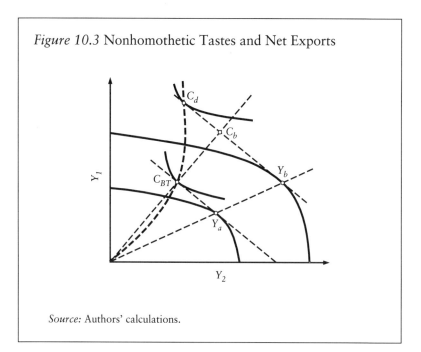

Source: Authors' calculations.

C_{BT} and C_d is the consumption expansion path for the case where Y_1 is the superior good. In other words, consumption point C_d is the point of tangency between the constant relative price line and an indifference curve that tends to favor the consumption of Y_1 relative to the indifference curve that runs through the lower consumption point C_{BT}. The main result from this simple analysis is that net exports of the inferior good Y_2 are higher and net exports of the superior good Y_1 are lower than expected under the homothetic-preferences assumption. Another plausible deviation from the homothetic-preferences assumption is Armington's (1969) home-bias in consumption. In terms of figure 10.3, the income expansion path would tend to bend toward good Y_2 since it is not imported. The empirical models presented below, therefore, include income per capita as a control variable for the possibility that the level of development (income) determines the composition of consumption and thus, also determines the pattern of trade.

Trade barriers and transport costs also present relevant deviations from the standard HOV model. Leamer (1984, 28) shows that such impediments to the international flow of goods are reflected in domestic prices deviating from international prices. Hence, the HOV model represented by equation (10.6) needs to be amended so that net exports and the values of the endowments are evaluated at domestic factor prices, while the world's endowments should be evaluated at international prices. This approach is virtually impossible to implement for a large sample of countries and goods—and over time. For this reason, Leamer (1984) only informally analyzes the impact of outliers on econometric estimates of the elements in the inverse of matrix A (that is, the inverse of the factor intensities matrix). The hope is that trade barriers and international transport costs only lead to HOV-inconsistent estimates in a few exceptional cases. As discussed further later, in our empirical models we do control for countries' deviations from a measure of "free-trade trade intensity." Also, we systematically discarded the top and lowest 1 percent of all annual observations of the net exports variables, and we do not expect our results to be severely affected by outliers. Finally, our preferred models are nonlinear, which reduces the influence of outliers affecting the magnitude of net exports across countries and commodities, as long as there are few outliers concerning the sign (that is, positive or negative) of net exports. These issues are further discussed.

Technology and skills have been important elements in the theoretical and empirical literature on the determinants of trade patterns since the early 1990s (Grossman and Helpman 1991; Wood 1994; Leamer and Levinsohn 1995; Trefler 1995). Trefler (1995) showed that an expanded version of the HOV model that includes both technological differences between developed and less developed countries as well as home-market biases in consumption a la Armington (1969) empirically outperforms the simple HOV model, as well as an expanded HOV model with unbalanced trade. Grossman and Helpman (1991) emphasize the role of patented knowledge, which in effect acts as a production endowment that is not transferable across countries. In practice, differences in technology and know-how across countries are difficult to measure. Trefler (1995) econometrically estimates country-specific deviations from the factor intensities matrix of the United States. While the validity of the resulting estimates derived from this approach can be assessed with model-selection tests comparing the results to those from models without factor-intensity heterogeneity, this approach does not tell us where the differences come from. This chapter controls for cross-country technological heterogeneity by including a composite index of "home knowledge," based on data on patents, research and development expenditures, and the stock of technical workers. This aggregation was statistically necessary due to the high correlation that exists among these variables. Finally, it should be recognized at the outset that trade in goods and foreign direct investments (FDI) are associated with international flows of knowledge (Keller 2001; Lumenga-Neso, Olarreaga, and Schiff 2005).

Another limiting assumption of the basic HOV model concerns the presumed linear relationship between excess factor endowments and the structure of net exports (Leamer 1984, 1987; Leamer and Levinsohn 1995), although this limitation is not fatal. It arises from the restrictive assumption that all countries produce all possible goods; however, this should be relaxed since many countries, especially developing countries, do not produce certain goods. In Leamer's (1987) terminology, there are "multiple cones of diversification." In practice, empirical work should not be limited to linear models, but rather, as done by Trefler (1995) among others, it should aim to test the endowments theory of trade patterns with nonlinear models. Hence, our preferred empirical models presented are nonlinear estimates of the relationship between (arguably) internationally immobile factors and know-how, on the one hand, and patterns of trade, on the other.

Finally, an important issue that affects the inference of empirical results but not the interpretation of the basic theory is the presence of specialized factors of production (Leamer 1984, 32–33). When certain factors, especially land, but also perhaps specialized capital equipment and labor skills, cannot be easily transferred or adapted for production of different goods, then the basic model needs to be amended. The theorem linking country endowments to trade patterns still holds: countries with large endowments of specific factors will specialize in the production and, therefore, will be net exporters of goods that use these factors intensively. However, estimates of the elements inside the inverted A matrix in equation (10.6) need to be interpreted with caution. First, the matrix is invertible only if the number of factors of production is equal to the number of products. However, this theoretical limitation cannot be implemented because of the implausibility of identifying large numbers of factors. Moreover, this assumption is necessary only for the pure HOV model, where production technologies are identical across all countries. Second, the elements inside the matrix A can be negative in the presence of sector-specific factors of production. For example, countries with large endowments of forest land that tend to export forestry products attract capital and labor inputs into this sector. Therefore, abundance of forest land reduces the production and net exports of other goods, including other agricultural and manufactured products. To reiterate, the elements in matrix A can be negative in general equilibrium when factors of production are industry-specific.

Nonlinear Estimates of Comparative Advantage with Trade Intensity: The Heckman Selection Model

In using the Heckman selection model (Heckman 1976, 1979), we simultaneously estimate a model of the determinants of comparative advantage and another of export (and separately, import) intensity. Factor endowments, broadly defined, determine whether the country is a net exporter (or a net importer); then trade policy (that is, "adjusted openness"), real exchange-rate fluctuations and volatility, and economic size determine the value of net exports (imports). Formally,

$$I^*_{it} = X^c_{it}\beta_c + \varepsilon_{it} \qquad (10.8)$$
$$I_{it} = 1 \text{ if } I^* > 0$$
$$NX_{it} = X^E_{it}\beta_E + u_{it}$$
$$\text{where } \text{cov}(\varepsilon_{it}, u_{it}) \neq 0$$

where I^*_{it} represents the index function for exports (imports); a positive value of the function leads to the status of net exporter (importer). The NX_{it} function represents the value of net exports (imports) per worker. Note that the unobservables for the selection equation and the main equations are allowed to be correlated. The equation of the determinants of export (import) status is the "comparative-advantage equation." The equation of the determinants of net export values is the "trade-intensity equation." In estimating the import and the export segments separately, we allowed the coefficients for the net export equation to differ across the net-export and the net-import subsamples, which provides an intuitive way to allow for nonlinearities in our estimates of the determinants of trade intensity. Finally, the selection of the explanatory variables included in the comparative-advantage and the trade-intensity equations followed statistical criteria discussed next.

Data

The Dependent Variables

The dependent variables are the net exports of Leamer's (1984, 61–66) commodity clusters. All empirical models presented below were estimated for each of nine commodity clusters. The names of the sector clusters are the following: (i) raw materials, (ii) forestry, (iii) live animals, (iv) tropical agriculture, (v) cereals, (vi) labor-intensive manufactures, (vii) capital-intensive manufactures, (viii) machinery, and (ix) chemicals. We excluded Leamer's cluster of petrochemicals from the econometric analysis because we were unable to gather data on petroleum reserves (stocks), which are likely to be the main determinant of net exports of this category. Moreover, export and import values of petroleum products are extremely difficult to explain due to the influence of oil price movements. The cluster of raw materials includes most mining activities, which is a more diversified lot than petroleum.

The net exports of each sector by country and year were divided by the total labor force. The dependent variables for our preferred models are the natural logarithm of a constant plus net exports of each commodity cluster per worker, in U.S. dollars. Table 10.A1 (in the annex) lists the countries in the sample, and table 10.A2 contains the summary statistics for the dependent and explanatory variables, including the top/bottom 1 percent of net exports by clusters, which were not included in the regressions mentioned in the previous section of this chapter.

The Explanatory Variables

Endowment Indicators   This chapter uses a broad definition of "endowments," which focus on a broad set of country characteristics that are more or less immobile (or transferable) internationally. Hence the following discussion is divided into seven categories of country characteristics. Table 10.A3 (in the annex) describes the variables and their sources.[4] The criteria used to place explanatory variables in the comparative-advantage or trade-intensity equations of the Heckman-selection models are discussed at the end of this section.

    1. *Traditional endowments.* Land, labor, and capital are the traditional factors considered by the textbook models of international trade. They are also the most commonly used factors in empirical studies of patterns of trade across countries and across industries within countries. The treatment of land and unskilled labor as endowments is less controversial than the use of capital.

    The inclusion of capital stocks in trade regressions has been criticized on two grounds. First, capital might be mobile across countries. As mentioned earlier, international capital markets are shown empirically to be less than perfect, as indicated by the high correlation between domestic savings and investment (Feldstein and Horioka 1980), and financial portfolio holdings show significant home-market biases (Lewis 1999; Kraay et al. 2000). As mentioned, some argue that if capital is considered to be country-specific, then the appropriate variables to include in trade regressions are domestic real-interest rates rather than the capital stock (Wood 1994). Based on this research, we follow Leamer et al. (1999) and use capital stock data (from Kraay et al. 2000, divided by the number of laborers) in our regressions. This decision was reinforced by the fact that available time series of interest rates across countries (from the IMF's *International Financial Statistics* database) are not always comparable, and those from many developing countries are of questionable quality. Finally, since the existing capital stock in each country is the result of past investment decisions, the stock itself can be considered to be predetermined relative to the pattern of trade.

The data on land endowments on the hectares of cultivated forest and crop land come from Leamer et al. (1999). Unfortunately, we were unable to gather data on mining reserves, and thus an important weakness of our analysis is that we do not control for the endowment of natural resources in each country. This limitation is taken into account in the interpretation of the econometric results.

2. *Knowledge and schooling.* These factors are country-specific only to the extent that efforts toward knowledge creation and schooling actually stay within national borders. In the case of expenditures in research and development (R&D), either private or public, patent rights embody the institutions that secure the property rights on the created knowledge. In the case of education, international limits on the migration of people make the educational attainment of the adult population a country-specific feature. In this chapter, we use R&D expenditures as a share of gross national product (GNP), the total number of patent applications in each country, the number of patent applications in the United States (that is, submitted to the U.S. Patent Office), plus the number of technicians (that is, engineers and other workers involved in R&D activities) to construct a composite index of "knowledge." The decision to aggregate these variables into a single index was motivated by the fact that these variables are highly correlated—half of the 10 pair-wise correlations among the five variables are above 0.60; and they conceptually belong together. We use the first principal component of these variables as the index of knowledge.[5] As a proxy for educational attainment, we use the average years of schooling of the adult population with 25 or more years of age. Finally, since education and knowledge may be complements in the determination of comparative advantage,[6] our explanatory variables also include an interactive term between schooling and the knowledge index. To facilitate interpretation, in the results tables we only show the marginal effects of these variables, which are calculated at the mean value of these variables for each sample.

302   LEDERMAN AND XU

3. *Domestic transport infrastructure.* Internationally immobile factors of production should also include the extent and quality of domestic infrastructure. Since industries have different transport-intensities for delivering their products to the main export markets, these factors have the potential of affecting the composition of net exports and comparative advantage. As a parsimonious way to capture this notion, we constructed a composite index of paved roads and railways using the principal-component method.

4. *Institutions and transaction costs.* Clearly, institutions are immobile across borders, and they tend to be persistent and change slowly over time. To the extent that institutions affect the sector choices—for instance, a poor protection of property rights would raise the relative return to an autarchy sector versus transaction-reliant sectors (Murphy, Shleifer, and Vishny 1993; Li, Xu, and Zou 2000)—we include an index of institutional quality as a determinant of sectoral net exports. The index of the quality of domestic institutions is constructed based on subjective data on corruption, law and order, and the perceived quality of the public sector's bureaucracy from the *International Country Risk Guide* (ICRG) database.

The value of net exports might also be affected by the availability of information and communications technologies (ICT). Since ICT-intensity varies across sectors (see, for instance, the evidence presented in Wheatly 1999), the level of ICT development might also determine comparative advantage (that is, what a country exports), as well as the amount that a country exports or imports.[7] The level of ICT development is proxied in this paper by an ICT index, constructed as a principal-component index based on the number of telephone lines, personal computers, mobile phones, fax machines, and Internet hosts per capita.

Overall, the explanatory variables mentioned so far include the following factors of production, although some of them were aggregated into composite indexes due to the very high correlation among them: total labor (included implicitly as the denominator in some of the explanatory variables); two types of land (crop and forest); capital; technical workers (included in the knowledge index); patented knowledge and R&D expenditures; general education; domestic infrastructure; institutions; and ICT. Altogether we have nine factors of production, and we implicitly work with Leamer's 10 commodity clusters. Thus, we satisfy the condition for the invertibility of matrix A in equation (10.6). However, the debate over what constitutes a factor of production and what does not is endless, and we refuse to be drawn into this impractical discussion. The remaining explanatory variables are qualitatively different.

Determinants of Trade Intensity In our preferred econometric models, we distinguish between variables that explain comparative advantage and variables that explain how much of each industrial cluster a country exports per worker—that is, "trade intensity." Most of the latter are macroeconomic variables that capture domestic demand and scale effects, neighborhood effects (that is, characteristics of the closest neighboring countries), relative prices, and macroeconomic volatility. As discussed in the theory section of this chapter, these variables could determine the pattern of net exports (that is, whether they are positive or negative). However, the over-time variance of these variables and of the value of net exports is much higher than that of the factor endowments discussed earlier. Consequently, we include them as determinants of the value of net exports per worker in our preferred econometric models.

5. *"Openness."* As mentioned, trade protectionism can affect the composition and intensity of international trade. Ideally, research should aim to control for industry-specific protection. Unfortunately, the necessary data to control for policy distortions across industries, countries, and time are not readily available. Consequently, we use an index of the exogenous portion of the trade-to-GDP ratio as proposed by Pritchett (1996). This index measures the portion of the trade dependence ratio that is not correlated with international transport costs, the size of the national territory and population, and a dummy variable for industrialized countries as done in Burki and Perry (1997, chapter 2).

6. *Domestic demand and scale effects.* Total domestic demand is captured by the (log of) GDP per capita and (the log of) total population. As discussed earlier, GDP per capita can also reflect consumption preferences that are correlated with income. However, it may also capture, together with the (log of the) domestic population, the size of the domestic market. If income per capita captures pure demand effects, then the sign of this variable on the value of net exports should be negative, because imports rise and exports fall with domestic demand. This is especially true for the superior goods, as explained earlier. In contrast, if scale effects are significant, then the expected sign of the income and population variables can be positive.

7. *Relative prices and volatility—the real effective exchange rate.* To control for the potential effects of movements in the relative price of tradable goods (and, hence, for a potential determinant of the trade balance), we include the annual change in the (log of) International Monetary Fund's trade-weighted real effective exchange-rate index. We also construct a measure of the volatility of this variable for the whole period covered by the data, 1976–1999, which is the standard deviation of the annual change of (the log of) this variable. The inclusion of this variable is motivated by existing evidence showing that export performance in some developing countries is affected by macroeconomic volatility (for example, Maloney and Azevedo 1995).

Criteria for Selection of Explanatory Variables The explanatory variables discussed earlier were divided into two categories: those that appear in the comparative-advantage equation and those that appear in the trade-intensity function. In theory, all explanatory variables could determine either the sign of net exports (that is, comparative advantage) or the value of net exports. In practice, however, due to the over-time stability of the condition of being a positive net exporter relative to the over-time variance of some of the explanatory variables, the variables for each portion of the system need to be chosen with caution. The pure cross-country and traditional panel-data estimates are discussed next, but for now it suffices to say that their performance is quite unsatisfactory, in part due to the stability of some explanatory variables.

Table 10.1 shows the standard deviations for the dependent (the sign and value of net exports) and explanatory variables. The first column shows the standard deviation of the variables across countries. The second shows the average over-time standard deviation within countries. The third column shows the ratio of the first divided by the second. The first obvious observation is that the cross-country variance for all variables is greater across countries than within countries. The trade data, namely the value of net exports and the condition of being a positive net exporter, change less over time than many of the explanatory variables. The cross-country variance of the value of net exports is 2 to 9 times greater than the within-country variance. The condition of being a net exporter has an even higher relative cross-country variance than the value of net exports for most sectors, except animal products, and to a lesser extent labor-intensive manufactures and cereals.

All explanatory variables in the comparative-advantage equation (shown in bold in table 10.1) are more stable over time than the value of net exports. The only exception is the index of ICT, whose over-time variance is surprisingly high. This is due primarily to the very fast growth of the number of registered Internet hosts in the late 1990s, when many countries went from having zero to having positive numbers. Therefore, we opted to include it in the comparative advantage together with the other endowment variables that change little over time. All of the characteristics of the neighbors were put in the trade-intensity function, thus limiting the variables in the comparative-advantage equation to relatively stable home-country characteristics.

Results We now present the results of the Heckman selection model, which relies on the premise that the direction of trade for each cluster of goods is determined by comparative advantage (and therefore by country endowments), but that the quantity of net exports is determined by trade policies, trends in real exchange rates and their volatility, and growth of domestic demand and supply, which is captured by each country's GDP per capita.

Determinants of Comparative Advantage Table 10.2 contains the results from the comparative-advantage equations. The model for raw materials is not very informative: only the coefficient on crop land is statistically significant. This is likely because we do not have data on mining endowments, and it is possible that crop land is positively correlated with this unobserved variable. However, the corresponding results about the deter-

Table 10.1 Variance of Variables of Interest across and within Countries

Variables:	(1) between standard deviation	(2) mean within standard deviation	(3): (1)/(2)
Net exports of:			
Raw materials	0.40	0.07	5.71
Forestry	0.54	0.08	6.75
Tropical agriculture	0.17	0.05	3.40
Animals	0.48	0.08	6.00
Cereals	0.19	0.05	3.80
Labor-intensive	0.31	0.13	2.38
Capital-intensive	0.21	0.07	3.00
Machines	0.85	0.27	3.15
Chemicals	0.31	0.10	3.10
Raw materials greater than 0	0.46	0.06	7.67
Forestry greater than 0	0.44	0.05	8.80
Tropical agriculture greater than 0	0.46	0.05	9.20
Animals greater than 0	0.43	0.15	2.87
Cereals greater than 0	0.43	0.12	3.58
Labor-intensive greater than 0	0.42	0.19	2.21
Capital-intensive greater than 0	0.40	0.10	4.00
Machines greater than 0	0.30	0.06	5.00
Chemicals greater than 0	0.34	0.05	6.80
Annual rate of change of REER	0.33	0.25	1.32
ICT (index)	1.79	1.27	1.41
Institutions (index)	1.55	0.44	3.52
Capital per worker (log)	1.29	0.30	4.30
Income per capita (log)	1.03	0.22	4.68
Adjusted openness (log)	47.09	8.39	5.61
Years of schooling (log)	2.67	0.46	5.80
Knowledge (index)	2.49	0.38	6.55
Crop land per worker (log)	0.72	0.07	10.29
Forest land per worker (log)	1.43	0.10	14.30
Land transport (index)	1.48	0.10	14.80

Source: Authors' calculations.

minants of trade intensity for raw materials are more informative and are discussed next. The other models are quite satisfactory, and the rest of the analysis compares the impacts of the explanatory variables on comparative advantage across the remaining eight commodity clusters.

The probability of having a comparative advantage in forestry exports, defined as being a net exporter of these goods, is affected positively and

Table 10.2 Determinants of Comparative Advantage:
Marginal-Effects Coefficients from Heckman's Selection Equations

	(1) Raw materials	(2) Forestry	(3) Tropical agriculture	(4) Animals	(5) Cereals	(6) Labor-intensive	(7) Capital-intensive	(8) Machines	(9) Chemicals
A. Traditional endowments (per capita)									
Crop land (log)	-0.121 (1.14)	-0.143 (4.84)***	0.116 (3.08)***	0.320 (8.27)***	0.257 (5.52)***	0.070 (2.24)**	0.004 (1.72)*	-0.086 (6.39)***	-0.051 (2.17)**
Forest land (log)	0.176 (5.66)***	0.240 (15.68)***	0.005 (0.27)	-0.007 (0.46)	-0.128 (7.32)***	0.008 (0.58)	-0.009 (1.32)	0.011 (1.50)	-0.194 (7.97)***
Capital (log)	-0.020 (0.37)	-0.127 (5.21)***	-0.149 (3.37)***	-0.221 (6.88)***	-0.103 (3.17)***	-0.033 (1.35)	0.014 (1.04)	0.028 (1.77)*	0.150 (5.81)***
B. Knowledge and schooling									
Knowledge (index)	0.074 (1.01)	0.261 (7.51)***	0.300 (3.12)***	0.077 (2.23)**	0.442 (8.45)***	0.398 (8.77)***	0.052 (4.60)***	0.093 (5.23)***	-0.158 (5.60)***
Years of schooling (log)	0.001 (0.11)	0.005 (0.37)	0.079 (5.10)***	0.108 (8.20)***	0.028 (1.64)	-0.060 (5.35)***	0.022 (1.76)*	-0.006 (0.74)	-0.083 (4.72)***
Knowledge * schooling	-0.016 (1.82)*	-0.030 (6.99)***	-0.046 (3.90)***	-0.016 (4.22)***	-0.052 (8.41)***	-0.031 (8.10)***	-0.009 (5.72)***	-0.005 (2.66)***	0.023 (6.69)***

(continued)

Table 10.2 Determinants of Comparative Advantage:
Marginal-Effects Coefficients from Heckman's Selection Equations *(continued)*

	(1) Raw materials	(2) Forestry	(3) Tropical agriculture	(4) Animals	(5) Cereals	(6) Labor-intensive	(7) Capital-intensive	(8) Machines	(9) Chemicals
C. Land transport infrastructure									
Infrastructure (index)	0.004	0.014	−0.069	0.121	−0.171	0.056	−0.004	0.032	0.161
	(0.06)	(0.66)	(2.80)***	(5.64)***	(5.34)***	(2.62)***	(2.86)***	(2.46)**	(5.12)***
D. Transaction costs and institutions									
ICT (index)	0.012	0.038	0.014	0.030	0.054	0.022	0.007	0.013	0.000
	(0.61)	(3.56)***	(1.27)	(2.47)**	(2.97)***	(2.01)**	(2.05)**	(2.90)***	(0.06)
Institutions (index)	0.047	0.050	−0.001	0.005	0.000	−0.106	0.007	−0.049	0.033
	(1.73)*	(2.53)**	(0.03)	(0.25)	(0.01)	(4.56)***	(6.25)***	(3.47)***	(1.65)*
Rho	−0.078	−0.601***	0.981***	−0.704***	−0.513***	0.401	1.000	−0.919***	−0.424***
	(0.814)	(0.105)	(0.017)	(0.074)	(0.099)	(0.396)	(5E-15)	(0.034)	(0.105)
Observations	872	872	872	872	872	872	872	872	872

Source: Authors' calculations.

Note: Intercepts are not reported. The marginal effects were calculated at the mean of each variable as $\beta_i P(\text{export}_{it} > 0$ evaluated at the mean of $X_{it})$ where β_i is the Probit coefficient and X_{it} is the vector of explanatory variables.
* significant at 10 percent, ** significant at 5 percent, *** significant at 1 percent.
Marginal-effects coefficients from Heckman's selection equations
Dependent variable: Probability of being a net exporter of each commodity cluster
(t-statistics in parentheses)

significantly by the availability of forest land per worker. This variable reduces the likelihood of comparative advantage in labor-intensive and chemicals. The estimated coefficients imply that a 1 percent increase in forest land per worker is associated with a subsequent increase in the probability of being a net exporter of forestry commodities of 0.240 percentage points, with a corresponding decline in the probability of being a net exporter of chemicals by 0.194 percentage points, as well as a decline of 0.128 percentage points in the probability of being an exporter of cereals. Most coefficients presented in this table can be interpreted in the same way, and thus, for the sake of brevity, we do not discuss in detail the magnitude of the remaining coefficients. The other land endowment included in the regressions, crop land, raises the probability of comparative advantage in cereals, animals, and, to a lesser extent, tropical agriculture. Surprisingly, this variable also has a positive and significant coefficient in the model on labor-intensive manufactures. The endowment of capital per worker increases the probability of comparative advantage in the most sophisticated manufactures, namely machines and especially chemicals, while it reduces the likelihood of being a net exporter of agricultural commodities.

The knowledge index is associated with higher probabilities of comparative advantage in cereals, labor-intensive manufactures, tropical agriculture, forestry, and machines, in that order, in terms of magnitudes of the marginal-effects coefficients. Somewhat surprising results are, first, that the likelihood of comparative advantage in chemicals on average falls with knowledge, and second, that the corresponding probability for forestry commodities rises with knowledge. In contrast, educational attainment raises the probability of comparative advantage in animals and tropical agriculture. Education also reduces the likelihood of comparative advantage in two of the four clusters of manufactured products. The only sector where there is evidence of complementarities between schooling and knowledge is in chemicals, which is reflected in a positive coefficient on the interacted variable. In all of the other sectors, including the agricultural activities and raw materials, the results suggest that schooling and knowledge might be substitutes, thus implying that developing a comparative advantage in those sectors can be achieved by raising either educational attainment or knowledge. In any case, it is clear that both knowledge and general educational attainment affect comparative advantage, but these variables are not necessarily exclusively associated with comparative advantage in manufactured products. Knowledge is more likely to be associated with comparative advantage in manufactured products than general education, however.

The results also suggest that domestic land-transport infrastructure increases the probability of comparative advantage in animals, as well as in labor-intensive manufactures, machines, and especially chemicals. Thus the data seem to reflect patterns of comparative advantage where nontraditional factors—in this case infrastructure—affect agricultural activities in a similar fashion as manufacturing activities. Moreover, since infra-structure can be developed through public investments, these results fur-ther support the contention that natural resources are not destiny.

Likewise, the quality of domestic institutions is positively correlated with the probability of comparative advantage in forestry and chemicals. This result clarifies the role of knowledge: on average, the key to develop-ing a comparative advantage in chemicals is not necessarily the endow-ment of patents and technicians, but rather the institutional environment that regulates the creation of knowledge related to chemicals, with patents being the key example. In other words, the data on patents, technicians, and R&D might reflect outcomes related to the quality of domestic insti-tutions, which then drives comparative advantage in chemicals. In fact, the results indicate that institutional quality tends to increase the likelihood of comparative advantage in chemicals, possibly at the expense of compara-tive advantage in other manufactures, such as labor-intensive goods and machines. The results concerning the ICT index are also provocative. They show that ICT development (broadly defined) is associated with a subse-quent increase in the probability of comparative advantage in labor-intensive manufactures, possibly at the expense of chemicals. This is not entirely surprising: the biggest beneficiary of ICT technology is possibly services (Wheatly 1999), with which labor-intensive manufacturing is more closely related than chemicals.

The estimated correlations between the errors from the comparative-advantage equations with the errors from the corresponding trade-intensity equations are shown in the bottom row of table 10.2. These results suggest that the portion of trade intensity (that is, net exports per worker) that is not explained by openness, relative prices, and macroeco-nomic volatility (that is, the explanatory variables used in the trade-inten-sity equations) is significantly correlated with unexplained comparative advantage. Thus, the estimates of the determinants of both dependent variables would be biased if this link were not considered.

Table 10.3 provides additional insights concerning the explanatory power of two sets of explanatory variables. It shows the ranges of the per-centage of the variance of the probability of being a net exporter of each commodity group that is explained by two sets of variables. The first set comprises the traditional factor endowments (land and capital per worker); the second concerns "new" endowments that are probably affected by public policies (knowledge, schooling, infrastructure, ICT, and institutions). The results presented in table 10.3 were derived from a set of analyses of variance (ANOVA) that entailed alternative assump-tions regarding the degree of exogeneity of the two sets of explanatory variables. For each sector, we estimated the share of the variance of the probability of being a net exporter across countries and over time. We then assumed that one set of variables is more exogenous than the other and vice versa. In any case, the evidence suggests that for most sectors, the

Table 10.3 The Role of Traditional and "New" Endowments in
Accounting for the Variance in Comparative Advantage across
Countries and over Time

	Percent of variance accounted	
	Traditional endowments: Crop land, forest land, and capital intensity	*"New" endowments: Knowledge, schooling, infrastructure, ICT, and institutions*
1 (export raw materials)	0.74–0.84	0.14–0.25
1 (export forest product)	0.71–0.74	0.14–0.17
1 (export tropical agricultural products)	0.14–0.38	0.61–0.85
1 (export animal products)	0.03–0.52	0.48–0.97
1 (export cereals)	0.30–0.53	0.42–0.65
1 (export labor-intensive products)	0.31–0.43	0.53–0.65
1 (export capital-intensive products)	0.02–0.17	0.79–0.93
1 (export machinery)	0.07–0.62	0.29–0.84
1 (export chemicals)	0.14–0.47	0.24–0.56

Source: Authors' calculations.

Note: The dependent variable in the ANOVA exercises for each row is the predicted probability of exporting the specific product; the underlying model is the selection equation of the Heckman model. The reported numbers in the cells are the share
of variance attributable to each group of variables. Since the share depends on the
order of appearance (for example, order of exogeneity) in the ANOVA equation, we
report the range of shares under alternative combinations of the complete explanatory
variables.

patterns of comparative advantage are better explained by the set of new
endowments than by the traditional endowments. In fact, only in the raw
materials and forestry sectors do the traditional endowments predominate in terms of the share of the explained variance of comparative
advantage. Hence, it seems that traditional endowments, including land,
are not destiny.

We now turn our attention to the remaining part of our empirical models, the determinants of trade intensity across sectors and countries.

Determinants of Trade Intensity   Four types of explanatory variables
were included in the estimates of the determinants of trade intensity for
exporters and importers as shown in table 10.4. The most important finding that emerges is that there are strong asymmetries in the estimates of the
effects of the explanatory variables between the import and export segments across the net export line.

Table 10.4 Determinants of Trade Intensity

	(1) Raw materials	(2) Forestry	(3) Tropical agriculture	(4) Animals	(5) Cereals	(6) Labor-intensive	(7) Capital-intensive	(8) Machines	(9) Chemicals
I. Subsample of net exporters									
Real exchange rate	0.024	0.122	0.005	0.008	0.066	0.000	−0.027	−0.063	−0.383
	(1.19)	(2.37)**	(0.91)	(0.70)	(2.90)***	(0.01)	(0.98)	(0.41)	(0.61)
Real exchange-rate volatility	−0.049	−0.635	−0.028	0.004	−0.058	−0.118	−0.100	0.995	0.356
	(0.42)	(3.61)***	(3.33)***	(0.15)	(1.55)	(4.91)***	(2.49)**	(3.19)***	(0.48)
Adjusted openness	0.005	−0.004	0.000	0.001	−0.000	0.001	0.001	0.008	0.004
	(7.17)***	(6.63)***	(3.06)***	(3.51)***	(1.00)	(3.20)***	(5.56)***	(3.64)***	(1.58)
GDP per capita (PPP, log)	0.182	0.447	0.002	0.064	0.209	0.115	0.117	0.550	0.207
	(6.06)***	(9.08)***	(0.24)	(6.81)***	(11.50)***	(11.05)***	(6.69)***	(3.34)***	(2.14)**

(continued)

Table 10.4 Determinants of Trade Intensity (continued)

	(1) Raw materials	(2) Forestry	(3) Tropical agriculture	(4) Animals	(5) Cereals	(6) Labor-intensive	(7) Capital-intensive	(8) Machines	(9) Chemicals
II. Subsample of net importers									
Real exchange rate	-0.040	-0.023	-0.070	-0.019	-0.044	-0.034	-0.028	-0.108	-0.035
	(3.43)***	(2.54)**	(2.49)**	(2.22)**	(1.61)	(1.60)	(17.63)***	(4.17)***	(4.62)***
Real exchange-rate volatility	0.012	-0.000	-0.448	-0.001	0.034	0.026	0.032	0.048	0.008
	(1.50)	(0.10)	(4.23)***	(0.28)	(3.03)***	(3.68)***	(19.12)***	(2.54)**	(1.24)
Adjusted openness	0.001	-0.000	-0.001	-0.000	-0.001	-0.001	0.001	-0.005	-0.000
	(5.39)***	(0.32)	(5.19)***	(3.35)***	(2.78)***	(6.79)***	(23.74)***	(6.17)***	(1.30)
GDP per capita (PPP, log)	-0.091	-0.074	-0.056	-0.036	-0.148	-0.069	-0.066	-0.304	-0.092
	(18.02)***	(18.23)***	(7.15)***	(9.17)***	(8.02)***	(10.78)***	(71.52)***	(11.59)***	(17.78)***
Observations	872	872	872	872	872	872	872	872	872

Source: Authors' calculations.

Note: Intercepts are not reported.

* significant at 10 percent, ** significant at 5 percent, *** significant at 1 percent.

Results from Heckman's "second-stage" equations estimated simultaneously with the selection (comparative advantage) equation

Dependent variable: log (constant + net exports per worker)

(*t*-statistics in parentheses)

The results indicate that growth in GDP per capita is generally associated with increases in the value of net exports for all commodity groups, and only the corresponding coefficient for tropical agriculture is not statistically significant. In contrast, this variable has a negative and significant coefficient for all sectors for the subsample of net importers. These results imply that economic growth is associated with increases in net exports in the sectors where countries have a comparative advantage, but with declines in the value of net exports (or increases in net imports) in sectors where countries do not have a comparative advantage. These results are consistent with the idea that positive supply-side effects reflected in a positive coefficient of the GDP per capita variable predominate in the subsample of net exporters, whereas demand-side effects that increase imports relative to exports predominate in the subsample of net importers.

Another interesting result concerns the adjusted openness variable. In the sample of exporters, net exports for most sectors seem to increase with the level of openness. The only significant exception is forestry. In contrast, in the sample of importers, openness is negatively correlated with subsequent net exports in most sectors, with two exceptions, namely raw materials and capital-intensive manufactures. In general, these results imply that trade liberalization (or other policies or economic shocks that raise the incidence of international trade) tends to strengthen the patterns of comparative advantage, as net importers tend to experience declines in net exports whereas exporters tend to experience improvements in net exports.

While macroeconomic volatility, captured by the volatility of the real-exchange rate, seems to have significant effects on trade intensity, these effects seem heterogeneous across both sectors and subsamples of countries. That is, volatility seems to affect trade intensity differently, depending on whether countries have a comparative advantage in a certain sector and across sectors.

Finally, the evolution of the real-exchange rate also seems to have heterogeneous effects across different sectors and countries. For instance, depreciations (that is, increases in the rate of change of our indicator of the real-exchange rate) seem to be associated with increases in the value of net exports in forestry and cereals when countries are net exporters of these commodities. In contrast, depreciations seem to be associated with declines in net exports (or increases in net imports) in several sectors when countries are net importers of those commodities. These results suggest that changes in the relative price of tradable goods have significant effects on national trade intensities that seem to be consistent with existing patterns of comparative advantage.

Conclusions

The main question posed by this chapter is whether traditional endowments are destiny in terms of determining the pattern of comparative advantage across countries and over time. The evidence presented herein indicates that traditional endowments—namely land, labor, and capital—do play an important role in determining comparative advantage. However, they are not destiny, because other country characteristics, which are arguably affected by public policies, also play an important role. In fact, the econometric evidence discussed suggests that the observed sectoral patterns of net exports are associated with international differences in schooling, knowledge, infrastructure, information and communications technology, and institutional quality. Perhaps more important, schooling and knowledge seem to be key factors that determine comparative advantage in agricultural commodities, and infrastructure seems to be important for obtaining a comparative advantage in animal products. Thus, comparative advantages in natural-resource sectors, such as agriculture, depend not only on land endowments, but also on endowments of human capital, knowledge, and infrastructure.

There are obviously important issues to be studied in the future that are related to trade structure across countries. An important weakness of the current chapter is that it did not consider the potential effects of trade agreements, especially preferential agreements. Also, an important question regarding the structure of trade concerns the degree of concentration of export and import flows across products. Both of these issues require further study in order to inform policy discussions in various regions, especially in Latin America and the Caribbean, where regional trade negotiations are underway and concerns about the impact of trade concentration on economic volatility are also being debated.[8]

Annex

Table 10.A1 Countries in the Sample

1. Argentina	30. Kenya
2. Australia	31. Korea, Democratic People's
3. Austria	Republic of
4. Bolivia	32. Malawi
5. Brazil	33. Malaysia
6. Cameroon	34. Mexico
7. Canada	35. Netherlands
8. Chile	36. New Zealand
9. China	37. Nicaragua
10. Colombia	38. Norway
11. Costa Rica	39. Panama
12. Dominican Republic	40. Paraguay
13. Ecuador	41. Peru
14. Egypt, Arab Rep. of	42. Philippines
15. Finland	43. Portugal
16. France	44. Sierra Leone
17. Germany	45. South Africa
18. Ghana	46. Spain
19. Greece	47. Sweden
20. Guatemala	48. Syrian Arab Rep.
21. Honduras	49. Thailand
22. Hungary	50. Tunisia
23. India	51. Turkey
24. Indonesia	52. Uganda
25. Ireland	53. United Kingdom
26. Israel	54. United States
27. Italy	55. Uruguay
28. Japan	56. Venezuela, R. B. de
29. Jordan	57. Zambia

Table 10.A2 Summary Statistics:
Annual Observations Used in the Regressions

Variable	Observations	Mean	Standard deviation	Minimum	Maximum
A. Explanatory variables (in alphabetical order)					
Adjusted openness	719	0.32	49.45	−87.76	282.53
Annual change in log of REER	719	−0.19	0.49	−4.95	0.35
GDP p.c. (log)	719	8.59	0.99	5.82	10.26
ICT index	719	1.04	2.32	−1.20	8.58
Institutional index	719	0.51	1.62	−3.08	2.92
Knowledge index	719	0.87	2.48	−2.32	10.91
Land transport index	719	0.46	1.47	−2.50	3.74
Log of capital per worker	719	2.31	1.22	−1.73	4.19
Log of crop land per worker	719	−0.14	0.71	−1.84	1.90
Log of forest land per worker	719	0.45	1.40	−2.28	3.48
Log of population	719	16.28	1.38	13.99	20.54
Standard deviation of annual change in log of REER	719	0.25	0.41	0.02	3.41
Years of schooling	719	5.97	2.63	1.05	12.20
B. Log (constant + net exports per worker)					
Raw materials	705	0.05	0.37	−0.53	1.93
Forestry	699	0.03	0.32	−0.58	1.85
Tropical agriculture	715	0.03	0.17	−0.67	0.82
Animals	715	0.13	0.49	−0.63	3.19
Labor-intensive	717	−0.02	0.36	−1.53	1.65
Capital-intensive	701	−0.08	0.21	−1.24	0.44
Machines	715	0.13	0.49	−0.63	3.19
Chemicals	704	−0.40	0.78	−5.50	2.29
Raw materials	711	−0.09	0.23	−0.80	1.16

Source: Authors' calculations based on data from the World Bank.

Note: The panel-data and Heckman-selection models were estimated with a subsample that excludes the top and bottom 1 percent observations of the net exports data.

Table 10.A3 Variable Descriptions and Sources

Variable	Description	Source
Net exports per worker on 10 commodity aggregates as in Leamer (1984 and 1995)	Petroleum and derivatives (SITC 33) (not used) Raw materials (SITC 27, 28, 32, 34, 35, and 68) Forest products (SITC 24, 25, 63, and 64) Tropical agriculture (SITC 5, 6, 7, 11, and 23) Animal products (SITC 0 to 3, 21, 29, 43, and 94) Cereals, oil, textile fibers, tobacco, and others (SITC 4, 8, 9, 12, 22, 26, 41, and 42) Labor-intensive (SITC 66, 82 to 85, 89, 91, 93, and 96) Capital-intensive (SITC 61, 62, 65, 67, 69, and 81) Machinery (SITC 71 to 79, 87, 88, and 95) Chemicals (SITC 51 to 59)	Author's calculations. Original data from UN COMTRADE, accessed with World Integrated Trade Solution
Adjusted openness	Calculated as the difference between the actual and the "structural" trade intensity (the trade-to-GDP ratio). STI is the estimated value of trade to GDP from the following regression: STI $= -7.273 \cdot \ln$ (area) $-5.212 \cdot \ln$ (population) $+ 2.663 \cdot$ (CIF/FOB) $\cdot 100 - 14.260 \cdot$ industrial country dummy	Method from Pritchett (1996); as applied in Burki and Perry (1997, chapter 2)
Capital stock	Capital stock at constant U.S. dollars, PPP.	Kraay, Loayza, Serven, and Ventura (2000)
Crop land per worker	Crop land per worker in hectares. One observation per decade: 1970s, 1980s, and 1990s.	Leamer, Maul, Rodriguez, and Schott (1999)
Forest land per worker	Forest land per worker in hectares. One observation per decade: 1970s, 1980s, and 1990s.	Leamer, Maul, Rodriguez, and Schott (1999)

(continued)

317

Table 10.A3 Variable Descriptions and Sources *(continued)*

Variable	Description	Source
GDP per capita	GDP per capita at current U.S. dollars, PPP.	WDI
Information and communication technology	FAX machines per thousand people Mobile phones per thousand people Personal computers per thousand people Internet hosts (computers with active Internet protocol (IP) addresses connected to the Internet) per thousand people. All hosts without a country code are assumed to be located in the United States. Main telephone lines in operation (number)	WDI
Infrastructure	Railroad length (km). Source: WB-WRS Paved roads length (km). Source: IRF Roads length (km.). Source: IRF Main telephone lines (number). Source: ITU Telephones. Connection capacity of local exchanges (number). Source: WB-WDI	Kraay, Loayza, Serven, and Ventura (2000)
Institutions: bureaucracy	Measures the expertise and autonomy of the bureaucracy. Low scores reflect "low-quality" bureaucracy	ICRG
Institutions: lack of corruption	Measures the extent to which bribery is present within the political system. Forms of corruption given in the ICRG are related to bribes in areas of exchange controls, tax assessments, police protection, loans, and the licensing of exports and imports. A lower score reflects high corruption levels	ICRG

(continued)

Table 10.A3 Variable Descriptions and Sources *(continued)*

Variable	Description	Source
Institutions: law and order	Measures the legal system and the rule of law. Low scores indicate weak, biased legal systems	ICRG
Knowledge	Expenditures for R&D as share of GNP. Includes overhead and other capital expenditures intended to increase the stock of knowledge	WDI and USPTO (http:www.uspto.gov/go/taf/tafp.html)
	Persons in R&D per million people. Includes technicians (vocational and technical training), scientists, and engineers (complete tertiary education)	
	Patent applications by residents and nonresidents as share of worldwide patents applications	
	Patent applications by residents as share of worldwide patents applications	
	Patent applications in the United States by origin of the applicant. Expressed as share of total patent applications in the U.S.	
Labor force	Economically active population. Includes employed and unemployed. It also includes first-time job-seekers. Excludes homemakers and other unpaid caregivers and workers in the informal sector	WDI
Real Effective Exchange Rate	Trade-weighted foreign consumer price index in domestic currency divided by domestic consumer price index	IMF, IFS
Years of schooling	Average schooling years in the population under 25 years old	WDI

Notes

*Eric Bond (Penn State University) and anonymous referees provided useful comments. Discussions with Marcelo Olarreaga and participants in the 2001 Latin American Econometric Society meeting were also helpful. Ana María Menéndez compiled data used in this paper. Remaining errors should be attributed to the authors.

1. Leamer (1984) and Balassa and Bauwens (1988) are notable attempts to estimate Heckscher-Ohlin-Vanek models of international trade where trade patterns are explained exclusively by traditional factor endowments such as labor, capital, and land.

2. The proportional-consumption assumption is rather implausible and is used for the sake of simplicity, but it is not a fundamental part of the argument. We discuss deviations from this assumption.

3. An important detail here is that what matters is the income per worker. Hence the two economies in figure 10.3 are not necessarily different due to differences in factor endowments, but rather due to differences in Hicks-neutral technology in the production of both goods. See next discussion concerning technological differences and the HOV model.

4. Some of the explanatory variables have missing values. In our analysis, we delete the observations for which the traditional endowment variables have missing values; for auxiliary variables, instead of deleting all observations with one of them being missing, we impute the value of the missing auxiliary variables. In particular, the missing values for the explanatory variables were imputed by regressing each variable on period dummy variables, regional dummy variables, (log of) GDP per capita, and (log of) the size of labor force.

5. In particular, the knowledge index was constructed as a linear function of the five variables, with coefficients of the variables ranging from 0.37 to 0.52. On the right-hand side, each variable is normalized into a variable with mean 0 and standard deviation of 1.

6. For example, schooling might aid countries to develop a comparative advantage in sophisticated manufacturing processes if such schooling yields a stock of technical laborers, such as engineers.

7. Preliminary results indicated that this variable had no significant effect on comparative advantage.

8. The authors are currently following up on these issues.

References

Armington, Paul S. 1969. "A Theory of Demand for Products Distinguished by Place of Production." *International Monetary Fund Staff Papers* 16 (1): 159–78.

Balassa, Bela, and Luc Bauwens. 1988. *Changing Trade Patterns in Manufactured Goods: An Econometric Investigation.* Amsterdam: North-Holland.

Burki, S. Javed, and Guillermo E. Perry. 1997. *The Long March: A Reform Agenda for Latin America and the Caribbean in the Next Decade.* Washington, DC: World Bank.

de Ferranti, David, Guillermo E. Perry, Indermit S. Gill, and Luis Servén. 2000. *Securing Our Future in a Global Economy.* Washington, DC: World Bank.

Deardorff, Alan V. 1984. "Testing Trade Theories and Predicting Trade Flows." In *Handbook of International Economics, Volume 1, International Trade*, ed. R. W. Jones and P. B. Kenen. Amsterdam: North-Holland.

———. 1994. "Exploring the Limits of Comparative Advantage." *Weltwirtschaftliches Archiv* 130 (1): 1–18.

Feldstein, Martin, and Charles Horioka. 1980. "Domestic Saving and International Capital Flows." *The Economic Journal* 90 (358): 314–29.

Grossman, Gene M., and Elhanan Helpman. 1991. *Innovation and Growth in the Global Economy*. Cambridge, MA: MIT Press.

Harrigan, James, and Egon Zakrajsek. 2000. "Factor Supplies and Specialization in the World Economy." International Research Department, Federal Reserve Bank of New York. http://www.federalreserve.gov/Pubs/feds/2000/200043/200043pap.pdf.

Heckman, James. 1976. "The Common Structure of Statistical Models of Truncation, Sample Selection, and Limited Dependent Variables and a Simple Estimator for Such Models." *The Annals of Economic and Social Measurement* 5: 475–92.

———. 1979. "Sample Selection Bias as a Specification Error." *Econometrica* 47: 153–61.

Irwin, Douglas. 1996. *Against the Tide: An Intellectual History of Free Trade*. Washington, DC: American Enterprise Institute.

Katz, Jorge. 2000. "Cambios estructurales y productividad en la industria latinoamericana, 1970–1996." *Revista de la CEPAL* 71 (agosto): 65–84.

Keller, Wolfgang. 2001. "The Geography and Channels of Diffusion at the World's Technology Frontier." NBER Working Paper 8150, Cambridge, MA.

Kraay, Aart, and Jaume Ventura. 2001. "Comparative Advantage and the Cross-Section of Business Cycles." NBER Working Paper 8104, Cambridge, MA.

Kraay, Aart, Norman Loayza, Luis Serven, and Jaume Ventura. 2000. "Country Portfolios." NBER Working Paper 7795, Cambridge, MA.

Leamer, Edward E. 1984. *Sources of International Comparative Advantage: Theory and Evidence*. Cambridge, MA: MIT Press.

———. 1987. "Paths of Development in the Three-Factor, n-Good General Equilibrium Model." *Journal of Political Economy* 95 (5): 961–99.

———. 1995. "The Heckscher-Ohlin Model in Theory and Practice." Princeton Studies in International Finance 77, Department of Economics, Princeton University, Princeton, NJ.

Leamer, Edward, and Jerome Levinsohn. 1995. "International Trade Theory: The Evidence." In *Handbook of International Economics*, volume 3, ed. G. M. Grossman and K. S. Rogoff. Amsterdam: North-Holland.

Leamer, Edward E., Hugo Maul, Sergio Rodriguez, and Peter K. Schott. 1999. "Does Natural Resource Abundance Increase Latin American Income Inequality?" *Journal of Development Economics* 59: 3–42.

Lewis, Karen. 1999. "Trying to Explain Home Bias in Equities and Consumption." *Journal of Economic Literature* 37: 571–608.

Li, Hongyi, Lixin Colin Xu, and Heng-Fu Zou. 2000. "Corruption, Income Distribution, and Growth." *Economics and Politics* 12 (2): 155–82.

Lumenga-Neso, Olivier, Marcelo Olarreaga, and Maurice Schiff. 2005. "On 'Indi-rect' Trade-Related R&D Spillovers." *European Economic Review* 49 (7): 1785–98.

Maloney, William, and Rodrigo Azevedo. 1995. "Trade Reform, Uncertainty, and Export Promotion: Mexico 1982–88." *Journal of Development Economics* 48: 67–89.

Murphy, Kevin M., Andrea Shleifer, and Robert W. Vishny. 1993. "Why Is Rent-Seeking So Costly to Growth?" *American Economic Review* (May): 409–14.

Pritchett, Lant. 1996. "Measuring Outward Orientation in LDCs: Can It Be Done?" *Journal of Development Economics* 49: 307–35.

Ramos, Joseph. 1998. "A Development Strategy Founded on Natural Resource-Based Production Clusters." *CEPAL Review* 66 (December): 105–27.

Schott, Peter K. 2000. "Do Countries Specialize?" Yale School of Management, New Haven, CT. http://www.som.yale.edu/Faculty/pks4/files/research/papers/schott_hts_cones.pdf.

Trefler, Daniel. 1995. "The Case of the Missing Trade and Other Mysteries." *American Economic Review* 85 (5): 1029–46.

Vanek, Jaroslav. 1968. "The Factor Proportions Theory: The N-Factor Case." *Kyklos* 21 (4): 749–56.

Wheatly, Jeffrey J. 1999. *World Telecommunication Economics.* Exeter, England: Short Run Press Ltd.

Wood, Adrian. 1994. "Give Heckscher and Ohlin a Chance!" *Weltwirtschaftliches Archiv* 130 (1): 20–48.

11

Outgrowing Resource Dependence: Theory and Developments

Will Martin

COUNTRIES VARY GREATLY IN THE SHARE of their exports derived from resource-based activities. In countries that obtain a large share of their export revenues from resource-based activities, the goal of reducing resource dependence is frequently a major influence on policy. The importance placed on this goal is particularly marked in resource-dependent developing countries, but it has also emerged in high-income countries such as Australia and the Netherlands in the form of concerns about deindustrialization during periods of growth in resource-based industries (Gregory 1976; Snape 1977).

There are many reasons why policymakers may wish to reduce the share of a country's export revenues obtained from commodities produced using resource-intensive procedures. These include (i) concerns about potentially adverse trends in the terms of trade for commodities raised by Raúl Prebisch; (ii) concerns about the perceived instability of returns from commodities and possible resulting problems of unemployment and output loss (Cashin and McDermott 2002) (iii) perceptions that the rate of technological change in resource-dependent activities may be lower than in manufactures or services; and (iv) concerns that resource-intensive production may promote rent-seeking activities, lower growth rates, and increase the risk of civil war (Sachs and Warner 1995; Collier 2000).

Clearly, given the potential stakes involved in decisions about changing resource dependence, as well as the fundamental nature of many of the policies advocated for achieving this objective, there is a great need for carefully formulated policies if this objective is to be realized. Unfortunately, much of the policy debate surrounding these objectives takes place at a sufficiently high level of abstraction that it does not provide much guidance. Consequently, many of the policies adopted to this end seem ad hoc and potentially counter-productive. A very common response, for example, is a relatively arbitrary set of protectionist measures designed, perhaps, to promote activity and learning in manufacturing sectors. But, as we shall see, protectionist policies may have quite contrary effects.

The policy options for dealing with this problem need to be chosen through good diagnostics, and they must be considered with a broad view. It is possible, for instance, that a country relying on a set of different commodities may find that the variance of returns from the resulting portfolio is not excessive—or that shifting from commodities to manufactures would not reduce the variance of returns (see Martin 1989, for example). Further, if the problem of excessive instability of export returns is identified as a problem, then the most effective solution may lie in portfolio-management approaches that allow reductions in the volatility of consumption without attempting to reduce the volatility of annual earnings. Such a solution is consistent with the general principle in economic policy of targeting the policy solution as closely as possible to the problem at hand.

Policies that attempt to deal with the risks associated with commodity dependence by diversifying the structure of output should not generally be undertaken unless analysis indicates that (i) there are market failures that are reducing the extent to which the production structure should shift away from commodities; and that (ii) policy options that will diversify output and improve overall economic performance are available. While these criteria might appear daunting, there are many cases where they will be fulfilled.

Potential causes of resource dependence in the structure of output and exports include (i) unusually large endowments of natural resources; (ii) limited supplies of factors, such as capital and human capital, that are used more intensively in manufactures and services than in resource-based industries; (iii) low productivity in manufactures and services; (iv) trade and pricing policies that discriminate against export-oriented manufactures and services; and (v) high transport and communication costs. Since countries would not generally wish to reduce their endowments of natural resources,[1] the policy solutions to what is regarded as an "excessive" level of dependence on natural resources are likely to lie in the four areas (ii) to (v).

These four influences on resource dependence are clearly strongly related to the basic determinants of structural change identified in the classic Chenery, Robinson, and Syrquin (1986) study of industrialization and structural change. One other influence on the structure of output and exports identified by Chenery, Robinson, and Syrquin is nonhomotheticity of consumer demand; this, however, is difficult to use for policy purposes. Low-income elasticities of demand may, in fact, cause a country undergoing unbiased growth to become more reliant on exports of commodities.

A wide range of policies designed to promote the development of favored sectors has been discussed under the rubric of industrial policy (see Pack 2000 and Stiglitz 1996). Industrial policies include many specific aspects, such as provision of infrastructure, support for education, export promotion activities, technology promotion programs, duty exemption and drawback arrangements for exporters, and preferential allocation of credit to exporting industries. All of these policies can be seen as ultimately affecting the level and structure of output through one of the three channels considered in this chapter.

The process of developing growth models that go beyond balanced growth is only now getting under way (see, for example, Kongsamut, Rebelo, and Xie 2001). Specifying model features in a way that will allow them to be useful in analyzing the profound structural changes associated with reducing resource dependence seems likely to require more sources of structural change than are included in most current growth models.

As noted in World Bank (2003) and in Martin (2003), there have been dramatic changes in the participation of developing countries in world trade. The share of manufactures in total merchandise exports has increased dramatically, at the expense of the traditional stalwarts—agricultural products and minerals. This change has been associated with dramatic shifts in policy toward trade openness, as well as with increases in factor endowments, which raise the available capital and skills per worker.

In this chapter, a simple equilibrium framework sufficiently general to incorporate the structural changes associated with reductions in resource dependence is specified. It is then used as an organizing framework to examine some of the indicators of influences on resource dependence. This analysis is then followed by consideration of policies that might be used to reduce resource dependence.

A Framework

For this chapter, we need a formulation sufficiently general that it can encompass changes in factor endowments, changes in technology, and changes in price policies. The dual approach popularized by Dixit and Norman (1980) provides this flexibility. The production side of the economy can be represented using a restricted profit function specifying the value of net output in the economy as a function of the domestic prices of outputs and intermediate inputs:

$$\pi = \pi(p, v) = \max_x \{p.x|(x, v) \text{ feasible}\} \qquad (11.1)$$

where π is the value added accruing to the vector of quasifixed factors, v, in the economy given the vector of domestic prices, p, for gross outputs of the vector of produced goods, x. The vector v includes economywide stocks of mobile factors, any sector-specific factor inputs, and public goods such as infrastructure that may not be readily allocable to particular sectors.

As Dixit and Norman (1980) note, the specification in equation (11.1) represents all of the properties of production technology. It is extremely general, being able to represent many different types of technology depending on the particular functional form used to specify the GDP function. These specifications may include the familiar 2*2 Heckscher-Ohlin model with two factors and two outputs, and no intermediate inputs, through a range of specifications of much greater generality. It may also include specifications such as the Leamer (1987) model in which there are more goods than factors, and small, open economies move between different cones of diversification in which the set of commodities produced change. The specification is also sufficiently general to include forward and backward linkages induced by input-output linkages and transport costs.

Over the range where the profit function is differentiable, its derivatives with respect to the prices of output yield a vector of net output supplies:

$$\pi_p = \pi_p(p, v) \tag{11.2}$$

Depending on the specification of the profit function, it may be possible to identify the gross outputs of each good, as well as the quantities of these goods used as intermediate inputs in production. For some purposes, such as estimating the incentives created by a protection structure, it is very important to be able to identify the net outputs.

The derivative of the profit function with respect to the factor endowments gives the vector of factor prices.

$$\pi_v(p, v)$$

One additional important expression is the matrix of Rybczynski derivatives. Differentiating the vector of price derivatives, π_p, by the vector of resource endowments (or equivalently by Young's theorem, differentiating the vector of factor prices by the price vector) yields a matrix, π_{pv}, of changes in the net output vector resulting from changes in factor endowments. Although this matrix is clearly critical for our analysis, its exact structure depends heavily upon the particular situation.

In the simple, two-factors, two-output model used in textbook treatments, the Rybczynski responses take a very clearly defined form in any economy that is producing both outputs. As the supply of one factor increases, the output of the sector in which that factor is used intensively increases. The output of the other good declines, despite the increase in the total resources available to the economy. Importantly, factor prices do not change. The required change factor use is achieved by changing the mix of outputs, rather than by changing factor prices. As long as the number of factors and the number of outputs remain the same, this mechanism can be generalized to economies in which there are multiple factors and multiple outputs. The concept of relative factor intensity can be generalized to indicate the increase in the cost of producing a good when the price of a factor increases (Dixit and Norman 1980, 57). The most difficult case to analyze is the realistic situation in which there are more goods than factors. Leamer (1987) and Leamer et al. (1999) provide an extremely useful analytical framework for analyzing this problem where there are three factors and many goods. In simple cases,[2] countries with three factors will specialize in the production of three goods. Over some range, the features of the Rybczynski theorem will hold and changes in factor endowments will result in changes in the mix of output without changes in factor prices. However, changes beyond that point will result in shifts into a new cone of diversification, with a change in the mix of output and a fall in the return to the factor whose relative supply is being augmented. As Leamer (1987, 967) points out, the location of these cones of diversification depends on commodity prices, and thus it is not merely a function of technology.

In the case of resource-poor economies, Leamer et al. show that the adjustment path associated with accumulation of human and physical capital is likely to be relatively smooth, with increases in the supply of capital raising the demand for raw labor as the economy moves through different cones of diversification. For resource-abundant economies, however, the path may involve reductions in unskilled labor as the economy moves from, say, peasant farming to resource-based systems involving greater use of capital. This move may be associated with reductions in the returns to unskilled labor that increase income inequality.

For some problems, such as situations where some goods are non-traded, we need to consider the consumption side of the economy as well as the production side. The consumption side of the economy can be represented similarly using an expenditure function:

$$e(p, u) \qquad (11.3)$$

where e represents the expenditure required to achieve a specified level of utility, u, and represents all of the economically relevant features of consumer preferences. Assuming differentiability of the expenditure function, the vector of consumer demands can be obtained as the following:

$$e_p(p, u) \qquad (11.4)$$

An important feature of real-world consumer preferences is their non-homotheticity, with commodities like basic food having small or negative responses to income increases, while luxury goods have large positive income effects. The vector of Marshallian income effects can be derived from (11.4) as the following:

$$c_Y = (e_{pu}/e_u)$$

where e_u is the marginal impact of a change in utility on expenditure, and e_{pu} is the marginal impact of a change in utility on the consumption of each good.

The vector of net imports of commodities is given by m, which is the difference between the vector of consumption and the vector of net outputs:

$$m = e_p - \pi_p$$

World prices of traded goods are determined by the market-clearing condition that the sum of the net trade vectors for all regions must equal zero. Where some goods are nontraded, the relevant subvector of m is exogenously equal to zero, and equilibrium in the market for these goods is achieved by adjustments in the prices of these goods. Similarly, where trade in some goods is determined by binding quotas, the relevant subvector of m is set exogenously at the quota level and equilibrium is achieved by endogenous determination of these prices.

Trade policy distortions are represented very simply as creating a difference between the vector of domestic prices, p, and world prices, p_w, for the small representative economy. It is frequently useful to define a net expenditure function $z = (e - \pi)$. The derivative of this function with respect to prices, $z_p = (e_p - \pi_p)$, is also equal to the vector of net imports. This function also provides a compact way of representing the revenues accruing from trade distortions as $R = (p - p_w).z_p$

Finally, the welfare impacts of any exogenous shock can be represented using the balance of trade function (Anderson and Neary 1992; Lloyd and Schweinberger 1988). This function takes into account the effects of trade distortions on the cost of expenditures, the revenue to producers, and the revenues from trade distortions (or domestic taxes, which are only levied on expenditures or producer revenues). The specification of this function is based on the assumption that all revenue from trade distortions is returned to the representative consumer. If this is not the case, the function needs to be modified to take into account losses of such revenues to, for example, foreign governments or foreign traders. The balance of trade function, B, can be specified as the following:

$$B = z(p, v, u) - z_p(p - p_w) - f \tag{11.5}$$

where f is an exogenously specified financial inflow from abroad. When u is held constant, and changes are made in any of the exogenous variables of the system, changes in B show the change in the financial inflow needed to maintain the initial level of utility in the face of the changes in the exogenous variables. This change in income is a measure of the compensating variation associated with the change.

Before the system can be used to analyze the consequences of changes in productivity, we need to augment this standard system to include the impacts of technical change on producer behavior and producer profits. As noted by Martin and Alston (1997), there are a number of ways in which this might be done, but perhaps the most appealing in terms of flexibility and consistency with economic theory is to represent technological change as resulting in a distinction between actual and effective units of an input or output. In the case of an output-augmenting technological advance, such a change might be one that increases the actual output achieved from the same bundle of inputs—such as an increase in the grain available for consumption from a given amount available for harvest in the field. In the case of an input-augmenting technological advance, the change might be one that reduces the actual quantity of the input required to achieve the same outcome—such as a reduction in the amount of labor needed to complete a task. Product quality improvements and promotion policies might create a similar augmentation of the product from the viewpoint of the user—a product augmentation, rather than a process augmentation.

Such technological changes have two important impacts on behavior and profitability. The first is the *direct* response of output associated with the initial level of inputs in the case of an output-augmenting technical change, or the change in required inputs to achieve a given level of output. The second impact is the *induced* impact resulting from changes in the effective prices of inputs. In representing such technical changes, it is necessary to take into account both the direct impacts on output or inputs and the indirect impacts working through induced changes in the effective prices of outputs or inputs.

In the case of output-augmenting technical change, we can define effective output i as the following:

$$x_i^* = x_i.\tau_i \qquad (11.6)$$

where τ is a technical change parameter equal to unity before the technological change. We can define a corresponding output price as the following:

$$p_i^* = p_i/\tau_i. \qquad (11.7)$$

In the case of an output-augmenting technical change,[3] the effect of the technological change is to increase the effective output associated with any given bundle of inputs and to raise the effective price of output. Clearly, both of these effects operate in the same direction, tending to increase output at any given output price. The first does so by increasing the outputs obtained from any given level of inputs, and the second by drawing additional inputs into production of this good. In the case of an input-augmenting technical change, the direct effect is to reduce the inputs required to achieve a given level of output, while the indirect effect is to increase output as producers substitute the input whose effective price has fallen for other inputs. In this case, the effect on input use is ambiguous, depending on whether the direct input-saving effect is outweighed by the substitution effect.

Rewriting equation (11.2) in terms of effective prices and quantities as defined in equations (11.6) and (11.7) allows us to assess the impacts of an improvement in technology in sector i on output from that sector in a small, open economy. Differentiating the supply of output in actual units with respect to τ yields

$$\frac{\partial \pi_p}{\partial \tau} = \pi_p^* + \tau \frac{\partial \pi_p^*}{\partial \tau}$$

which can be rearranged to yield

$$\frac{\partial \pi_p}{\partial \tau} \cdot \frac{\tau}{\pi_p} = 1 + \eta_{ii} \qquad (11.8)$$

where η_{ii} is the own-price elasticity of supply for good i. The intuition behind equation (11.8) is that a technological advance proportionately increases the output generated by the resources originally committed to production of the good. In addition, it increases the effective price of the output and, hence, induces an additional increase in output equal to the own-price elasticity of supply.

Another influence on the response of output and resource use is the impact of the technological change on the actual price of output. In a small, open economy, the actual price is unaffected by technological changes, unless the technical change is global, when it will affect world prices. However, for a closed economy, technical changes can be expected to affect the price of output. The higher the elasticity of consumer demand in this situation, the smaller the decline in the actual price of output and the more likely it is that input use will rise when production of a particular output benefits from a technological advance. Matsuyama (1992) distinguished between an open-economy situation in which improvements in agricultural technology increased input use in agriculture and a closed-economy case in which improvements in agricultural technology allowed the demanded level of output to be produced with fewer inputs. When trade in a good is quantity-constrained, either for natural reasons such as transport costs or because of policy constraints such as quotas, we can readily modify the derivation of equation (11.8) to take the consequent changes in actual output prices into account. For a single nontraded good in an undistorted economy, the (compensated) impact[4] on prices is given by

$$dp/p = (1 + \eta_{ii})/(\varepsilon_{ii} - \eta_{ii})d\tau/\tau \qquad (11.9)$$

where ε_{ii} is the compensated elasticity of demand for good i.

One informative limiting case is the one where the elasticity of demand is very small relative to the elasticity of supply. While this case appears very restrictive, it is probably a realistic approximation in many cases, since general-equilibrium supply elasticities for a single industry in a Heckscher-Ohlin setting are determined only through impacts of changes in its output on factor prices and are likely to be very much larger in absolute value than demand elasticities. In this case, (11.9) reduces to

$$dp/p = -(1 + 1/\eta_{ii})/d\tau/\tau$$

This identifies two components of the price reduction. The unit impact is the price reduction required to exactly offset the impact of the technical change on the effective price of output and, hence, on the supply of actual output. The second is the decline in the domestic price needed to offset the direct stimulus to supply (at any given level of inputs) resulting from technical change. Given the dramatic growth rates feasible in some export-oriented sectors, this difference could result in very large differences in the welfare benefits obtainable from technical change.

Empirical Evidence

The framework just outlined provides a potential basis for analysis of changes in the structure of the economy in general and resource dependence in particular. Such a framework is vitally needed, as there have been dramatic changes in the composition of exports from developing countries during the past 20 years. The extent and rapidity of these changes is highlighted in figure 11.1, which shows that developing countries as a group have reduced their reliance on exports of agricultural and mineral commodities. In the late 1970s, agricultural and mineral commodities accounted for close to three-quarters of exports from developing countries. By the late 1990s, this share had fallen to less than a fifth.

As is clear from the data presented in annex table 11.A1, the decline in the importance of resource-based products has not been confined to merely a few countries. Manufactures have become the dominant exports of a wide range of developing countries. Even countries in Sub-Saharan Africa such as Malawi, Mozambique, Tanzania, Zambia, and Zimbabwe have increased the share of manufactures in their total exports to the point where manufactures make up almost a quarter of the exports of the group (Martin 2001b).

To ensure that the changes in figure 11.1 reflect changes in output volumes rather than simply changes in product prices, the commodity output shares were reestimated in 1965 prices using deflators from the World Bank's Development Prospects' Group. Specifically, agricultural exports were deflated by the World Bank's index of agricultural product prices for developing country exports, mineral exports were deflated by the price of oil, and manufactures

Figure 11.1 The Changing Pattern of Merchandise Exports from Developing Countries

Source: Global Trade Analysis Project (GTAP) 5 Database.
http://www.gtap.org.

export prices were deflated by the United Nations manufactures' unit value index. The resulting commodity shares are presented in figure 11.2.

The numbers presented in figure 11.2 show that the changes in the composition of developing country exports have been the result of shifts in the quantities of exports they produce, rather than solely in the prices received for outputs. This figure shows that the increase in the importance of manufactures exports began in earnest in the 1970s rather than in the 1980s, as suggested by the graph in nominal values. The dramatic increase in the price of oil and hence the share of minerals during the 1970s obscured this fundamental shift in figure 11.1.

Developing countries' dependence on exports of resource-based products has been further reduced by an increase in the importance of services exports. Figure 11.3 presents data on the shares of commercial[5] services in the exports of goods and services from major country groups. Although these numbers are the only ones available as a time series, they appear to considerably understate the importance of services exports.

Figure 11.2 Change in Developing Country Export Shares at 1965 Prices

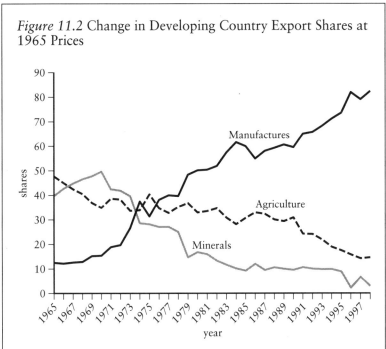

Source: GTAP 5 data for agriculture and minerals deflated by price series from Development Prospects Group, World Bank; prices for manufactures deflated using data from the UN MUV index.

Karsenty (2000) estimates that this category of services now accounts for only around 60 percent of the total exports of services covered by the four modes of the General Agreement on Trade in Services (GATS). In the early 1980s, commercial services made up 17 percent of the exports of high-income countries—a share that has since risen to 20 percent (shown as High in the figure). In the low- and middle-income countries (LMC in figure 11.3), services trade started out much less important—at 9 percent—but rose much more rapidly, to 17 percent. Among the relatively poor countries of Sub-Saharan Africa (SSA), the share also grew rapidly, from 10 to 15 percent.

A key challenge is clearly to understand and to explain the changes in the structure of output and exports that underlie these sharp changes in the structure of exports from developing countries. These changes are so profound and rapid as to call into question much previous discussion of developing-country trade policy, which typically postulates developing countries as reliant almost exclusively on exports of agricultural and

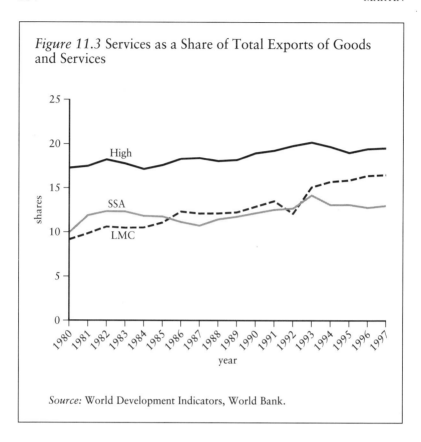

Figure 11.3 Services as a Share of Total Exports of Goods and Services

Source: World Development Indicators, World Bank.

natural resource products (see, for example, Buffie 2001, 151). Clearly, the policy implications for reducing resource dependence, and for development policy more generally, will differ greatly depending upon the causes of this dramatic change. In the next three subsections of the chapter, we examine the available evidence on the factors most likely to influence the composition of exports. Changes in factor endowments are considered first, followed by changes in protection policy. Finally, the role of technological advance is examined.

Factor Accumulation

For factor accumulation to have a major impact on the structure of output and exports, two conditions need to be satisfied. The first relates to the structure of the π_{pv} matrix and requires that changes in relative factor endowments result in substantial changes in the composition of output à la Rybczynski, rather than in changes in factor proportions within sectors, as in the neoclassical growth model. The second is that there must be sizeable changes in relative factor endowments, that is, that Δ must be nonuniform. In this section, the evidence on the impacts of changes in factor endowments is first examined, followed by the evidence on changes in relative factor endowments. Finally, attention turns to the extent to which the Rybczynski assumption of exogenous, or at least predetermined, factor endowments can be taken to be realistic.

Whether changes in relative factor endowments will affect the composition of output is a question that can only be resolved through empirical studies. If, for instance, the factor intensities of different sectors were not greatly different, or if different factors were near-perfect substitutes, this effect would not be expected to be large. The empirical impact of factor accumulation on the share of output and hence on export patterns has received considerable attention in recent years. A number of studies using quite different approaches have concluded that changes in factor endowments can have quite strong impacts on the composition of output and exports, rather than on factor prices, confirming the potential empirical importance of the Rybczynski theorem.

Martin and Warr (1993) examined the determinants of the rapid decline in the share of agriculture in Indonesian gross domestic product (GDP). Using time-series data, they estimated a profit function that incorporates the factor endowment and technological change effects discussed in this study, as well as relative price changes that include the impacts of changes in trade policy. Their conclusion was that the most important determinant of the reduction in the share of agriculture in the Indonesian economy was increases in the capital-labor ratio. The output price effects that take into account the effects of factors such as changes in protection policy and in worldwide technical change played a much smaller role. Technological advance was found to be biased toward agriculture and, hence, tending to increase agriculture's share of output, other things equal.

Gehlhar, Hertel, and Martin (1994) used a completely different analytical tool—the Global Trade Analysis Project (GTAP) computable general equilibrium model of the world economy—to examine the changing structure of the world economy. This model incorporates the nonhomotheticity in consumer demand that plays such an important role in discussions of the decline in agriculture's share of output in the world economy. It also includes input-output tables with the differences in the factor intensities of different sectors that drive the Rybczynski effects when relative factor endowments change. Further, it includes forward and backward linkages through its input-output structure and the transport costs that loom large in the new economic geography. The model was first validated over the 1980s to ensure that it could realistically replicate the changes in sectoral shares of exports in the Asia-Pacific region. Then the structure of output was projected from 1992 to 2002. A key conclusion of the analysis was that the most important determinant of likely changes in agricultural output and trade patterns, and particularly a sharp decline in reliance on agricultural exports in East Asian developing economies, was likely to be differential rates of factor accumulation, rather than nonhomotheticity in consumer demand.

Harrigan (1997) examined the impact of technological changes and changes in relative factor endowments on the structure of manufacturing output in a panel of Organisation for Economic Co-operation and Development (OECD) countries. His econometric results caused him to conclude that factor endowment changes, as well as technological changes, have large effects on output shares. Kee (2001) reached the same conclusion in a study of the manufacturing sector in Singapore.

In a completely different literature, Hanson and Slaughter (2002) examined the implications of changes in the supply of workers with different skill levels in states of the United States. They found that a key part of the adjustment to changes in the supply of workers of a particular type was a change in the structure of output of the type suggested by Rybczynski effects.

There remains some controversy about the relevance of the Rybczynski theorem in some cases. Cohen and Hsieh (2000) focused on the very large immigration of Russian Jews into Israel in the early 1990s and found results more in line with the single-sector neoclassical model: a short-run fall in the wages of native Israelis and a rise in the return to capital. Equilibrium was restored through an increase in the capital stock associated with increased external borrowing. This case was considerably complicated by the ambiguous skills endowment of the immigrants. Although they were much more highly educated than the native population, they suffered substantial occupational downgrading following their immigration, which made it difficult to assess whether the output response should have involved outputs intensive in skilled or unskilled labor.

If one accepts the potential validity of the Rybczynski theorem as a potential cause of structural change, a key question is whether there have been major changes in relative factor endowments that would cause changes in the composition of developing country output away from dependence on resources. Recent data on accumulation of human and physical capital suggest that there have been quite sharp changes both between developed and developing regions, and between different developing country regions. The most comprehensive such database known to this author is that by Nehru and his coauthors (Nehru and Dhareshwar 1993; Nehru, Swanson, and Dubey 1995).

Table 11.1 shows the growth rates of physical and human capital relative both to labor and to output. The first column points to quite rapid increases in physical capital per worker (K/L) in both industrial and developing countries. The 5.1 percent per year growth rate for East Asia implies more than a quadrupling of capital per worker over the 30-year period of observation. The 2.4 percent a year increase in Latin America implies more than a doubling of the capital-labor ratio over the period. Even the 2.1 percent per year increase in Sub-Saharan Africa implies a near doubling of capital per worker. The stock of education per worker, measured by years of schooling completed, grew at quite high rates in most developing country regions, although it grew very slowly in the industrial countries. This was particularly the case for secondary and tertiary education stocks, which grew extremely rapidly in most developing country regions. The 9.2 percent annual growth in the stock of secondary school education in East Asia, for instance, implies a 14-fold increase in this stock over 30 years.

Before placing too much emphasis on the apparent increases in capital and in education per worker in developing countries as indicators of changes in factor endowments, it is important to examine the capital-output ratio (K/Q). One of Kaldor's key stylized facts of economic growth (Branson 1979, 465) was a constant capital/output ratio and a rising capital/labor ratio. This is frequently interpreted to imply that technical change is Harrod-neutral, with capital per worker increasing in line with effective labor. If true, this would imply an absence of changes in factor endowments, implying no long-run changes in factor endowment ratios, and hence no role for Rybczynski effects.

In fact, it appears from table 11.1 that the physical capital-output ratio increased quite substantially over the period in both developing and industrial countries. For human capital, the education-to-output ratios have increased substantially in developing countries, but fallen quite rapidly in developed countries. These results have potentially important implications for our interpretation of the process of growth and structural change. Before going too far, however, it is important to check the data used by Nehru, Swanson, and Dubey against other data sets to ensure that these results are not merely artifacts of the data construction process. A check against the

Table 11.1 Annual Changes in Factor Endowment Ratios

	K/L %	K/Q %	Edn/L %	Edn/Q %	Secondary Edn/L %	Tertiary Edn/L %
Industrial	3.7	1.1	0.3	−2.3	2.2	4.9
Developing						
East Asia	5.1	2.3	4.2	1.4	9.2	3.4
South Asia	3.2	1.4	3.3	1.5	4.3	6.4
Latin America	2.4	1.4	2.0	1.0	5.3	6.7
Sub-Saharan Africa	2.1	2.1	4.2	4.2	9.7	12.6
Middle East &						
North Africa	3.4	3.2	2.3	2.1	1.9	6.3

Sources: Nehru and Dhareshwar 1993; Nehru, Swanson, and Dubey 1995.
Note: Rates for physical capital refer to 1960–90 and for education 1960–87.

well-known Penn World Tables data (see http://www.nber.org) for a range of countries suggests that physical capital/output ratios were generally rising quite rapidly in the 1970–90 period for which the capital accumulation data are available. The fact that the growth rates of K/Q and Education/Q are generally lower than their growth relative to the labor input does, however, give reason for caution about common assumptions, such as the Hicks-Neutral technical change in all sectors used by Harrigan (1997) and Kee (2001).

Despite the evidence from many different types of empirical studies on the potential role of Rybczynski effects, the coincidence of high rates of accumulation of physical and human capital over the period and the rapid shift of developing countries into exports of manufactures and services is clearly not definitive evidence of causation. However, it is strongly suggestive, and it needs to be examined in conjunction with changes in trade policy and in technology.

Protection Policies

Protection policy is frequently advocated as a means of promoting industrial development. It can certainly do this for import-competing activities, such as production of consumer goods. However, this production pattern locks producers into small, and typically slow-growing, markets for their output. Further, it introduces a major discontinuity. Under a protectionist policy regime, an exporter must not only have sufficient comparative advantage to be able to compete in world markets, he or she must have sufficient advantage to be able to compete *despite* the cost increases resulting from protection levied on his or her intermediate inputs, as well as the adverse effects of real exchange-rate devaluation on his or her costs for factors and nontraded goods.

Developing countries have increasingly come to recognize the adverse impacts of protection on their export performance and have begun to adjust their policies toward more open trade regimes. The most profound and far-reaching manifestation of developing countries' interest in greater participation in trade is evident from the wave of unilateral trade reforms that has swept the developing countries. These reforms have affected all regions and all of the major types of policy distortions. As discussed in *Global Economic Prospects and the Developing Countries, 2001* (World Bank 2001, chapter 2) and presented in figure 11.4, average tariff rates in developing countries have halved, from around 30 percent in the early 1980s to around 15 percent in the late 1990s. The absolute reductions in tariff rates in developing countries have been much higher than in industrial countries and, of course, decreases from a higher level are likely to have a much greater welfare benefit than corresponding decreases from a lower base (see Martin 1997). In addition, the dispersion of tariff rates, which typically increases the welfare cost of any given average tariff rate (Anderson 1995), was substantially reduced.

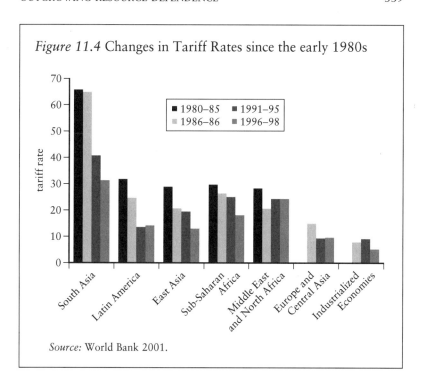

Figure 11.4 Changes in Tariff Rates since the early 1980s

Source: World Bank 2001.

Table 11.2 Frequency of Total Core Nontariff Measures in Developing Countries, 1989–98 (percent)

Country	1989–94	1995–98
East Asia and the Pacific (7)	30.1	16.3
Latin America and the Caribbean (13)	18.3	8.0
Middle East and North Africa (4)	43.8	16.6
South Asia (4)	57.0	58.3
Sub-Saharan Africa (12)	26.0	10.4

Source: World Bank 2001, based on Michalopoulos 1999.
Note: Figures in parentheses are the number of countries in each region for which data are available.

One must be careful when examining changes in tariff rates, because a decline in tariffs may reflect substitution of nontariff barriers for tariffs. However, during this period, the coverage of nontariff barriers, including state-trading monopolies, in developing countries also appears to have fallen considerably, as is evident in table 11.2.

Another important dimension of reform has been a sharp reduction in the number of countries using foreign-exchange restrictions on current account and in the average foreign-exchange premia. The World Bank (2001) reports that the number of developing countries applying foreign-exchange restrictions on current account has fallen sharply. Table 11.3 shows foreign-exchange premia for a range of countries in the 1980s and 1990s. This table highlights two things: first, that average foreign-exchange market distortions were enormous in the 1980s, and second, that these premia in most developing countries, in most regions, have fallen to very low levels. While the simple average foreign-exchange rate premium is highest in the Middle East and North Africa, at 46.5 percent, this high rate is almost entirely due to large premia in Algeria and Iran. If these two outliers are excluded, the average rate falls to only 1.4 percent. When Nigeria is excluded, the average premium in Sub-Saharan Africa is less than 10 percent, down from 112 percent in the mid 1980s. Clearly, for most countries, the premia are now small enough to imply that foreign-exchange distortions impose relatively small taxes on trade.

There are good reasons to expect that, in this situation, a high-protection regime will lock countries into continuing dependence on resource-based commodities that are typically less dependent on purchased intermediate inputs than is manufacturing, particularly in this era of production fragmentation. To allow further examination of this difference, table 11.4 presents data on the cost structure of output and the effective rates of protection imposed on export-oriented activities for a number of countries. A striking feature in the top section of the table is the much lower dependence of primary agriculture and resources commodities on intermediate inputs. This gives resource-based activities an opportunity to survive even in situations of very high protection.

It is, of course, possible that the greater vulnerability of manufacturers and agricultural processors to high-protection regimes would be off-

Table 11.3 Average Black-Market Premium, 1980–97 (percent)

	1980–89	1990–93	1994–97
Total[a]	82.0	78.2	20.3
East Asia	3.6	3.6	3.2
Middle East and North Africa	165.6	351.6	46.5
Excluding outliers[b]	7.1	8.8	1.4
Latin America	48.7	13.1	4.4
South Asia	40.8	45.1	10.1
Sub-Saharan Africa	116.5	28.6	32.2
Excluding Nigeria	112.1	25.8	9.6

Source: World Bank 2001.
Notes: a. Sample of 41 developing countries.
   b. Algeria and Iran.

set by a type of tariff escalation that involves lower-than-average protection on intermediate inputs to agricultural and manufacturing sectors. To see whether this is the case, the second panel of table 11.4 examines the effective rates of protection applying to exporters. These effective rate calculations are done very simply, taking into account only the effects of intermediate input shares and tariff rates. They therefore ignore the additional burdens imposed on exporters by nontariff barriers on inputs, or by the real exchange-rate appreciation associated with protection. What the results of these calculations strongly suggest is that the pattern of tariff protection does not provide any relief to exporters of manufactures or processed agricultural products. In fact, it appears that the pattern of real-world protection adds to the discrimination against exporters of manufactures and processed agricultural products resulting from their greater dependence on intermediate inputs.

Table 11.4 Shares of Intermediate Inputs and Effective Rates of Protection for Exporters, 1997 (percent)

	Agriculture	Ag. proc.	Resources	L manuf	K manuf	Services
Input shares						
Argentina	21.8	61.9	11.9	58.9	57.7	24.2
Chile	40.8	76.8	46.3	65.5	65.2	39.6
China	42.9	80.0	48.4	74.0	78.3	61.3
India	32.0	82.3	27.6	69.6	76.8	40.6
Malawi	40.3	58.2	35.7	55.9	50.9	30.3
Morocco	34.9	82.7	35.6	62.2	75.7	52.1
Pakistan	35.0	84.2	18.7	72.2	79.3	41.2
World	44.5	72.2	37.3	64.5	68.0	39.7
ERP-X						
Argentina	−2.7	−13.6	−0.8	−16.2	−13.7	−2.9
Chile	−5.2	−22.5	−5.6	−11.2	−13.2	−2.6
China	−15.1	−54.0	−7.3	−34.8	−27.9	−13.7
India	−5.4	−38.5	−3.3	−22.6	−34.8	−6.3
Malawi	−7.3	−16.4	−5.0	−15.0	−8.9	−3.9
Morocco	−8.5	−50.4	−1.9	−27.5	−17.9	−8.1
Pakistan	−8.4	−45.4	−5.6	−40.5	−54.0	−12.2
World	−7.2	−25.0	−1.0	−8.5	−5.7	−1.4

Source: GTAP 5 database. http://www.gtap.org.
Note: ERP-X measures the reduction in value added caused by protection on intermediate inputs under the assumption of homogeneous products. Results for Pakistan are based on the composite region "Other South Asia," which also includes Afghanistan, Bhutan, the Maldives, and Nepal.

Given the negative effective rates of protection seen in the lower panel of table 11.4, the structure of protection is clearly a daunting problem for putative exports of manufactures or processed agricultural products, particularly if there are fixed costs involved in entering export markets. However, it is clear that this problem is much more manageable in many countries than it was in the early 1980s. If we triple China's protection level from its 1997 base to align it with the tariff rates that applied in China in the early 1990s, we find ERP-X's of –78 percent for processed food and –62 percent for labor-intensive manufactures—and this is before the direct adverse impacts of licensing, quotas, and nominal exchange-rate overvaluation, as well as the indirect effect of real exchange-rate appreciation, are factored in.

Direct evidence on the implications of increased openness for exports of manufactures is provided by a wide range of empirical studies using traditional computable general equilibrium (CGE) models. A recent econometric study by Elbadawi, Mengistae, and Zeufack (2001) builds on recent economic geography models developed by Redding and Venables (2004) and concludes that increasing openness in African countries would considerably expand exports of manufactures.

Overall, it seems highly likely that the sharp reductions in developing-country trade distortions since the early 1980s have played a vital role in allowing developing countries to so sharply increase their exports of manufactures and, hence, reduce their dependence on resource-based products.

Technological Change

Technological change is a very important determinant of changes in both resource dependence and economic growth and development. Unfortunately, it is relatively poorly understood because of the complexity of many of the processes that lead to it, as well as because of the problems involved in measuring it.

Much thinking on the role of technological change in promoting structural change has been confused by a failure to distinguish between open and closed economies. The oft-encountered argument that technical advance in agriculture promotes industrialization by freeing up resources formerly used in agriculture is, as pointed out by Matsuyama (1992), likely to be relevant only in a closed economy. In an open economy, technical change that increases productivity in agriculture, or any other sector, will generally increase the size of that sector by drawing additional resources into the sector because of induced increases in the profitability of production.

Assuming a relatively open economy, a key determinant of whether resources are likely to shift from agricultural and other resource-based products into manufactures and services is the relative rate of technical change. Many economists, including Matsuyama (1992), follow a tradition dating back to Adam Smith and assume that productivity growth in agriculture is very slow. However, more recent empirical studies (for example, Martin and Mitra 2001) suggest that the average rate of total-factor productivity (TFP) growth in agriculture has been higher than in manufacturing. This appears to represent a change from results from earlier periods surveyed by Syrquin (1986), in which there was no consistent tendency for TFP in agriculture to grow more rapidly than productivity in manufactures. This apparent change may reflect the substantial investments in international research and dissemination of rural technologies during recent decades.

Key results from the Bernard and Jones and the Martin and Mitra studies are presented in table 11.5. The Bernard and Jones analysis is based on data from OECD countries over the period 1970 to 1987, while the Martin and Mitra study is based on data collected by Larson and Mundlak (see Larson et al. 2000) for 1966 to 1992. While this evidence is somewhat limited as a basis for judgment, further support for the proposition that agricultural TFP has been more rapid than that in manufacturing is provided by a number of single-country studies, including Jorgenson, Gollop, and Fraumeni (1987). The Bernard and Jones estimate of a small, negative rate of TFP growth in mining is surprising, given the manifestly rapid changes in the technology used for mining, and may reflect resource depletion in some OECD countries.

The apparently robust finding of relatively rapid technical change in agriculture suggests that the decline in developing countries' dependence on agricultural exports cannot simply be explained by higher rates of productivity growth in manufactures. This difference, alone, would seem to increase the importance of the other possible explanations for increased exports of manufactures from developing countries—Rybczynski effects and reductions in protection.

Table 11.5 Sectoral Productivity Growth (percent per year)

	Agriculture	Manufacturing	Mining
OECD	2.60	1.90	−0.2
Low-income countries	1.99	0.69	n.a.
Middle-income countries	2.90	0.97	n.a.
All developing countries	2.60	0.90	n.a.
Industrial countries	3.50	2.80	n.a.
Overall average	2.90	1.60	n.a.

Sources: OECD results from Bernard and Jones 1996. All other results from Martin and Mitra 2001.

Note: TFP estimated using factor shares.

n.a. = not applicable

There is a possibility of a strong positive interaction between increased export orientation and productivity growth in manufacturing exports. This does not appear to result from the traditional anecdotal model in which exporters "learn by doing" or from their interactions with their foreign customers. Rather, recent studies suggest that the firms that choose to export generally have higher productivity and produce higher-quality products when they begin exporting (Tybout 2001; Hallward-Dreimeier, Iarossi, and Sokoloff 2001). In this situation, it becomes particularly important to have a policy environment that encourages entry of firms—whether new or old—into exporting activities. Further, the productivity gains from entry can be compounded by the expansion of these firms, at the expense of less efficient firms, following entry. Finally, as noted in the discussion of technical change, the gains from technical change may be much greater when firms have the opportunity to expand than in cases where their market size is restricted.

Transport Costs

One change that has received a great deal of attention as a potential cause of greater developing-country participation in world trade in manufactures is falling costs of communication and transport. It is very clear that communication costs have fallen dramatically in recent years. New technologies for communication (for example, fax and, subsequently, e-mail and the World Wide Web) have greatly increased the ability of firms to coordinate activities undertaken at distant locations. Transport costs have also fallen in many, although not all, cases.

The cost of transport has been shown to have a major impact on trade flows. Limao and Venables (2002) found that halving transport costs increased trade volumes by a factor of five. They also found that freight costs vary enormously, depending on the quality of infrastructure and whether a country is land-locked. Amjadi and Yeats (1995) found that transport costs were particularly high in Africa and had increased as a share of export value since 1970. Using a model based on trade in manufactures, Redding and Venables (2004) showed that transport costs for trade in output and intermediate inputs could be profoundly important for poverty in developing countries that were integrated into world trade in manufactures. They concluded that up to 70 percent of the variation in incomes between countries could be explained by such geographical factors.

It is widely believed that the costs of ocean shipping have fallen dramatically, and that this has been a major factor contributing to globalization. However, as in some earlier episodes of globalization (O'Rourke and Williamson 2000), changes in shipping rates have been anything but consistent[6] over the period since 1950. Hummels (1999) concluded that liner shipping rates increased by more than 50 percent between 1954 and 1983, although they declined substantially after 1985 to bring them back close (in real U.S. dollar terms) to their 1954 level. Other costs that depend on infrastructure quality, such as port charges, the costs of clearing customs, and internal freight costs, frequently exceed the cost of ocean freight by a multiple of two or three and whether they have declined varies greatly depending on the regulatory environment in individual countries. Hummels (2001) found that time costs appear to have an impact equivalent to very high transport costs, with every day saved in shipping time equal to a cost saving of 0.8 percent ad valorem.

Given the great importance of transport costs for income levels and for economic development, it seems clear that reform of maritime shipping services should be a high priority in future negotiations. Even though reform in this area has proved very difficult under the multilateral system in the past, there seems to be an enormous opportunity to make progress that would be important for developing countries in the future. Such progress could be particularly important for African developing countries, which face disproportionately high transport costs.

Policy Implications

Any consideration of action to deal with resource dependence needs to begin with an assessment of whether a country's current level of dependence on agricultural and resource-based products is excessive in relation to policy goals such as growth and stability or considerations of poverty and vulnerability. The analysis of the problem should aim to specify the problem very carefully, as the policy solution is likely to depend heavily upon the specific nature of the problem. A problem of excessive income variability in a context of, for instance, rigid wages that translate terms of trade shocks into unemployment may have quite different solutions than a problem of resource rent dependence that leads to rent-seeking, or provides funding for civil insurgencies (Collier 2000). If the problem is one of excessive income variability, then there is a prima facie case for dealing with it through a financial policy instrument such as the use of futures contracts, rather than through changes in the mix of output in the economy (Priovolos and Duncan 1991).

If the analysis of the problem suggests that the situation requires action to change the structure of the country's output and export mix, then policy should focus on achieving this change in ways that overcome market failures and maximize the development payoff. A key priority is likely to be stimulating the accumulation of physical and human capital. Not surprisingly, attempts to stimulate the development of sectors that are more intensive in physical and human capital than the current output mix without providing additional capital inputs are likely to distort resource use throughout the economy. The fact that financial capital remains relatively immobile internationally (Gordon and Bovenberg 1996) means that attempts to increase the accumulation of physical capital are likely to focus on stimulating domestic saving. Loayza, Schmidt-Hebbel, and Serven (2000) draw on a large number of studies to provide policy recommendations to this effect. Even if factor accumulation is less important for overall economic growth than has previously been thought (Easterly and Levine 2001), it seems likely to provide a strong stimulus to a shift in the composition of exports toward manufactures and services.

Given the weakness of capital markets in financing intangible assets like human capital, governments tend to play a much larger role in guiding the accumulation of human capital than of physical capital. Accumulation of human capital is likely to have both level and growth effects on output and to facilitate the transformation of the economy into one that produces relatively more human-capital-intensive goods. As Dessus (1999) notes, the impact of human capital accumulation on both output and on poverty reduction depends a great deal on the emphasis of the education system and on its effectiveness. As Leamer et al. (1999) note, provision of education may need to be very proactive, attempting to take into account demands in the next cone of diversification associated with economic development, rather than in current activities. As they note further, this may imply training workers for much more sophisticated activities than are undertaken in an initially very resource-dependent economy.

Attracting foreign direct investment may help to augment the available capital stock, although this source of capital is typically small relative to total investment. However, it is possible that foreign direct investment or subcontracting relationships (Deardorff and Djankov 2000) can help transfer the knowledge needed for rapid productivity growth. If attracting foreign investment leads to a focus on developing the institutions needed to improve the investment climate—for domestic as well as foreign investors—then it can play a particularly important role in development. Use of foreign investment implies a need for greater caution in the use of protection policies. Since foreign investors' returns are based on the private returns to their capital, investments in import-substituting industries are very likely to reduce national income. Second-best mechanisms such as export performance requirements have been used, very imperfectly, to reduce these problems in the past (Rodrik 1986), but they are likely to be largely unavailable in the future because of the Uruguay Round agreement on trade-related investment measures.

There is a strong case for relying on an open trade regime as the best approach to development and economic restructuring. Activist trade policies can only work in a dynamic sense if they promote sufficiently rapid learning in the favored sectors to overcome their certain short-run efficiency costs. However, analyses such as the one performed by Krueger and Tuncer (1982) have failed to find any significant stimulus to productivity from infant-industry protection, let alone enough to justify static inefficiencies. An open trade regime overcomes the discontinuities resulting from positive protection to import-competing sectors and negative protection to exporting activities. These sharp discontinuities threaten the viability of manufacturing and service sectors that may represent the next step in development as a resource-dependent economy moves from one cone of diversification to the next. In the presence of such sharp discontinuities, import-competing industries are likely to be constrained to grow very slowly after they experience a positive shock to productivity—unless the boost to productivity is sufficiently large as to make the activity competitive in export markets despite the negative impacts of protection on its input costs and the real exchange rate. Constraints on output growth in this situation can greatly reduce the welfare benefits from increases in productivity.

If a very low and uniform protection regime cannot be achieved, a case can be made for the use of duty exemptions or duty drawback mechanisms to reduce the burden of protection on exporting activities. This type of second-best response remains fully legal under World Trade Organization rules, even though it effectively provides an export subsidy designed to offset the burden of import barriers. If implemented properly, such mechanisms can reduce the variance of effective rates of protection across importing and exporting activities by increasing the effective rate on exporting activities to zero. Duty-exemption schemes have certainly been important in stimulating the development of manufacturing exports from East Asia (Rodrik 1994; Martin 2001a). However, such schemes are costly to implement and frequently stimulate corrupt behavior. Further, they reduce the incentives for exporters to press for lower tariffs on their inputs and may, therefore, lead to higher protection than would be the case in their absence (Cadot, de Melo, and Olarreaga 2001).

Buffie (2001) makes a second-best case for an escalating tariff to provide high effective protection to domestically oriented industry in the presence of an irremovable wage distortion in the import-competing manufacturing sector. However, this case is heavily dependent on the unknown mechanism determining this wage differential. If the wage determination mechanism responds to greater protection to the import-competing sector by increasing the real wage in this sector, this mechanism could be extremely costly. Further, it is inferior to a duty exemption arrangement in providing the flexibility needed to allow the emergence of new export sectors.

A key issue for policy is to stimulate technological advance in all sectors, but particularly in the manufacturing and services sectors that are likely to lie on the evolution of the country's comparative advantage. In this area, Navaretti and Tarr (2000) stress the importance of increasing the absorptive capacity, particularly through increasing education. Increasing export orientation of the manufacturing sector through trade reform and factor accumulation appears to help increase productivity in this sector—not by learning by doing, but more through the entry of higher productivity firms. Foreign direct investment may also help promote technical advance. Finally, of course, the provision of an appropriate level of protection of intellectual property rights can help stimulate innovation.

Policy options for reducing transport and communications costs include domestic, unilateral reform options; regional agreements; and multilateral reform options through GATS. Hummels (1999) feels that one possible explanation for the increase in shipping freight rates up to the mid-1980s, despite the introduction of cost-saving innovations such as open registries and improvements in shipping technology, was that containerization may have helped strengthen shipping cartels. In the shipping arena, Clark, Dollar, and Micco (2004) conclude that improving port infrastructure and liberalizing restrictions on cargo handling and provision of port services could substantially reduce overall transport costs. Fink, Mattoo, and Neagu (2000) agree that government restrictions on entry into port services raise shipping costs substantially. However, they conclude that the policies that allow shipping conferences to collude in ways that raise rates are a much more important source of cost increases. They estimate that removing restrictions on trade in maritime services would result in a 9 percent reduction in the average costs of liner shipping. Enacting policies that would eliminate the collusive practices that are endemic in the industry would have a much greater payoff, allowing a further 25 percent reduction in costs. They suggest the use of the GATS to challenge these restrictive practices, some of which cannot be tackled by governments acting unilaterally.

Conclusions

This chapter examines the options for policymakers interested in reducing the potential adverse consequences of dependence on resource-based products. It argues that any such action should follow a careful examination of the nature of the problems created by resource dependence. If the conclusion is that economic output should be restructured to reduce resource dependence, then appropriate policy responses are likely to involve (i) increasing accumulation of the types of physical and human capital needed in the manufactures and service activities most appropriate to the country's comparative advantage, (ii) developing a trade regime that allows the emergence of new export activities as comparative advantage shifts, and (iii) promoting technological change in manufactures and services.

Over recent decades, developing countries have greatly diversified their exports, to the point where manufactures account for more than 80 percent of developing-country merchandise exports. While declines in commodity prices have played a role in this change, it appears that there have been other contributing factors—in particular, relatively rapid accumulation of human and physical capital in developing countries, as well as a dramatic shift toward more open trade regimes. Biases in technical change do not appear to have played a major role in this transformation. If anything, increased productivity in developing-country agriculture has tended to increase the share of agriculture in individual developing countries, although it has inhibited continuing to rely on agricultural exports by putting downward pressure on world agricultural prices.

Declines in communication costs have unambiguously helped developing countries participate more fully in global manufacturing production. Reductions in air transport costs have been helpful to developing countries, while liner freight rates actually increased in the period up to 1983 before beginning to decline. Policy action at the national level, and potentially through GATS, has an important role to play in reducing transport and communication costs.

Annex

Table 11.A1 Shares of Manufactures in Total Merchandise
Exports (percent)

Japan	98.1
Taiwan, China	96.3
Singapore	96.0
Hong Kong, China	95.9
Korea	94.4
Sweden	94.3
Finland	92.7
Austria	92.2
Italy	92.2
Germany	92.1
Portugal	91.4
China	90.7
Philippines	89.3
Bangladesh	89.3
Rest of Central European Association	89.0
Rest of South Asia	87.7
Switzerland	87.5
United States	86.8
Belgium/Luxembourg	86.3
Sri Lanka	85.9
United Kingdom	85.3
France	84.2
Malaysia	84.1
Thailand	83.2
Hungary	83.2
Mexico	81.7
Ireland	81.6
Spain	81.4
World Average	**81.2**
Turkey	79.8
Poland	77.4
India	76.8
Canada	76.5
Netherlands	73.6
Morocco	69.3
Denmark	68.4
Rest of World	62.3
Indonesia	62.1
Greece	61.8
Central America, Caribbean	61.0

Table 11.A1 Shares of Manufactures in Total Merchandise
Exports (percent) *(continued)*

Brazil	59.1
Vietnam	56.8
Uruguay	47.4
Rest of South African Customs Union (Namibia)	47.1
Former Soviet Union	44.6
Rest of North Africa	44.2
Argentina	39.7
Venezuela, R.B. de	37.7
New Zealand	36.3
Rest of European Free Trade Association	34.5
Colombia	33.6
Australia	32.1
Rest of Middle East	31.8
Zimbabwe	31.2
Other Southern Africa	25.5
Chile	24.3
Mozambique	19.6
Peru	18.3
Rest of Sub-Saharan Africa	17.3
Rest of South America	14.9
Rest of Andean Pact	14.1
Tanzania	11.8
Malawi	9.8
Zambia	9.7
Uganda	1.2

Source: GTAP 5 database. http://www.gtap.org.

Notes

1. Although they may wish to consider the timing of exploitation of nonrenewable resources.

2. In the absence, for instance, of nontraded goods.

3. It is also possible to consider input-augmenting technical change, as in instances where technical change is factor-biased; this is true in the frequently adopted case of Harrod-Neutral technical change. In this case, the direct impact of the technological change is to reduce the quantity of the input required to achieve the initial level of output and to increase demand through the associated reduction in the effective price of the input.

4. We focus on compensated impacts, as these are simpler and more relevant to the calculation of compensated measures of welfare change in distorted economies (see Martin 1997).

5. Commercial services is a balance-of-payments concept covering services traded across borders (GATS mode 1) or through movement of the consumer

(GATS mode 2). It excludes services traded by establishing a service-providing firm in the consuming country (GATS mode 3) or by temporary movement of service providers (GATS mode 4).

6. Historical analysis in O'Rourke and Williamson (2000) shows that freight costs between Europe and the Far East varied substantially between 1700 and 1760 without evidence of a downward decline. Only in the 19th century was a sharp decline in evidence.

References

Amjadi, A., and A. Yeats. 1995. "Have Transport Costs Contributed to the Relative Decline of African Exports?" Policy Research Working Paper 1559, World Bank, Washington, DC.

Anderson, J. E. 1995. "Tariff Index Theory." *Review of International Economics* 3: 156–73.

Anderson, J. E., and J.P. Neary. 1992. "Trade Reform with Quotas, Partial Rent Retention, and Tariffs." *Econometrica* 60 (1): 57–76.

Bernard, A., and C. Jones. 1996. "Productivity across Industries and Countries: Time Series Theory and Evidence." *Review of Economics and Statistics* LXXVIII (1): 135–46.

Branson, W. 1979. *Macroeconomic Theory and Policy,* 2nd ed. New York: Harper and Row.

Buffie, E. 2001. *Trade Policy in Developing Countries.* Cambridge, United Kingdom: Cambridge University Press.

Cadot, O., J. de Melo, and M. Olarreaga. 2001. "Can Duty Drawbacks Have a Protectionist Bias? Evidence from Mercosur." Policy Research Working Paper 2523, World Bank, Washington, DC.

Cashin, P., and C. J. McDermott. 2002. "Riding on the Sheep's Back: Examining Australia's Dependence on Wool Exports." *Economic Record* 78: 249–63.

Chenery, H., S. Robinson, and M. Syrquin. 1986. *Industrialization and Growth: A Comparative Study.* New York: Oxford University Press.

Clark, X., D. Dollar, and A. Micco. 2004. "Port Efficiency, Maritime Transport Costs, and Bilateral Trade." NBER Working Paper 10353, Cambridge, MA.

Cohen, S., and Chang-Tai Hsieh. 2000. "Macroeconomic and Labor Market Impacts of Russian Immigration in Israel." Unpublished manuscript, Princeton University.

Collier, P. 2000. *Economic Causes of Civil Conflict and Their Implications for Policy.* World Bank: Washington, DC.

Deardorff, A., and S. Djankov. 2000. "Knowledge Transfer under Subcontracting: Evidence from Czech Firms." *World Development* 28 (10): 1837–47.

Dessus, S. 1999. "Human Capital and Growth: The Recovered Role of Education Systems." Policy Research Working Paper 2632, Research Group, World Bank, Washington, DC.

Dixit, A. and V. Norman. 1980. *Theory of International Trade.* Cambridge, United Kingdom: Cambridge Economic Handbooks, Cambridge University Press.

Easterly, W., and R. Levine. 2001. "It's Not Factor Accumulation: Stylized Facts and Growth Models." *World Bank Economic Review* 15 (2): 177–220.

Elbadawi, I., T. Mengistae, and A. Zeufack. 2001. "Geography, Supplier Access, Foreign Market Potential, and Manufacturing Exports in Developing Countries: An Analysis of Firm-Level Data." Unpublished manuscript, World Bank.

Fink, C., A. Mattoo, and C. Neagu. 2000. "Trade in International Maritime Services: How Much Does Policy Matter?" Policy Research Working Paper 2522, World Bank, Washington, DC.

Gehlhar, M., T. Hertel, and W. Martin. 1994. "Economic Growth and the Changing Structure of Trade and Production in the Pacific Rim." *American Journal of Agricultural Economics* 76 (December): 1101–10.

Gordon, R. H., and A. L. Bovenberg. 1996. "Why Is Capital So Immobile Internationally? Possible Explanations and Implications for Capital Income Taxation." *American Economic Review* 86 (5): 1057–74.

Gregory, R. 1976. "Some Implications of the Growth of the Mining Sector." *Australian Journal of Agricultural Economics* 20 (2): 71–92.

Hallward-Driemeier, M., G. Iarossi, and K. Sokoloff. 2001. "Manufacturing Productivity in East Asia: Market Depth and Aiming for Exports." Unpublished manuscript, World Bank.

Hanson, G., and M. Slaughter. 2002. "Labor Market Adjustment in Open Economies: Evidence from U.S. States." *Journal of International Economics* 1: 3–29.

Harrigan, J. 1997. "Technology, Factor Supplies, and International Specialization: Estimating the Neoclassical Model." *American Economic Review* 87 (4): 475–94.

Hummels, D. 1999. "Have International Transport Costs Declined?" Unpublished manuscript, Purdue University.

———. 2001. "Time as a Trade Barrier." Unpublished manuscript, Purdue University.

Jorgenson, D., F. Gollop, and B. Fraumeni. 1987. *Productivity and U.S. Economic Growth*. Cambridge, MA: Harvard University Press.

Karsenty, G. 2000. "Assessing Trade in Services by Mode of Supply." In *GATS 2000: New Directions in Services Trade Liberalization*, ed. P. Sauvé and R. Stern. Washington, DC: Brookings Institution.

Kee, Hiau Looi. 2001. "Productivity Versus Endowments: A Study of Singapore's Sectoral Growth 1974–1992." Unpublished manuscript, World Bank.

Kongsamut, P., S. Rebelo, and Danyang Xie. 2001. "Beyond Balanced Growth." IMF Working Paper WP/01/85, Washington, DC.

Krueger, A., and B. Tuncer. 1982. "An Empirical Test of the Infant Industry Argument." *American Economic Review* 72 (5):1142–52.

Larson, D., R. Butzer, Y. Mundlak, and A. Crego. 2000. "A Cross-Country Database for Sector Investment and Capital." *World Bank Economic Review* 14 (2): 371–92.

Leamer, E. 1987. "Paths of Development in the Three-Factor n-Good General Equilibrium Model." *Journal of Political Economy* 95: 961–99.

Leamer, E., H. Maul, S. Rodriguez, and P. Schott. 1999. "Does Natural Resource Abundance Increase Latin American Income Inequality?" *Journal of Development Economics* 59: 1–42.

Limao, N., and A. Venables. 2001. "Infrastructure, Geographical Disadvantage, Transport Costs, and Trade." *World Bank Economic Review* 15 (3): 451–79.

Lloyd, P., and A. Schweinberger, A. 1988. "Trade Expenditure Functions and the Gains from Trade." *Journal of International Economics* 24: 275–97.

Loayza, N., K. Schmidt-Hebbel, and L. Serven. 2000. "Saving in Developing Countries: An Overview." *World Bank Economic Review* 14 (3): 393–414.

Martin, W. 1989. "Implications of Changes in the Composition of Australian Exports for Export Sector Instability." *Australian Economic Review* 89 (1): 39–50.

———. 1997. "Measuring Welfare Changes with Distortions." In *Applied Methods for Trade Policy Analysis*, ed. J. Francois and K. Reinert. Cambridge, United Kingdom: Cambridge University Press.

———. 2001a. "Trade Policy Reform in the East Asian Transition Economies." Policy Research Working Paper 2535, World Bank, Washington, DC.

———. 2001b. "Trade Policies, Developing Countries, and Globalization." Background paper for World Bank, *Globalization, Growth, and Poverty*. http://econ.worldbank.org/prr/doc.php?type=5&sp=2477&st=&id=2866

———. 2003. "Developing Countries' Changing Participation in World Trade." *World Bank Research Observer* 18: 187–203.

Martin, W., and J. Alston, 1997. "Producer Surplus without Apology? Evaluating Investments in R&D." *Economic Record* 73 (221): 146–58.

Martin, W., and D. Mitra. 2001. "Productivity Growth and Convergence in Agriculture and Manufacturing." *Economic Development and Cultural Change* 49 (2): 403–23.

Martin, W., and P. Warr. 1993. "Explaining Agriculture's Relative Decline: A Supply Side Analysis for Indonesia." *World Bank Economic Review* 7 (3): 381–401.

Matsuyama, K. 1992. "Agricultural Productivity, Comparative Advantage, and Economic Growth." *Journal of Economic Theory* 58: 317–34.

McKibbin, W., and P. Wilcoxen. 1999. "The Theoretical and Empirical Structure of the G-Cubed Model." *Economic Modeling* 16: 123–48.

Michalopoulos, C. 1999. "Trade Policy and Market Access Issues for Developing Countries." Policy Research Working Paper 2214, World Bank, Washington, DC.

Navaretti, G., and D. Tarr. 2000. "International Knowledge Flows and Economic Performance: A Review of the Evidence." *World Bank Economic Review* 14 (1): 1–15.

Nehru, V., and A. Dhareshwar. 1993. "A New Database on Physical Capital Stock: Sources, Methodology, and Results." *Revisita de Análisis Económico* 8 (1): 37–59.

Nehru, V., E. Swanson, and A. Dubey. 1995. "A New Database on Human Capital Stock in Developing and Industrial Countries: Sources, Methodology, and Results." *Journal of Development Economics* 46: 379–401.

O'Rourke, K., and J. G. Williamson. 2000. "When Did Globalization Begin?" NBER Working Paper 7632, Cambridge, MA.

Pack, H. 2000. "Industrial Policy: Elixir or Poison?" *World Bank Research Observer* 15 (1): 47–67.

Priovolos, T., and R. Duncan, eds. 1991. *Commodity Risk Management and Finance*. New York: Oxford University Press.

Redding, S., and A. Venables. 2004. "Economic Geography and International Inequality." *Journal of International Economics* 62 (1): 53–82.

Rodrik, D. 1986. "The Economics of Export Performance Requirements." *Quarterly Journal of Economics* 102 (3): 633–50.

———. 1994. "Getting Interventions Right: How South Korea and Taiwan Grew Rich." NBER Working Paper 4964, Cambridge, MA.

Sachs, J., and A. Warner. 1995. "Natural Resource Abundance and Economic Growth." NBER Working Paper 5398, Cambridge, MA.

Snape, R. 1977. "Effects of Mineral Development on the Economy." *Australian Journal of Agricultural Economics* 21 (3): 147–56.

Stiglitz, J. 1996. "Some Lessons from the East Asian Miracle." *World Bank Research Observer* 11 (2): 151–79.

Syrquin, M. 1986. "Productivity Growth and Factor Reallocation." In *Industrialization and Growth: A Comparative Study*, ed. H. Chenery, S. Robinson, and M. Syrquin. Oxford: Oxford University Press.

Tybout, J. 2001. "Plant and Firm Level Evidence on 'New' Trade Theory." NBER Working Paper 8418, Cambridge, MA.

World Bank. 2001. *Global Economic Prospects and the Developing Countries, 2001.* Washington, DC.

World Bank. 2003. *Global Economic Prospects and the Developing Countries, 2003.* Washington, DC.

Index

Note that *f* indicates figure, *n* indicates note (*nn* is notes), and *t* indicates table.